IN PURSUIT OF COMPETENCE

A Life as a Westminster Nomad

Norman Warner

Grosvenor House
Publishing Limited

First published in Great Britain in 2021

The right of Norman Warner to be identified as the author of this
work has been asserted in accordance with Section 78
of the Copyright, Designs and Patents Act 1988

This book is published by
Grosvenor House Publishing Ltd
Link House
140 The Broadway, Tolworth, Surrey, KT6 7HT.
www.grosvenorhousepublishing.co.uk

A CIP record for this book
is available from the British Library

ISBN 978-1-83975-841-6

About the author

Norman Warner is a Crossbench Member of the House of Lords, having left the Labour party in 2015. In 2003 he became a Health Minister in the Blair Government and in 2006 he was made a Privy Councillor. In 2014/15 he was appointed Commissioner for Birmingham's Children's Services following critical Ofsted reports. In 2010/11 he was a member of an independent Commission on the Funding of Care and Support.

He was the Senior Policy Adviser to the Home Secretary after the 1997 Election. He set up and chaired the Youth Justice Board for England and Wales from 1999 to 2003. As Kent's Director of Social Services from 1985 to 1991 he was very involved in reform of community care. He has chaired voluntary organisations and a government inquiry, as well as working as a management consultant. Earlier in his career he was a senior civil servant in the Department of Health and Social Security.

Norman lives in London with his wife Suzanne.

Dedication

In Memoriam, Albert Warner: 1915 to 1994

If we want things to stay as they are, things will have to change.

Guiseppe di Lampedusa, 1957 The Leopard

Rules are for the guidance of wise men and the obedience of fools.

Oliver Wendell Holmes, US Supreme Court Judge (attributed)

Only a crisis – actual or perceived – produces real change.
When that crisis occurs, the actions that are taken depend on
the ideas that are lying around.

Milton Friedman, 1982 Preface to Capitalism and Freedom

Sacred cows make the best hamburgers.

Attributed to Abbie Hoffman US 1960s radical

Problems are never solved permanently.

John Stuart Mill

Contents

Introduction

Lockdown provided an opportunity to wade through diaries, speeches, newspaper cuttings, pamphlets, briefings and numerous documents I had accumulated over half a century. They revealed a somewhat haphazard nomadic journey in and around government from the 1960s to Brexit and the pandemic. I have been involved with some big spenders – the NHS, social security, the Home Office and criminal justice, social care and children's services. A lot of time has been spent trying to curb public expenditure or getting better value for it. Insofar as there was a common thread to my activities it was change and improving service delivery.

I have handled subjects from different perspectives: senior civil servant, special adviser and Minister, but also as a management consultant and chair of public bodies, charities and public inquiries. I've been politically promiscuous by working for and with Conservative, Labour and Coalition Governments. Sometimes the political cards had been dealt on a subject, sometimes they weren't. What surprised me was how often the same issues cropped up. Poor management was a common theme. Few problems seemed to stay fixed. Many of the problems I've wrestled with are still around today.

In the 1950s there was an inquiry into NHS affordability. Two decades ago, police and public were agitated about knife crime. There is nothing new about homelessness and rough sleepers in our cities. We've spent 20 years discussing inadequate funding of social care without fixing the problem. Every decade produces hospital scandals, with the NHS promising to learn lessons but failing to do so. Child sexual abuse first hit the headlines in the 1980s and we're still trying to deal with it. In the 1990s we were worried about a prison population of 60,000 but now accept one 50% higher. Harold MacMillan was the last Housing Minister to build enough affordable social housing - over 60 years ago.

Rereading papers I was reminded of the problem of institutional memory that had bothered me when I returned to the Health Department as a Minister in 2003. I found then I had a better knowledge of what had worked or failed in the past than most of the civil servants advising me. I thought this odd, given that so many Ministers have little management experience, are learning on the job and stay in post for relatively short periods of time. Government is difficult enough, without being unable to recall past successes and failures.

The recurring nature of public policy issues and the weakness of institutional memory persuaded me to try to map my nomadic government journey. That decision was reinforced by the growing evidence that UK public services face serious challenges in our post-Brexit, post-pandemic world. The long post-war consensus on the welfare state has been fracturing for some time as intergenerational inequalities have grown. Geographical levelling up has become the political trope, as considerable variation in local service quality and volume is exposed. Public expectations of services and their personalisation keep rising, usually faster than public willingness to pay the taxes to fund improvements.

Even though the way public services are delivered may change with new technologies, the basic service needs of the public are unlikely to alter that much. Health services and care have to be delivered; children need to be educated and looked after; people require affordable housing, the public want protection from crime, homelessness, domestic violence and child abuse. Those left in poverty may well increase unless inequalities are reduced. Public services will continue to be labour intensive, with staff needing good training and effective management. Whoever is governing would do well not to forget past experience – successes and failures - as they try to provide a new future.

The pandemic has demonstrated the fragility of governmental systems – political and official. Few Ministers have had much preparation for what they are asked to do, often at short notice. Rarely do they stay long in jobs. Inevitably they rely heavily on a permanent civil service that I never believed was the Roll Royce machine some mandarins claimed. I came to that conclusion when Dominic Cummings was still in short trousers. As Covid19 has shown, government competence can be in short supply when you need it most. Yet it is competence that most public service users expect and rely on, whatever their political affiliations. Brexit may have been inevitable, but people expected it to be handled competently. I doubt even the most enthusiastic Brexiteer would claim it was.

Our post-Brexit civil service looks nervous about speaking truth to power. It needs to find its voice and collective memory. Talented people seem less willing to expose themselves and their families to the tough and not very well-paid life as a Minister. Capital, ideas, people and dangers fly across international boundaries and can make a mockery of national governments claiming sovereignty and control. In battling Covid19 the role of the State has been critical globally and is likely to remain so in the aftermath. But the pandemic has also exposed very worrying deficiencies in government planning, purchasing and organisation, despite a rally with the vaccination programme. Our public services will need to increase, at pace, their management capacity and competence.

This book is not a manual on how to do this. It is an account of a journey and reflections on it that may be useful. Some changes haven't lasted, others have. Where possible I have tried to show what happened after I moved on. Many areas described, especially the NHS, continue to be major challenges. In government individuals count, some more than others. People behaving badly or incompetently goes with the territory When thwarted, I have tried to be fair to those responsible, without being mealy-mouthed. I have often had a lot of support and have tried to acknowledge this. Most successful change is a team effort, not a solo performance. It rarely benefits from being oversold as fantastic, world-class or a moon shot.

I have adopted a broadly chronological approach starting with an unusually varied and meritocratic civil service apprenticeship. The rest of the book provides four main perspectives: senior civil servant, Director of Social Services, Home Office Special Adviser and Health Minister. Politics and significant personalities crop up frequently to influence the narrative. That is inevitable in government, as is the prevailing economic and political context of the times. The 1970s were a period of relentless economic crises which dominated decision-making. In 1997 the Labour Party had been out of government for 18 years, so I have used the diary I kept, to show what it was like to take over a major department of state and work with No.10 on a new Government's reform programme.

I have devoted space to unfashionable and neglected service areas like child protection, social care and youth justice where I have put in long shifts. These areas deserve far more attention and investment than governments usually provide. There are five chapters on the NHS, the biggest spender of them all, apart from cash benefits. My time as Health Minister was a rollercoaster ride of pharmaceuticals regulation, financial meltdown, a mega IT programme, quango culling and pursuing a market approach to an NHS that was underperforming relative to its investment. I have been involved with the NHS over a good part of my working life and take a more critical view of it than most commentators.

I recognise that the NHS is an iconic public service with committed staff and huge public support verging on uncritical adulation. But I consider we have failed to apply to the NHS the critical scrutiny applied to other public services. Alongside NHS strengths – free at the point of clinical need and relatively cheap – are some serious shortcomings. It is largely an ill-health service, not a health service. Its business model is suspect, with insufficient investment in primary care, community services and public health, relative to what it spends on hospitals. The public is very concerned about mental health, but the NHS has never given these services the same parity of esteem given to physical health. The result is excessively long waits for mental health services, especially for children and young people. Despite the large proportion of the NHS budget spent on acute hospitals, their performance is highly variable, as a 2016 independent report demonstrated. The NHS will need a step change in performance if it is to eliminate the backlog of over 5 million patients awaiting treatment, following the pandemic.

The book ends with an Epilogue on my two decades in the House of Lords and some thoughts on reforming government drawing on my experience. If the UK is to build back better after Brexit and Covid19, politicians, civil servants and public sector managers and professionals will need to raise their games significantly.

Prologue: A Galaxy Far, Far Away: 1940-1959

Early Years

I was born when young men, trained in six weeks to fly primitive fighter planes, were defending Britain over the fields of Kent. My mother had been evacuated to London's periphery and my early years were spent moving between host families. In late 1944 my father returned from duty as a Chief Petty Officer repairing planes on aircraft carriers. We settled in Brockley in South-East London. I recall clambering into a green cage under my parents' bed when V2 rockets attacked London in late 1944. One V2 demolished nearby Depford's Woolworths killing over 150 people. The Government said these were gas explosions – an early example of fake news. Shortly after Hitler's last fling with the V2s, we moved along the road where I lived until 1961.

Our Victorian house was rented from a private landlord who collected rent on Friday evenings after Dad was paid by his gas company employers. The heating was coal fires. We had electric lighting but my grandparents still had gas lighting until the late 1940s. Milk and bread were delivered by horse drawn carts. Refrigerators were a rarity until the 1950s so shopping was done daily. Bread, petrol, sugar, confectionery, meat and other foods were rationed throughout the 1940s, finally ending in 1954. Rationing was a major issue in the 1951 Election, with the Conservatives promising to end it and Labour favouring retention. The 1945 landslide majority was reduced to 5, showing Labour the dangers of 'Nanny Statism.'

My educational relationship with the LCC began at Mantle Road School, one of many large Victorian schools in London that had survived Luftwaffe attention. I was taught for six years in three schools by a string of formidable ladies. They did a good job of educating me and establishing a lifelong love of reading. My second school, Turnham Road School, is now a Foundation school but was then a candidate for Ofsted turnaround. My disgruntled Dad had me transferred. to Edmund Waller – one of many schools then named after 16th and 17th century poets and playwrights.

Here, in classes of over 40 children, we were prepared for the 11-plus exam. The top stream went to grammar schools and a few public schools; the middle stream to central and technical schools; and the remaining poor devils were consigned to secondary moderns which they left at 15. The only man on the staff, apart from the Head, was Mr Horan who took all boys for football and cricket. I ended up taking the 11-plus twice. Despite passing first time I was forced to stay another year and repeat the experience. This improved my cricket, football and captaincy skills but did little for compliant behaviour. A few encounters with the Headmaster led to canings which were solemnly recorded in an LCC register.

Much of my education took place outside school, with a rich diet of comics – Dandy, Beano, Film Fun and later Eagle, Champion, Wizard, Hotspur and Adventure. These were supplemented by the Children's Newspaper and books as presents or from the local library. Biggles, Just William, Frank Richards and Greyfriars, John Buchan, Treasure Island and many others were all consumed at pace. I became a newshound with my Dad's News Chronicle and, when it closed, the Daily Express – then a proper newspaper robustly supporting Lord Beaverbrook's strong pro-Commonwealth views. A newspaper round enabled me to read other newspapers and the occasional magazine not intended for young eyes. It also introduced me to capitalism and the merits of having my own money that I decided how to spend.

Post-war London was full of bomb sites which served as playgrounds; and its children had much more freedom than in today's risk-averse and security obsessed world. We walked to school with our mates and could travel cheaply on our own on buses, trams and trains. I could take the tram on Saturday mornings to the New Cross Gaumont and watch Tarzan, Roy Rogers, cartoons and newsreels. Later, in school holidays, Brockley's Ritz and Rivoli cinemas enabled me to indulge my lifelong love of the cinema, especially westerns. Any Michael Curtis film with Errol Flynn was a must see, especially Robin Hood. With an experienced gang, a single payer could get a couple of freebies in through the fire exits.

From an early age London was my oyster. I could go to the Oval and sit on the grass to watch Test matches. I usually went to football matches with my Dad because the crowds were so big: Arsenal v

Charlton at the Valley would have 70,000 people standing on now forbidden terraces. I went to Millwall on my own and watched the Fisher brothers stub out their cigarettes in the tunnel before running on to the pitch. In 1951 there was the great excitement of the Festival of Britain on London's South Bank which I went to twice. Anxiety about their children's safety outside the home was not a strong feature of London's post-war parents.

My parents were not religious but I was sent to Sunday school from an early age. I won bible-reading prizes and sang in the church choir, a nice little earner from weddings. I also joined the Church Lads Brigade who had an annual camp on the Isle of Wight. The older boys had to dig latrines, while younger ones like me went to Sandown in the deputy leader's Austin 7 for the beach and ice-cream. At the time, this all seemed entirely innocent and I never experienced anything untoward. Modern revelations have made me wonder if I had a narrow escape from the two confirmed bachelors who ran the local CLB. Or perhaps they were just loyal partners surviving in a harsh pre-Wolfenden world?

1940s diets and exercise kept children reasonably healthy, apart from infectious diseases: I caught everything. There was the hazard of London's pea soup fogs. I still remember the great London smog of December 1952. This was said to have killed 4000 people and led to the 1956 Clean Air Act that created smoke free zones. I survived my two pre-NHS hospital experiences. The first was several weeks in the Brook Fever Hospital in Woolwich, with scarlet fever, then requiring hospital admission. Like most children then, I had my tonsils removed as part of childhood. My parents paid these hospital costs, drawing on their weekly payments to the Hospital Savings Association.

My first NHS health encounter was nearly my last. It started with painful stomach aches diagnosed as indigestion by our GP, a Scottish Dr Finlay's Casebook lookalike. Increased pain and frequency could not deflect him from his diagnosis and the supply of yet more indigestion pills. When I collapsed my Dad took me by tram to the Miller Hospital in Greenwich where I was whisked into the operating theatre with acute peritonitis and 24 hours to live. This first NHS experience encapsulated the frustrating mixture of competence and incompetence that has been my lifetime's experience of the NHS.

7

The Dulwich Experiment

In 1952 I eventually escaped from my LCC holding pen and passed the selection process for entry to Dulwich College. I was part of the 'Dulwich Experiment,' the brainchild of Christopher Gilkes who had been the Master there since 1941. (His brother ran a similar scheme at St Paul's in West London.) Dulwich had been founded in 1619 by a successful actor/manager, Edward Alleyn, a contemporary of Shakespeare. In 1870 a new Dulwich College opened, built in an Italianate style by Charles Barry Junior, the eldest son of Sir Charles Barry who built the Houses of Parliament. I have spent 30 years in the flamboyant buildings of the Barry family. The school was badly damaged in the war and its academic reputation and finances were in decline when the 1944 Education Act came to its rescue.

Local education authorities (LEAs) could fund secondary education for boys who passed the 11-plus. Gilkes used this to expand the intake of LEA scholarship boys. He made no secret of his wish to drive up academic standards by creaming off bright boys from State schools. But he continued running Dulwich as a traditional boys' public school, with its CCF, school song in Latin and emphasis on sporting achievement. LEAs paid tuition fees and travel expenses but parents paid for school uniforms and sports kit. These had to be bought from the school Commissariat run profitably by two prosperous-looking men. When the bills arrived, my Dad must have had his doubts but he never moaned, even when London's conversion to electricity bankrupted his gas company employer and made him unemployed. (He joined the Post Office and later excelled as a trade union organiser, especially in the 1971 postal strike.)

Apart from sciences, where I was evicted too many times to learn much, I performed reasonably well academically. I enjoyed good relations with all the History and English masters. Some were outstanding, like Laurie Jagger (to whom the novelist Graham Swift has paid tribute) and Eric Williams, a noted historian, who was always busy researching his latest book. These teachers encouraged wide reading and taught me to think, analyse and express myself coherently. I owed them a lot, as I did those who coached the cricket, rugby and hockey teams I played in. A lifelong enthusiasm for competitive sport was shaped on the playing fields of Dulwich - literally by one rugby master, who forgot he was refereeing and tackled me when I was about to score a brilliant try and broke my collar bone.

Dulwich taught me an invaluable life lesson about plausibility. After your second year you were supposed to join the CCF, unless you were a member of the scouts. I discovered that you could tell the CCF you were in the scouts and the scouts that you were in the CCF. No-one checked my stories and this left my Tuesday evenings free. It came as no great surprise that my end of year reports indicated that I showed leadership qualities but too often in the wrong direction. I was clearly not a reliable enforcer of school rules so couldn't be a prefect. This didn't upset me much as teenage life outside school then was much more fun.

Growing up in 1950s London

Although hardly the Swinging 60s, 1950s South London offered more tempting alternatives than a traditional boys' public school. Young people could leave school at 15 and earn their own money to spend on new fashions, new music and coffee bars and jazz clubs. Here the young could hear their heroes. Elvis, Buddy Holly, Chris Barber, Humphrey Lyttelton, Lonny Donegan all became available according to taste, often live. You could even experience the great Louis Armstrong and his All-Stars or Count Basie live in concert, as I did. But for a working-class boy to participate in this teenage scene, he needed a source of income.

I had a series of jobs while still at school. It started with paper rounds, progressed to working in the local newsagents and the Coop grocery store. I then moved on to checking Zetters football coupons and selling Walls ice-cream door-to-door and at motor racing events at Crystal Palace – then a Formula 1 venue with good proximity to the cars. These income-generating activities helped me purchase my pride and joy – a blue suede jacket - and the start of a jazz and pop music collection.

The local Coop youth club provided a ready-made teenage social life with girls, music, table tennis, amateur dramatics and even debating competitions. My first experience of chairing a meeting was in a Coop teenage debating competition. We could travel the country at the Coop's expense for competitions and holiday breaks. The youth club was run by a cheerful middle-aged man who worked in a hospital. Unfortunately he was caught later supplementing his income by defrauding the NHS. His conviction coincided with the rise of supermarkets and the demise of many Coops and the closure of their youth clubs.

At the end of the 1950s our household budget was not in good shape and Dad's fitness was deteriorating from a leg damaged in a war-time accident. Going to Cambridge to read history, as Eric Williams tried hard to persuade me to do, seemed inappropriate. Dad never tried to stop me or pressurise me to join the labour market. I had just become increasingly disenchanted with Dulwich and wanted to earn my own living. Impetuously, as Christmas approached, I announced my departure from Dulwich.

1. Government Apprenticeship - 1960s Style: 1959-1973

Auditing the NHS

After a few months as a temporary clerk in the Treasury, I passed the exam for the civil service Executive Class and was posted to the Ministry of Health. There I was assigned to the Accountant General's Department to become an NHS auditor. You learned then to be an auditor on the job through a postal course. Audits were done in teams of four led by a Higher Executive Officer. Groups of teams were managed by a senior auditor. I was assigned to a team auditing most of the then Hospital Management Committees in the South-East Hospital Board Region (including the big psychiatric hospitals); the Regional Board itself; some London teaching hospitals then managed by Boards of Governors and the London Executive Council managing the capital's GP, dentist, pharmacist and optician services.

An auditor looked for two things: did the accounts accurately reflect an authority's financial position and was there scope for fraud. Audit lore identified likely areas for fraud: 'ghosts' on the payroll; fraudulent invoices; stealing supplies (especially beer and spirits); theft of patients' money; and embezzling staff recreation funds and hospital farms. These last three items were real issues in the large psychiatric hospitals with which London had been ringed by the Victorians. My time as an auditor taught me a lot about the NHS including how it could be ripped off. Forty years later as the Minister for fraud prevention I found fraud had become an even bigger problem.

We did find frauds where financial control systems were lax. Spot checks on stores might reveal someone on the take. In a Bermondsey hospital the Supplies Officer (a former jailbird) was doing this on an industrial scale. Persuading the Chairman – later a Labour Chief Whip – to sack him was an uphill struggle. Payroll 'ghosts' were a regular hazard. Senior staff were paid according to the number of beds; and in some hospitals the audit team found wards with an unusually large number of empty beds and no staff. Executive Councils produced their own problems – inflated GP lists to claim more capitation fees; dentists who carried out improbable numbers of fillings ('drill and fill' as it was called); false claims for prescriptions dispensed by pharmacists. Some Board members fiddled their expenses.

The most difficult places to audit were the large mental illness and mental handicap hospitals – as they were called then. We had three on our books– Darenth Park near Dartford (with 2000 patients plus two smaller hospitals, Stone House and Mabledon with its Polish patients); Netherne Hospital near Coulsdon (with about 2000 patients); and Leybourne Grange in Kent which was a colony of largely Downs syndrome patients. All these places have now been closed and largely demolished. Back then they were large communities with their own way of doing things and suspicious of outsiders asking awkward questions.

These long-stay hospitals were dreadful places. Dark, physically neglected, forbidding and overcrowded, with patients hanging around the wards with nothing to do. Some very disturbed individuals were mixed up with sad, gentle people forgotten by society. There was little occupational therapy except for the few working on the farms or making baskets Ward staff were usually long-serving, and often as institutionalised as their patients. They belonged to the same union as prison officers and it often showed. Handling patients' money was a ripe area for theft but difficult to prove, as were frauds in staff social funds which were often very large. Each hospital group had a Medical Superintendent; but there were few psychiatrists for the number of patients and heavy reliance on new drugs like Largactil.

The most suspicious places were the farms – a large one at Darenth Park and a smaller one at Netherne. Pig fraud was relatively easy and common because the farm manager could keep back a piglet or two from each litter and fatten them up for private sale. To find a fraud you needed to examine the tagged ears of each pig and check the numbers against breeding records: untagged pigs were suspicious as were small litters. All this involved going into the pens and looking at the tag number in their ears. Pigs tend not to be co-operative with a city boy; but I did uncover one fraud and despatched the farm manager.

While I was an auditor, shock waves hit the long-stay psychiatric hospitals. In 1960 Enoch Powell returned to MacMillan's Cabinet as Health Minister and in early 1961 he astonished everybody with his apocalyptic 'water towers' speech. He said he wanted to see the

Victorian mental hospitals demolished or left derelict, likening them to funeral pyres to be torched. It would be another 30-40 years before this happened and Powell would be long gone from politics. But I never forgot Powell's speech when as Kent's Director of Social Services, I helped to close these long-stay hospitals and rehouse their residents in the community in small group homes (see Chapter 4).

Back in 1963 I was suddenly catapulted into a policy job as a guinea pig for a new scheme testing my ability to join the administrative class. This involved working with an experienced Principal for 2 years on a policy project and then passing a two-day process run by the Civil Service Selection Board. My new job was based in the Health Ministry's new HQ in Alexander Fleming House (AFH) on the Elephant and Castle roundabout. This was a controversial new building by Erno Goldfinger that won a RIBA award. People either loved or hated AFH. Ian Fleming hated it so much he named a Bond villain after Goldfinger; and when Erno threatened to sue him, Fleming said he'd change the name to Goldprick. One of my later bosses liked AFH so much, in 1990 he bought his old office converted into a flat.

Salmon Committee on Senior Nursing Staff

I was apprenticed to the former Permanent Secretary of the Nigerian Ministry of Education, a casualty of the 'Winds of Change' in Africa. David Williams commuted from Surrey each day with a rolled umbrella and bowler hat. We rubbed along well for 2 years with no outside social contact and no common interests. David turned out to be a stickler for good grammar and drafting clarity which improved my prose style. My main job was to assist David in his role as Secretary to a new Committee set up to consider senior nurse management. The Salmon Committee was a response to pressure from senior nurses for more say in the running of hospitals. They disliked the Hattie Jacques 'Carry on Matron' image of nursing and being regarded as the handmaidens of doctors. They still revered Florence Nightingale's legacy but thought it entitled them to equality with doctors and administrators in running hospitals.

Half the committee were top nurses – 4 matrons and a psychiatric hospital chief male nurse - with 2 doctors, a hospital administrator, and a Scottish professor of management. Its chairman was a businessman, Brian Salmon, a member of the family controlling J Lyon and Co, a hotel, restaurant, grocery and electronics company best known for its Lyon's corner teashops. At the time we didn't realise the company was on a slide that led to its demise and break-up. This was my first encounter with a Conservative businessman engaged in public service, a phenomenon I saw much more of in Margaret Thatcher's time (see Chapter 3).

The Committee met monthly to consider papers David and I produced. It soon became clear that nurses would get a status boost and arguments were needed to deliver it. This made our management guru, Tom Paterson, very influential. He formed an alliance with the nurses led by Dame Muriel Powell, Matron of Hyde Park's St George's Hospital, then one of the most powerful hospitals in the country – unlike today's troubled Wandsworth version. The nurses discovered 'management speak.' It appeared they had great 'sapiential' authority because of their professional knowledge but insufficient 'structural' authority. If nurses were to punch their weight in hospital hierarchies, they needed more 'structural' authority. Their flat management structure was said to require more posts between ward sisters and Matrons.

After many hospital visits, the Committee settled on replacing 'Matrons' with 'Chief Nursing Officers'- the title used for top nurses in psychiatric hospitals who were usually men. CNOs would have direct access to governing bodies and equality with senior positions on executive management teams. A new grading structure was proposed, with Staff Nurses at Grade 5, Ward Sisters at Grade 6 and the new Chief Nursing Officers at Grades 9 or 10. This left several new grades for senior nursing posts above ward sister level. The Committee defined the responsibilities of the different grades. For the final report, I produced a set of organisation charts showing how the grades might be used in different types of hospitals, using place names from Trollope's Barchester novels. The report recommended management training and improved selection processes - issues I would return to in future jobs.

Thus, was a new nursing bureaucracy born after Ministers accepted the recommendations and gradually implemented them. There was disgruntlement among ward sisters who saw layers of management imposed between them and their ultimate nursing bosses. Cries of 'bring back Matron' have rung out periodically and sometimes successfully. But the Salmon report led to a boost in senior nurses pay; more nurses going into management and, later, nurses becoming chief executives. Looking back on this now I think we rather over-egged the management roles with too many grades between 6 and 10. These changes didn't last long and were replaced by another Conservative government in Keith Joseph's 1974 NHS re-organisation.

I also became the Secretary to two advisory bodies set up under the NHS founding statute – the Central Health Services Council and the Standing Nursing Advisory Committee. The CHSC was chaired by the Chief Medical Officer, the formidable, George Godber, with his unnerving monocle. Nothing much was settled on medical matters without Godber's approval with which Ministers found it wisest to agree. He was strongly anti-smoking and had ashtrays removed from meeting rooms, much to the consternation of visitors who lit up only to find no ashtrays. I handled some Merseyside regional matters like trying to complete Liverpool's new teaching hospital, started a decade ago and still way off being finished.

I wrote a report on relieving hospital nurses of non-nursing duties. This was part of boosting the professionalism of nursing and making better use of scarce nursing skills. At the time this made sense. But later, as nursing became a degree-entry profession, this issue became tangled up with an argument about making nurses 'too posh to wash' their patients. Discussions about the role of nurses which started in the 1960s still continue.

During my time on nursing, I became a fully-fledged member of the Administrative Class as an Assistant Principal – an apprentice mandarin. Enoch Powell had been replaced by Kenneth Robinson in October 1964 following Labour's election victory. Robinson was the son of a GP with a longstanding interest in the NHS. But GPs were on the war path over falling numbers and their pay and expenses system. With the Salmon Report completed in the Spring of 1966, I moved to GPs. Negotiations with the BMA had started already, against a backcloth of 18,000 GP resignations from the NHS allegedly being held at BMA headquarters.

Renegotiating the GP contract with the BMA

The BMA's lead negotiator was Jim Cameron, a moderate Scot with a prosperous London practice. Alongside him was a feisty Welshman, Ivor Jones, who had been labelled a 'pirate' by Kenneth Robinson – which got into the press. Jones was a strong advocate for private practice and wanted to move GP pay from a capitation system to item of service payments. When I saw these two in action, sometimes through a fog of cigarette smoke, I thought they had a rather effective hard cop, soft cop routine. This of course irritated enormously the more cerebral civil servants.

The BMA negotiators were always looking over their shoulders at their membership's varied views on the GP pay system. They regularly flourished the signed resignations, although we never actually saw them. I thought the BMA held all the high cards. Since 1948, hospital consultants had done much better financially than GPs whose payment system didn't reward those who invested in practices to improve patient services. Many GP premises were in poor condition; and GPs were leaving the NHS and emigrating. If the Government wanted to save NHS general practice, I thought it would have to meet many of the BMA's demands. These had been well marshalled in a Family Doctors Charter - much of which the BMA had lifted from a rival doctors' organisation – the Medical Practitioners Union.

Kenneth Robinson wanted to move GPs to a salaried service, as envisaged when the NHS was being set up. That proposition was doomed to failure because GPs owned most of their premises and the Government couldn't afford to buy them out. In any case most GPs didn't want to be in new health centres controlled by local authorities. Robinson was not prepared to move to an item of service payment system, as in the US which would have been very expensive and possibly the end of the UK family doctor model. Jim Cameron, later, acknowledged Robinson had been right about that. It took a while to move the BMA away from the item of service model. In the end Robinson abandoned a salaried service and accepted a few item-of-service payments for public health items like immunisations and cervical smears. This was enough for the BMA to abandon a full item-of -service system.

To end the dispute, the Government had to agree a major package of sweeteners in respect of GP premises, training and staffing. This package included a basic practice allowance, loans to set up group practices, a cost-rent scheme, improvement grants for repairing premises, paying for practice staff and a post-graduate education and training scheme for new GPs. There would also be incentives to practice in under-doctored areas. As well as recording the negotiations and preparing papers for them, I worked up a new improvement grant scheme for GP premises. The package of changes negotiated were codified in a red book - a substantial contract rule book, not a slim Maoist tract. The contract was priced by the doctors pay review body who awarded GPs a 33% pay rise.

Kenneth Robinson saved the NHS GP service with this new contract. Without wholesale reform and a more generous financial settlement, many GPs would have left the NHS, with no replacements in sight. The new contract led to significant improvements in GP services and lasted until 1990. Then Margaret Thatcher and Ken Clarke imposed a new contract on the BMA that was all about competition, commissioning and GP fundholding.

A First Stab at NHS Reform

In April 1967, a few months after the birth of our first child, I left GPs to join a new Long-term Planning Unit. Given the trouble with settling the 1948 tri-partite structure – hospitals, executive councils and local authorities – there had been little enthusiasm for tampering with it. The hospitals were a law unto themselves. The family practitioner services were independent contractors who didn't want to be managed by anybody. Local government had the bits left over - health centres, district nursing, health visitors, as well as old people's homes and home helps. Their local medical officers of health were responsible for local population health and prevention programmes.

As the NHS approached its 20th anniversary, its structure and lack of integration began to be questioned. Any change that cut costs had Treasury support and Robinson, an ex- hospital board member, was interested in streamlining NHS administration. In November 1967 he announced a Departmental inquiry into the NHS structure, with a small advisory group of trusted outsiders to oversee work by the new Long-term Planning Unit. Our remit was to produce a Green Paper on reform of NHS administrative structures for public discussion. We did this in July 1968 in a slim document with the less than compelling title of 'The Administrative Structure of the Medical and Related Services in England and Wales.'

My involvement in producing the final version of this Green Paper was limited by four months away at the civil service college being taught economics and statistics by high quality economists like Alan Williams, the first real health economist, and the late Maurice Peston, father of Robert, and later a Labour Peer and colleague. On my return I found this first stab at reorganising the NHS had few friends; and was abandoned by Robinson's successor, Dick Crossman. I was deemed ready for a stint as a Minister's private secretary.

Kenneth Robinson and the Scientologists

When I moved to Kenneth Robinson's private office I was spoilt for choice in terms of political action. 1967 saw the 6-day Arab-Israeli war in June which proved a disaster for Palestinians. De Gaulle rejected Britain's second EU membership bid. Then in November, Harold Wilson devalued the pound and changed Chancellors from Jim Callaghan to Roy Jenkins whose belt-tightening impacted the NHS. Jenkins gave Robinson the choice of prescription charges or suspending the hospital building programme started by Enoch Powell. Robinson chose to re-introduce the prescription charges he'd abolished in 1965 because he suspected that once halted, the building programme wouldn't restart. He then secured a raft of prescription charge exemptions – for children, pensioners, the chronic sick and those on supplementary benefit. These halved the Treasury savings and are still in place today.

Like all his predecessors since Nye Bevan, Robinson wasn't in the Cabinet but attended when invited. He had the Ministerial job he wanted and was very involved in day-to-day decision making. His Ministerial support was one limited Parliamentary Secretary, Julian Snow, who was reputed never to have made a speech from the backbenches. Snow had a diet of late-night adjournment debates in which he regularly read out explanatory notes marked 'not to be read out in any circumstances.' In the House of Lords, a Government Whip, Baroness Nora Phillips, handled health matters. I helped brief her, ensured she stuck to her brief and went to Hansard to remedy any 'infelicities,' as the civil service called them. It was a different era.

Robinson was a committed liberal with a track record of social reform. He had campaigned to end suicide being a criminal offence which led to the change in the 1961 Suicide Act. He had introduced a Private Members Bill to legalise abortion in 1961, well before David Steel's successful 1967 Bill. He was a campaigner for homosexual law reform and in 1960 had introduced the first Parliamentary debate on the Wolfenden Committee's report. He had been the first chairman of the National Association of Mental Health, now known as Mind, and remained committed to mental health reform.

I was responsible for Ministerial correspondence and he expected replies for his signature to reflect his social liberalism, whatever the more cautious civil service might wish. He was meticulous in replying to his colleagues, MPs and a wide range of interest groups. He was a competent speaker but no great orator. He was seen as a technocratic Minister, unattached to any Labour Party faction. But on issues he cared about he was very determined. He limited promotional advertising for cigarettes (despite Crossman's opposition) and was a staunch critic of the tobacco industry. I became very involved with his battle with scientologists.

In the 1960s the so-called Church of Scientology had not achieved the scale and following of today. Founded in the 1950s by L Ron Hubbard, a Californian science fiction writer, it aimed at implementing a self-help book he had written called Dianetics. Scientology's central tenet was that people were immortal spiritual beings who had lost their true nature. Essentially, they needed to rediscover their 'thetan', the source of the life force said to have created the universe and which had been trapped in human bodies. To enable its release a person should go through 'auditing' to enable them to re-experience painful events in their past that needed confronting. In the 1960s 'auditing' was a crude process, with the person and the auditor each holding an E-meter which was effectively two cans joined by wire. It looked like any other flaky Californian creed of self-discovery.

In 1959 Hubbard set up his worldwide headquarters in a Georgian manor in East Grinstead. From here he ran his operations in the UK, the USA, Australia and South Africa, including delivering his UK courses. Scientology had become an organised commercial cult that recruited vulnerable people and relieved them (or their families) of large sums of money and then left them in a damaged state. We received a growing number of complaints about activities in East Grinstead. Harrowing accounts of people who had experienced scientology "treatment" began to attract national media coverage. There was pressure to do something, particularly following the Australian Anderson Report's scathing criticisms of Scientology. Robinson wanted to act, but Crossman – now his boss – was unconvinced.

In the end, Robinson persuaded the Home Office that the immigration rules should be used. On 25 July 1968 the UK became the first country to introduce national restrictions on Scientology. Foreign scientologists were banned from entering the country and Hubbard was branded as an 'undesirable alien.' In the Commons Robinson laid into the scientologists.

> *"The Government is satisfied, having reviewed all the available evidence, that Scientology is socially harmful. It alienates members of families from each other and attributes squalid and disgraceful motives to all who oppose it. Its authoritarian principles and practices are a potential menace to the personality and well-being of those so deluded as to become its followers; above all its methods can be a serious danger to the health of those who submit to them."*

The scientologists campaigned vigorously against the ban. A huge petition was delivered to AFH with hundreds of signatures and letters. I collected it but declined to be filmed doing so. I passed it to officials for filing. In the short term, it was a victory for Robinson and common sense. About 140 people were banned from entering the UK and Hubbard left in 1969, never to return before his death in 1986. He was convicted of fraud in France; removed his worldwide HQ from the UK; but kept a property in East Grinstead.

Before the end of 1968 Dick Crossman – now fully in charge - tried to reverse Robinson's robust approach with an inquiry that proved inconclusive. Civil liberties organisations continued to campaign against the ban with support from the Guardian; and there were several legal challenges. Margaret Thatcher asked Willie Whitelaw to lift the ban, but this was derailed by Hubbard's wife's criminal conviction in the USA. Eventually, the pressure told and in 1996 Michael Howard, then Home Secretary, lifted the ban. Today, all Robinson's determined opposition to Scientology, a cult masquerading as a religion, has been undone. Scientologists even set up a recruiting tent outside the burned-out shell of Grenfell Tower.

Changing Ministers: Dick Crossman

On 6 April 1968 Harold Wilson announced a major Cabinet reshuffle with the headline appointment of Barbara Castle as First Secretary of State in charge of the new Department of Employment and Productivity, making her the most senior female Cabinet appointment. There was another bombshell. Dick Crossman who had been Lord President and Leader of the House of Commons was given overall responsibility for health and social security, with their two Ministers, Kenneth Robinson and Judith Hart, staying in post. Crossman remained Lord President and initially was to act as a co-ordinating Secretary of State for Social Services based in the Cabinet Office with a small staff. A new Department of Health and Social Security (DHSS) would be formed, some said, large enough for Crossman's ego.

Initially we saw little of Crossman who was preoccupied with a new pension scheme, working with Judith Hart and his own brains trust. Robinson and Crossman disliked each other. Robinson made it clear he didn't want to work for Crossman; but for the time being pursued his own agenda. Few of us in Health realised what a big political beast Crossman was. He remained Lord President and the chairman of many Cabinet Committees. By office and temperament, he remained heavily involved in the big political issues of the day – immigration (following Enoch Powell's 'Rivers of Blood' speech); House of Lords reform; Scottish devolution; and the whole area of prices and incomes policy and public expenditure.

This was a period of economic turbulence, shifting Cabinet alliances and occasional Prime Ministerial paranoia about plots. In the

Private Office we were simply unused to a powerful Minister who played for high political stakes and could get the Prime Minister's attention whenever he liked. We soon learned that Crossman was more interested in Labour Party manoeuvrings than briefs on the NHS. Finally, on 18 October the DHSS was announced alongside the merger of the Foreign and Commonwealth Offices. Judith Hart joined the Cabinet as Paymaster-General. Kenneth Robinson did not, and instead became Minister for Planning and Land in Housing and Local Government – a post abolished a year later. (He left Parliament in 1970, a sad loss in my view.)

Sir Clifford Jarrett from social security became DHSS Permanent Secretary and Alan Marre – who had helped set up the NHS – was the No. 2. On 4 November, Crossman and his new team "took over Alexander Fleming House, the great skyscraper at the Elephant and Castle" – as he described it in his Diaries. Crossman hated AFH and wanted his headquarters to be at social security's elegant Georgian offices in John Adams Street. Jarrett decreed this was too small to accommodate the top brass. Crossman insisted his driver did timed runs between the two places and his London flat and Parliament. There wasn't much time difference so the hated AFH it was. Later Crossman asked me to arrange a meeting with Erno Goldfinger. I had to rescue an ashen Goldfinger from Crossman's lengthy tirade on AFH's shortcomings.

Crossman had two new Ministers of State – Stephen Swingler for social security and David Ennals for health and two journeymen Parliamentary Under-Secretaries, Julian Snow and Norman Pentland. He inherited Robinson's private office, plus a social security equivalent to me. Fortunately, his longstanding secretary, Janet Newman, came with him to keep his diary, organise his energetic social life and save our bacon by rescuing confidential Cabinet papers from under his bed or elsewhere in his London and Oxford homes. Janet was the only one who knew how to handle Crossman, a physically imposing intellectual bully used to getting his own way. Later we discovered he had serious stomach problems which may explain a lot.

The early months with Crossman were total chaos as this bull elephant charged around our small farmyard. Fortunately, on social security, Crossman inherited from Douglas Houghton and Peggy

Herbison much good work on pensions, means-tested benefits and the idea of tax credits. Despite a regular diet of visits and meetings, Crossman struggled with the culture and conduct of the NHS. He saw health officials as cautious bureaucrats, used to getting their own way with Kenneth Robinson. He thought senior officials were hiding things from him and would search through files for advice contrary to their recommendations. I often hunted through files to find where he had scribbled his views; or brought young dissidents to see him, without wrecking their careers. His tongue-lashings of the luckless Alan Marre were painful to behold. With the exception of George Godber, few were exempt. We tried to explain that his approach didn't get the best out of the civil service but not a lot changed in my time.

In this chaos, Crossman still had a capacity to surprise on health issues. His experience as a local councillor in Oxford and as Minister of Housing and Local Government gave him a good understanding of local government. He was a supporter of health centres and kept a map in his room showing progress on the health centre building programme- even if his arm-waving periodically knocked all the pins off the map. He wrestled with the problem of the NHS and local government boundary as he attempted another Green Paper on NHS reform. Crossman also understood the NHS scope for political patronage at a time when few people worried about standards in public life. He wanted to get as many Labour supporters as possible on hospital boards while he could, because he knew Conservative Ministers would do the same when they were in office. He was canny enough to put nothing down on paper but to use the Party machine and not his private office, thankfully.

I thought Crossman's greatest NHS achievement was the way he handled Geoffrey Howe's ground-breaking report on the scandalous conditions and treatment in Ely Hospital - a mental handicap hospital in the Cardiff constituency of the Welsh Secretary of State, George Thomas. After a heated political battle, Harold Wilson backed Crossman's wish to publish the damning report in full on 27 March 1969. Crossman then brushed aside civil service reservations and robustly tackled the isolation of long-stay hospitals by setting up in November 1969 an independent Hospital Advisory Service. This was to inspect and report on standards in hospitals, initially long-stay

23

hospitals. Crossman appointed Dr Alex Baker, a psychiatrist, as its first director. This was the forerunner of today's Care Quality Commission.

In February 1969, Stephen Swingler unexpectedly died. Harold Wilson came up with possible replacements that Crossman rejected on competence grounds and asked for Roy Hattersley, who Wilson in turn rejected, later it appeared on loyalty grounds. In the end the bold decision was taken to appoint Baroness Bea Serota, a Lords Whip, as the Health Minister of State and to switch a disappointed David Ennals to social security. This caused a small insurrection by Julian Snow who couldn't understand why he hadn't been promoted.

By then, I'd had enough of the long hours and Crossman's approach to people. On several occasions I had simply walked out of his room when he started shouting at me, once telling him I'd come back when he'd calmed down. The Department wanted to promote me. Surprisingly, Crossman wanted me promoted but to stay on working for him. I rejected the idea and the Department supported me. This did not go down well with Dick and I never appeared in his Diaries. I left just before our second child, a girl, was born in April 1969.

Executive Councils and Disciplining Doctors

Just before Neil Armstrong walked on the moon, I moved to the sleepy world of Executive Councils. I was now on the Mandarin ladder as a Principal, with my small piece of DHSS to run. I was responsible for Executive Council administration; disciplinary procedures for independent contractors providing GP, dental, pharmaceutical and optical services; and the Medical Act governing the professional standards and conduct of UK doctors. With no management training I found myself managing 20 executive and clerical staff whose performance I had to appraise. I had joined the club of 'gifted amateur' generalists who could turn their hand to anything. The Fulton Report, published in 1968, was supposed to change this; but I never did receive any management training in my time in the civil service.

Executive Councils were organised by Counties, with a mega Council for London. They held the contracts with individual contractors and had professional bodies to advise them, the most powerful of which were Local Medical Committees elected by doctors. In the 1960s the professions operated a tight grip on Councils, especially the LMCs who were the major source of national officers of the BMA - a registered trade union. Responsibility for Executive Council administration meant their offices, their costs, their governance and any serious problems that arose. I had regular meetings with the Council Clerks and attended their annual conference. Most Clerks had been in post since the start of the NHS and didn't want a new kid at HQ interfering in their affairs. Only when big problems arose, like an expensive new office in London, was I useful. Surprisingly, I found myself in charge of the 1971 currency decimalisation for Executive Councils which I promptly delegated to my deputy.

I doubt if the NHS founders realised the implications of establishing a contractual relationship between the Health Minister and tens of thousands of independent contractors. This had produced a contractor disciplinary system that involved proving breaches of those contracts and applying sanctions for the breaches. This was the main part of my job. Initially cases were decided by Executive Council Service Committees in accordance with national regulations, usually after an oral hearing at which practitioners could be legally represented. Appeals and serious cases came to DHSS where they were considered by a small panel chaired by my boss, an Assistant Secretary, with a professional adviser and me. We would determine the outcome on behalf of the Health Secretary. I usually ended up being prosecuting counsel and judge. Each week we spent a morning deciding these cases.

There were three types of case: fraud, poor quality care and professional misconduct. Fraud cases typically involved dentists, pharmacists or opticians claiming for treatments not given. Poor quality care and professional misconduct might also be involved – for example where a dentist was repeatedly filling the same tooth. The medical cases were usually more serious matters of poor practice with adverse consequences for patients, such as failure to refer a patient to a specialist or to make a home visit. There were even cases where a GP, phoned in the night for an emergency visit, had gone back to sleep and a child died.

Once 'guilt' was established we had to decide a sanction for the breach of contract. There were several levels of sanctions - warnings, fines and reporting serious cases to the GMC and other professional bodies. The latter could end up with a practitioner being struck off the professional register. If it was a first offence and not too serious, we would let the practitioner off with a warning. The remaining offences were usually dealt with by a fine and a stiff letter. About once a month a case we thought constituted professional misconduct would be sent to the professional body. I soon concluded that the fines were derisory - often as low as £100 for quite serious failures. I agitated for a substantial increase – basically adding a nought to the current 'tariff.' A row with the professions predictably followed. But I was able to show fines had not increased for years and had not even kept pace with inflation. I secured higher-level support and after a consultation the fines were increased substantially. I also started sending more cases to professional bodies because of my concerns about clinical competence.

My third area of responsibility was legislation governing the work of the General Medical Council (GMC). In those days the GMC was elected by the medical profession and had over 100 members but no lay people. The GMC Chairman was Lord Cohen of Birkenhead, a 70-year-old formidable Professor of Medicine, occasionally seen with a top hat. Bureaucrats and politicians were not Henry's favourite people. I minimised contact with him when I had to handle the passage of the modest 1971 Medical Act. This made no changes to the GMC's medical self-regulation model. That took another 30 years following the 2001 Kennedy Inquiry Report into the Bristol Royal Infirmary paediatric surgery deaths. Only then was the GMC Council reduced to 35 members, 40% of whom were lay members. Now the Council has only 12 members, half of them lay people.

The sleepy 1940s world of Executive Councils that I inherited in 1969 was long overdue for change. By a series of later NHS re-organisations, they became Family Health Service Authorities, Primary Care Trusts and then, in 2013, Clinical Commissioning Groups. NHS England now contracts with groups of GPs for services supplied under nationally agreed contracts and operates a system of contract breaches, sanctions and terminations all set out in a complex contract document. But individual 'offenders' still go to the professional bodies to see if they should be retrained or struck off the register. Further changes are now in prospect.

By late 1970 I had become bored, despite rising rapidly in the civil service. I had always wanted to live and travel in the USA and, by luck, spotted a scheme open to a civil servant each year for study in the US. After backing from DHSS, I produced a plausible project to study US healthcare financing and delivery and gained a Harkness Fellowship. In September 1971, my then wife and our two children (aged two and four) gallantly set sail with me from Southampton on the SS France. My parents came to see us off, fearing no return. Having sold our house, I wasn't sure we would.

US Government and Healthcare Reform

The SS France was elegant and luxurious, with the Atlantic bumpy and grey. After four days we eased past a misty Statue of Liberty into the Hudson River and a berth on Manhattan's lower West Side. To US immigration authorities we looked typical drug smugglers, so they turned out our trunk of children's clothes and toys on the customs hall floor. Finally, we made it to our hotel and the Central Park Zoo. After a few days sightseeing in a steamy New York and collecting Harkness funding we flew to Washington DC. After grappling with letting agents, insurance companies and banks, we ended with an apartment in the Maryland suburb of Rockville and a gas-guzzling yellow Dodge estate wagon which was to take us on our American odyssey over the next two years.

Our arrival was three years into Richard Nixon's first administration. Nixon had just surprised the world by announcing he would visit China following Kissinger's secret negotiations with Zhou Enlai. The Vietnam War was still the No.1 political issue although Nixon had reduced the number of US ground forces in Vietnam from over 500.000 in 1969 to well under 100,000. Instead, he had intensified bombing, including Cambodia and Laos, which was killing many civilians. America was very divided, particularly after the National Guard had shot 4 students at Kent State University the previous year. Nixon's mind was on his second term and he wanted a distracting domestic issue. What better than health care?

In his 1971 State of the Union address Nixon had launched a $100 million campaign to find a cure for cancer, pushing health up the political agenda. At the same time the Democrats had Senator Ted Kennedy focussing on healthcare as part of his political rehabilitation after the Chappaquiddick incident. Kennedy co-sponsored a Bill providing even more money than Nixon for cancer research; and in 1971 became Chair of the Senate Health Sub-Committee. Using this platform, he launched his 'Health Security Act' calling for a universal single-payer plan financed through payroll taxes.

With the support of organised labour, Kennedy held hearings across the US on his proposed legislation and published a report, 'The Health Crisis in America.' Worried that Kennedy might run against him for President, Nixon published his version of reform legislation – the National Health Insurance Partnership Act. This preserved private insurance but required employers to provide coverage to all employees who contributed 25% of premiums and also gave some support to health maintenance organisations. The political battle lines were drawn: some Democrats arguing for a single payer system, like the NHS; and a Republican President trying to extend coverage by tweaking the traditional US health insurance system. It looked as though I had chosen a hot political topic for study as we arrived in Washington DC.

My base was an agency of the Health Education and Welfare Department (HEW). This was the National Centre for Health Services Research and Development based in a new Federal Building in Rockville. It was headed by Dr Paul Sanazaro, a political appointee, who promptly put me under the wing of Dr Gil Barnhart, a permanent civil servant. I never saw Sanazaro again. The Centre seemed like a giant cash dispensing machine for academic researchers in nice parts of the US like Albuquerque that needed visiting regularly to see how research was going. Most Centre's staff had little interest in my subjects, funding systems, healthcare coverage and service delivery.

I decided to use the Centre as a research base and organise my own programme of visits from there. I wasn't able to meet the Secretary of HEW, Elliot Richardson, a liberal Republican, who filled five Cabinet posts and later became US Ambassador in London. I met many of his staff in the HEW headquarters and regional offices and was struck by how well-regarded Richardson was by staff largely overtly Democrats. He was to achieve national fame in October 1973 when he resigned as

Nixon's Attorney General for refusing to sack the Special Prosecutor, Archibald Cox, then investigating the Watergate scandal (see below).

Over six month I met experts in health insurance and health care organisations. I travelled to New York, Chicago (Blue Cross, Blue Shield and the AMA), Philadelphia, North Carolina, Atlanta, Harrisburg, Virginia and Baltimore (Social Security Administration who ran Medicare). I even secured an interview with Ted Kennedy who interrogated me about the virtues of the NHS, but thought it was a bridge too far for the US: I met him again a few years later. I gave a lecture at Richmond's Medical School to an audience hostile to 'socialised medicine' and full of GP critics of the NHS who had fled to the US.

The picture that emerged was of an expensive, provider dominated healthcare system with high administrative costs because of its health insurance funding system. At least a third of the country had no insurance coverage. They relied, in an emergency, on overcrowded public hospitals, some of which I visited. Those with insurance usually received good quality care but many doctors practiced very defensive medicine, with large numbers of diagnostic tests. Payment was by item of service so there was every incentive to order more tests than needed, particularly if you had a stake in the diagnostic services or the hospital you used. Conflicts of interest were abundant but seemed not to bother anybody. The lack of primary care 'gatekeepers' meant many people went straight to a specialist whether they needed to or not. Negligence claims were rising, along with the cost of medical insurance. The generosity of insurance coverage usually depended on your employer, so this influenced job choice.

At the heart of the US healthcare debate were three issues: the large number of people with no healthcare insurance; the rapidly rising cost of healthcare as a proportion of GDP; and the effect of these costs on employers. These problems were greatest for people of working age because the Johnson era Medicare scheme now looked after the needs of the elderly. Although there was much public dissatisfaction with coverage and costs, few people seemed optimistic about the prospects of reform. People I interviewed had some interest in the NHS, but disliked the idea of 'socialised' medicine and the perceived lack of choice over specialist care. There was interest in Kennedy's single payer system but those involved with healthcare rarely thought it would never happen. The insurance industry, the private hospital sector and the AMA had too much political clout for Kennedy and organised labour to win.

I concluded that item of service payment was hard-wired into the hospital and medical reimbursement systems. This put healthcare spending on a perpetually rising escalator. The transaction costs of a private health insurance system in the 1970s added over 10% to healthcare costs with no patient gain. Medicare was restricted to older patients and although it was a single-payer system, providers were still paid by the inflationary item of service system. Medicaid and the public hospitals provided a safety net for the poor without insurance but were not care models acceptable to the middle-classes. The nearest the US got to an NHS was the Veteran's Administration (VA) which was nationwide, was a direct provider of both inpatient and outpatient care and had its own funding stream provided by Congress. I returned to see the VA's IT advances when I was a Minister (see Chapter 11).

By the Spring of 1972 I came to the conclusion that, apart from the VA, the Kaiser Permanente healthcare system and a few brave Health Maintenance Organisations, most of the US working age population were trapped in a provider-controlled healthcare system with no effective ceiling on costs. The lessons for the NHS were to avoid going down this road. The Vietnam war continued to dominate American politics, especially following the publication of the 'Pentagon Papers' by the New York Times. Although there were plenty of health reform bills floating around Congress – Javits, Griffiths, Kennedy – the Democrats chose Senator George McGovern as their 1972 Presidential candidate. He had fallen out with organised labour and had no interest in campaigning for healthcare reform.

I went to some Congressional hearings, but healthcare reform had gone off the boil. There was no prospect of any bi-partisan agreement on reform, with the Republicans only interested in small tweaks to the system and the Democrats uncertain about how to proceed. Ted Kennedy lacked the political heft to secure a single-payer system. The Clintons would have another go at healthcare reform in the 1990s without getting close to achieving it.

The US had to wait another 40 years until 2010 for any significant expansion of healthcare coverage with Barack Obama's Affordable Care Act. Even with Obamacare, the improved coverage was well short of universal and proved vulnerable to Trumpian attacks. Moreover, Obamacare never really tackled the problem that continues to bedevil US healthcare – excessive price inflation from a provider dominated system. US health spending remains at about 18% of GDP whereas the UK and EU average is about half that.

By mid-1972 there was nothing more for me to do in Washington; but I still wanted to drive across the USA and spend time in California. I tracked down an Anglophile Professor of Public Health at Berkeley, Henrik Blum, who was willing to let me do a two-year Master of Public Health course in one-year, starting in September 1972. The Commonwealth Fund agreed to pay, and DHSS agreed I could stay longer. I finished my paper on US healthcare; and prepared for four of us to drive across the USA. Nixon beat McGovern in a landslide in November 1972; and US healthcare reform died a death. Little notice was taken of a burglary at the Democratic National Committee's offices in DC's Watergate Building.

Living in the USA

To understand America and Americans you have to stay on the ground and experience the diversity, surprises and contradictions. In 1970s America travel with young children was affordable and easy. Petrol was cheap, so were motels and good quality campsites and eateries. You packed your station wagon with camping gear and set off on spacious Interstate highways for well-preserved and spectacular national and state parks - FDR's inheritance. The surprises and contradictions were plentiful on a trip to the South.

George Washington's Mount Vernon home is modest. Thomas Jefferson's Monticello reveals his ambivalent attitude to slavery. The Disneyland version of C18th Williamsburg can produce a guide describing the Governor's House as a "scene of British tyranny." The Civil War battlefields like Gettysburg were slaughterhouses where more Americans died than in any other US war. The local heroes in Virginia's capital, Richmond, are Jefferson Davis and Robert E Lee, not the Founding Fathers. The humidity of ante-bellum Charleston and Savannah and the Okefenokee swamp help to explain Southern difference.

Just four years after the assassination of Martin Luther King we drove into Alabama from the tourist playgrounds of Florida to be greeted by a huge welcoming picture of the segregationist Governor, George Wallace. In Biloxi, Mississippi, hostile Daughters of the American Revolution took us round the home of Jefferson Davis (first and last President of the Confederacy) thinking we were Yankees. Shortly after we met our first Native American Indians when we camped in their Tennessee campsite.

Even a century after the Civil War, for some in the South it hadn't really ended. The Ku Klux Klan was still in evidence. It was only a few years since Federal law enforcement officers had been despatched to Mississippi to investigate the deaths of two civil rights campaigners. When I visited an LBJ 'Great Society' project for the black community in South Atlanta, life there provided a stark contrast with the shiny new glass skyscrapers in nearby Peachtree Avenue. Both then and now racism remains a major problem; but a New York experience made me realise the dangers of racial stereotyping. Window shopping in Times Square I became aware I was surrounded by six large black guys. I was considering my best option when two of them asked me about my suit with its flared trousers. We had an amicable discussion about Manhattan and London tailors.

It took a drive across America in June 1972 to appreciate the scale and natural beauty of the USA and how different it is to Europe. The first stop was Boston, followed by camping in the White Mountains and then on through Vermont to Niagara Falls. There we donned oilskins to walk behind the Falls. There are always boring bits like a three-day drive round the Great Lakes and across Iowa and Nebraska. Arriving late at night in Cheyenne, Wyoming, we found a diner/bar full of rednecks unused to hungry children well past their bedtime. Then on to Denver and Rocky Mountain National Park. This was the start of a lifelong love affair with the American national Parks – nearly ended by a tyre blow out coming down the Rockies.

We made it to Durango after crossing the Rio Grande. Staying in a cabin on top of a mesa we explored the astonishing cliff dwellings of

Mesa Verde, built by the Anasazi Indians around the C12th. From the man-made phenomenon of the Anasazi Cliff Palace, we drove to the extraordinary colours of the Grand Canyon's sunrises and sunsets. I walked halfway down the Kaibab Trail before giving in. Then on to Utah's exotic rock formations, first in Zion National Park and then walking among the multi-coloured, wind-eroded columns of Bryce Canyon. Descending from 7,000 feet, we headed to Salt Lake City (depressing), Reno in Nevada (equally depressing) and finally to California and a home on the San Andreas Fault.

California is a country in its own right, then the fifth largest economy in the world. Ronald Reagan had been re-elected Governor in 1971 after tackling California's financial deficit problems and was becoming a national figure. San Francisco's Haight-Astbury district was its radical heart with the patron saint of LSD, the Harvard psychologist Timothy Leary, still encouraging everyone to "turn on, tune in and drop out." Berkeley was beginning to change, with its anti-war People's Park in decline and more Republican fraternity boys - a contrast to the long-haired Berkeley police. We lived in student accommodation in the Berkeley Hills. My son went to an Oakland primary school where most pupils were black and sang the star-spangled banner each morning with his hand on his heart.

I thought I should try to see Ronald Reagan in Sacramento. Although unable to meet the man himself, I spent a morning with his Health Secretary discussing UK and US healthcare. At the end of this he offered me a job as a policy analyst, but I thought I wouldn't last long with Reagan and his views on welfare. Later, as a Minister, I could boast I was the only member of the Labour Party who'd been offered a job by Ronald Reagan.

The liberal School of Public Health used positive discrimination to recruit more students from minority groups. I was friendly with a Navajo Indian doing a post-graduate course so that he could set up primary care and public health services on his reservation. My civil service drafting skills secured good grades for the written work that determined my degree. I learned a lot about psychology, changing human behaviour and public health practice; and I undertook a project in the local authority to reduce alcoholism - whether it did or not I never found out. All this enabled me to return to the UK as a Master of Public Health.

As the end of my time in Berkeley approached, US government provided a new drama - the Senate Watergate Hearings. The burglary of the Democrats' offices was not straightforward, although it had not stopped Nixon winning the 1972 Election easily. Washington Post's reporters, Woodward and Bernstein, had relentlessly pursued a link to Nixon. In May 1973 the Senate set up bi-partisan hearings under the chairmanship of North Carolina's Democrat Senator, Sam Ervin. The Public Broadcasting Service (PBS) decided to broadcast these hearings live and so did the commercial news channels, with repeats in the evenings. Across the US, Americans watched the skewering of their President live: over 80% of Americans saw part of over 300 hours of broadcast hearings. In Berkeley life became organised around the afternoon's live hearings from Washington.

We sat in bars with jugs of beer, faculty and students together, glued to the screens. The interrogation of witnesses was conducted by Ervin and the leading Republican, Senator Howard Baker from Tennessee. Baker developed the catchphrase questions – 'what did the President know and when did he know it.' It was gripping stuff, especially the discovery of the tapes of Nixon's Oval Office meetings. It didn't seem to matter to most Americans that JFK and Johnson also taped meetings. The hearings were like a thriller, but we wouldn't know the ending until after we returned to the UK.

The Senate's huge report was published in June 1974. Over 40 officials were prosecuted, including White House Counsel, John Dean. Nixon refused to release the tapes but the Special Investigator, Archibald Cox, continued to demand their release. Nixon fired Cox and his new Attorney General, Elliot Richardson, and continued to deny knowledge of the burglary. Eventually a 'smoking gun' tape emerged revealing Nixon's early knowledge of the break-in. Nixon had a choice, resign or face impeachment. He resigned in August 1974 and Gerald Ford became President and promptly pardoned Nixon. Ford, the former House Minority Leader, had only become Vice President in October 1973 when Spiro Agnew resigned over a corruption scandal when he was Governor of Maryland. And this was 40 years before Donald Trump.

There was time for one last trip down the Pacific Coast and across country to Las Vegas and Death Valley where we raced a flash flood washing away the dirt road behind us. We soothed our nerves with the calm of the giant redwoods in King's Canyon and Sequoia National Park and later in Yosemite. Although I had enjoyed my time in the US, I realised I was a European social democrat who was unlikely to flourish in US government. I had major reservations about living in a country with a written constitution framed in the 18th century by slave-owning Founding Fathers. The US version of capitalism, its gun laws and racial tensions were decided downsides. As we flew back to the UK in August 1973, I knew that the USA was a place I would visit to see friends but would never live there.

NHS Reorganisation and Management as the New Religion

On my return to DHSS in September 1973 I found it absorbed in two issues – Keith Joseph's reorganisation of the NHS and its new religion – management. The two overlapped. Joseph had decided that the NHS needed better management and the Department had fallen into the clutches of management gurus. McKinsey were advising DHSS and Brunel University was leading on NHS reorganisation. I was assigned to the latter and had to learn new doctrine.

I was surprised how much government had changed while I had been away. In 1972 Heath had taken us into what was to become the European Economic Area. He had encouraged government to take a longer-term view with the establishment in 1971 of a new 'Think Tank,' the Central Policy Review Staff (CPRS) chaired by Lord Rothchild. Heath had also tried to reduce the size of the Cabinet by combining some Departments. Attempts were being made to make the civil service more professional following the 1968 Report of the Fulton Committee that had recommended more management training, with top civil servants having wider experience in the outside world. The civil service class structure had been abolished and more officials were attending courses at the new Civil Service College.

As part of this cultural shift DHSS tried to apply management efficiency to itself and the NHS. The problem was the Department tended to see 'management' as a new policy to be introduced like any other policy, rather than as something people had to learn to do. They found it difficult to apply to themselves the expensive advice they were receiving. McKinsey partners invited me to lunch to discuss their frustration with the DHSS top management. When they left for yet another top-level meeting, they described these encounters as "wrestling with a jellyfish." Of course, they consoled themselves with their fees from this new source – government – which was to serve them well for decades to come.

The NHS reorganisation was not going smoothly. On 5 July 1973 Royal Assent had been given to the NHS Reorganisation Act. In the 1960s Joseph had toyed with the idea of an insurance-funded NHS but had now shifted his focus to management efficiency and organisational change. He had discarded Dick Crossman's NHS re-organisation plans in favour of integrating NHS bodies and reducing their number. Joseph had ended up replacing 700 hospital boards, boards of governors, management committees and executive councils with 14 regional health authorities, 90 area health authorities (AHAs), each with a linked family practitioner committee and 200 district management teams, each with a community health council to represent patient views.

To help deliver the changes Joseph had brought in as consultants, Brunel University, led by Professor Elliott Jacques. A large multi-disciplinary study group oversaw the detailed planning of new structures using a management 'bible' produced by Brunel called the 'Grey Book.' The aim was consistency of grading and job descriptions at all levels – regional, area and district. As each staff and professional group tried to protect their interests, the sheer lunacy of this was revealed. Some of the DHSS meetings I attended were dire, as we descended into theological debates about whether there should be district remedial gymnasts and the finer points of grading new posts. A casualty of Joseph's reorganisation was the Salmon Committee's senior nursing changes I had worked on less than a decade ago.

The NHS was taught new management speak. Maximum delegation downwards was to be accompanied by maximum accountability upwards – whatever that meant. Things were to be run on a basis of 'consensus management' – in practice a recipe for endlessly referring issues upwards. As NHS staff scrambled for jobs at the new regional, area and district tiers, it was unclear to some of us who would be left to manage the hospitals. There seemed to be no credible implementation plan for a start date that was less than 6 months away. When I asked to see the file on the allocation of functions to regions, areas and districts I was told there wasn't one - despite the NHS needing a circular on the division of responsibilities. A couple of us drafted a circular and whizzed it round the Department. After a few tweaks, we issued it to the NHS to give them some guidance.

Joseph's focus on NHS management was sensible, as was reducing the number of bodies. But the detailed grading system was daft, as was neglecting hospital management where so much of the money was spent. I also thought he had one tier too many, but it was too late to change the structure. Despite all the detailed work put into the 1974 NHS reorganisation it was fundamentally flawed and planted the seeds for an unproductive NHS bureaucracy. The new DHSS Permanent Secretary, Pat Nairne, who arrived later in 1974, aptly summed up this reorganisation as "tears about tiers."

The changes were not entirely bad. They improved slightly the balance between hospital and community services. Little noticed at the time, Joseph's Community Health Councils gave patients a say in running the NHS for the first time and there was a better complaints procedure. But the bureaucratic cost of the changes was very high. A few years later Professor Rudolph Klein revealed that administrative and clerical staff had increased by nearly a third to make the re-organisation work. The public took little interest in the changes, regarding them for what they were – a reshuffle of the bureaucratic chairs which didn't affect services much. This reorganisation caused none of the fuss of later ones. Labour opposed the changes, but when they took office in March 1974, they declined to halt them because of the chaos it would cause. Too many people had already changed jobs. There was little national publicity and Barbara Castle left David Owen to handle implementation.

While NHS reorganisation was limping along there was a tremendous shock to the global political system. October 1973 saw the Yom Kippur war and the resulting OPEC oil embargo because of US support for Israel. Oil prices soared and a UK financial crisis followed. The Chancellor, Anthony Barber, introduced a package of public expenditure cuts and a policy of wage restraint. Resisting wage demands soon led to industrial unrest and the miners overtime ban in

January 1974. Heath took emergency powers and imposed a 3-day working week, with Patrick Jenkin memorably telling people to clean their teeth in the dark. Heath tried a trial of strength with the miners over who ran the country. The miners closed every pit. Heath then called an Election and lost a commanding poll lead in the election campaign. After Heath failed to clinch a coalition deal with the Liberal Democrats, Harold Wilson found himself, to his surprise, forming a Labour Government on 4 March 1974.

With constraints on public expenditure following the oil price hike, the high administrative costs of Joseph's NHS reorganisation continued to be a problem. There was a growing recognition that there was one tier too many, but no agreement on which one to abolish. David Owen wanted to remove the regional tier, but DHSS officials were keen to keep it for reasons of control. I rather agreed with them and thought districts were the problem. They drained managerial talent from the acute hospitals who spent so much of the NHS budget and added little value. There was some discussion of merging districts and AHAs and devolving more authority to areas but nothing much changed.

Neither DHSS nor the NHS wanted another re-organisation. Even better alignment of NHS and local authority boundaries was off-limits. Barbara tried to build a relationship with AHAs, but officials preferred running the NHS through regions. Labour pledged in the March Election campaign to increase democratic accountability in the NHS; and increased the number of local authority members on AHAs from a quarter to a third. This did little to improve service integration and was Labour's only contribution to the 1974 reorganisation.

By April 1974 I was being sounded out about a new job – Principal Private Secretary to the new Secretary of State, Barbara Castle. On 18 June I was interviewed by Barbara and was able to flourish my working-class credentials and trade union father. We seemed to hit it off, and I took up the job the following month. My apprenticeship was over and a two-year roller-coaster ride was about to begin.

2. Life with the Red Queen: 1974-1976

Life as Barbara Castle's Private Secretary

Working for Barbara Castle involved much more than dealing with the NHS and BMA. There was a new state pension scheme to be settled; an independent Supplementary Benefits Commission to be established; and the replacement of family allowances with a new child benefit scheme that would be controversial. Barbara also wanted to raise the status of social services, play a leading role in Cabinet and oppose membership of the EEC in a referendum campaign. This policy range was huge, with no devolution then and a budget that accounted for about 25% of public expenditure. Barbara was supported by just four other Ministers. Today it takes a Secretary of State, five other Ministers, plus NHS England and several other quangos to just run the NHS and social care in England. The backdrop was economic crisis, pay restraint and a seemingly endless review of public expenditure.

The Private Office consisted of me and two other private secretaries and a diary secretary. To my surprise I found I was the line manager for all staff in the Ministerial offices and that this involved intervening if Ministers and their private secretaries fell out – this happened in David Owen's office when a more experienced private secretary had to be found. I also managed the branch that dealt with Parliamentary Questions and the Ministerial correspondence section. The latter handled the growing avalanche of letters from MPs, other Ministers and some celebrities and friends. The 1970s was really the beginning of MPs becoming social workers and passing on constituents' woes to Ministers at scale. It also saw a big increase in 'write-in' campaigns, sometimes sponsored by newspapers.

Barbara had long ago learned to delegate to her junior Ministers – Brian O'Malley, Alf Morris, Alec Jones (later, Michael Meacher) and David Owen (first as Parliamentary Secretary and later a Minister of State). Barbara particularly trusted O'Malley who was in charge of social security. She delegated a large amount of running the NHS to David Owen; but their relationship went through some difficult patches in the dealings with the BMA. I kept a close eye on Morris and Meacher.

Alongside the Ministerial team were Barbara's special advisers (SPADs): Professor Brian Abel-Smith (an LSE social policy academic who had worked for Dick Crossman); Tony Lynes (a prickly social security expert concerned with claimants' rights); Jack Straw (a political adviser and Islington councillor, appointed by Barbara for what she called his "low cunning."); and David Piachaud, (a young LSE academic). In the 1970s SPADs were a new feature of government; and civil service traditionalists still had reservations about them. Cabinet Ministers were only supposed to have one SPAD, but Barbara had secured Wilson's agreement to four. This gave her considerable alternative policy capability to the civil service. The SPADs worked fairly well with civil servants who used them to float ideas.

There were others to keep on good terms with. Ministers' drivers are important sources of Whitehall gossip and usually know about reshuffles before anybody else. Ministers still have to get re-elected, so you have to pay attention to their constituency staff, who in Barbara's case were excellent. Perhaps, most importantly, was regular contact with the Permanent Secretary: initially this was Philip Rogers (whose obituary I later wrote for The Guardian) and then, Patrick Nairne (whose calligraphic notes and sketches at meetings were often more interesting than the discussion). The most regular attendants at my desk were the Information Director, Peter Brown (who had also worked for Dick Crossman) and his sidekick, Ian Gillis. They were neurotic about Barbara's covert access to the media and suspicious that I was selective about what I told them, which I was. Brown renamed me the 'Prince of Darkness.'

Barbara Castle had hitched her political star to Harold Wilson. She still had relatively easy access to him but was suspicious of his deviousness. After the trauma of 'In Place of Strife' and the failure of her Cabinet colleagues, led by Jim Callaghan, to support her trade union reforms, Barbara was keen to rebuild her reputation at the DHSS. Given her age it was her last throw of the political dice, but it didn't stop her mixing it with her male counterparts if she thought it necessary.

Barbara cared about her personal appearance, particularly as politics entered the age of television. Her weekly appointment with her hairdresser was as sacrosanct as Cabinet meetings. At times of crisis a dash to the hairdresser for a comb out was as important as any civil service briefing If all else failed there was always the reliable wig nicknamed 'Lucy.' The wig nearly came to grief when Barbara and I were touring the burnt-out shell of an old people's home after a terrible fire in Nottingham in December 1974. With the TV cameras rolling, 'Lucy' caught on a stray wire and was lifted off Barbara's head. Fortunately, a Ben Stokes reaction catch by the accompanying fire chief returned the wig to Barbara who plonked it back on her head. Not a word was spoken, and nothing appeared on television.

Barbara had a strong commitment to home and her family, despite being childless. Her husband Ted was her rock and politically active in Islington. Her niece Sonia and her family were very important to Barbara. Nothing pleased her more than being at her main home, Hell Corner Farm, in Buckinghamshire, gardening and walking her dogs. Entertaining friends and parties were important; and there were few problems that could not be solved over a good meal and wine. (She introduced me to the delights of Volnay.) She regularly visited her mother who suffered from dementia in her care home.

Barbara was an experienced Minister who got on well with her civil servants and dealt with her red boxes conscientiously. Cabinet attendance was sacrosanct because she wanted to keep a beady eye on her colleagues, especially the Prime Minister. This meant a heavy briefing load because Cabinet often met twice a week and in one week in November 1974 met four times. Occasionally it met all day and there were many more Chequers meetings than now. The briefing load was shared between officials and the SPADs. It was the job of the private office to assemble this material into a red Cabinet folder. I realised Barbara was keeping a diary when a sheaf of her verbatim notes fell out of a Cabinet folder. I returned them without comment and told no-one.

An important part of the weekly routine was the Husbands and Wives dinner with Michael Foot, Tony Benn (known to his irritation as Wedgie), John Silkin and Peter Shore (whose wife was a senior DHSS doctor). This group preserved their left-wing credentials and was the core of what we would today call 'Eurosceptics' who campaigned against EEC membership in the 1975 referendum. When the referendum was announced they became the core of the 'Dissenting Ministers' Group.

My key role was to keep Barbara reasonably content without destroying my civil service career by alienating the senior mandarins. If a big speech was to be written, it was best to leave her alone with a cigarette and a gin and tonic so she could return to her journalist past. She could write as well as any civil servant and quicker, which was just as well given how many big speeches were left to the last moment. The mid-1970s Labour Governments never had a comfortable majority and late night and all-night sittings were common. Exhaustion was a part of life for leading politicians then and the civil service made little allowance for it.

I slowly realised I had a strange mix of roles as adviser, manager and general factotum – a kind of civil service Jeeves trying to keep a lot of plates spinning. I have selected what I regard as the most important and interesting topics to write about here; but there were many others that Barbara took an interest in, such as Scottish Devolution or Southern Rhodesia independence (where Arnold Goodman acted as Wilson's agent). Dominating my time with Barbara was the increasing power of white-collar public sector unions at a time of pay restraint and rising inflation. None were more difficult to deal with than the BMA.

A Second Election with Doctors in Revolt

When I arrived in Barbara's office in July 1974 the NHS agenda had largely been set – pay, pay beds and funding. Public expenditure was tight. Wage restraint was the order of the day. Labour's majority over the Conservatives was wafer-thin – 301 to 297; and they were 34 votes short of an overall majority. The Government was focussed on another Election to try to increase its majority, with a referendum on EEC membership a key issue. (Enoch Powell had said he voted Labour in the last election because they promised an EEC referendum.) Drafting a manifesto had started; and the NHS unions were limbering up for a fight, with an anxious Michael Foot, the Employment Secretary, trying to maintain a cap on pay increases.

The first groups agitating for more pay were the radiographers (led by the ASTMS union and its fiery leader Clive Jenkins) and the nurses. The BMA were also seeking more money for the NHS (about £500 million) something they had not been pressing the Heath Government on. Peace was patched up over the summer by using the Halsbury Review of non-medical pay and the end of the statutory pay policy. By July there was a temporary lull in hostilities that enabled us to go on holiday, with Barbara fretting more about a new swimsuit than the BMA.

Harold Wilson set the General Election for 10 October with a Manifesto promise of a referendum on EEC membership within 12 months, despite the protests of Roy Jenkins and the Labour Europhiles. The outcome was a Labour victory winning 42 seats more than the Conservatives: but the seats won by other parties meant the Government's overall majority was only 3 votes. The end of a statutory pay policy and a new Labour Government had the NHS unions queuing up for pay increases, with the BMA demanding a new consultants' contract. Now the fun began, with three restive medical groups – hospital consultants, junior doctors and GPs – posing the greatest pay challenges to the new Government.

The consultants had been discussing a new contract with Keith Joseph since 1972 and had made little progress. They were now being gingered up by a new militant rival to the BMA – the Hospital Consultants and Specialists Association (HSCA). The essence of the problem was that the 5000 or so full-time hospital consultants were working lengthy extra hours without pay; whereas the 6 to 7000 maximum part-time (9/11ths) consultants could control their hours more easily and supplement their NHS income with private practice. This was particularly attractive to surgeons where long waiting lists could be 'queue-jumped' by going private. This involved using either the nearly 4000 beds then available in private hospitals or the 4500 or so private pay beds in NHS hospitals.

Theoretically pay beds and the consultant contract were separate issues; but just before my arrival in the Private Office, an unofficial strike about queue-jumping pay beds at Charing Cross Hospital had linked the two issues. 'Granny' Brookstone a NUPE (National Union of Public Employees) shop steward who led the strike wanted NHS pay beds – part of Nye Bevan's 1948 deal with the BMA – abolished. The strike was called off by Barbara pledging to phase out pay beds and referring the matter to the negotiating committee with the BMA on the consultants' contract chaired by David Owen.

Thus, one already big problem (the consultants' contract) became an even larger one with pay beds added to the mix alongside the long-running dispute with junior doctors over their hours and pay. Harold Wilson tried to calm things down by stopping Barbara's attempt to put the pay bed pledge in the October Queen's Speech. This didn't stop her referring to the pledge in her speech in the Queen's Speech Debate. This turned out to be the incendiary moment that intensified a trilogy of smouldering bad-tempered disputes with the BMA and medical profession that came to dominate Barbara Castle's time in office.

Battleground One – the Consultants' Contract

The work on the consultants' contract drifted on until December in the Owen joint working party, with a threat of industrial action hanging over the outcome. It was clear that some extra payments would have to be conceded to the full-time consultants without benefitting the part-timers; and that a Labour Government could not be seen to encourage private practice and patient queue-jumping. By mid-December, the Top Salaries Review Body had recommended huge increases for senior civil servants, admirals and generals and judges but the Government wanted to limit pay increases for high earners. Barbara struggled to get her proposals for the new consultant contract through Cabinet. Finally, on 19 December the Cabinet agreed she could offer the BMA the new consultants' contract but without a funding commitment when it was priced by the independent pay Review Body.

The next day a meeting was scheduled of the Owen joint working party but a larger BMA contingent gate-crashed the meeting, including three powerful players, Walpole Lewin, Derek Stevenson (the BMA General Secretary) and the appropriately named surgeon, Tony Grabham. In the office meeting beforehand Barbara announced that there would be no review of an item of service pay system for doctors – something promised the BMA by David Owen. (Barbara had already told me that she thought David had conceded too much, before involving her.) She also said she did not want to go into the meeting until Harold Wilson's statement on top salaries increases had been made at 3.30pm. Unsurprisingly the 50 or so doctors who had turned up became very restive and threatened to walk out.

The meeting was a disaster. The doctors had the contract proposals before Barbara arrived and wouldn't let her explain them. They were furious about no review of item of service payments; considered the Government had made a 'take it or leave it' offer; and exploded when told that Barbara was going to send the contract offer direct to all NHS consultants rather than via the BMA. They asked to talk amongst themselves and we withdrew.

Unfortunately, Barbara's room had been taken over (with her agreement) by the Private Office Christmas Party which was in full swing. I ushered everybody into Brian O'Malley's room. When we returned, another hour of chaotic discussion took place, with the BMA rejecting the contract and saying they were mandated to take industrial action, with a strike threatened for 2 January. People started drifting away and at about 8pm Barbara had had enough. She told them that this would have to be settled in the court of public opinion. She went to talk to the massed ranks of the media and then to ITN's 10 o'clock news.

The New Year brought a resumption of hostilities. We had industrial action by the consultants, with the medical Royal Colleges trying to act as mediators. The GPs joined in because they were cross over the Doctors and Dentists Review Body's rejection of their claim for an 18% interim pay award and being told they would have to wait for the final report. To add fuel to the flames, the junior doctors wanted payment for the hours over 40 they worked each week. Barbara met representatives of the juniors and GPs on 8 January and calmed things down. The consultants remained recalcitrant.

As we moved through January, officials were buckling. They wanted to ditch the new contract and negotiate add-ons to the existing contract. Barbara, rightly in my view, thought the doctors would stick out for very expensive add-ons and try to secure more benefits for the part-timers with private practice. She made a neutral statement to Parliament on 13 January which conceded pricing the new contract before asking the profession to agree it. We met the Royal College Presidents who seemed to me scared stiff of upsetting the BMA. When asked, I told Barbara how useless I thought they were.

The CMO took over as intermediary with the consultants who immediately changed tack and produced a shopping list of add-ons to the current contract, including limiting part-time consultants' obligations to the NHS. This produced an emollient but unenthusiastic response from Barbara and weeks of discussions with the CMO and no progress. We were by now into mid-February with the CMO's discussions going nowhere. There was a highly stressed CMO, continuing industrial action and an irritated Barbara. She was, however, cheered up by the election of Margaret Thatcher as Leader of the Conservatives and the prospect of a female Prime Minister. This was soon offset by the suicide of Dick Crossman's teenage son, Patrick, less than a year after his father's death.

At the end of February, we spent a weekend of telephone activity about how to reply to the BMA's request to meet the Prime Minister to discuss the consultants' contract. I suggested that if the PM was to see them, they should call off their industrial action first. Barbara liked it, officials didn't, but No. 10 did, so that was the reply. The BMA asked the PM to reconsider his position and then asked for an independent adjudicator. At the time inflation was running at 30% and wage increases at 20% which hardly made it the easiest time to drive a hard bargain with the BMA.

We drifted into March with a desperate CMO buying into the BMA's half-baked idea of an independent 'fact-finder;' and their rivals the HCSA becoming more militant. Barbara was much more pre-occupied with the EEC referendum and whether Cabinet Ministers could campaign against continuing EEC membership – the Cabinet's position. Media coverage looked as though the consultants were losing public support. A rather desperate BMA asked to see Barbara but the meeting on 20 March was a re-run of the chaotic December meeting with another list of demands and no progress. By this time Barbara was in disgrace with Harold Wilson over her decision to actively campaign against EEC membership.

In the coming weeks discussions with officials narrowed matters down to improving the existing contract and trying to agree an interpretation of what the maximum part-time consultants contract meant. The Government's position was that maximum part-timers had the same NHS service obligations as full-timers; but the BMA wanted part-timers to be able to charge for extra sessions beyond nine. The upshot was a document, by officials called optimistically the Option Agreement, for discussion with Barbara on return from the USA.

Hostilities were resumed on 16 April after a tough Budget and a tightening of public expenditure. But unknown to the BMA the Doctors and Dentists Pay Review Body's recommendations for higher pay awards had been agreed, subject to staging. Fractious negotiations on the Option Agreement began at 4pm on 16 April and lasted until 6.30am on 17 April. My main role was to keep up the spirits of the Government side, with food, drink and good humour; and to try to starve the BMA into submission. The BMA nit-picked their way through the text, hour after hour. Trying to increase the pay of maximum part-time consultants. At 5.30am Barbara had had enough. She told the BMA she had an important Cabinet that morning and she would tell her colleagues that no agreement was possible.

The doctors' negotiators clearly thought that Cabinet would be discussing the Pay Review Body report, even though it had been agreed. The BMA cracked and even asked Barbara what wording would help her with Cabinet. She told them they must call off industrial action and they agreed to recommend this. All this was to be put to the Consultants' Central Committee on 18 April. The doctors agreed the deal; and the Government announced its acceptance of the Pay Review Body's report. This was just round one with the consultants. The indefatigable Barbara was now determined to move on to reducing pay beds.

The Pay Beds War

I had considerable personal misgivings about Barbara's policy on pay beds. This was partly because, in a democracy, I thought people could spend their money how they wished; and partly because I thought if we drove private practice out of NHS hospitals there would be more private hospitals competing for staff. Despite these misgivings, I recognised there was a Manifesto pledge to deliver change. So, I arranged a small meeting with officials to take Barbara through the obstacles. This led to a consultation document which Harold Wilson insisted on clearing from Jamaica where he was attending the Commonwealth Conference.

The document was launched on 5 May 1975. It announced legislation to phase out NHS pay beds and to extend licensing powers over the size of the private sector. Authorised NHS pay beds would be reduced by about 500 from 4500, using the argument of under-utilisation. Consultants would be encouraged to have common waiting lists for NHS and private patients – a totally unenforceable proposition. Barbara secured in June a provisional legislative slot for a Pay Beds Bill in the next session.

In early July I brought officials to a meeting with Barbara to report on their policy work on licensing private sector beds which needed cross-Whitehall approval before legislation could be drafted. I knew the work was not going well. A new policy on regulating the quality of private hospitals and nursing homes was hammered; out and Barbara accepted that it might not be possible to phase out NHS pay beds by November 1976. Officials continued to work up a consultative document. "The Separation of Private Practice from NHS Hospitals,' was published on 11 August when Barbara and Ted Castle were safely in Corfu.

Over the summer, NHS discontent increased, with more personal attacks on Barbara and a background of funding reductions and pay constraint. Pay beds added to the mix. Doctors were said to be emigrating in droves – the reality was about 500 a year left, with 200 a year coming in. At the same time Barbara was locked in rows with the Chancellor over NHS funding and with Michael Foot on pay policy. In mid-1975 the most pressing medical dispute was with the junior doctors (see below) and for the rest of the year this was used by the BMA to pressurise Barbara on pay beds.

When Cabinet discussed the Queen's Speech on 23 October, Harold Wilson helped Barbara get the Pay Beds Bill included against a lot of opposition. The issue of licensing the private sector was left for later legislation. Despite this success, David Owen started to have cold feet about pay beds legislation and provoking the BMA. When Barbara asked me for my views, I told her I thought this was not the time to flinch, having come this far and given the NHS censure debate on 27 October. Just to make life interesting, the police phoned me on 27 October to tell me that Barbara was on an IRA hit list. The following day an official told me someone claiming to be from the Ministry of Defence asked for an AFH building plan: this was denied by MoD when I called them.

The BMA were incandescent over the Pay Beds Bill being in the Queens Speech on 19 November. They linked their anger to the unresolved juniors pay dispute. Harold Wilson now decided to intervene and phoned Barbara on 20 November to say that his personal lawyer, Arnold Goodman, had been retained by the Independent Hospital Group (IHG) to fight the pay beds legislation. He asked if she wanted to meet Arnold privately. Barbara did and then swore me to secrecy on our next move. Unbeknownst to anyone in DHSS, including David Owen, Barbara and I set off the following Monday (24 November) to see Arnold at his Portland Place flat: this was shown as 'personal engagement' in her circulated diary. 10 days of cloak and dagger then started that did little for my career prospects.

On entry to Arnold's flat was a flight of stairs at the top of which was a large portrait of Arnold by Graham Sutherland that made him look like Peter Lorre, the film star. (Arnold was much fonder of this portrait than Winston Churchill was of his Sutherland portrait which his wife, Clemmie, burnt.) Arnold was late, so his housekeeper brought us tea and cucumber sandwiches, most of which were eaten by Arnold when he arrived. Oozing charm, Arnold said he wanted to avoid a collision course and to bypass Grabham on the BMA team. His clients wanted the pay bed issue referred to the Royal Commission on the NHS (see below) and he asked if licensing of the private sector could also be referred to the Commission as doctors saw this as a threat to private medicine.

Barbara welcomed his involvement; but told him Grabham couldn't be excluded because he was their best negotiator. There was no possibility of referring everything to the Royal Commission because of NHS union opposition. She wanted a firm date for phasing out pay beds, but she would take powers to vary it locally. She wasn't against referring the licensing issue to the Royal Commission providing there were constraints on excessive private hospital developments in the meantime. We explained how common waiting lists might have stopped the row and I undertook to send Arnold a paper on the idea. It was a useful meeting, even if I couldn't show anybody my notes.

When I spoke to Arnold three days later, he thanked me for the waiting list paper, but was coy about what he was up to. Barbara had a private word with Wilson before Thursday's Cabinet to tell him what

49

had happened with Arnold. She was happy to discuss the phasing arrangements providing the legislation stopped a massive expansion of private hospitals. She was willing to negotiate through Arnold provided the Cabinet was kept out of it. There was a Cabinet row about giving Barbara powers to limit private hospital development. Wilson said it was necessary, but he would oversee negotiations. Legislation would go ahead but so too would consultant industrial action.

I had a discussion with Arnold that afternoon and he told me that he had tried to get the BMA to postpone industrial action until 1 January but without success. We agreed that overtures from the Government would look as though it wanted to concede. He suggested that a letter to the profession next week followed by a meeting was the best way forward. He wanted the PM involved but I discouraged that and said the negotiations should be left to Barbara. I reported to Barbara. We had managed to keep things under wraps for a week.

On Monday (1 December) Barbara agreed I should find out where Arnold was with the BMA. He told me he was meeting them at 6.30pm and this might be his last meeting with them as he disapproved of their industrial action. He would try to get them to spell out their minimum requirements for a settlement. I asked him if it would be a good idea to meet Barbara before he saw the BMA and he agreed. Barbara and I trotted along to Arnold's flat at 5pm. First, he tried to get Barbara to accept that timing of phasing out should be left to the Royal Commission which she flatly rejected but was willing to discuss timing with the BMA. He then tried to get her to agree to an independent review body to consider the phasing out of pay beds in different areas. She said there could be a professional body to advise her, but the final decision should rest with her. I told Barbara I thought the BMA wanted to delay matters to put new private facilities in place.

Later an upbeat Arnold called saying the meeting had gone well. He thought the BMA would be willing to discuss a settlement along the lines that there would be legislation to phase out pay beds; the timetable for phasing out would be agreed with them; and pay beds would remain in particular areas until alternative private facilities were in place. Arnold told me he was meeting the BMA again tomorrow and if they were willing to put this proposal to Barbara, he thought agreement could be reached in 48 hours. I was more doubtful.

The next day there was a bombshell that totally undermined Barbara's position – the handiwork of the duplicitous Arnold. Before another of our secret meetings with him, No. 10 called to tell me that the PM had agreed to meet the full BMA tomorrow without them calling off industrial action. I checked with the PM's Principal Private Secretary, Ken Stowe, - with whom I would have a dust up a decade later – and he confirmed Wilson had agreed this personally and the press had been told. Wilson was now in Rome and Barbara couldn't speak to him. Barbara was incandescent but still went to meet Arnold who unwisely was late. He received a furious dressing down about undermining her position and made matters worse by revealing he had been in touch with Wilson in Rome. He had put to Wilson the idea of an independent review of pay bed phasing, already rejected by Barbara. She pressured him to accept that the PM should listen to the BMA without commitment and pass them back to negotiate with her. Barbara and I went to the House of Commons to decide what to do.

I phoned No.10 to seek a meeting for Barbara with the PM before tomorrow's meeting with the BMA at 11.30am; and helped Barbara draft a strong minute to Wilson saying he should push the BMA back to her. I delivered this to No.10 around 10pm, leaving Barbara to write her Nye Bevan lecture on the 'NHS Revisited' due for delivery in Oxford tomorrow night. The next morning, No.10 failed to contact Barbara about a meeting with the PM, so she simply turned up at Downing Street and insisted on seeing Wilson before the BMA meeting. She grabbed five minutes which was apparently very bad-tempered and ended with Goodman joining them to go into the BMA meeting together. Wilson, who had returned from Rome at 3am, seemed to confuse everybody as to his position; but did push the BMA back to Barbara to discuss some vague proposals from Goodman. Despite a friendly drink with Wilson after the meeting, Barbara was convinced he was going to sell her down the river. She spent the afternoon completing her Nye Bevan lecture before dashing to Oxford.

When I arrived at the office the following morning (4 December) I found an irate CMO accusing me of letting Barbara negotiate with the BMA behind his back. I denied this but went to confess all to Pat Nairne, to protect my position. I then dashed to No.10 to meet Barbara before Cabinet to warn her that Stowe had told me Wilson was angry over the Mail's and Telegraph's coverage of her Nye Bevan lecture. He thought this showed him and her in conflict. I explained we needed a meeting that afternoon to tell David Owen and officials what we were up to with Arnold and the PM. She agreed the meeting and said she would draft a mollifying note to the PM during Cabinet. I collected it for typing later. The meeting with the top of the office that afternoon went surprisingly well. Only the CMO was curmudgeonly about being kept in the dark. Pat Nairne encouraged Barbara to have a further meeting with Goodman that evening which I set up.

Arnold was late as usual but was a bit chastened by his dressing down at our last meeting. He outlined the note he had done for Wilson on the way forward. The unacceptable passage was that the phasing out of pay beds should be certified by a 3-person independent commission set up by the Government but agreed with the BMA. Barbara told Arnold she wanted the commission to be a board or tribunal; that the legislation should include a Schedule of a 1000 plus pay beds to be phased out by a given date in areas with plenty of private beds; there would be a second category, with a later date, where new private beds could be provided quickly, with joint waiting lists until phasing out; a freeze on all new private hospitals until everything was agreed; and consultation with NHS unions on such a deal. After lengthy argument, we persuaded a reluctant Arnold to put all this to the BMA at lunch the next day. Barbara would meet the unions at the Gay Hussar at the same time.

If all went well Arnold would meet Barbara again tomorrow evening. The PM would be kept out of things for now. Arnold and I exchanged phone numbers and we left. Everybody had gone home in the private office, so Barbara and I set up tomorrow's lunch with the unions. The next morning No.10 told me the PM wanted Barbara's comments on Goodman's formula by 2pm so I drafted something for Barbara to sign and sent it over to her in Cabinet. She then established with a flurry of notes in Cabinet that Harold was content for her to carry on with Arnold negotiating with the BMA. She and David Owen went to lunch with the Unions who took the proposed deal well, especially a Schedule in the Bill phasing out a lot of pay beds. Arnold had gone to ground. When I finally tracked him down it was clear that he was a long way from clinching anything with the BMA but wanted Barbara to meet them that evening. I fixed for her, David Owen, Pat Nairne, Jack Straw and me to meet Arnold at his flat, before cancelling a phone-in programme with an irate Capital Radio presenter.

At Arnold's flat, the BMA contingent had been parked in his dining room while he briefed us in the sitting room. Virtually nothing had been agreed. Barbara made it clear that the minimum she could agree was a Schedule of pay beds to be phased out and a time limit for the Board's existence. The BMA joined us with Arnold presiding from an armchair and refreshments arriving. At first, Grabham and Rodney Smith of the Royal College of Surgeons opposed the schedule of closures. Then Smith introduced a clever new argument. Surgeons needed access to specialized facilities like radiotherapy and neurosurgery for their private practice, but most private hospitals couldn't provide these services. Denying doctors access to these services would deprive them of their right to private medical practice. Rather shrewdly, Barbara agreed to consider Smith's point if they would accept the schedule of closures and agree the criteria the independent board would use for closures. Grabham refused to sign an agreement because they disagreed with the legislation; but if there was an agreement, they would call off industrial action. At 11pm Arnold suggested we go away and draft a document and meet again on Sunday evening. All agreed.

Saturday brought a draft statement from David Owen which Barbara thought too conciliatory. Owen produced a revised version when we assembled at the Department on Sunday afternoon (7 December). Three hours later we had a revised draft statement that I left with a typist I had persuaded to come in. We went to Arnold's flat where chaos reigned. Eventually the BMA produced some strange pieces of paper they called tentative proposals from Arnold that would form the basis of Government proposals for the medical profession to consider. These had no proposals for phasing out pay beds. We gave Arnold our proposals and left. On Monday I fixed a meeting with the BMA for 8.30pm but they didn't show up. I took a note to No.10 telling the PM where things stood.

On Wednesday (10 December) we considered comments on our draft statement by one of Arnold's partners and responded with a clear message that the legislation would phase out 1000 beds within six months. Arnold returned to the charge with a detailed critique but continued to say how reasonable Barbara's proposals were. We responded on Friday and called the revised document a statement on the phasing out of pay beds agreed between the government and the profession. This produced an angry response from the BMA who were not prepared to say they had agreed anything and wanted the document to be Barbara's proposals for phasing out pay beds having watered everything down. There was a flurry of telephone exchanges about drafting changes with Arnold over the weekend which ended up with the BMA requesting a letter from the PM. In essence this would say that clarification had taken place through Arnold and, as a result, proposals had emerged that would be put to the BMA Council and consultants' negotiating body. If agreed and industrial action was called off, the proposals would form the basis of legislation.

On Monday (15 December) negotiations continued at DHSS but Goodman continued to move between the BMA in a conference room and Barbara's office. Words continued to be added and deleted but exhaustion was setting in. Finally, a letter the PM could send was agreed. Barbara showed Derek Stevenson the statement she would make to the House of Commons that afternoon and gave the BMA a drink. Grabham was still arguing over consulting other NHS unions. This meeting ended this phase of the negotiations with the pay beds battle moving to the Bill itself (see below). Before Christmas we tried to settle another long-running medical dispute – with junior doctors.

Battleground Three – Junior Doctors

The new contract for juniors had been agreed by Barbara in January 1975 for payments to begin after they had worked 40 hours a week. It was to be priced by the Pay Review Body but with no extra money. The new overtime payments had to be paid for from the pot already used for extra duty payments. This pot only had enough money to pay overtime to everybody after they had worked 44 hours a week. This turned out to make some juniors receiving hefty extra duty allowances worse off. The shortage of money was partly because the Review Body had given the juniors such a large basic pay rise. Unofficial strikes of juniors broke out over doctors made worse off. There was a good deal of public and backbench Labour sympathy for the juniors because of the long hours many worked – sometimes 120 hours a week. Michael Foot, as guardian of pay policy, was unwilling to make juniors a special case.

In mid-October, Harold Wilson tried to calm medical unrest with a Royal Commission on the NHS. He said Barbara could tell the BMA in advance to help defuse the juniors' dispute. After a lot of haggling with the BMA, on 16 October I finally extracted from Derek Stevenson in an angry phone conversation – with Barbara, David Owen and officials listening in – an agreed text of a statement they would issue. This said the BMA accepted there were some overriding national issues and the juniors would be balloted on the Government's pay offer. Wilson made his Parliamentary statement on the Royal Commission and agreed to see the BMA on 21 October. Flanked by five Cabinet Ministers, Wilson told the BMA that the Government was still going ahead with legislation on pay beds, despite their protests. Now he and other Ministers had seen the BMA in action, sympathy for Barbara increased.

The juniors' dispute rumbled on through November with numerous meetings – largely with officials and some with Barbara – but no progress was made. The juniors were split over the deal, with BMA consultants stoking opposition. By 17 November the ballot looked likely to show half the juniors in favour of industrial action. With the Queen's Speech announcement on pay beds on 19 November the consultants came to Barbara's meeting with the juniors the next day. Michael Foot attended to explain to them yet again why Barbara couldn't breech the Government's pay policy, only to be told their proposals were consistent with pay policy. Afterwards the BMA told us that because of the pay beds policy the consultants' leaders were calling a meeting to agree to join the juniors in attending to emergencies only from 1 December. They would start collecting undated resignations from the NHS.

Barbara had another inconclusive meeting with the juniors on 15 December. My sense was that juniors wanted an industrial contract with all hours over 40 per week attracting overtime payments. The wider BMA were becoming nervous about exchanging a professional contract – which suited consultants – for a straight industrial contract. The juniors worked the back channels with Jack Straw to emphasise they were arguing for the principle of a shorter working week, with their basic salary tied to that. An independent audit of Review Body

55

figures was offered to see if more money was available without breaking pay policy.

Then we held a marathon meeting starting after lunch on Thursday (18 December) and concluding at 3am on Friday morning, with an energised Barbara and a flagging Michael Foot. The government and the juniors agreed to an independent audit of the Review Body's figures and to making a joint approach to the Review Body about accepting the basic salary was for 40 hours per week. It would be left to the Review Body to determine the basic salary from time to time. A Jesuit would have been proud of the agreement's final text. It settled this long-running dispute with an agreement in principle but no guarantee of extra money.

A statement was made to Parliament the next morning and the juniors agreed to accelerate calling off their industrial action. Wrangling over details continued for months with sporadic threats and local industrial action. There was a growing realisation that the deal's complex system of overtime payments would cost a lot more than DHSS and the Treasury had calculated. Ironically, there was also brief industrial action by the Admin and Clerical staff about their own back pay for paying the juniors' overtime back pay. But by the end of 1975 the war with the junior doctors was finally over.

The Pay Beds Bill and Private Medicine Aftermath

Although the consultants were still taking industrial action while they were balloted on the pay beds deal, the close of 1975 saw a reduction in hostilities with the BMA. Unfortunately, Barbara fell down some stairs at the TUC Christmas party on 16 December and her leg needed an X-ray. The press obsessed over whether she would receive preferential treatment or whether doctors would refuse to treat her. She kept refusing treatment until her GP and I convinced her to be x-rayed at the Whittington Hospital which was not on strike. I received a rocket for telling the hospital in advance that she was coming but she calmed down when I told her that the hospital manager had told me how fond they were of her.

With the New Year there was still the loose end of who would chair the Wilson peace gesture of a Royal Commission. The search for a chairman had produced Alec Merrison, a Professor of Physics at Liverpool University who later became Vice Chancellor of Bristol University. He received the thumbs up from a trade union leader Barbara trusted; and he flourished his family's left-wing credentials when Barbara interviewed him. After a tussle about whether his remit covered pay beds, Barbara resolved the matter by specifically excluding them in the press notice announcing his appointment on 20 January. The Commission eventually reported to Mrs Thatcher in mid-1979. Its report saw no problem with the expansion of the private health sector, provided the NHS was safeguarded. It didn't consider the presence or absence of NHS pay beds was significant.

Back in 1976 the mood music on pay beds was very different, with Harold Wilson in serious procrastination mode. Goodman complained to me about BMA treachery in encouraging rejection of the pay beds agreement. No surprise there I told him. Then in February, the BMA messed up the ballot and had to re-run some of it. DHSS tried to consult the NHS informally about where pay beds would be phased out in order to produce a Schedule for the Bill; but No. 10 vetoed the idea until the ballot result was known. The final ballot result was a great flop for the BMA. Only 54% of consultants voted with 4,438 voting to accept Barbara's package and only 2048 voting to reject it. Wilson then wanted a White Paper before the Bill went to Parliament; and second reading couldn't happen before Easter. The BMA began to wonder if the Goodman proposals were being ditched.

I arranged a briefing of Stevenson by Barbara, followed, a few days later, by a lengthy meeting with the massed ranks of the BMA. After a grumpy hour or so the BMA leadership calmed down, accepted the legislation would go ahead and made it clear that for now they didn't want a public row. Goodman – who hadn't been well – made it clear he wanted to detach himself from pay beds issue and wouldn't speak on the Bill in the Lords. In a private meeting in early March, Harold Wilson told Barbara he wouldn't be Prime Minister much longer. She remained confident he would not stop her getting the Pay Beds Bill through. I thought she and the Bill were living on borrowed time but said nothing to anyone.

Throughout March there were meetings with the BMA, Goodman and the Independent Hospital Group (IHG) trying to secure agreement on what was now the Health Services Bill. Most of the arguments were over the licencing provisions for private hospitals and the schedule of pay beds to be abolished. The IHG wanted to licence only hospitals with over 250 beds but Barbara wanted all those with over 75 beds. Cabinet agreed a number nearer the IHG-figure. Eventually we ended up with a Bill that would remove a 1000 NHS pay beds within 6 months of passing, with the remainder to be phased out by an Independent Board but with no time limit. The Bill received its Second Reading on 27 April, with Barbara, now a backbencher, a member of the Standing Committee on the Bill.

Was all the Castle blood sweat and tears over abolishing pay beds worth it? Not really. When the Independent Board was abolished in 1980 by Mrs Thatcher it had still not eliminated 1000 NHS pay beds. By the time Labour left office in 1979 private hospital beds had increased by 80% in three years, with many new and better equipped private hospitals being built to serve the growing number of people with private health insurance. Moreover, after the 1979 Election, the wily Grabham, then the BMA Chairman, did a deal with Patrick Jenkin on the Consultants' Contract which effectively undid what had been agreed by Barbara Castle and David Ennals. This involved a pay deal under which the limited money available was used to give the maximum part-time consultants a 10% pay increase; and the whole-time consultants were able to increase their earnings from private practice.

As some commentators remarked Barbara Castle had inadvertently become the patron saint of private medicine, aided and abetted by Harold Wilson's delaying tactics. To add insult to injury the BMA had later persuaded a more emollient Health Secretary to allow whole-time NHS consultants to secure private practice earnings, previously prohibited. The political mudwrestling had produced little long-term gain; but it had revealed the BMA negotiators in their true male chauvinist colours and how tough it was for a woman in front rank politics. These medical wars would be long remembered by participants but plenty of other dramas were being played out alongside them. Life with the Red Queen had few dull moments.

The 1975 EEC Referendum

Before the March 1974 Election, Enoch Powell decided not to stand as an MP and said he was casting a postal vote for Labour because it was the only Party promising to give people a vote in a referendum on remaining in the European Economic Community (EEC). In mid-1974 there was a heated Labour Party debate about what should be said in the next manifesto about a referendum. This ended in a compromise between the strong pro-EEC Cabinet Ministers like Roy Jenkins and Shirley Williams and the others. The compromise was holding a referendum or election within 12 months of the end of a period of renegotiation with the EEC on the UK's terms, especially on agricultural subsidies/tariffs and state aid for industries like steel. During the October Election campaign Jenkins and Williams said they would leave active politics if people chose to leave the EEC.

On Labour's return to Government in October 1974 Harold Wilson didn't rush to tackle this contentious issue but open warfare broke out between Cabinet Ministers in December. At the end of January Cabinet agreed to hold a referendum in June 1975. Wilson then told Cabinet on 21 January that as soon as they had agreed the terms of the referendum the minority in Cabinet would be free to campaign in the country for their point of view but without personal attacks. This approach was agreed. My conversations with Barbara suggested that she would campaign to leave the EEC but didn't expect to win and didn't want to split the Labour Party or Government on what she saw as a second-order issue. She recognised that as a civil servant I couldn't help her with any campaigning.

Wilson followed up his Cabinet peace-making by instructing Ministers to clear speeches with him and Jim Callaghan, the Foreign Secretary; and not to oppose EEC membership in principle. There was a Ministerial skirmish over an EEC directive on language tests for doctors which weakened our English language tests. Within Government, Ministers began raising the issue of Parliament's sovereignty over particular EEC directives: but the pro-EEC Callaghan said it was too late to raise this issue now in the negotiations, as that pass had been sold by Ted Heath's EEC legislation. The Government published a White Paper on the EEC Referendum at the end of February which announced that the referendum would be held by the end of June. An EEC summit was set for 10 March to decide the EEC's position on the negotiations with Callaghan.

A week later there was a totally mad four days. It started with the Government's pro-EEC position being settled at a mammoth two-day

Cabinet Meeting on 17 and 18 March, with Barbara writing much of her Pensions Bill Second Reading speech during the second morning's meeting. The anti-Marketeers had gathered beforehand but didn't seem to me to have their hearts in a major confrontation with the Wilson/Callaghan axis, although a group called 'Cabinet against the Market' was established. They launched an Early Day Motion that attracted a lot of signatures. Wilson made a Statement to the House on the afternoon of 18 March, effectively launching the EEC Referendum campaign. Barbara followed this by moving the Second Reading of the Pensions Bill before dashing off to a 'Cabinet against the Market' press conference. She then decided – against advice – to speak at the following morning's FT pensions conference.

As if this was not enough, the afternoon of 19 March was spent in a lengthy, bad-tempered meeting with the BMA on the consultants' contract (see above). We got Barbara home about 9pm only for an irate Prime Minister calling her about the activities of the 'Cabinet against the Market' group and a motion delivered to Labour's National Executive Committee calling for an active campaign of opposition to the Government's EEC position. She then rushed to the Commons and spent two to three hours trying to calm down Wilson and Callaghan. The next morning (Thursday) Wilson held a political Cabinet with no papers and no civil servants present; and Barbara spent most of the afternoon in Labour Party meetings.

Things then calmed down a bit. Arguments continued in the Labour Party with Barbara's participation but with meetings outside DHSS. In the Easter break Barbara and I went to the US for her to deliver a lecture and to look at health issues, including a meeting with Ted Kennedy who was still attempting to get his National Health Insurance Bill through Congress. On 9 April Wilson secured Parliament's approval to his negotiated EEC terms with the support of the Conservatives. 170 Labour MPs voted against him.

The Labour anti-Marketeers were now operating through a 'National Referendum Campaign' with public funds. The Government was using the better funded 'Britain in Europe' campaign to convince the public to stay in the EEC. The Dissenting Ministers Group met most weekends; and they increased their campaigning during May, with more television activity and Jack Straw doing most of Barbara's briefing. Barbara and

Jack did a shopping trip to Brussels with her niece Sonia and her daughter: this was followed by a press conference to show how high EEC prices were. There was intense media activity at the end of May and early June, culminating with a televised Oxford Union debate on EEC membership on 3 June, two days before polling: Ted Heath and Jeremy Thorpe spoke for and Barbara and Pete Shore spoke against.

Despite all the dissenters' efforts, it was clear from the polls that they were going to lose – as Barbara expected. Their campaign was less well-run than the Government's whose focus on the threats to jobs from leaving the EEC seemed likely to carry the day. And it duly did. On 5 June there was a two to one vote in favour of staying in the EEC in a poll turnout of 65%. Immediately after the referendum result, Harold Wilson held a political Cabinet telling everybody that all the special dispensations of the referendum campaign were over and normal collective Cabinet responsibility resumed.

Wilson also decided to reshuffle his Cabinet, with Tony Benn going to energy with Eric Varley replacing him at Business; and Reg Prentice demoted from Education to Overseas Development placed back under the FCO. This put Judith Hart out of a job. Her dissenting friends Michael Foot, Tony Benn and Barbara went to confront Wilson to try change his mind. This caused Barbara to tell me she might be sacked on the morning of the Report Stage of the Pensions Bill. In the end Judith Hart resigned. All Barbara lost was her junior Minister, Alec Jones, to the Welsh Office, replaced by Michael Meacher.

Although the Cabinet wounds of the referendum campaign did not totally heal, they moved into the normal left/right splits that marked most Wilson Cabinets. The 'Great Ringmaster' managed to keep his troops together rather better than David Cameron and Theresa May did during the Conservatives' Brexit schism 40 Years later. Nevertheless, the Wilsonian unifying skills were tested to the limit during the continuous Cabinet battles over public expenditure that dominated the 1974 Labour Governments.

Public Expenditure Battles and the Social Contract

James Carville's political advice to Bill Clinton in the 1990s that "It's the Economy Stupid", was never more relevant than during the 1970s

Wilson Governments. Hostilities with the BMA and Cabinet divisions over EEC membership were played out in a context of continuous economic crisis. This arose from hefty oil price hikes, long-standing balance of payments problems and rapid inflation. The situation was made worse by a difficult relationship with the unions over a long period of pay restraint. In this situation, Labour didn't help themselves by generous social security promises in their February Manifesto.

The centre piece of these promises was a £10 per week increase in pensions and other benefits for single people and a £16 increase for married couples. Thereafter these benefits would be increased annually in line with earnings. Labour had also committed to replacing the Conservative pension scheme with one that was not means-tested and gave equality to women. There was also to be improved financial help for the disabled. To relieve child poverty, family tax allowances were to be replaced by new "child cash allowances" for all children (not just second and subsequent children) and paid to the mother.

When I arrived in Barbara's office the increase to pensioners and others was already in train; and in a March Budget, Denis Healey had taken one and a half million people out of tax. In DHSS work had already started on the other social security changes; but in the Treasury, Healey and his Chief Secretary Joel Barnett, had already kicked off an exercise to restrain next year's public expenditure. On return from the summer holidays Barbara was told by Healey that her proposals took up all the Contingency Fund for 1975/76 and she needed to cut further. There was then a lull for the Election and subsequent Queen's Speech, but the public expenditure Cabinet battles resumed at the end of October.

Prior to this the Government worked hard with the TUC, led by Len Murray, on a measure to assist pay restraint – a "Social Contract" – in which Barbara played a key role. This attempted to sell the idea that Labour and the unions were not just about pay but had a wider social fairness agenda. This involved commitments such as full employment and fairer distribution of national wealth and that the unions had wider loyalties than just to their members. Unions would recognise that pensioners, the unemployed and disabled were also entitled to a fair share of limited national resources, not just those in employment. Also in this social mix was a free NHS and free education.

At their conference in September the TUC committed themselves to the Social Contract – just in time for 1974's second Election in October.

Despite saying the top priority was attacking inflation, Labour's Election Manifesto continued to commit the Government to expensive social security increases. It would replace the Tory pension scheme with an earnings-related pension scheme for everyone, fully protected against inflation. Family allowances would be increased and extended to the first child through a new scheme of 'child credits.' New ways of helping one-parent families would be examined. There would be a new non-contributory benefit for working-age disabled people; an Invalid Care Allowance for those who gave up their jobs to look after a disabled relative; and a new Mobility Allowance for seriously disabled people.

These commitments gave Barbara a measure of protection when in the 1974 Autumn Budget, Denis Healey said the £60 billion surplus held by oil-producing countries was depressing world trade and causing unemployment and inflation to rise everywhere. The UK's trade deficit and public sector borrowing requirement were far too high; and resources had to be switched to investment and exports, with growth in public expenditure restricted to 2.75% in 1975/76. Although this seemed serious at the time, it was much less harsh than George Osborne austerity in the 2010s. While the Manifesto commitments protected the social security budgets there was no such protection for the NHS.

The DHSS official in charge of negotiations with the Treasury, Dick Bourton, was used to doing deals with the Treasury official responsible for public expenditure, Peter Baldwin, a near neighbour. Bourton was accustomed to Ministers and his senior colleagues giving him a round of applause on his deals. The first of a number of frosty exchanges took place at the end of October when Barbara refused to accept his side-deal for the NHS on the grounds that she wanted first to see what was proposed for other spending Departments, especially Defence; and she would take her chances in Cabinet. There was much civil service harrumphing and dire warnings of a bad outcome for the NHS.

At the Cabinet on 5 November Barbara found that she had achieved most of what she wanted on social security apart from family allowances for the first child. But Healey was holding her to a 2.8% increase for the NHS in 1975/76 which was two-thirds the Heath Government's annual increase – still more generous than George

Osborne. Wilson sent the Chancellor away for further discussions with Barbara. A week later, when the Budget was announced, the Chancellor had given no ground but had infuriated Barbara by giving away £280 million in tax reliefs to the working elderly. This prompted her to write a fierce letter to Healey, much to the consternation of DHSS officials. This produced a private acknowledgement from Healey at Chequers that he had been wrong on the elderly tax reliefs but there would be no public admission and no more money for the NHS or family allowances.

Barbara gave up on the NHS but carried on her campaign for family allowances for the first child. She returned to the issue at Cabinet on 25 November where she persuaded Wilson to agree to the setting up of an Anti-Poverty Committee to consider family allowances for the first child as its first item and to report by Christmas. She enjoyed telling DHSS officials, especially finance chief Bourton. In the New Year her joy was complete when Cabinet accepted paying family allowance for the first child, with the Chancellor announcing it in his next Budget statement. Officials complained about hardening Treasury attitudes, with Barbara telling them she had no problems with Denis Healey and Joel Barnett.

By the end of January, the Chancellor was telling the Cabinet, the Unions and anybody else listening, that things couldn't go on as they were with wages rising even faster than an already high inflation rate. The UK's economic position worsened, with earnings for 1974 turning out to have risen by 29% and retail prices up by 20%. Business confidence was falling, as unemployment rose. The Social Contract was having little impact on union behaviour. As Joel Barnett memorably said, the Social Contract was about give and take – government gave, and the unions took.

In April, Dennis Healey produced a budget to reduce private consumption and public expenditure by nearly £1 billion, with VAT and income tax rising. But to Barbara's joy and my astonishment, Healey announced that family allowances would be paid for the first child in April 1976 with the replacement of family allowances by child benefit to start in April 1977. The economic situation deteriorated further and on 22 May the Cabinet met to consider the Chancellor's proposal for a £3 billion annual public expenditure cut by 1978/79. Inflation had reached 25% by mid-June. The TUC recognised they had to deliver on the Social Contract and were considering a voluntary incomes policy. This was agreed eventually at no more than £6 a week.

Healey said the country faced a further run on the pound that could mean a massive in-year cut in public expenditure: the pound had fallen nearly 30% since it was floated in 1972. The word hyperinflation was beginning to be used; and by the middle of July there was a major Cabinet row about whether the Chancellor could announce a large cut in public expenditure for 1978/79 – the period of the next Election. DHSS officials claimed this would mean the first real terms cut in the NHS budget since 1948.

During this period Barbara undertook to produce a popular version of the Social Contract and calling it the "Social Wage." Early in March I went to a meeting she and Brian Abel-Smith had in the Commons with a sozzled Hugh Cudlipp then editor of the Daily Mirror. She persuaded him to release a Mirror journalist, to help write this pamphlet, using contact with me, not civil servants. Discreetly, I worked with the journalist, David Tattersall, on producing a popular version without involving DHSS who regarded this as a political matter. I liaised with the Treasury who kept trying to swap their deathly prose for that of the Daily Mirror. In July Harold Wilson insisted on publishing a version Tattersall and I had negotiated alongside the new pay restraint policy. We had had no help from DHSS officials.

On 4 August Wilson summoned the Cabinet to Chequers to have another go at future public expenditure cuts. Barbara decided to take her two dogs, I suspected to butter up Wilson who loved dogs. She deployed Brian Abel-Smith's arguments that defence expenditure should not be excluded from cuts, and that tax increases should be an alternative to some of the public expenditure cuts. No decisions were taken, other than to commission more work. Everybody went on holiday. When they returned Barbara initially avoided proposed increases in dental and optical charges but bowed to the inevitable in Cabinet at the end of October.

Unemployment continued rising and the NHS was said to be collapsing. The BMA duly said this was all Barbara's fault. Healey wanted public expenditure cuts and the Treasury moved to a tried and tested approach – across the board formula cuts of 10% on revenue budgets and 25% on capital. This would save £2 billion a year by

1978/79. The Chancellor said this wasn't enough and started looking at cutting the social security budget by changing the historical method of uprating. Rumours started of a 'secret' Treasury paper and £5 billion of public expenditure cuts. I knew DHSS officials had the paper and were withholding it. I thought this was wrong and persuaded the Permanent Secretary to have it released.

The situation worsened in November when the boss of Chrysler told the Government that it needed to take over his company with £75 million of debts and invest a similar sum. If it didn't, the company would go bust with the loss of 25,000 jobs The Chancellor piled on the agony by demanding nearly £4 billion of public expenditure cuts. He forced Barbara to choose between reducing the pensions uprating or NHS cuts. 1975 ended without a public expenditure settlement but with Barbara having to give ground on social security, social care and the NHS. A big handout for Chrysler was agreed to save jobs but with the EEC forbidding import controls to protect the British car industry.

By early February 1976, the Chancellor reached his savings target of £3 billion for financial year 1978/79. When the White Paper on Public Expenditure was finally published in mid-February it showed Barbara as having secured all her prospective social security reforms; and secured a better deal for the NHS than that for most other public services. She had generally protected her Department's large budget and done this through a political route rather than leaving it to officials to negotiate. A bit of judicious 'advance briefing' gave her a relatively good press. The only DHSS downside was the large staff cuts required because Wilson wanted cuts to the civil service. On a personal level I attracted criticism from some mandarins for not controlling Barbara by getting her to follow official advice – some chance.

The modest NHS growth posed some problems for the new resource allocation formula for regions on which David Owen had put in so much effort. This work was meant to even out the per capita allocation of money to the regions; and was the first attempt to do this since the start of the NHS. The new allocations favoured the northern regions who had often been underfunded in the past. It meant that the London regions, with their numerous teaching hospitals, had standstill allocations while others caught up. This went down badly in parts of the NHS but compared with BMA rows, the noise level was modest.

Exports Drive: Saudi Arabia, Kuwait and Iran

These public expenditure battles consumed a huge amount of time but did not stop Barbara – and therefore me – working on her own exports drive. The idea of this started in May 1975 with a meeting with an enterprising civil servant I had found in charge of the DHSS Exports and Industries Branch. Later I arranged a dinner for her with Sir Derek Rayner, the CEO of Marks and Spencer who was advising the Ministry of Defence on procurement. (I became closely involved with Derek when Margaret Thatcher was Prime Minister – see Chapter 3). At the dinner we discussed how best to exploit the UK's healthcare expertise and centralising NHS purchasing to achieve better commercial deals. The DHSS top brass were not keen on this Ministerial initiative, particularly after I drafted a minute for Barbara to tell the PM what she was going to do on health exports.

As the balance of payments deteriorated further, exports rose up the Cabinet's agenda. We held a drinks reception for NHS suppliers to encourage them to export more. Barbara told them she would use the Christmas Recess to promote UK health expertise in oil-rich countries. I was tasked with arranging a programme of visits to Kuwait, Saudi Arabia and Iran in January: the visits were set up with FCO help and despite DHSS officials. The starting point was Jeddah, then the capital of Saudi Arabia.

In the mid-1970s you could only fly to Jeddah on Middle East Airlines whose flights were alcohol-free. We smuggled two bottles of gin on to the plane in a black official bag to enhance Barbara's in-flight orange juice. Twenty minutes before landing there was a rush to the loos by Saudis to change into Arab dress. On arrival, there was a terrible clanking noise from our black bag as we crossed the tarmac and an Embassy official quickly confiscated the bag. It showed up again in the evening in the Ambassador's walled garden where we had a sundowner. We were treated to the sight of a Saudi Prince opening a door in the wall, coming to the drinks table, downing a couple of large whiskies and leaving without a word spoken. The Ambassador told us he did this every evening. I was warned my hair length would attract attention from the religious police. It duly did but I was rescued by Embassy staff.

We met the Saudi Health Minister, a young surgeon trained at St Thomas's Hospital. His room was awash with plans for new hospitals which he had to approve personally after detailed scrutiny. Dr Al Jazairy told us about British firms trying to sell him shiny new hospitals with scant understanding of the healthcare needs of a population of 5 million people scattered over a million square miles of desert. It was clear that the leaders of this newly rich country were deeply suspicious of western companies ripping them off with expensive buildings that they would struggle to run and maintain. Jazairy accepted our offer to send out some officials to advise on health care needs and hospital design. Below the leaders there was virtually no technocratic class to provide expertise.

This absence of technocrats was clear when I went to Riyadh, the proposed new capital, and then a giant building site. I was taken to a recently opened hospital but there was no sign of any patients and very few staff. This was rather like the episode of 'Yes Minister' when Jim Hacker was told that patients got in the way of the smooth running of the hospital. The Saudis said they had to hire technicians from Egypt to maintain and operate equipment and doctors and nurses from wherever they could. Despite these obstacles, nothing was going to stop the Saudis building a new city and moving the capital from Jeddah. The King had spoken. Or more accurately Crown Prince Fayed had.

There was no doubt who ran the country when we had our audience in a giant carpeted room with King Khalid. The elderly King exchanged a few pleasantries through an interpreter and then moved to the other side of the room. Crown Prince Fayed then strolled across to welcome us to his country, chatted briefly and then left us to sit and talk among ourselves while he had a conversation with his colleagues. After several cups of bitter coffee, we got the message that we were supposed to leave and Fayed shot across the carpet to say goodbye. The official dinner later followed a similar pattern of limited warm words but with great interest in whether the westerners would pluck out the eye from the sheep's head placed before Barbara. I declined her offer to let me do the honours. Throughout this visit the older Saudi men found it difficult dealing with a senior female political figure

The next stop was Kuwait which had an office in London that booked hospital treatments for wealthy Kuwaitis. We were welcomed at the airport with TV cameras and everybody in western dress apart from an irritable Barbara still wearing her full-length high-necked Saudi dress. The UK Ambassador, Archie Lamb, was an exports enthusiast, unlike his fellow countryman in Saudi Arabia. I realised then the huge variation in Ambassadorial enthusiasm for trade issues. The Kuwaiti Health Minister, Dr Awadhi, was pro-British and knew what help he wanted from us. Like the Saudis, Awadhi made it clear he was not going to be ripped off. He was worried about Barbara's policy on pay beds in case that made it difficult for Kuwaitis to get private health care in London. Barbara tried to reassure him that 200 NHS beds could be made available each year for Kuwaitis. I explained to her later that it wasn't NHS beds the millionaire Kuwaitis wanted.

The Kuwaitis laid on a lavish reception at which we were presented with a huge model Arab dhow which I quickly redirected to a civil servant. Before we left Kuwait, the Ambassador insisted that we experience a desert picnic. We sat in the stony desert with the wind sand-blasting our faces, determined to enjoy our wine like Brits making the best of a bad bank holiday on Brighton beach. We didn't know if we were in Kuwait or Iraq but thankfully Saddam Hussein was not checking up on us.

We then flew on to Tehran where we were followed in the streets by two beefy men in ill-fitting suits with bulging jackets. We were told Savak officers were there for our protection. We heard the same story of Westerners trying to rip off oil-rich countries as we had heard in Kuwait and Saudi Arabia. The only difference here was that the Minister of Social Affairs, Dr Shaikh, another surgeon, wanted to argue about an excessively high tender for a new hospital from a British firm. We haggled a bit and then went to see the Prime Minister, Mr Hoveyda, who was more sympathetic after we said the same company had built a similar hospital in the UK. We invited them to come and see it. They later sent a deputation to see our 'Best Buy' hospital; but Dr Shaikh continued to dispute the price, and nothing was settled before the 1979 Iranian Revolution ended the project.

I liked Hoveyda and his Chief of Staff for whom I arranged a short UK government study tour. Hoveyda had been Prime Minister for 10 years and was one of the great survivors in the Shah's autocratic regime. He was reputed to be one of the liberals in the Iranian elite who was trying to convince the Shah to share more of the country's wealth with the people rather than spend it on grandiose projects. When the Shah fled at the time of the 1979 Revolution, Hoveyda bravely stayed behind to try to help manage a transition. Sadly, this civilised man was hanged by the Mullahs for his pains.

It was clear to us that the Pahlavi regime was completely out of touch with the needs of the Iranian people and flaunted its wealth. A few women were given Government appointments and the Shah's sister presided over some worthwhile social programmes; but these were token gestures rather than real reform. When I went on holiday to this stunning country in 2015, I realised that the luckless Iranian people had exchanged an autocratic and greedy monarchy for a failed intolerant theocracy. They still await the government they deserve.

I never found out how much these visits did for UK exports; but Barbara was the first DHSS Minister to encourage senior health civil servants to be more commercially aware. On the flight home from Tehran, Barbara told me in strictest confidence that she intended to retire in the autumn after the pay beds legislation was passed and she had implemented her social security reform agenda.

Social Security Reforms

Looking back, it was extraordinary that Barbara managed to push through Cabinet a raft of social security reforms and expansions during a period of low economic growth, high inflation and curbs on public expenditure. She did this by making herself the guardian of the 'Social Contract' with the Unions and by relentlessly reminding everyone of the Manifesto commitments. The decisions to provide a big boost to pensions and uprate them annually in line with the most favourable of prices and earnings had been taken before my arrival in Barbara's office. (The only Conservative criticism had been that up-ratings should be six-monthly.) In May 1974 Barbara had announced the scrapping of Keith Joseph's Reserve Pension Scheme due for introduction in April 1975 and replacing it with a more generous earnings-related scheme.

The political work on what was now the third new pension scheme in three years – Crossman, Joseph and now Castle – was done mainly by the two Brians – Abel-Smith and O'Malley. The detailed work was done by many of the civil servants who'd worked on the earlier schemes. By the end of July 1974, a White Paper on the new 'National Superannuation Scheme' was produced with little involvement by Barbara. She, however, had to take it through Cabinet which she did successfully before disappearing on holiday to Mauritius. The White Paper was published to a favourable press reception on 11 September.

With an Election looming, benefits announcements came thick and fast. Then it was the turn of the disabled. A Joseph benefits policy had come unstuck in 1973 when a Commons revolt forced him to accept an amendment committing him to a review by October 1974 of the benefits for the chronically sick and disabled. Although not a Manifesto commitment, this review had given Alf Morris the opportunity to work, with support from Barbara and Harold Wilson, on a suite of new benefits for the disabled. (Alf, who had piloted the 1970 Chronically Sick and Disabled Act through the House of Commons as a Private Members Bill, was now the Minister for the Disabled.) Despite trouble with a reluctant Treasury, on 13 September Barbara and Alf launched a package of new benefits and mobility measures.

There was a non-contributory invalidity pension for people of working age unable to work; an invalid care allowance for those forced to stay at home to look after a disabled relative; and an invalidity pension for disabled housewives. All these were to be introduced in stages starting in 1975. In addition, a mobility allowance of £4 a week was to be paid for some 100,000 disabled people, irrespective of their ability to drive. The mobility measures would initially cost only £1.5 million. The problem of the invalid three-wheeler car was deferred. The first two disability benefits were included in the November Bill uprating benefits.

Brian O'Malley worked away with officials on the Pensions Bill, but Barbara insisted on doing the Second Reading on 18 March 1975. Ken Clarke, who was handling the Bill for the Conservatives, kept provoking her by calling it the 'O'Malley' Bill. (Ken owned up to doing this deliberately in his memoir, 'Kind of Blue.') The debate took place to a virtually empty House following Harold Wilson's statement on the EEC referendum. O'Malley carried on taking the Bill through Committee and sorting out many details with Ken Clarke, including using Ronnie Scott's jazz club as a bi-partisan venue. But Barbara attended a few Committee sessions and handled amendments, so by the end of May when Committee Stage finished, Ken Clarke had started calling it the 'Castle' Bill.

In the middle of the Castle/Foot row with Wilson over moving Tony Benn from the Business Department, Barbara handled the Report Stage on 11 June and saw off Tory /Labour rebels – aided and abetted by Alf Morris – seeking more money for mobility allowance. Finally, what was the Social Security Pensions Act 1975 received Royal Assent on 7 August. Barbara insisted we organise two parties for those who worked on it, with one of them at Hell Corner Farm where Barbara undertook the catering and Ted handled drinks.

The third legislative prong of the Castle social security reforms – the Child Benefit Bill – had a much rockier passage. It had two parts: extending the old family tax allowance to the first child which was uncontroversial; and turning the tax allowance into a benefit payable to the mother which was not. Although child benefit paid to the mother was Party and Government policy, many trade unionists and men in the Cabinet were either opposed to or nervous about transferring money from the male wallet to the female purse. The Cabinet male chauvinists turned out to be a bigger obstacle than the Tory frontbench. There was also the Whitehall 'wrinkle' that Treasury convention regarded the new cash benefit as public expenditure while the old family allowances were not because they were a tax relief. This was significant at a time of public expenditure restraint.

It took until the end of April 1975 to get the Child Benefit Bill introduced and to the middle of the night on 8 July for the Bill to be passed by the Commons. Even then there was another month of wrangling in the Lords. The Bill still had no rate for child benefit because the Chancellor wouldn't agree one while the Cabinet public expenditure battles were still raging. The new scheme was not due to start until April 1977 and the rate would end up not being fixed while Barbara was still in office. Her nemesis, Jim Callaghan, would fight a rear- guard action to have the scheme deferred (see Chapter 3).

Barbara also beefed up the independence of the Supplementary Benefits Commission. The Commission had been set up in 1966 and had taken over responsibility for administering means-tested benefits

– formerly the responsibility of the National Assistance Board. Since 1969 the Commission had been chaired by Lord Collison, an amiable trade union leader and Government 'trusty.' Collison was due to retire; and his deputy, an academic, David Donnison, wanted his job. Early in 1975 he made a pitch to Barbara about giving the already independent Commission a more positive role in shaping social policy and tackling poverty using the Commission's annual report to float new ideas.

Barbara was keen on exposing Government to a wider range of ideas on social policy; but the civil servants were not. Barbara asked for my views. I told her I thought the civil servants were overstating the problems of expanding the Commission's role She asked me to fix to see Kay Carmichael, another Commission member and wife of an MP. Despite this being International Women's Year, Barbara chose Donnison as the new Commission chairman and made Kay his deputy. (Little did she realise that they would later develop a very close working relationship.) Before making the appointments, Barbara took a paper to the Cabinet's Social Policy Committee widening the Commission's scope. Predictably the Treasury opposed it, fearing extra DHSS expenditure demands but the paper was approved.

It was clear that poverty was a growing problem despite the benefits improvements. The publication in 1974 of the Inquiry Report into the death of 7-yearold Maria Colwell had revealed the darker side of family life and the problems for the State in protecting children. Around the same time, Barbara fought and won a six-month battle with the civil service over upgrading the rank of the DHSS's Director of Social Work Services from Under-Secretary to Deputy Secretary because she wanted social work to feature more prominently within DHSS. As part of that she and David Owen had private lunches with Directors of Social Services as an attempt to find out what was happening in the real world: I attended and knew how much the civil service disliked this alternative source of advice.

Little did I know then that my next job would be working with the Supplementary Benefits Commission and that a decade later I would be a Director of Social Services. Despite David Donnison's best efforts, the Thatcher juggernaut rolled over creative social policy and the Commission was abolished in 1980.

Jeremy Thorpe and Norman Scott

Social security played a significant role in a bizarre episode in early 1976. Some strange stories began emerging about Jeremy Thorpe, the Leader of the Liberals. Thorpe had been helpful as Labour's small Parliamentary majority dwindled. Wilson had a good relationship with Thorpe who had attacked the South African Government over apartheid. Wilson had developed a view that Thorpe was a victim of smears by the South African secret services (BOSS – the Bureau of State Security) and he decided to try to help Thorpe. Wilson's intervention arose from a court case in Barnstaple in which a Norman Scott had been charged on 29 January with dishonestly obtaining £14.60 of supplementary benefit.

In court Scott had alleged he was being harassed because of a sexual relationship with Thorpe. This relationship was denied by Thorpe, but the media had been full of stories of hush money being paid to Scott by Peter Bessell, a former Liberal MP, who was apparently now in America. At the centre of the Scott court case was a strong suggestion that Thorpe had employed Scott; but the National Insurance record that would show this seemed to have disappeared. On 5 February 1976 Wilson asked Barbara, in whose name as Secretary of State Scott was being prosecuted, to find out more about this. She asked me and Jack Straw to look into this discreetly and to do a note for the Prime Minister. Although somewhat unorthodox, Warner and Straw, the Holmes and Watson of DHSS, were on the case.

The first step was to get Scott's local records. I went to see the Second Permanent Secretary, Sir Lance Errington, a rather Dickensian character, and told him I was tasked by the Secretary of State, on behalf of the Prime Minister, with getting the local office documents on Norman Scott. I asked him to do this quickly and without revealing the reasons. He was, understandably, somewhat reluctant; but I pointed out that he would have to explain to Barbara why this could not be done.

The following Monday I received a folder on Norman Scott from the local social security office. In it was plenty of evidence in terms of National Insurance stamped cards that showed Scott had indeed been employed by Thorpe at his home address. There was also other material about the nature and length of Thorpe's relationship with Scott that should not have been in a local social security office file. Jack Straw and I shut ourselves in his room to look at the material and I left him to prepare a note for Barbara which we later agreed. She gave it to the Prime Minister before Cabinet on 12 February. Wilson cooled on his support for Thorpe but not on his suspicions about the activities of BOSS.

Thorpe had a rough time with his Party; and was criticised over his conduct as a non-executive director of a bank, London and Counties Securities, that had collapsed. He hung on as Liberal leader until May when he resigned. Strange stories appeared about a gunman being hired to shoot Scott; and his dog was found shot on Dartmoor. At the end of 1978 Thorpe was committed for trial at the Old Bailey with others for conspiracy and incitement to murder Scott but was acquitted the following year.

Some years later two journalists – Barrie Penrose and Roger Courtier – turned up on my doorstep to talk to me about a strange interview Harold Wilson had given them around the time of his resignation. This was all about MI5 plots and the efforts of South Africa's BOSS in bringing down Jeremy Thorpe. I gave them a less colourful account of what had happened and heard no more from them. Nearly three decades later Hugh Grant played Jeremy Thorpe in a BBC film about the Scott affair, 'A Very British Scandal.' In this the Norman Scott character (Ben Whishaw) talks about his missing social security file. I never knew what happened to it after it was returned to Lance Errington. It looked as though the BBC's film Director didn't either.

Finale

Work on social security ended on a sombre note. On 23 March 1976 Brian O'Malley walked out of the House of Commons in the middle of DHSS oral questions, complaining of feeling ill. He left Barbara and David Owen to deal with his questions. It turned out to be a subarachnoid haemorrhage and he died early on 6 April – the second social security Minister to die while I worked for his political boss. I tracked down Brian's wife Kate at the Nervous Diseases Hospital, Bloomsbury and took Barbara over to see her. Afterwards Barbara insisted we go to Fortnum and Masons and buy food for Kate who clearly hadn't eaten for some time. I subsequently had a bit of a battle with the Government

Car Service about allowing Brian's driver to take Kate and his daughter back to their home in Rotherham. Two days later Barbara was sacked.

I had known since early 1976 that Barbara wanted to retire in the autumn and had assumed I would leave Private Office then. I had already been promoted and Pat Nairne was warming me up for a move. Then on 16 March Harold Wilson dropped his bombshell and told the Cabinet that he was standing down with immediate effect – still some months before his 60th birthday. A leadership election followed with Barbara in the stop Callaghan camp and supporting Michael Foot with Denis Healey as his deputy. Callaghan won and became Prime Minister on 7 April.

Barbara had been fearing the worse but did her Benefits Uprating statement the same day with Callaghan sitting beside her. The axe duly fell the next day, when I was in the middle of a house move. Barbara had been told by Callaghan that he needed her portfolio to reduce the age of the Cabinet when he was only a year younger. I rushed back to the office. We had Barbara's resignation letter typed and I organised a farewell party. The announcement was delayed to 5pm when all the changes were announced. The farewell party was more like a wake. David Owen made a very generous and warm speech. An emotional Barbara thanked everybody. I had to slip away briefly to talk to David Ennals, Barbara's successor.

On my return, I managed to get Barbara's private papers packed up. I removed the Persian picture given to her in Iran; and took a just about holding it together Barbara down to the DHSS soulless car park. I told her driver to take Barbara to her London flat and to stay on to take her to catch her train to Blackburn. After my triumph with Mrs O'Malley, I told her I would square the Government Car Service. I gave Barbara a kiss and packed her into the car before the tears came. Then back to my house move.

3. Servicing the Government's ATM: 1976-1985

The Child Benefit Leak

I knew David Ennals from his time as Minister of State under Dick Crossman and liked him. He was determined to show he wasn't a Callaghan patsy who would reverse Barbara's policies. He pushed on with the Pay Beds Bill which had its Second Reading on 27 April. Implementing the new Child Benefit scheme was a trickier proposition. Although the scheme was to start in April 1977, the benefit rates had not been set. Callaghan had never liked the scheme because it transferred take home pay in male pay packets to women's purses. Cabinet discussed child benefit four times in April and May. On two occasions a No.10 private secretary contacted me to say Callaghan was asking how much a week a woman with two children would get. Resisting the temptation to tell him to read the Cabinet paper, I told him.

All to no avail. Healey and Callaghan majored on the drop in male take home pay and would not agree rates for the new benefit that ensured no families would be worse off. At the fourth Cabinet, Ennals was told to announce the deferment of the scheme but with the introduction of family allowance at a £1 a week for the first child. Over 80 Labour MPs put down an Early Day Motion calling for the decision to be reversed; and Barbara, still a member of the TUC/Labour Party Liaison Committee got them to set up a working party to look at the issue.

Shortly after this, an article by Frank Field (then Director of the Child Poverty Action Group) appeared in a weekly magazine, New Society. It was headed 'Killing a Commitment: The Cabinet v the Children.' It was a detailed description of the Cabinet discussions and could only have been written with access to Cabinet papers. Frank called his source, as per Watergate, 'Deep throat;' and made things worse by lurid descriptions of brown bags of Government documents being left on the steps of CPAG's offices. Callaghan was outraged.

After an abortive civil service leak inquiry, the PM asked the Metropolitan Police to conduct a full-scale criminal investigation. I came in one morning to find Commander Haberson of the Bomb Squad waiting to talk to me. He was not a happy man, having been brought back from his overseas holiday to conduct the inquiry. He had a list of all the people with access to the leaked papers and was going to give them the full works. Everybody, including Permanent Secretaries, were to be finger-printed and interviewed under caution. I arranged for tables to be set up in the corridor outside my room for Habershon's people to finger-print everybody. It was one of the great sights of my civil service career to see the queue of senior civil servants waiting to be finger-printed and worrying whether their fingerprints would be held by the police. I established they would be returned.

The investigation produced nothing. At the time most people assumed the leaker was a Minister, with Tony Benn the prime suspect. Four decades later Malcolm Wicks, at the time a Home Office civil servant, and later a Labour Minister owned up to the leaking in a posthumous autobiography. As far as I am aware Frank Field has never revealed his source. The leaks worked politically. The Government was in disarray and increasingly dependent on the support of the Liberals, now led by David Steel. After the summer break, rates were agreed for a phased introduction of the child benefit scheme to be completed in April 1979 at a rate of £4 a week per child. Despite its controversial start, child benefit has largely survived as a universal benefit and was strongly supported by John Major. Residence tests were later applied; and George Osborne withdrew it for higher taxpayers, but the benefit is still around.

Life was much less interesting than with Barbara. The only other excitement I recall was going with David to Prague to sign a health agreement with the then hard-line Communist Government. This was to take place in the President's residence - the imposing Prague Castle. We marched through endless corridors accompanied by a posse of armed soldiers in splendid uniforms. Suddenly two of them stopped me and took away an apprehensive David under armed guard. I had visions of returning to London to report the capture of the Secretary of State who I thought had been in intelligence in the war. All ended well when we were re-united for a toasting ceremony with a lethal Czech spirit in mid-morning.

Eventually, Pat Nairne secured my release and told me his cunning plan. My predecessor in Barbara's office was on a trajectory to be the Permanent Secretary of the health side. I was to transfer to social security, inject some social policy thinking and progress to heading it up. My immediate destination was the Supplementary Benefits Division where a review was starting, aided and abetted by Barbara's re-energised Commission led by David Donnison. I had no interest in a career in social security with its two tribes - the upmarket contributory benefits tribe and the means-tested benefits tribe who dealt with the poor and indigent. These tribes barely mixed with each other, let alone a health type like me. With deep reluctance I accepted my fate, for the time being.

Supplementary Benefit Chaos

The world of supplementary benefits was in bad shape. The safety net for the poor that Beveridge had assumed would be small, had grown into a monster. The 1966 change to supplementary benefit from national assistance – the modern successor to the 1601 Elizabethan Poor Law – had simply not worked. What had started as a scheme to help the unemployed, a few pensioners and others without entitlement to contributory benefits, was now making payments to nearly 5 million people, about 10% of the population.

There were still many supplementary pensioners, but also increasing numbers of unemployed, single parents and students. The means tests for supplementary benefits were not aligned with different systems of housing assistance run by local authorities. The National Assistance Board's legacy of discretionary payments had expanded enormously, with the discretion being exercised in totally different ways geographically. Glasgow's children seemed to need their shoes replacing through special needs payments far more frequently than anywhere else in the UK. In Manchester and the North West, local office staff were unusually tough on applications for special needs payments.

What had originally been national assistance administered by peripatetic local officers with a lot of discretion, had now become "benefits" to which people were entitled and could press their entitlement through appeals. A growing army of welfare rights officers helped them appeal. The case law expanded each year so that the portable handbook for local national assistance officers had grown into a multi-volume code – the A Code - occupying many shelves in local offices. Within a decade the new system was handing out one-off special needs discretionary payments to half the claimants. Although the staff numbers had doubled in a decade, the local office clerical systems were in total disarray with phones unanswered, giro cheques going missing, appeals rising and huge variations in local decisions.

The public and press criticism of this chaos had reached a political tipping point. It was made worse by two other public and political criticisms of this shambolic system. One, usually made by the political left, was that too many claimants – usually pensioners - were not getting the benefits to which they were entitled. The second, usually made by the political right, was that too many claimants – usually the unemployed - were work-shy scroungers ripping off the system. A focus of the latter critics was claimants using benefit to buy coloured televisions with free-standing legs: it was the legs that seemed to cause most offence. A Conservative MP, Iain Sproat led the charge on scroungers and forced DHSS to strengthen their anti-fraud activity.

To respond to the public criticism, David Ennals had been persuaded by Donnison to set up a review of the supplementary benefit system by civil servants, with the participation of Donnison and his Commission. This review had been started before my arrival and without my participation. In agreeing to the Review, the Treasury required it not to incur extra expenditure. My job seemed to be to keep the existing rickety system going until the Review was completed; but I had no control over the benefits delivery system which was in the hands of the Regional Directorate. The delivery system was highly unionised; and the unions were effective at protecting local and regional jobs.

A bizarre aspect of my role was that I was supposed to support and help the independent Commission but at the same time advise Ministers on the merits of the Commission's advice to them. Talk about marking your own homework. This situation was made more complicated by the presence of an activist Chairman who had his own agenda for the Review. David Donnison was a quietly spoken, politically-savvy, academic with an egalitarian view of social policy, reinforced by his unwillingness to wear ties – a problem when a Permanent Secretary took him to lunch at his club.

Donnison was strongly opposed to a benefits system based on a subsistence level of daily living; and wanted to see the poor more empowered to secure better support. He considered the social security system as rigged against the poor, which in many ways it was; and he wanted this system to be placed more clearly in a wider social policy context for alleviating poverty that involved housing, transport, health and education/training. His views were summed up in the memoir he later wrote on his time at the Commission entitled "The Politics of Poverty." I had a good deal of sympathy with his more holistic approach, but it was never going to be delivered by the shambolic 1970s benefit system.

I agreed with Donnison that we should reduce officer discretion with a simplified benefits system based on entitlement. But as someone with a working class background, I thought he had a rather romantic view of that social group, particularly their budgeting skills. He seemed very keen on claimants deciding how to spend their benefits, irrespective of whether that produced debt causing hardship for dependents, especially children. I could see the case for aligning all the means tests; but I had reservations about replacing all rent and rates subsidies and allowances by a single housing benefit, particularly as many people would be worse off.

Under the proposed new housing benefit scheme, rents would be fixed by the average of local market rents that in turn were determined by landlords. This was the direction in which the review was heading. It seemed to me a landlords' charter that central government would end up funding - as later proved to be the case. Future Governments have struggled to control the budget for that scheme. This was unsurprising given that the scheme produced a market based on 'provider capture.' I suspect, from what friends later told me, that I was seen as a bit of a 'hard' man at meetings, challenging well-meaning liberal views.

I decided to confine myself to modest changes to the existing system. After a struggle, the A Code was published as a means of removing fantasies about cunning bureaucratic rules cheating claimants. We tried a benefit take-up campaign for pensioners without moving the dial much; and only succeeded in annoying the Treasury. We published benefit leaflets in different languages like Urdu and Gujarati with mixed success: the text of one edition in Gujarati was published upside down through the absence of a Gujarati-speaking proof-reader. We managed to discreetly dispose of the offending leaflets.

There was one success when my attention was drawn to a small outfit called the Salford Market Forum who specialised in simplifying official documents used by the public. This was run by a former benefits claimant, Chrissie Maher. We visited Salford and commissioned them, against DHSS advice, to simplify some of our supplementary benefit leaflets - which they did to considerable acclaim. After I left, DHSS dropped them. However, the energetic Chrissie turned the unit into "The Plain English Campaign" in 1979. She caught the attention of Margaret Thatcher with a demonstration outside No10 and the Campaign became a great success winning many awards and an OBE for Chrissie. It is still going as far as I know.

1978 saw the Review published as a document called 'Social Assistance.' Its two main recommendations were to replace most of the discretionary payments by benefit entitlements determined by local benefit officers; and the creation of a single housing benefit with the same means test. This new benefit would cover 100% of housing costs for all supplementary benefit claimants; would taper off as income rose above supplementary levels; and would be administered by local authorities. The faltering Callaghan Government pushed the report out for public consultation, and it was left to Patrick Jenkin, after the 1979 Election, to implement a low-cost version of the new scheme.

Unemployment was rising, along with inflation, at a time of wage restraint. The Government was kept in office by David Steel's Liberals. We civil servants watched closely the weekly meetings between Steel and Michael Foot – the Leader of the House – to settle the following week's Parliamentary business so that the Government didn't fall. Finally, the 'Winter of Discontent' strikes, with rubbish piling up on the street and the personal health issues of some Labour MPs, enabled the Conservatives to win a confidence motion by one vote at the end of March 1979. (All this was later captured entertainingly in James Graham's play 'The House.') Callaghan duly called an Election for 3 May 1979.

Before then I had been moved to a new Management Services and Computers Division that was to improve the efficiency of social security management and prepare a new Operational Strategy for the use of computers. By this time, I had realised that the social security system was basically a giant cash dispensing machine. I thought that if

I couldn't change the policy, I could at least make the machine more efficient. Much more significantly I had fallen in love with the person who was to become my partner for life.

Thatcher's Efficiency Drive and Derek Rayner

In my new role, Pat Nairne used me to organise and edit the briefing for incoming new Ministers. This briefing was on commitments in Manifestos and 'must do' topics that had to be attended to quickly. Each paper had the same factual analysis but with different conclusions based on the known Parrty political preferences, including Liberals because of their potential 'kingmaker' role. Folders even had different colours - blue, red and yellow. The Conservatives campaigned on controlling inflation and curbing the unions. They won an overall majority of 43 and Margaret Thatcher became the first female Prime Minister. At the same time, she was joined in the Commons for the first time by her successor, John Major.

On arrival in No.10 Thatcher made clear her commitment to both a smaller State and more efficient government. To help deliver these flagship policies, she brought in Derek Rayner, the CEO of Marks and Spencer, to lead a central government efficiency drive. She saw retail as her business model for shaking up public sector management. Perhaps more worryingly for her Cabinet colleagues, she wanted Ministers to demonstrate that they were managing their Departments: only Michael Heseltine seemed to take this seriously. She wanted to apply the management message to Permanent Secretaries and senior mandarins. as well. Each Department was to undertake a Rayner efficiency scrutiny. The idea was to see if the civil service could improve its own efficiency by using short, focused, studies, supported by a powerful external figure (Rayner) with access to the PM. Each scrutiny was to be completed in 3 months.

Pat Nairne asked me to come up with an impressive sounding scrutiny. It had to be large given the size of the DHSS budget and avoid the NHS, given there was a Royal Commission on this area. Even Mrs Thatcher wouldn't be keen on stirring the NHS pot at this stage. I suggested the way social security benefits were paid. This looked managerial and could produce impressive savings without, as I thought then, causing huge political controversy. How wrong I turned out to be.

In 1979 the cost of social security administration was about £750 million compared with the £15 billion spent on benefits – some 30% of public expenditure. About a third of those administrative costs went on the method and frequency of paying benefits. Nearly two-thirds of that money went to the Post Office to meet encashment charges and the postal costs of enabling the public to cash social security order books and giro cheques in post offices. At the time of the scrutiny about 95% of these payment instruments were cashable weekly, with 90% in the form of order books containing individual payment foils. If a person received more than one benefit, they had separate order books. Payment went to about 9 million retirement pensioners, 7 million child benefit recipients and about 4 million recipients of supplementary or unemployment benefits.

The job of the 3-person scrutiny team I led was to see if we could reduce administrative costs by changing the methods and frequency of those benefit payments. Our inquiry involved a wide range of discussions within the civil service and externally. We sought suggestions from staff and unions. I even took Derek Rayner to a local social security office in Hackney but suggested his chauffer driven, expensive car remained out of sight, a couple of blocks away. We undertook market research among benefit recipients – then novel for DHSS. At the end of this process we concluded that the existing payments arrangements were anachronistic.

Nearly 40% of the working population and 3 million occupational pensioners were already paid monthly, usually through bank accounts. Across the EU (apart from Ireland) and North America most social security benefits were paid monthly or less frequently and often through bank accounts. Moreover, our market research revealed a public appetite for changes in the methods and frequency of paying benefits. For example, 70% of mothers said they would find it very or fairly easy to manage if child benefit was paid every four weeks. Only war pensioners were allowed to have their pensions paid through banks. Three years earlier the DHSS had looked at paying benefits through banks but not pursued the idea.

We recommended three main changes. First that nearly all benefits paid weekly should be paid fortnightly, apart from child benefit which should be paid four-weekly. Some protection of weekly payments should be available for vulnerable groups. The second recommendation was that DHSS should make available quickly payment by direct credit to bank accounts on a four-weekly basis: this should also be available on a three-monthly basis for retirement pensioners who wanted it. Third, we identified a raft of procedural simplifications for benefit payments. We calculated that if this package was implemented as a whole, DHSS could reduce their administrative costs by £50 million a year at 1978 prices. We estimated it would take them 3 to 4 years to implement the changes.

From the outset we knew the Post Office would be the people most upset. Payments for each transaction covered a chunk of their overheads and provided full cost protection. There was no effective competition because the banks had shown no interest in entering the social security market. They thought weekly payments would leave accounts too quickly to be worthwhile. The Post Office had no incentives to improve efficiency. In the previous decade their charges for paying retirement pensions had increased by double the rate of inflation.

Two-thirds of DHSS business was transacted through sub-post offices – many in Tory heartland rural areas. That is why we suggested that the Government should remove the legal barriers to the Post Office obtaining new counter business; and that the Agency Service Agreement with sub-offices should be amended so that enhanced payments could be made to protect rural sub-post offices. Our report pleased Derek Rayner and was supported by the DHSS top brass and the responsible Junior Minister, Lynda Chalker (now Baroness Chalker).

Ours was the largest Rayner scrutiny and Derek chose our report and a Ministry of Defence scrutiny led by Clive Ponting to take to Mrs Thatcher. (Clive was to achieve notoriety when in 1985 he was tried for leaking papers relating to the sinking of the Argentinian cruiser, Belgrano, which cast doubt on the UK government's version of events: he was acquitted following a 'public interest' defence.) We duly appeared before the Prime Minister to give a brief account of our studies. She seemed more interested in taxing me about the NHS hospital building programme than my study; but I seemed to have acquitted myself satisfactorily because Derek told me I was to accompany him to the Cabinet to present my study.

I did my turn the next day to a Cabinet that seemed more concerned with keeping their heads down and avoiding eye contact with Thatcher. Derek's paper was noted, with not a word of concern about the sub-post offices. Years later I was reminded of this Cabinet experience when told the joke about Thatcher at a Cabinet dinner being asked by a waiter, "Vegetables, Prime Minister?" and allegedly replying, "They'll have the same as me."

Despite the apparent Cabinet blessing, the scrutiny report still had to be considered by DHSS and a submission made to the Secretary of State, Patrick Jenkin. Before this could be done a leaked version of our report found its way into a speech by the then Chairman of the Post Office, William Barlow – the rumour was this came from an exchange with Jenkin on a train journey. The result was a major campaign against the report between mid-December 1979 and the end of February 1980. Claims were made that pensioners would be compelled to open bank accounts and hundreds of sub-post offices would close. Over a thousand letters and dozens of petitions were sent to DHSS. The National Federation of Sub-Postmasters organised hundreds of members to march to the House of Commons. At a meeting with their leaders I tried, unsuccessfully, to reassure them with minimal support from Patrick Jenkin and Keith Joseph, the Business Secretary, who spent much of the meeting doing his constituency correspondence.

In a subsequent Parliamentary debate, Jenkin promised wide public consultation when the report was published. However, at Prime Ministers Questions on 28 February, Thatcher cracked when she conceded that retirement pensioners would be able to have their pensions paid weekly through post offices if they wished. Effectively she had given away the main recommendation that accounted for 40% of the savings before the report had even been published. So much for the 'Iron Lady.'

The controversy continued with the scrutiny report still not published but with more media focus on Derek Rayner's work, including a BBC programme. Patrick Jenkin and I appeared before the House of Commons Social Services Select Committee in March 1980: Derek Rayner sent a supportive letter but declined to appear saying the report was a matter for Ministers. The Committee had to make do with a summary of the report but they still endorsed most of our ideas, provided beneficiaries had the right to continue with weekly payments if they wished. The Committee also said the Post Office should increase its counter business from new sources.

With the Government considering what to do, the DHSS brass despatched me to Canada for three weeks to participate in a Duke of Edinburgh study tour. This was intended to promote harmony between industrialists and trade unionists from different Commonwealth countries, with a few civil servants providing a government perspective. On my return there were months of Government silence. Eventually, on 9 December 1980, DHSS replied to the Select Committee and published the Scrutiny Report.

It proposed offering from mid-1982 four-weekly payment of benefit by direct credit to bank accounts for most beneficiaries. Secondly it would only pay retirement pensioners less frequently than weekly if they opted for payment to banks. Third it proposed paying child benefit four-weekly but with our recommendation of vulnerable groups retaining weekly payment. Last, they would implement all our administrative streamlining proposals. The Government also proposed amending legislation to allow the Post Office to compete for more public sector business but not for more private sector work that would threaten building societies or travel agencies. An interesting perspective on competition.

These proposals effectively cut our savings by about 25%; and they shrank further with more changes as implementation proceeded slowly through the 1980s and 1990s. I wandered into the House of Lords Chamber one evening in the early 'noughties' and listened to the final touches being put to some Post Office changes that flowed from our 1979 scrutiny report. It illustrated how slowly change happens in the public sector.

By the end of this saga the Rayner scrutiny programme had been well established across Government. Within a few years, there were reviews producing significant manpower and financial savings. In DHSS alone – and on top of my scrutiny - there were savings from a Government-wide scrutiny of the Government Statistics Service; a shake -up of the health care exports programme; reductions in the cost of the national insurance contributions scheme; and big manpower savings in running job centres and paying unemployment benefit from a joint scrutiny with the Department of Employment. The Treasury set up a Financial Management Unit to run the Government-wide Financial Management Initiative which started in September 1982. The FMI aimed to give civil servants managing resources clear objectives, a means of measuring achievement, information on costs and responsibility for securing value for money.

Whatever one thinks of Thatcher she deserves credit for persisting with her attempts to turn mandarins into managers. Many Permanent Secretaries, as Accounting Officers, found it difficult to embrace this agenda. It could expose shortcomings in the way their Departments managed taxpayers' money and the limitations of the 'good chaps' way of governing. The approach encouraged people to ask awkward questions, not always welcomed by government bureaucracies. I noticed over time, however, that many civil servants involved with the Rayner scrutiny programme had blighted civil service careers. I was later to join their ranks.

I remained on good terms with Derek, later to be Lord, Rayner, and learned more about management from him than from the civil service. Visits to Marks and Spencer headquarters were always instructive, particularly on the use of data and measurement - not strong features of civil service management in those days. I remember being impressed that at the end of each day he could find out which cheeses had sold well in each store. He remained a strong supporter of my next efficiency project.

Before the end of the benefits payments project, my new partner and I experienced the joy of the birth of twins, only to have to handle the awfulness of their early death. We battled on coming to terms with this through the summer of 1980. I was then asked by the DHSS top brass in October 1980 to lead another, much larger, Rayner-type project. This was to examine the flow of business ("traffic") between social security local and regional offices and between the latter and headquarters. The real purpose of what became known as the Traffic Study was to cut the costs of administering social security. This would guarantee another group of people I'd make unhappy – those who worked in regional offices.

Reforming Social Security's Regional Organisation

By the autumn of 1980 it was clear the Thatcher government would cut the size of the civil service substantially: the aim was to come down from about 740,000 to 630,000. The sheer size of DHSS – then about 90,000 staff - made it a candidate for substantial cuts. I was under no illusions about the purpose of the Traffic Study and nor were the trade unions; but I tried to avoid making it a crude cost-cutting exercise. During the previous decade there had been a drift of decision-making away from the local offices to regional offices and headquarters, without any clear reason. I made the purpose of the study finding out what had happened and do something about it. I was chosen to lead it because I was independent of the Regional Directorate and my connection to Derek Rayner.

When our team of four started, social security expenditure was about £35 billion a year and the cost of administration was over £1.5 billion a year – 70% of which went on staff. There were nearly 67,000 people in the regional organisation, nearly all of whom were in the 530 local offices; with about 3,500 in the 12 regional offices. Another 300 worked in headquarters. We started by looking at the way different types of cases were referred upwards and with a disposition to reduce upward referral. After a range of visits and discussions we found local office staff were keen to make more decisions, but with more senior people reluctant to devolve decision-making. The latter had rigged the codes covering the handling of cases to require a lot of upward referral to regions and headquarters. It looked like a giant job creation programme; but we needed to prove it.

We conducted two surveys of senior people at regional offices about their workloads and scope for change: these produced reasonably honest answers They revealed that many decisions could be left to local managers but many of the requirements for upward referral came from headquarters staff whose job was supposed to be policy formulation, not case work. My masterstroke was the third survey – of local managers. For this I hired a survey organisation who designed for us a 22-page questionnaire with 55 questions. It was designed for easy completion, requiring only 'yes or no' tick box answers or a figure. We also made it anonymous and agreed it with the unions. The result was a 90% response rate. The analysis of the replies provided an authority our report would otherwise have lacked.

I wanted to look at organisations outside the civil service with dispersed local branches and regional organisations to see if they had similar problems to DHSS. So, we visited two retail companies, a clearing bank, a building society and a nationalised industry, plus another Government Department for good measure. None of them was perfect and they often had similar problems to DHSS. But they usually had clearer definitions of the roles to be played by each tier and the level of performance expected. They were much more willing than DHSS to make changes. One company told us that regional tiers needed regular culls.

Our analysis revealed that each year local offices referred upwards in writing or telephone at least a million cases. These were on issues like decisions to prosecute for fraud or non-payment of national insurance contributions. This increased 'traffic' was despite local office managers having been upgraded to take more decisions locally. The survey of local managers revealed that 84% wanted more authority to decide cases locally; 30% said they wanted much more authority; and none said they wanted less authority. Over the previous decade the Regional Directorate had used various management approaches to measure performance; but most of these systems measured case volume, rather than the quality of case decision-making. Local managers had become disconnected from the main business of local offices which was the quality of individual case decision-making. They also had too little control over decisions on personnel and office administration costs.

Our recommendations were a three-year programme to remove whole slabs of casework from headquarters; and a wholesale delegation of casework decision-making to local offices in areas such as contribution liability, benefit entitlement, prosecutions, appeals and medical adjudication. We also wanted to replace detailed controls of administrative costs by annual budgets; and a major overhaul of personnel matters to empower local managers, including simplification of many of the staff appointment, appraisal and training aspects.

This would reduce the 3500 regional office staff by at least 1600, offset by an increase in local office staff by about 600. Even allowing for estimating errors, I couldn't see how DHSS could fail to reduce administrative costs by upwards of £15 million a year and reduce staffing by at least 1000. We also recommended, as a consequence, reducing the number of regional offices from 12 to 7; and placing

Group Mangers in their territories and having charge of more local offices, as was the case in other organisations we had seen.

Ministers agreed our report in principle late in July 1981. They made the report public with an announcement that the 12 regional offices would be reduced to 7; the first merger – Wales and the South West Region should take place at the end of August; and discussions would open with the unions with the aim of completing implementation by the autumn of 1983. This was faster than I had proposed. The unions were predictably outraged and refused to accept the report: they didn't engage with it for a year or so. In part this was because there had been a one-day civil service strike in May, ostensibly about pay, but really about Thatcher's attitude to the civil service.

Ironically, I was the Chairman of the DHSS branch of the First Division Association and had been out on strike for the day in May and on the picket line with other unions: I was also collecting cheques for the strike fund from senior civil servants who covertly supported the strike. Despite this the unions decided I was the Great Satan. Not only had I authored the Traffic Study report, from September I became the Controller of the newly created Wales and South West Region. I was implementing the report to show how it could be done. I added insult to injury by running this large region from London. Our new son had arrived in May and I refused to move home or do the job longer than two years.

I set up a new regional headquarters in Cardiff and appointed an integrated set of assistant controllers; and started about 10 micro-computer projects for topics like routine personnel work and supplementary benefit assessments. We helped re-write all the national procedures for a new delegated authority system. I let local managers talk to the local press and I started doing a radio phone-in benefits programme: when headquarters found out the brass were rather upset. I introduced a staff newspaper to improve staff understanding of the changes taking place: in those days this was an innovation. By mid-1983 the local managers were recruiting all clerical staff and promoting clerical assistants. A new budgetary system for controlling all administrative expenditure was being trialled.

I can't claim to have been popular. I was roundly booed at a regional staff dinner and dance in 1982. But by then the local unions had resumed talking to me. Implementation went reasonably harmoniously and there was no industrial action until I started shutting a few small national insurance offices in Wales. The region's experience was being disseminated nationally when negotiations resumed. By April 1983 all seven new regions had been established; and regional office staffing had been reduced by 600. By October most of the proposed changes had been introduced or were due to start in early 1984. Many local staff liked the greater trust in them and the more flexible ways of working. Local managers had better financial information and fewer regional and HQ people on their backs.

Many of the ideas in the Traffic Study were being disseminated by Ministers across Whitehall as part of the wider Rayner efficiency programme. I even persuaded Derek to come to Wales to speak to my managers. When I picked him up from Bath Station he called in at the local M & S to check up on the local manager; and emerged triumphantly with bags of unripe tomatoes he'd found. Unusually, the Treasury acknowledged the influence of the Traffic Study on its new Financial Management Initiative launched by Thatcher in late 1982.

Farewell to Mandarin Land

By autumn 1983 I was feeling pleased with the successful delivery of the Traffic Study and looking forward to a job change. During my time running the new region, I had remained involved in developing the new social security operational strategy and advising on efficiency issues. I had watched a few people being promoted ahead of me even though I knew I was marked as fitted for promotion. I assumed I had to finish the Traffic Study before my time came. However, a particularly bizarre promotion and some worrying exchanges with a few senior friends set my alarm bells ringing. Someone was blocking me.

The 'someone' turned out to be the DHSS Permanent Secretary, Ken Stowe, who in 1981 had replaced Pat Nairne. Stowe had been Callaghan's and Thatcher's Principal Private Secretary and run the Northern Ireland Office. My suspicion was that Stowe's view of me was nothing to do with work performance and more to do with my involvement in the civil service strike. I enlisted the help of John Ward, the General Secretary of the First Division Association and decided on frontal attack. I wrote to Stowe telling him I believed he was blocking my promotion despite my being marked fitted in several annual reports; and that I wanted a meeting with him. Eventually he agreed to meet me but was very evasive about my next job. He suggested a career break on a Gwilym Gibbon scholarship at Nuffield College, Oxford. John Ward thought the best thing he could do was to talk informally with Sir Robert Armstrong, then Head of the Civil Service.

I took a break in Oxford where I wrote up my 'efficiency' experiences for publication; gave a few talks; and met some interesting people. Unfortunately, the economists had taken control of the wine committee at Nuffield with adverse consequences. During this time, I was approached by Sir James Swaffield, the Director-General of the GLC, then led by Ken Livingstone and his deputy John McDonnell. Jim was struggling with handling this left-wing duo who had gained control in 1981 and whose high spending put them in constant conflict with the Thatcher Government just across Westminster Bridge. He wanted to create a new Assistant Director-General post to help him try to improve GLC/Thatcher relations. As I had worked closely with a number of Labour Ministers, he thought I might be acceptable to Livingstone and McDonnell. I was also interested in a stint in local government.

I was sceptical about my acceptability to Ken Livingstone; but I put in an application and was shortlisted along with two others. On paper I looked the best candidate. At interview I was faced with 25 or so GLC members seated in a horseshoe. We worked our way round the horseshoe with me giving balanced answers. I sensed this might not be what the 'lefties' were looking for. The next day Swaffield called to say I hadn't got the job, despite a good interview. It turned out that all the Labour Ministers I'd worked for – Castle, Crossman, Ennals and Robinson – weren't left-wing enough and were deemed to have 'sold out.' The job went to a Camden community organiser – clearly chosen to thwart Jim Swaffield. This turned out to be for the best because Thatcher lost patience with the GLC and abolished it in the 1985 Local Government Act, leaving London without a strategic political body.

In the Spring of 1984, I was summoned back to DHSS urgently. I was to be promoted and to take over as the Under-Secretary in charge of policy on supplementary benefit and housing benefit. (John Ward had done his stuff and Robert Armstrong had shown the fair-mindedness

93

I was to see when we became colleagues in the House of Lords.) I wasn't wild about another stint in social security. Thatcher had evicted most of the 'Wets' in her 1981 Cabinet reshuffle but had put a One Nation Tory, Norman Fowler, in charge of DHSS. There was concern about my political acceptability, particularly as supplementary and housing benefits weren't Margaret Thatcher's favourite subjects. I had to be checked out by Rhodes Boyson, a former headmaster and then the social security Minister of State. We chatted amiably for a while, mainly about Barbara Castle who Boyson liked. I was passed fit for purpose.

In 1984 Thatcher was in her pomp and Labour in total disarray. She had gambled and won the Falklands War, with a little help from her chum, Ronald Reagan, and after the controversial sinking of the Belgrano killing 800 Argentinian sailors. On the back of her military triumph, she had won the 1983 Election with a hugely increased majority – 397 seats to Labour's 209. Michael Foot had campaigned on a Manifesto described by Gerald Kaufman, as the longest suicide note in history. Labour had split after their Gaitskellite right, led by Roy Jenkins and David Owen, had left to form the Social Democrat Party. The SDP had allied themselves with the Liberals in the 1983 Election and together they had secured nearly 8 million votes – just fewer than Labour – but only 23 Parliamentary seats.

At the time it looked as though Thatcher would go on and on. I was unlikely to progress in the civil service under Stowe after challenging him. I thought I would do a year in the new job and then look to leave. Meanwhile, I would do the best I could to minimise damage to the welfare state by a Prime Minister who wanted individuals and families to do more to look after themselves rather than rely on the State. Work had been done on replacing the NHS with private health insurance; ending state funding of higher education; and removing price protection for social security benefits. There was little doubt in my mind that with a massive Parliamentary majority her ideological convictions would come into their own in the DHSS sphere, posing serious challenges to civil service neutrality.

Unemployment, which had been falling at the time of the 1979 Election to a little over 1 million, rose rapidly afterwards. It was given a major upwards push by Geoffrey Howe's 1981 deflationary budget. I had dealt with the direct impact of that budget as a Regional Controller when benefit claims in Wales soared: I used to say locally that social security was the only stimulus the Welsh economy was getting. By the end of 1981 there were nearly 3 million people unemployed. There were riots in Brixton – two miles from where I was living – Liverpool, Manchester and many towns and cities across the country. UB40, the unemployment benefit form, gave its name to a successful rock band led by Bono. After the 1983 Election, Nigel Lawson became Chancellor and immediately cut large Departmental budgets and made clear the social security budget was in his sights.

Norman Fowler was confronted with a series of social security challenges which became his main focus. The long-term affordability of the earnings-related pension scheme (SERPS) was placed in doubt by the growing number of elderly people, as we lived longer. Labour's reformed supplementary benefit scheme was out of control as welfare rights officers secured more of the benefits to which people were entitled and the number of individual special payments soared. Patrick Jenkin had tried to introduce the new Housing Benefit scheme with no extra money to avoid losers. The scheme's administration became very complex with different means-tests and faulty computers; and in 1983 Fowler cut the money available even further. There was growing political hostility to paying supplementary benefit to 16 and 17-year-olds and students. This was the 1984 social security world I had to handle.

Fowler's response was to have a review by a think tank, the Policy Studies Institute (PSI). This was not a bad decision in the circumstances, but it meant I was back to where I had been in 1976. There were reviews in policy areas for which I was responsible but which I had little control over. Thatcher and Lawson wanted to cut the social security budget; but Fowler wanted to avoid taking the blame for politically disastrous cuts that were difficult to justify and administer. Although the PSI review was presented as the biggest review of social security since Beveridge, it never actually produced a report. Instead, there were a series of papers with a good analytical underpinning that were discussed by officials, the Social Security Advisory Committee and Ministers. The aim was to keep budgets under some kind of control and not provoke the occupants of 10 and 11 Downing Street.

In January 1984 The Times called housing benefit "the biggest administrative fiasco in the history of the welfare state." The scheme

95

was totally out of control. It had had so many short-term fixes that few people understood it properly anymore, including me. During my time we added to the problems by using secondary legislation to close a variety of loopholes that had been exposed. We were like the Dutch plugging holes in their dykes, with the North Sea – claimants – creating new holes.

I tried to explain to Ministers that if you stopped 16 and 17-year-olds from claiming supplementary benefit, they wouldn't return to their families who were often the people they were fleeing from. They would sooner sleep rough on the streets of London and other cities. You could not re-invent the Speenhamland system in the 20th century. Ministers were told that if they wanted to cap the supplementary benefit single payment system, they would still need some kind of cash fund for hardship cases, with local discretion in administering it. That is where Ministers ended up with what later became the Social Fund.

As civil servants many of us became exasperated by the endless meetings and submissions on trying to cut benefits without appearing to do so. At one of these meetings, which had gone on for nearly three hours, one of my staff blurted out to a startled Tony Newton (who had replaced Rhodes Boyson) "we've all had to become Tories, Minister, why shouldn't you." The likeable and competent Newton paused and then went on with the meeting as though nothing had happened. Month after month the reality of the world that the social security system was dealing with was brought home to Thatcher's Ministers.

At the end of this grinding process SERPS survived in a cheaper form, with the public encouraged to make better provision for their old age. The Social Fund was set up to curb the growth of one-off payments in the supplementary benefit scheme. (This did at least stop some of the idiocy I saw, as in an appeal for failure to pay for a hot water bottle grinding its way through the system to the Social Security Commissioner; and even a claim for an inflatable life size Swedish doll for a lonely male pensioner.) Supplementary Benefit was renamed 'Income Support.' Benefit was withdrawn from 16 and 17-year olds with the sad results we had prophesised of many homeless young people sleeping in London shop doorways and underpasses. Norman Fowler's review tactics probably prevented the most draconian social security cuts, but it was grinding stuff. The reviews certainly did not lead to the fundamental changes claimed for them by Ministers.

Outside of these reviews, it became apparent to me that the supplementary benefit scheme was funding, unintentionally, a rapid expansion of private residential care and nursing homes. For some time, the benefit had been payable to people living in board and lodging accommodation, including care homes. If it wasn't practicable to move someone to a cheaper home then the benefit system would pick up the tab, no matter how large the bill. In 1978 there were about 7000 people having their care bills paid by the benefit system. But by 1984 the number had risen to over 42,000 and their average cost had increased six-fold. The number of private care homes doubled between 1979 and 1984 to well over 4,000. This sector was now larger than the local authority care homes sector.

This dramatic expansion of private care homes was often happening in seaside resorts along the south and east coast where the holiday trade was declining. Hotels became available cheaply for other uses. Some local authorities were even handing over their own care homes so that residents could claim benefit. In late 1983 the Government had tried to set limits on the costs they would meet from benefit. However, these were to be set locally and there was political anxiety about frail elderly people being evicted from homes. This change by my predecessor only made more would-be proprietors aware of the attractions of benefit-funded care homes. It also enabled more hard-pressed local authorities to sponsor people for admission to these private homes where the benefit system picked up the tab.

A joint working party between DHSS and local authorities was established – I was not a member. It reported in May 1985 just as I was leaving. It suggested that local authorities should pay for the care costs of eligible people in private and voluntary care homes and that DHSS should pay for their board and lodging. This would be very difficult to implement and would only be a solution for elderly people. No consideration had been given to homes for people with mental or physical disabilities or for those needing nursing homes. Meanwhile more people invested in private care and nursing homes and the benefits bill climbed. The Thatcher Government, intent on cutting the social security bill, had managed, on its watch, to let that budget accidentally fund the development of a private nursing and care home sector. DHSS had no idea how to fund that sector or regulate it. I helped tackle this in my next job.

I heartedly disliked the political and civil service climate and by early 1985 was determined to escape. Although interested in improving government efficiency, I was definitely not a 'One of Us' Thatcher supporter. A head-hunter approached me about the job of Director of Social Services for Kent County Council. I met privately the Chairman of the Council's Social Services Committee and we hit it off. I told him I'd never been in a Social Services Department let alone managed one. Their social workers had been on strike for a year and they wanted a manager who had worked with politicians. I had come to their attention from my work with Derek Rayner. Would I apply? I did and was successful. I had no idea what I was getting into, but there was a pay increase, it sounded interesting and I could continue living in London. Best of all, I escaped from DHSS, or 'The Department of Stealth and Total Obscurity' as David Owen called it. Thus began, six of the best years in my working life.

4. Replanting the Garden of England: 1985-1991

Working for Kent County Council

Kent County Council was very different from Ken Livingstone's GLC. After my interview the Council's Leader, Tony Hart, took me for a drink. He told me they knew all the candidates were 'pinkos' but I looked as though I could manage. They had been worried about my divorce and whether my former wife would chain herself to the County Hall railings. My predecessor, the Rev Nicholas Stacey, a former Olympic sprinter, had reminded them they were not appointing a Bishop.

Kent was a large County physically, with a population of about 1.5 million people, then the same as Northern Ireland. It was spot on the England average for wealth but with West Kent wealthier than other areas. The poorer areas were along the Thames Estuary and around the South Coast. It had significant ethnic minorities in the Medway towns, Dartford and Gravesend. Kent had been run by the Conservatives since County Councils were established in 1888. A century later, they still had a healthy majority on the Council. The Conservatives controlled most of Kent's District Councils; and had more MPs than any other political Party, with a sprinkling of Cabinet Ministers like Patrick Mayhew and Michael Howard.

Although there were a 100 Council Members, I soon realised the Council was run by a handful of Committee Chairmen. These used to be landowners and prominent family businessmen, but self-made men were increasing in number. The few women were usually confined to the social services and education committees. There were more Labour than Liberal Democrat councillors and surprisingly no Independents. It was an all-white Council.

Kent Tories' expectations of me were clear. End the social workers strike which had dragged on for a year. Balance the budget and inject some management. Avoid social services scandals. How I did this was up to me provided the Chairman of the Social Services Committee approved. I was comfortable with this agenda and had much more freedom than in DHSS. I had some tussles over funding, but the Tory leadership never stopped me doing what I thought was right. I made sure I never sprang surprises on them.

Compared with central government it was easy to get decisions taken. Papers had to be prepared for formal Committee decisions, but there was plenty of scope for informal discussion and securing agreement orally. Members liked to take credit for good news but were happy for me to keep popping up on their TV screens. For the most part Kent Members in the 1980s seemed to expect their senior officers to handle the media - another refreshing change from central government. Although Members appointed Chief Officers and their Deputies, other appointments in Kent were left to Chief Officers.

The big Council issue when I arrived was construction of the Channel Tunnel. Work on this brought about a surprisingly close relationship between Tory Kent and Socialist Nord-Pas de Calais. They both supported the tunnel project and thought it would bring economic benefits. This led them to making common cause on securing EU funding for joint projects, some of which benefitted social services. Margaret Thatcher was unenthusiastic about the Channel Tunnel and had delayed a knighthood for the Council's Leader. The Treaty of Canterbury was finally signed in February 1986 to enable Parliament to pass the Channel Tunnel Bill and for the project to proceed.

The first tunnel broke through in 1990 and the Queen opened the main tunnel in 1994 when trains began running. Throughout my time in Kent this project had a major impact on the Council's work. The road and rail issues were formidable, as were the planning implications. Local communities were disrupted and had to be helped to adjust. Kent's Chief Fire Officer found himself responsible for the tunnel's fire safety, including escape in the event of a fire. I had to close and sell a children's home that obstructed the tunnel's entrance. (I held out for an exorbitantly high price.)

Changing the Social Services Management Culture

I spent six months assessing my senior management. Two of the six Area Directors had to go and another one was so-so. The headquarters policy capability was weak, especially in relation to children's services. Area managers, who managed teams of social workers, needed more focus; and financial management and accountability were poor. I brought in a young policy analyst and hired consultants to help me re-organise the department.

But first I had to face down the unions. There were two unions: NUPE (National Union of Public Employees) representing lower paid, mainly care, staff; and NALGO (National Association of Local Government Officers) representing social workers and administrative and clerical staff. NALGO had been out on strike over disciplining a Dartford social worker. The Socialist Workers Party were active there and it became the epicentre of the strike. I invited both unions to a meeting.

NALGO were led by an SWP shop steward wearing a jacket with both lapels full of badges telling me every cause that he supported or opposed. He did the talking, mainly to tell me that he couldn't negotiate with me until I agreed to reinstate the sacked social worker. He was being paid from a national levy on NALGO members who were fed up with paying the levy. I said there would be no re-instatement and there would be organisational changes that I would like to discuss with them. They declined to talk to me. I made clear I would be making the changes needed. NUPE said they would meet me. NALGO stomped out.

I announced the appointment of management consultants; met NUPE; and learned that NALGO had stopped the levy. Virtually all Kent's social workers returned to work. NALGO eventually asked to see me and were led again by the same SWP steward. He told me that no re-organisation could take place without their agreement. I explained that wasn't how things worked. This produced a tirade about how my job was to secure the money social workers needed. I ended the meeting and told them that if they wanted another meeting, they could meet the Council's Personnel staff. I had virtually no further meetings with NALGO during my time in Kent; but had perfectly amicable relations with NUPE. There was not a peep from any Council Members, including Labour members.

The consultants produced their report which the Social Services Committee accepted. I appointed from outside Kent a new (female) Assistant Director for Children and Families Services; and two new Area Directors (one female) after suggesting two incumbents took early retirement. I brought in a new Finance Director to improve the financial management system; and eventually managed to secure a more effective HR director. Another Area Director left after threatening to resign if I wouldn't increase his budget for learning disability services to meet promises he had made. I asked him for his letter of resignation. It was clear that I had to change the Department's management culture, especially around social work; and.to create a greater sense of accountability for providing quality public services.

Social Services Departments came into being in 1971 following the 1969 Seebohm Report. Since then, their management had been dominated by a strong professional social work culture. The belief seemed to be that these Departments could only deliver services by direct public provision managed by people with a social work qualification. Scotland required such a qualification and most English local authorities did likewise. Brian Roycroft, the Newcastle Director, was so outraged by my appointment that he wrote to a professional journal saying: "Both the standing and credibility of the Chief Officer would be much diminished if he had to depend on professionals to provide social work advice." A few suggested Margaret Thatcher had personally authorised my appointment to sort out social work. If they only knew.

Unfortunately for the Seebohm purists a lot had changed in the 1980s. The myth of the all-purpose social worker was exposed for what it was, a myth. The legislation, knowledge and skills for particular client groups was rapidly changing and more specialised social workers were needed. Those protecting children were doing a very different job from those helping mentally ill patients or providing services for the frail elderly. More services from private and voluntary organisations were becoming available which threatened local authority direct provision. The latter were increasingly required to show they were value for money. This mixed economy of care required local authorities to develop new service commissioning and contracting skills which had little to do with social work expertise.

The 1980s also saw a surge of new legislation requiring new ways of working: the 1983 Mental Health Act, the 1984 Registered Homes Act, the 1986 Disabled Persons Act, the 1989 Children Act and at the end of the decade the 1990 NHS and Community Care Act. As a result, the budgets and staffing of social services departments increased considerably. As one of my few Director friends, David Townsend, said about the 1970s: "Budgeting then required vision, idealism and five or ten per cent on each of the previous years' activities." Between 1981 and 1991 personal social services staff in the UK rose from about 250,000 to over 300,000 while NHS staffing actually declined slightly.

What was happening, without most local authorities realising it, was that these departments needed a general manager. The same thing was happening in the NHS, following the recommendations of Sir Roy Griffiths. Kent was just ahead of the curve. A social work qualification was not much use in managing a large budget, 6000 or so staff, a diverse range of functions and playing a role in the corporate management of a big County Council. In the 1980s big changes were needed to social services management, irrespective of Mrs Thatcher.

Kent Social Services had virtually no IT, did not believe in staff appraisal, did no medium-term planning and had no system of cost-centre budgeting or financial accountability by managers. The social services budgeting system was described by Kent's political leadership as "a black hole into which the Council tipped money." Staff morale was at rock-bottom after a nine-month strike that had created a huge backlog of work. Social service managers had little incentive to improve their management competence. The Council's central departments for finance, personnel and property controlled these areas tightly and made it difficult to adapt these support services to social services' needs. There were few incentives for social services to seek efficiency savings to deploy on new services.

In 1985 Kent was similar to most social services departments, with many managers hankering after the good old days. I couldn't sack them all. I had to take them and the Council on a journey, with a change programme that had achievable objectives. A statement of organisational vision was needed that was linked to the performance of individual managers. My change programme had three key elements: three-year medium-term plans for all the main client groups, updated each year; annual business plans and budgets for each of the 6 operational areas and HQ setting out what would be achieved in each financial year; and resource accountability statements for each of the 40 or so senior managers setting the service levels they had agreed to achieve in a year with the money and manpower provided.

I had found that no individual manager was held to account for their performance. Gradually I introduced a new staff appraisal and development programme linking performance to pay which caused Kent to withdraw from national pay bargaining. Eventually all managers down to the fourth tier (team manager or head of a care home) were appraised each year against an action plan agreed with them and their pay increases were determined by their performance. Within this appraisal process a manager's development needs were identified. In five years, the annual expenditure on staff training was increased from under £100,000 to about £1 million, with staff receiving 4 to 5 days training a year on average. We sold some of the training to outsiders to offset some of our costs.

At the request of staff, a new staff counselling and support service was established in 1989 on a confidential basis: it could be accessed without contact with an individual's line manager. By 1991 this service was being offered on a commercial basis to other employers. Day care nurseries and holiday play schemes were established for staff with children. More women were appointed as managers. Personality profiling and critical reasoning and numeracy assessments were introduced as part of the senior management selection process: the aim was to have teams with a mixture of skills and personality types.

Rebranding Social Services and a Ferry Disaster

By 1987-88 there were new service-level agreements with all central support departments (personnel, finance, property, IT and legal) on what level of service they would provide each year. For personnel and finance functions I selected a senior person from the central department to work full-time in social services as a member of my management team. By this time, we had established Kent Social Services as a brand called 'KentCare' We used this brand to run national recruitment campaigns in The Guardian newspaper with a strip cartoon character who engaged with current political issues. This approach succeeded in attracting social workers and managers to Kent and the campaign won national awards.

I needed to improve communications with staff given the size of Kent. I wanted a vehicle in which staff could participate and which didn't come across as a heavy-handed creature of the boss. I hired a part-time journalist as editor of a new staff newspaper called 'The Ferret.' I pointed out in the first edition, 'ferret' meant 'to search out, to bring to light.' The title was also a bit of fun that provided the cartoon character who led our recruitment campaigns. The Editor knew he had editorial control provided he didn't slag off the County Council and campaign against departmental policies. It was circulated outside Kent and often had articles used by national journals and even national newspapers. The Ferret was launched in February 1987 and was still going strong well after I left Kent.

The introduction of new management approaches and disciplines into a traditional social services department was not without pain. Many social work traditionalists resisted the ideas I was plugging. Some thought we were too frivolous. When the idea of treating people as 'customers' was suggested some social workers were outraged. Many managers did not like being held to account and appraised. However, as I pointed out, we were never short of talented external applicants wanting to participate in this new management experience. When I asked them why they were coming to Kent their reasons were usually about wishing to make change happen and being given the freedom to innovate.

This change of management culture was put to the test when something totally unexpected happened. On the evening of 6 March1987 the Townsend Thoresen car ferry, 'Herald of Free Enterprise' capsized just outside Zeebrugge harbour on its way back to Dover. Fortunately, the water was shallow and the Belgian emergency services reacted quickly. They saved many lives but about 150 passengers (many children) and 50 crew died. Many of the survivors were injured and seriously traumatised. We soon learned that many other people were also traumatised, like relatives and those involved with the rescue and its aftermath. Dragging dead bodies out of water and examining large numbers of them takes its toll.

We had to set up from scratch a counselling and support service for three main groups: the bereaved, the survivors (including crew) and others, like the coroner, affected by the tragedy. I soon learned about "survivor guilt." Within 3 or 4 days we had established a 'Herald Support Team' in the Ferry offices and a 'Heraldline' in our Dover office. They contacted bereaved families across the country and secured help. We brought in bereavement counsellors from voluntary organisations and NHS professionals: and ran a 24- hour service. By the end of three months, we had provided – and were often continuing to provide – counselling and support to over 350 survivors and their families, 200 relatives of dead passengers and crew and 70-80 other people.

We kept these services going for two years with help from other organisations, particularly Bradford Social Services. They had dealt with the aftermath of a serious fire at the local football stadium killing 56 people and injuring over 250 others. We and Bradford spoke at many conferences so that others could learn from our experience and produced training material. This tragedy showed how a well-run and confident social services department could take a major disaster in its stride and work well with many voluntary bodies. This ability to work with other bodies was something I tried to develop in Kent.

Creating a Mixed Economy of Service Providers

I spent a year reviewing the scale and quality of the private and voluntary service providers in Kent, alongside our own traditional local authority services. Kent had always had a strong voluntary sector; but in recent years the private residential and nursing home sector had expanded rapidly with the increased supplementary benefit expenditure (see previous chapter). There was virtually no quality assurance for any of this expenditure and no comparison with Council services. The Council's old peoples' homes had received little investment and were struggling with increasingly dependent residents. The traditional home help services were not trained to meet the needs of an ageing population who wanted to stay in their own homes. A new registration and inspection regime for private and voluntary care homes was being developed nationally under new legislation; but Kent was struggling with the sheer number of new care homes that had sprung up.

The limitations of our registration regime were exposed by Yorkshire Television's 'The Granny Business,' shown in October 1987. This focussed on a selection of the 500 or so registered care homes in Kent, many occupied by people from outside Kent. Many of these homes were converted hotels and boarding houses in seaside towns. I co-operated with the programme and gave an interview, which was used selectively. The programme revealed inadequate staffing in homes, especially at night; gross breaches of registration conditions; incontinent residents left in wet beds; and a registration and inspection service too small to inspect the number of homes in Kent. Worst of all, there were dangerous people running homes, including an owner of several homes who had been in prison for firearm offences and been on a murder charge.

The Council protested that the programme was not balanced, which of course it wasn't. I thought protesting was a waste of time and I used the programme as a galvanising event to reform Kent's adult services. I referred potential criminal cases to the police and started beefing up the registration and inspection service. We trained more inspectors and made more unannounced inspections, including in the middle of the night. We computerised the information from inspections; did more criminal record checks; and set up a confidential inquiry line for residents, families and staff. I started closing homes with TV cameras rolling as we relocated residents. We developed quality standards for all Kent's care homes (public and private) and published them in attractive booklets. Gradually these standards booklets were extended to home care and other services.

Alongside the bad private homes there were some good new ones, especially those offering nursing services. In many of our own homes, we were struggling to cope with the growing number of people with dementia. Homes were having to create dementia wings to curb the impact of dementia residents on others. We began shifting to a system whereby all homes that met our standards could become approved care providers.

It was not just residential services that needed attention because many of Kent's ageing population wanted to stay in their own homes. The traditional Kent response of home helps, WRVS meals on wheels and Age Concern daycentres did not cut the mustard. Nick Stacey had recognised the problem and started a small project in which staff called 'care managers' had budgets to buy services to keep people in their own homes, including paying neighbours. This had been evaluated by Kent University and looked promising; but nothing had been done to expand it. This was my first example of something I would see a lot of in the UK's public sector, successful pilot schemes that never went to scale. I took the scheme to scale, and not just in Kent (see next section).

So was born the Kent care management scheme, or what Nick Timmins of the Financial Times later called "the cheque-book social worker." Except most of Kent's care managers weren't social workers. We decided to design our own training course for care managers and our own specification of the skills required. This was to be a scheme that required people to manage a budget and keep people in their own homes with the practical services they needed. Care managers could spend up to two-thirds of the cost of a place in a residential care home to keep a person in their own home, if that was what they wanted.

Kent's social workers for the elderly thought they should automatically be slotted into the new care manager posts. They found I disagreed, which caused a bit of a rumpus. I was convinced that Kent had a large number of women who wanted to return to work as their children grew up and would have the practical skills and temperament, after training, to be good care managers. This turned out to be the case when we advertised the posts on a basis of open competition. We also found many occupational therapists made good care managers.

We began discussions with the private and voluntary sectors about the standards we would expect if we contracted with them to provide community services. I contracted out most of our elderly day care to Age Concern Kent to deliver it through their local centres. We funded a wider range of services, such as reminiscence therapy. We put our meals on wheels services out to competitive tender to drive up quality and had a row with the WRVS about this. I discussed with Waitrose and Marks and Spencer whether they could provide more single portion meals but without success. We funded some parents of children with autism to develop a residential facility that became the basis for the Kent Autism Service. We persuaded retail employers to hire more people with learning disability; and funded some residential care homes to provide more community-based services. We worked with Carers UK to provide more support for carers.

We also expanded some of our own services, particularly the home help service whose management and productivity needed shaking up. We began the process of converting 35 of our old peoples' homes into linked service centres so that they could provide a range of community, as well as residential services. Perhaps more radically we looked seriously at buying places for the care of less dependent elderly people in Spain, but this proved a bridge too far for Councillors. Their unwillingness to invest in Council residential homes and hostels began to cause concerns but it took time to achieve a solution.

While these changes were happening, KentCare, as it now was, began working with the NHS to close two large long-stay hospitals, Leybourne Grange near Maidstone and St Augustine's near Canterbury. The former had a capacity of 1200 people with learning disability and the latter was a 2000-bedded psychiatric hospital with a chequered history. The NHS had decided to move most occupants into the community and close the hospitals. KentCare was to assume responsibility for the patients with funding from the NHS. The programme started in the mid-1980s but was not completed until the late1990s. We bought a lot of houses for conversion into small group homes, supervised by community teams we had to recruit and train.

Many of those being discharged from Leybourne Grange were very institutionalised. I remember meeting women who had been placed there as pregnant teenagers in the 1930s and 1940s by families who claimed they were mentally handicapped. We had to help these victims re-enter a society that would have preferred they stayed where they were. We purchased fencing on an industrial scale to screen their new community homes as best we could. Getting payments from the NHS was seriously hard work and a decade later Kent – like many others - was to find that the NHS had failed to fund adequately the service needs of those they had chosen to move into the community. Closing long-stay hospitals proved to be a seriously under-funded exercise geared to providing valuable capital assets for the NHS. Community care failures were largely the result of NHS underfunding community services.

The creation of Kent's mixed economy of providers was a success story that proved cost-effective and lasted. It could not have been done without the changes in management culture. Some Councils, mainly counties, followed Kent down a similar path, but few went as far or as fast. Many Labour authorities thought it more important to preserve public sector jobs than introduce challenge to existing providers or even consider whether the public wanted something different.

The Audit Commission was concerned about the unsatisfactory nature of much community care. In December 1986 it produced a critical report, "Making a Reality of Community Care." The Government was still concerned about the amount of social security funding going into private residential and nursing care homes. In 1987 Norman Fowler asked Sir Roy Griffiths "to review the way in which public funds were being used to support community care policy and to advise on options for action that would improve the use of those funds as a contribution to more effective community care." Because of Kent's work on care management and a mixed economy, I was drawn into Roy's orbit.

Reforming Care in the Community with Roy Griffiths

Roy Griffiths had been the Managing Director of Sainsbury's and in 1987 was the Deputy Chairman. In 1983 he was asked to look into NHS manpower, then thought to be out of control, but refused and told Ministers that the NHS's problem was management – or the lack of it. He then produced a 24-page report dismantling Keith Joseph's 1974 management structures. As Roy graphically put it, if Florence Nightingale was wandering round the NHS with her lamp, she would be trying to find who was in charge. He said consensus management should go; doctors should be involved in budgets; budget-holders should have targets. There was more in the same vein. I hoped he would sort out community care.

Roy came to Kent to see what we were doing, particularly our care management scheme. Ministers started visiting us frequently, including John Moore who had replaced Norman Fowler as Secretary of State. In early 1988 Roy produced his report – another slim document of 30 pages. It was very sympathetic to the problems of community care which Griffiths described as "a poor relation; everybody's distant relative and nobody's baby." As with his NHS report Roy wanted to put someone in charge so everybody knew who it was. He was clear that local authorities should be in charge of community care. He wanted them to take over joint finance from the NHS and to assess people for residential or nursing home needs.

Local authorities should organise individual packages of care – basically the Kent care management scheme. They should act as "the

110

designers, organisers and purchasers of non-health care services and not primarily as direct providers, making the maximum possible use of voluntary and private sector bodies to widen consumer choice, stimulate innovation and encourage efficiency." He wanted the same purchaser/provider separation that Ken Clarke would later propose for the NHS. Roy's report was straight out of the Kent playbook. He later confirmed to me that "I'd seen what worked in Kent and used that."

It was difficult to know who disliked this report most: John Moore the struggling DHSS Secretary of State, who complained he had not agreed the recommendations; or Margaret Thatcher. Relations between Thatcher and local government were poor after the abolition of the GLC and metropolitan authorities, all Labour strongholds. This was also the time of the Poll Tax legislation. DHSS sat on the report until in July 1988, the struggling Moore had his Department split in two and the ebullient Ken Clarke then took over as Health Secretary.

Clarke – pre-occupied with his NHS Review – turned out to be no fan of Roy's report either. With the aid of the DHSS Finance Department and the Treasury, Clarke cooked up an alternative to Griffiths' plan. This was a medical assessment of the need for residential or nursing home care funded by social security. (He later had the grace to call it a 'ding-bat' solution.) At my instigation Kent had gone public in its support for the Griffiths Report and so had the Association of Directors of Social Services (ADSS) and the Labour-led Association of Metropolitan Authorities. This only made Clarke more suspicious.

I went with the ADSS President to see David Mellor, Clarke's Minister of State. Mellor insisted on keeping his classical music playing but we managed to establish that he was a Griffiths supporter. We also found an unlikely ally in Nicholas Ridley the Secretary of State for the Environment who had taken through Parliament legislation requiring local authorities to use compulsory competitive tendering for their refuse collection, street cleaning and other services. Ridley wanted to apply this approach to other local authority services. The tussle in central government continued throughout 1988 and the first half of 1989.

Roy persuaded me to go with him to the Carlton Club to convince the Conservative Medical Society of the merits of his approach. It was one of my more bizarre political experiences. In September 1988 the ADSS annual conference supported a pamphlet I had written that proposed that Griffiths' ring-fenced money for community care should be distributed through a Community Care Development Agency to prevent it being syphoned off for other local government services, something the Government feared. In January 1989 I went with two ADSS colleagues and a Conservative MP to see Ken Clarke who in an hour's meeting was non-committal, except to say he would deal with mental illness differently from other groups.

By the summer of 1989 Roy had retired from Sainsbury's and was very fed up with the Government's indecision. He wrote a paper explaining why Clarke's scheme of medical assessments – now supported by John Major as Chancellor - wouldn't work. Clarke was in the middle of rows with the BMA over his proposed NHS internal market and wanted to shut down the Griffiths debate. Those of us lobbying for local government thought we had lost when Roy was summoned to see Thatcher. He told me afterwards that he didn't think he'd convinced her. A week or so later she told a Cabinet Committee that she supported Roy's report. On 12 July 1989 Clarke told Parliament that the Government had accepted the Griffiths Report's recommendations and that social security money would be transferred into a new funding system for local authorities starting in 1991. This was not the end of the saga.

The initial plan was to introduce the community care changes in April 1991 along with changes to children's services following the 1989 Children Act and the NHS reforms for a 'purchaser/provider split.' A White Paper was published in November 1989 with the upbeat title of 'Caring for People – community care in the next decade and beyond.' The Health Department organised working parties to work out the implementation details. We had semantic spats over 'care management' as in Kent or 'case management' – the social work view. I argued that people didn't like being called 'cases.' I lost but continued using my own terminology. Departmental guidance was issued but with no mention of budgets.

I geared up Kent to implement the community care changes in April 1991. We introduced the care management approach to people with physical and learning disabilities; and started working with the NHS to apply the same approach to mental health services. The Council was to become mainly a care enabler rather than a service provider and this meant reviewing which old people's homes we retained: many of them needed upgrading but we lacked the money to do this. The Council was expected to create a care market so that users could choose the home that suited them best. This meant training staff to commission services rather than manage them; and explain to the independent sector how we were going to operate in the future. This was a massive culture change for staff and councillors.

As we moved through 1990, Whitehall whispers began that local authorities would not be ready in time and implementation would have to be deferred. The ADSS conducted a survey which showed the great majority of local authorities would be ready. In June the House of Lords passed an amendment to the NHS and Community Care Bill requiring Ministers to provide an earmarked grant to support the community care changes. An ADSS survey showed that 88 Councils out of 116 supported an earmarked grant and only two Labour Councils opposed it. We lobbied Robin Cook, the Shadow Health Secretary but the Government reversed the Lords' amendment.

Talk of deferment increased. I asked Roy to find out what was going on. He reported back that "there is a complete obsession about Poll Tax, and I have tried the macro-economic argument as to the excessive use of income support. Kenneth Clarke and the Treasury are well on side but a few pounds on the Poll Tax seems to be the overriding concern." We secured Leaders in the FT, Times, Guardian and Independent arguing against delay. But government fears about Poll Tax increases triumphed. Implementation was deferred until April 1993, safely after the 1992 Election. In Kent, as elsewhere, we slowed things down which displeased staff and councillors geared up for an April 1991 start.

The delay gave me time to reduce the number of Council care homes. The success of our care management scheme had reduced demand for these. We converted 35 homes into Linked Service Centres that provided community as well as residential services. As one of my last acts, I persuaded the Council to close a few homes and transfer the remaining nine into the new Kent Housing Association. This enabled the Association to borrow in the money market to upgrade the homes, improve maintenance and provide better pay and conditions to the low paid staff working in them. It also took on the management of some hostels and group homes for the mentally ill and people with learning disability.

113

The saga of community care dragged on until April 1993 when the new system was finally implemented. After leaving the County Council, I spoke at many conferences about the work we had done in Kent. I discovered my approach to change management remained less than universally popular in the social work world.

Protecting Children

Alongside community care, I spent a lot of time reshaping children's services and dealing with the growing problem of child abuse. Some of Kent's inhouse children's services were working well and I saw no reason to change them. I recognised that the Council had an effective, arms-length Adoption Agency which was very successful at matching children to parents. I left this high-performing service alone, only intervening to support the idea of a 25th anniversary party where adopted children, now adults, met up with those who had adopted them. However, it was adoption that produced a difficult encounter with Kent MPs.

After the fall of the Romanian dictator Nicholas Ceausescu – executed on Christmas Day 1989 – TV screens were full of distressing pictures of children in State orphanages, estimated to hold 100,000 children. Convoys of concerned citizens were driving across Europe to try to rescue these children, some led by Kent residents. Two Conservative MPs asked to meet in Parliament to persuade me to send social workers with the convoys to bring children back to Kent for adoption. I explained that this was tantamount to kidnapping children across international borders and was not something I could do. I pointed them in the direction of Government Ministers, which was not the response they wanted. One of them was a future Home Office Minister in the Major Government.

Kent had put a lot of effort into fostering services by paying foster parents quite well and investing in their training. I met foster parents once a year to thank them; and we tried to pay up promptly if a child trashed their home. Some of the teenagers being fostered could be very challenging. Nick Stacey had recognised this by having a scheme of specially trained foster-parents who were paid at half the rate of a qualified social worker to look after challenging teenagers. I continued with the scheme.

114

Kent also had a multi-agency youth justice system involving police, social services, probation and education, with occasional NHS participation. It was presided over by a Board comprising the chief officers of these services who rotated chairing duties. This system had worked well with youth court magistrates in keeping young offenders out of custody. I drew on Kent's model in creating youth offending teams (YOTs) when reforming the youth justice system in the Home Office after the 1997 Election (see Chapters 6 and 8).

Nevertheless, I thought some children's services would benefit from a mixed economy of service providers, as we had done for adult services. As the number of child abuse cases rose it was clear that not all the children coming into our care could be coped with by fostering. I did not want to open more local authority children's homes, in large part because the few we'd run didn't have a great track record. An increasing number of reasonable quality private children's homes were opening, some with on-site clinical services we couldn't provide in our homes. In 1990 we began a tendering process to find a small number of approved contractors we could use when necessary.

We also found that attendances were dropping at our own Family Support Centres which offered help and support to families in difficulty, to prevent children coming into care. This was unsurprising when one looked at some of the public attitude surveys. Many people regarded social services as the people who took away their children, so why would they come to us for support and reveal their inadequacies? So, I began a process of transferring these centres to voluntary organisations like Gingerbread.

I began to realise that the work we were doing in treating adult users of our services as customers could be applied to children's services. I started off in 1989 with an 'in the round' event in the Medway towns with about 150 children. I wandered round the stage like a cut-price Jeremy Vine trying to engage these young people in a conversation about their views on care and what they would like to see changed. Some argued strongly for pocket money increases. But messages began emerging about their confusion over how care worked and how they wanted us to listen better to their concerns and complaints.

I thought the event was a flop but discovered that for some senior managers it was something of a light bulb moment. They and frontline social workers wanted to listen more to the views of children in care. I became more engaged with this issue which was at the heart of the new 1989 Children Act. With the help of young people, we produced a new booklet that they could keep 'Finding your way in Care.' It was light-hearted with cartoon illustrations and sections on keeping in contact with friends and family, having your say and how to get help. My and other phone numbers were in the booklet.

A Kent in Care Network was formed to bring children together. Slightly to the annoyance of some senior managers, a young man called Alex Saddington came to see me occasionally to talk about campaigning for children in care. He was speaking at conferences and helped to set up a campaigning organisation called the National Young People in Care (NAYPIC). I gave them some funding and paid for Alex to go on a study tour that included Russia. On his return he gave me a small bust of Lenin that I unwisely left on my desk, much to the annoyance of visiting councillors.

We discovered that children in care who had suffered criminal injuries, could lodge claims with the Criminal Injuries Compensation Board. In late 1989 we agreed a system with the Board for fast-tracking applications and helped children to make them. By mid-1991 we had made 120 applications and been successful with 59. In 18 months, this pioneering initiative had secured more than £500,000 for abused children. We invested the money in a building society for release at 18, or earlier if this assisted a young person's development.

The major problem we faced with children was the rapid increase in child abuse, particularly sexual abuse. Between 1984 and 1990 Kent experienced a five-fold increase in child abuse referrals. By late 1990 the annual rate of abuse referrals was over 2300, with half of them coming from members of the public. Nearly 1400 of these were registered after investigation and over a fifth were sexual abuse cases. Referrals were increasingly coming from family members as well as the general public, demonstrating greater public awareness of abuse. The Kent numbers per capita of the child population, were above the national average; and we had a higher proportion of sexual abuse cases.

We had to recruit more social workers and improve their joint working with the other agencies. I negotiated with the Chief Constable for more police officers to accompany social workers on home visits on some of the rougher council estates; and we arranged joint training of social workers and police officers in child protection work – the second local authority to do this. We set up a new Kent-wide Child Protection Committee with the other agencies which I chaired. A new child protection manual was introduced so that all the agencies adopted the same terminology and procedures. To improve social work practice, a specialist adviser was hired to support child protection teams.

The ground rules for social workers were stick to the procedures and we will always support you, whatever happens; but not if you ignore the procedures. The response from staff was excellent. Given the scale of the workload increases we had very few serious incidents. When things did go wrong, I remembered the advice given me by Patrick Mayhew, a Kent MP and former Northern Ireland Secretary of State – "If things have gone wrong Norman, put your paws up and apologise." Those who struggled most with this huge increase in child abuse, were the leading male councillors who hated the impact on the Council's budget.

The Chairman of the Finance Committee started saying I was sending social workers around Kent searching for child abuse to boost my budget. I suggested he commission an independent audit of our figures and that leading councillors should spend time with a social work team of their choice. This would enable them to see child protection work in action and the types of case social workers dealt with. The independent financial report at the end of July 1989 totally supported our figures and our response to the growth in referrals. It told councillors bluntly what the alternatives were. They could either put children at risk by not responding to referrals outside our control and ignore government guidance; or they could fund properly the increased workload. I lunched with some councillors (including a GP) after their visits to local social work teams. They told me how shocked they were at what staff had to deal with; and one said he felt physically sick after being shown a sexual abuse case.

Still not satisfied, the Council's Finance Committee called in Ernst and Young to crawl over my department. In January 1990, EY reported favourably on our social work practice and procedures and said we needed another £2 million or so in the next budget to maintain these standards. I heard no more about searching out child abuse and had no

117

further trouble funding children's services. The bean counters had made me a folk hero within my department.

Apart from strategic and political interventions I didn't interfere in the day-to-day running of children's services, leaving that to a very competent Assistant Director who later became a successful Director and personal friend. I did decide to sit in on interviews for social work team managers for a while so that we could secure a talent pool of future leaders. I had my disagreements with some social workers, particularly when I insisted – after a pilot study – parents should be able to attend and participate in the first half of case conferences so that they could put their views, face to face. I did however intervene in social work training.

I had never been a fan of Seebohm's generic social worker. The national overhaul of social work training was going painfully slowly. I decided that we should try to accelerate in Kent the work on a new Diploma as a basic qualification but with a special emphasis on working with children. We found a Further Education College that specialised in vocational training, Christchurch College in Canterbury. We agreed with them and the professional body a syllabus for a new Diploma in Social Work that devoted more time to working with children. That became the first new social work qualification in the country and increased Kent's supply of social workers.

In 1989 a major legislative change was introduced, a new Children Act. This required an overhaul of procedural manuals for frontline social workers and new in-service training. The biggest change was the emphasis in the Act on the paramountcy of the welfare of the child and the detailed checklist for courts in determining a child's welfare This new Act pulled together legislation scattered across several Acts; and turned the spotlight on social work training, particularly the expertise needed by social workers working with children. All this was timely given the increase in child sexual abuse work and public and media concerns.

The Rise in Child Sexual Abuse and Value of Social Workers

Until the 1970s the staple work of child protection teams had been neglect. The Maria Colwell case in 1973 changed that and revealed that

118

social workers had to look out for physical abuse of children within their families. What happened in the 1980s was a massive increase in abuse referrals and the revelation that child sexual abuse happened in families, as well as in institutions. We knew that children's homes attracted paedophiles; and were later to find that nurseries did too. My predecessor had reduced the number of Council children's homes in Kent to four, none of which were secure homes with locked doors: Lancashire, the same size as Kent, had over 30 Council children's homes. I had no wish to open new homes.

Unfortunately, one of our homes was managed by Peter Jaynes, a colleague of Frank Beck who was then under investigation for abuse in children's homes he'd managed in Leicester. Jaynes had been a Deputy Head of a home managed by Beck. I discovered that Jaynes was using the same 'regression therapy' as Beck: this involved children being dressed as infants and sitting on the manager's knee. I had Jaynes removed and reported him to the police for linkage to the Beck case. He subsequently received a three-year prison sentence for indecent assault and actual bodily harm for his activities in Leicestershire homes. After a two-year investigation, Beck was convicted in 1991 and received five life sentences for his abuse. Chapter 5 has more about the Beck case and my involvement in its aftermath.

In another of our children's homes the only black manager in Kent was found on top of a 15-year-old girl at 3am. An investigation also revealed substantial theft of food and other items. He was suspended before dismissal. He was the cause of my only appearance before an Employment Tribunal when he claimed his dismissal was the result of racism. Not long after, I had to persuade a Kent MP and his wife that inviting a promiscuous and vulnerable 15year-old girl in our care to their home for the weekend could well finish his political career.

The game changer on child sexual abuse was what happened in Cleveland and the subsequent enquiry. In the first half of 1987 about 120 children in Cleveland were diagnosed as sexually abused and removed from their homes, often in the middle of the night. The diagnoses of these children were made by two paediatricians in Middlesbrough, Marietta Higgs and Geoffrey Wyatt using a diagnostic technique of reflex anal dilation that was later discredited clinically. So many children were removed from their homes that there were

119

insufficient foster homes, so they were housed in a hospital. The public outcry led the Government in July 1987 to commission a report from a judge, Elizabeth (later Baroness) Butler-Sloss.

Her report published in July 1988 was highly critical of the poor communication and joint working between the different agencies and the excessively dogmatic decision-making by the two doctors. As a result, over 90 children were returned home, although about 40 remained wards of court. The big finding from this inquiry was that social services should not rely solely on medical examinations but on a wider multi-agency view of the child and their circumstances. The report led to a major overhaul of multi-agency procedures and working and the early passage of the 1989 Children Act.

Butler-Sloss recognised the difficulty of investigating sexual abuse within families. At the same time research had found that children were twice as likely to be sexually abused inside their own home as outside it; and that both parents and children might well avoid telling the truth about cases of sexual abuse. The same research by Professor Jean La Fontaine also revealed that the estimates of sexual abuse were likely to be inaccurate - on the low side; and it was wrong to believe that incest was limited to disadvantaged groups like the poor. In 1997 a controversial TV documentary suggested that more of the Cleveland children had been abused than was thought at the time of the Butler-Sloss Report. The two doctors, Higgs and Wyatt, continued claiming that the medical evidence supported their view that abuse had taken place in many cases where children had been returned home.

What all this meant for my staff was that investigating and unravelling evidence of child sexual abuse in families was extremely difficult and painstaking work. It required careful and collaborative work across the different agencies – with social services and police in the lead – if abused children were not to suffer repeat trauma through investigation and prosecution. It was certainly not true that you could rely on medical evidence as the only and conclusive evidence of abuse in the great majority of cases, as had happened in Cleveland. Events there had flashed warning lights about crusading hunts for child sexual abuse.

In 1989 we found we had a disciple of the Middlesbrough paediatricians working in Kent, Dr Heather Richardson. When she saw children for school medicals, she routinely examined them for sexual abuse and took anal and vaginal photographs without parental approval. This was despite the police saying this had no evidential value. She used similar controversial techniques to those used in Cleveland; and had a private social worker assessing children without telling the police or social services. She claimed that the size and responsiveness of a boy's penis could indicate he had been sexually abused. She routinely called back children for further examinations after agency case conferences had rejected claims of sexual abuse. Her part of Kent had more than double the referrals for child sexual abuse to the rest of the County. She caused a massive amount of unnecessary family distress and wasted work by other busy professionals, including fellow doctors.

Nobody claimed she was never right about sexual abuse: she sometimes was. But her working methods and conduct were not going to secure convictions and protect children. She ignored agreed procedures; and unnecessarily distressed children – some as young as three – and many innocent families. It took me two years to finally persuade the NHS regional authority to undertake an independent review of her conduct at which I gave evidence. Shamefully they found in her favour but did have the grace to move her to other duties. It took the Mail on Sunday later to expose her working methods to the public. Thankfully the NHS has become much better at dealing with errant doctors than it was 30 years ago.

Dr Richardson was involved to a limited extent in what became known as the 'Canterbury Sex Ring or Network' that first hit the national media at the end of 1990.This network of offences and prosecutions involved about 75 children. Many offences went back to early 1989 but the first trial was not concluded until December 1990. That trial involved 32 children and 17 adults. The second trial was concluded in March 1991 and involved 10 children and 11 adults. The third trial started in July 1991 and involved 17 children and 11 adults; and concluded after I left Kent. In all the trials the abusers were both men and women, some of the latter involved in incest with sons. Some boys were victims and perpetrators.

These children experienced very serious incidents of sexual abuse including multiple rape; multiple buggery; rotation of abuse by adults; child sex for sale; ritual beating; involvement of drugs and alcohol; and some exposure to bondage and animal involvement. This gruesome material was what two teams with about 25 social workers and managers had to cope with. The children were taken into care and made safe before prosecutions were mounted. Many of the children had to be interviewed more than once as new facts emerged and most of this was done jointly by social workers and police officers, usually women. This took a heavy toll on staff and children. A limit was set at no more than four interviews per child. The work was painstaking and slow in building evidence from the children for prosecution. They were now in care, either fostered or in a children's home. These children were very disturbed and scared; and some ran away.

The build up to the first trial took nearly a year. Children had to be prepared for court appearances without contaminating evidence. Adolescent boys who were perpetrators as well as victims had to be helped not to incriminate themselves: this needed careful negotiation with the police and CPS. Sometimes when giving evidence children froze or passed a note to the judge rather than speaking. On occasion their evidence was taken apart by an aggressive defence barrister. The outcome of the first trial was five convictions. The most serious offender received 10 years imprisonment for rape, buggery and indecent assault. There were 12 acquittals. Vigilantes expressed their views on one of those acquitted by setting his residential caravan on fire at night and killing him. I have been unable to track down the number of convictions in the second and third trials.

These events and many others elsewhere created a difficult atmosphere of anxiety and uncertainty for social workers which was not widely appreciated. The Cleveland inquiry had not produced a clear-cut outcome on the scale of abuse, despite highlighting procedural shortcomings. Rochdale and Nottingham produced lurid cases of alleged satanic abuse, with children said to have been taken to woods for ritual abuse. Adults dressing up as witches seemed to capture more media attention than the fact of defenceless children being sexually abused by their own family members. I tried to make clear to staff my scepticism about the more excitable stories about satanic and ritual abuse. All one could do was ask social workers to exercise their professional judgement within the framework of established multi-agency child protection procedures.

Only one national newspaper, the Guardian, covered the Canterbury case. I had given their reporter access to Kent social work managers throughout the cases on condition nothing was published until a trial was completed. I thought social workers failed to get the media credit they deserved and in April 1991 I wrote to The Independent a letter they published with the heading, 'Social workers can never win.' It included the following passages:

> *"This case [the Canterbury sex rings] was larger than any of the episodes in Nottingham, the Orkneys or Rochdale, all of which have been reported in depth. The trouble with the Kent case was that it showed the police and social services working closely together, observing sound procedures and achieving convictions. Pretty boring stuff really – just some routine incest and buggery."*

It went on to say:

> *"Unlike most professionals social workers are often doing their jobs in the living rooms of distraught and malfunctioning families rather than in the more detached arena of a courtroom or a hospital. Of course, social workers make mistakes but let us keep them in perspective. Doctors sometimes remove the wrong limb. Judges sometimes misdirect juries and deal incorrectly with appeals by long-serving prisoners. Journalists occasionally libel individuals and ruin their reputations."*

A few years after I left Kent, I came across research by the University of Southampton. This showed that between 1973 and 1993 annual child abuse deaths in England and Wales had fallen by two-thirds to 33 for children up to the age of 14. Comparable figures in the US were an increase from 92 to 110. From the third worst developed country we had become the fifth best. Child abuse continued but social workers were getting better at saving children from dying. I still believe the media undervalue social workers compared with other professions.

Leaving Kent in 1991

I decided not to renew my contract and left Kent amicably at the end of September 1991. I summarised for the Council what had been achieved during my tenure. In 1985 Kent Social Services was an under-managed, over-centralised organisation with low staff morale after a year-long strike. Now services were well managed, with able and self-reliant managers operating a structure with devolved decision making. There was greater concern for staff and their welfare with annual appraisals and personal action plans, supported by training funded by a guaranteed 1% of the budget. There were five-year strategic plans based on data and policy analysis; and annual performance plans for the top 40 managers whose pay had a performance element. There was more investment in support services like finance and IT.

Social services were more outward-looking with greater concern for the needs and views of its users. Kent had moved increasingly to providing packages of care tailored to individual needs. There was public consultation over service development, with a mixed economy of service providers and stronger partnerships with outside agencies and organisations. We had pioneered individual care management which had become national policy. Over 200 people had been transferred from long-stay hospitals to the care of community mental health teams. Better support for carers had been started.

Child protection had been strengthened enormously by multi-agency cooperation. Kent's social workers had coped with a five-fold increase in child abuse referrals and a large child sexual abuse network without scandal. We listened more to the children in our care. Four of my management team had gone or would be going to be Directors in their own right and another one was to be the Deputy Director of the Social Services Inspectorate.

Not everyone had enjoyed the journey, but I thought this was not a bad record for a guy who wasn't a social worker and had never been in a social services department before. At a time when the lifespan of a Director of Social Services averaged about that of a football manager, I had lasted six years and left on my own terms. Over 20 years later I had to dredge up my memories of Kent and apply the experience to Birmingham's failing children's services.

Postscript – Birmingham's Children Commissioner: 2014-2015

On 26 March 2014 I met, at his request, Michael Gove who was then Secretary of State for Education. He asked me to take on the role of

Commissioner for Birmingham City Council's children 's services. These services had been failing for nearly a decade and been the subject of numerous critical reports by Ofsted and others. Central government's patience had run out. I would have considerable powers to secure information and cooperation locally. I wasn't keen to take the job and made it clear that I was not prepared to act as his hatchet man. The civil servants looked apprehensive, but Gove was fine and accepted I would be independent. I agreed to do the job for a year only and a day a week. DfE officials followed up the meeting with a legal Direction under the 1996 Education Act. This set out my powers and a lengthy list of the work areas I was to investigate.

Seven weeks after my appointment I sent Michael Gove a progress report. This explained the Council's botched reorganisation a year earlier but said top management was working well on a three-year Improvement Plan. I had told them this needed high impact changes in the first year, particularly a big improvement in assessing children when the Council was first contacted – 'the front door.' Too many children at risk were not identified for safeguarding action. I had told the Council I wanted the Plan monitored and directed by a 'Quartet' – the Council Leader and children's Cabinet member, the Chief Executive and the Director of People's Services. They would be fully accountable if the plan wasn't delivered.

I told Gove it was clear that the Council's centralisation of children's services had not worked. The sheer size and complexity of Birmingham required a more devolved operational structure and work was starting on this in time for the new area structures to begin in the next financial year. The Council's funding was inadequate; and they now recognised that if their children's services were to improve, then they must recruit more qualified social workers, reduce their staff turnover and improve significantly social work practice and leadership using external expertise. I kept in touch with Edward Timpson, the Minister for Children, and DfE officials. I also wrote to Simon Stevens to ask for his help with improving NHS cooperation locally with the Council over safeguarding children. This was forthcoming.

Steady progress had been made by the time of my second report in October 2014 to Nicky Morgan who had replaced Gove. I had stayed in close touch with the Quartet on my regular visits to Birmingham and by phone. They were meeting fortnightly to monitor progress but were facing a lot of political pressure over so-called 'Trojan Horse' schools, where an Islamist or Salafist ethos was allegedly being introduced. I had agreed, after amendment, the 3-year draft Plan sent to DfE in July. The Council had clearly failed to identify significant numbers of children requiring safeguarding. A new Multi-Agency Safeguarding Hub (MASH) was being set up to reduce risk at the 'front door.'

If the Council was to rectify the problems with children's services, extra funding of about £140million would be required over three years. Although the Council had made children's services their top priority, they had not identified the money required to deal with all the problems. There was a budgetary stand-off between the Council and the Government: but I focussed the Quartet on preparing an itemised 3-year budget to rectify the shortcomings in children's services.

I persuaded management to develop a more credible performance scorecard at social work team level and to work on improving internal quality assurance systems for social work. I authorised the appointment of a Chief Social Work Officer with an independent brief to tackle unsatisfactory professional practice. A new devolved area management system started to be put in place; but the Council had failed to appoint an Executive Director to manage children's services. My review of social work capacity had shown shortages of quantity and quality; an inability to recruit and retain staff; excessive use of agency staff; and poor administrative support, with dysfunctional IT systems. I agreed a series of workstreams to tackle these problems, with the Chief Executive becoming responsible for carrying them out. Many of the problems were caused by HR corporate services and interference by councillors.

By the time I sent my third report to Nicky Morgan in January 2015, DfE had appointed two other Commissioners following concerns about alleged extremist Islamic penetration of Birmingham's schools. One of these was for education and one for security aspects: I kept in touch with both. There was also a review of the Council's governance by Sir Bob Kerslake. These extra actors and their activities were putting enormous pressure on senior officers, with Council elections and a General Election also looming. I recognised the Council's shortcomings but thought the Government had overdosed on external scrutiny. In my third report I drew particular attention to the support I received from top management, despite these other pressures from central government.

126

The new MASH system for dealing with referrals seemed to be working well. There was a much more purposeful air about the staff who were answering virtually all phone calls within 90 seconds. The children at highest risk were now moving through initial triage and into investigation at pace, with family support more easily available. There were still too many agency staff, but staff were volunteering to work at MASH. Referrals were up by over a third and there had clearly been under-reporting of children at risk. Better data collection also suggested continuing considerable under-reporting of children at risk in Asian and Asian British ethnic groups. My advice to DFE Ministers and officials was that independent research was needed into this sensitive issue.

A new Executive Director for Children's Services had finally been appointed. I had insisted on an independent competency assessment of the top 80 or so managers, from team manager to area director. This revealed considerable variation in performance but some potential in the younger lower grades. I told senior management how they should handle under-performers and promote some of the younger talent. I had insisted on the development of a credible scorecard/dashboard that measured children's safety for use from team manager to Executive Director. This was developed and installed by one of the Council's young social work managers. A similar system was being developed for family support. I persuaded the Council leadership to stop using the bureaucratic corporate system of performance assessment for social work staff and to replace it with a more relevant system.

I set out in this report the serious problems with the corporate HR members and management over producing a credible strategy for the recruitment and retention of social work staff, especially team managers. I told DfE I was close to recommending a change in the terms of my direction to require the Council to test the market for the outsourcing of the recruitment and retention of all social work staff. This would replace the Council's HR Committee who were blocking change. I wanted the chair of the HR Committee removed, which was done. Although some extra money had been found to fund the 3-year Improvement Plan there was still a budgetary shortfall of about half the £140million required to the end of 2017/18.

Early on I had asked for a review of the services for looked after children where I thought there was scope for improving efficiency and effectiveness, especially over the use of expensive out-of-area residential care. The review set out a programme of change with scope for savings, if implemented at pace by the new Executive Director. I also suggested improving support for families to reduce the number of children coming into care.

Progress had been made on partnership working to safeguard children and this would be overseen by a new chief officer group of the Council, police and local NHS. I suggested DfE replace the Birmingham Safeguarding Board which was too big (50 members) and ineffective. I set out proposals for expanding the commissioning of children's services to bring in a wider range of service providers and chaired a conference for DfE to assist this process. CAFCASS were brought in to improve Birmingham's failing Independent Review Officer system that was supposed to challenge poor professional social work decisions.

In April 2015 I sent my final report to Nicky Morgan. The first part described the decade of failure Birmingham's children's services had experienced. The second part described the steady progress made during financial year 2014/15 but identified the risks and vulnerabilities that remained. These were a continuing budgetary shortfall; doubts about their capacity to improve social work practice fast enough; and concerns about whether senior management at the centre and in areas could deliver change quickly. But the greatest risk of failure resided in the weakness of the Council's ability to recruit and retain good quality social workers.

The final part of my report described the situation in each of the work areas I had been required to examine in the legal direction that specified my remit; and set out the direction of travel for the next three years. I thought the Council's final version of its Improvement Plan for 2015-17 was a good basis for moving forward, apart from the section on workforce. This was just a set of aspirational numbers, unconnected to labour market reality. I doubted the Council's ability to reduce their dependence on agency staff to 5%. I was also concerned that, against my advice, they had not confirmed their Area Directors in post so they could exercise the robust leadership required. The funding of the Improvement Plan had little contingency provision if service demand exceeded expectations or there was slippage on implementation.

I concluded my report by saying I remained far from convinced that the Council could deliver its updated Improvement Plan and I could not encourage DfE Ministers to approve the Plan as it stood. I had warned the Quartet that I would be doing this, but they seemed unable to change their approach. I declined to extend my tenure and left in May 2015. I received no response from DfE Ministers to my report or to the separate letter I had sent Nicky Morgan about the under-reporting of children at risk in Birmingham's Asian community and the possibility this was happening in other cities.

Birmingham City Council seem to have continued with their Improvement Plan; but another part-time Commissioner was appointed in December 2015. In 2018 the Council's children's services were placed in a trust with its own board and separate from the Council The trust was chaired by the Commissioner. In January 2019 an Ofsted inspection report judged Birmingham's children's services as "requires improvement to be good." This was the first time for over a decade that they had not been judged inadequate. In July 2019 DfE finally issued a statutory direction withdrawing a children's commissioner from Birmingham. I felt vindicated in not signing off the 2015 Improvement Plan.

5. Portfolio Man and Preparing for Government: 1991-1997

Frank Beck Scandal and Chairing a Children's Homes Inquiry

When I left Kent, I was determined to avoid managing a large organisation. After a holiday, I set up a small consultancy company. I had read a few books by Charles Handy who had coined the term 'Portfolio Man' for a person with a mix of jobs. This appealed after 30 years in big organisations. I was in no rush to start work but the Government had other ideas.

On 29 November 1991 Frank Beck was sentenced to five life-terms for sexual and physical assaults, including rape, against more than 100 children in his care. His sentences remain one of the most severe in British legal history since the ending of the death penalty. Beck had been acquitted in 1983 of a charge of bodily harm to a 10-year-old boy after dubious testimonials from senior managers in Leicestershire. There were further complaints of sexual abuse of adolescents; and he was known to practice his own brand of 'regression therapy' (see Chapter 4). He resigned from Leicestershire, but still practiced as a social worker in London on an agency basis using favourable references from his previous employer. He had finally been arrested in 1989 following a complaint about historical sexual abuse made by a young mother who had been in a home managed by Beck. This led to Britain's largest investigation into institutional child abuse, with the police taking statements from nearly 400 former children in care during a two and a half years investigation in the UK and abroad.

On the day Beck was sentenced, the Health Secretary, William Waldegrave, announced two Inquiries. The first by Andrew Kirkwood QC was into the management of Leicestershire's children's homes between 1973 and 1986. The second was an Inquiry chaired by me into the methods of recruitment, selection and appointment of staff for children's homes; and to examine management and other issues relevant to the protection of children. There had been a tussle between Waldegrave and his Minister of State, Virginia Bottomley over the choice of chairman: Waldegrave, an Etonian, wanted a Permanent

Secretary; Bottomley, a former Psychiatric Social Worker, wanted someone who knew the territory. Bottomley won and was Health Secretary by the time I reported a year later. It took until the end of January 1992 for the rest of the Committee to be assembled.

We began by examining four of the many other inquiry reports into scandals in children's homes. There was the 1986 Hughes Report into nine boys' hostels and homes in Northern Ireland involving homosexual acts and prostitution, with allegations of official cover-ups and linkages to loyalist para-military organisations. The Staffordshire Pindown Inquiry in 1991 had revealed unacceptable practices for controlling children in local authority homes by deprivation of liberty and use of social isolation. The Leeways Report related to the manager of a children's home in South London who was convicted of various offences involving indecent photography of young children. Towards the end of our inquiry, we saw the Williams Report on Ty Mawr Home in Gwent which recommended immediate closure of the home after incidents of suicide and self-harm. These reports, and others by Social Services Inspectorates, revealed how dangerous children's homes were and how bad those in authority were at protecting children. Despite regular claims that lessons would be learned, few were.

Given how dangerous they were, surprisingly little was known nationally about children's homes. The Government didn't know how many there were or how many children were in them. We commissioned the first comprehensive national survey of the characteristics, staffing and employment practices in all types of children's homes – public, private and voluntary: we were not allowed to look at boarding schools described as children's homes. We found that in mid-1992 there were about 15,000 places in children's homes, two-thirds of which were run by local authorities. However, the local authority sector was shrinking and had lost 2500 places in the previous three years. The private sector, which had not been inspected until just before we were appointed, had been growing rapidly.

From this survey we obtained a picture of the children in these homes. About two-thirds were there because they had emotional or behavioural problems that made other placements inappropriate. Typically, they were aged 13-14 and had had a succession of failed foster placements. Nearly a third had been sexually abused before their arrival in a home which made children's homes particularly attractive to paedophiles. Looking after these demanding children was a largely unqualified and sometimes untrained workforce. About 80% of care staff and 40% of heads of homes in local authority homes had no relevant qualification: the position was much better in private homes. Few homes had a professional ethos around them.

Over the following months we visited a variety of homes in 10 English local authority areas and had discussions with senior personnel. We visited Scotland, Wales, Northern Ireland and the Netherlands for discussions on the management and staffing of children's homes. We took evidence from over fifty UK organisations and individuals and three Government Departments, as well as on children's residential care across Europe. It was clear that this sector was a mess. Over the past decade more and more difficult children had been placed in a shrinking number of homes. Apart from the high proportion of sexually abused and behaviourally disturbed children in these homes, many were also substance abusers, self-mutilating and victims of violence in their own family homes.

Children's homes were no longer full of the orphans and truants of a bygone era. Yet the management, staff qualifications and training and clinical support were totally inadequate for the job these homes were being asked to do. The homes were looking after the most difficult children in local authority care with the least well-qualified and trained staff. These were closed institutions that needed close monitoring but received the least attention from senior management or elected councillors. When I asked a senior Kent councillor why he never visited children's homes, he said because the children there were so rude to him.

A striking feature of children's homes was low esteem, both among the children and among the staff. For the public, these homes were out of sight and out of mind. Unlike children's homes in other European countries there was no willingness to invest in the homes and their staff to help vulnerable children to thrive and rebuild broken lives. There were some remarkable people working in these homes, but they were doing good work despite the system, not because of it. The homes rarely received sustained attention from senior management. Inquiry after inquiry had highlighted poor management as a major contributor to abuse in homes, but politicians and senior officials – national and local – had done little to change culture and practice.

These managerial shortcomings showed up alarmingly in the way staff were recruited, selected and appointed. Too often, there was little probing of people's employment record or checking criminal records before staff were allowed unsupervised access to children. Relying on interviews as the primary means of selection was about as good as tossing a coin for choosing people. The result was appointing too many people without the aptitude for working with children. A common complaint by staff was the absence of knowledge and training about how they should care, control or attend to the development needs of very disturbed children. No suitable qualification provided the knowledge and skills that staff needed to cope with children's homes as they were at the end of the 20th century. Perhaps even more worrying, there was no consensus on what that qualification should be and how a culture of quality care in children's homes could be attained.

I wanted to report within a year with practical proposals for making homes better and safer for children and staff. We spent six months working up our ideas. We then set up two seminars to discuss the ideas with interested parties, including civil servants who would have to implement our proposals. In the summer of 1992, I worked with the Inquiry's secretariat to draft our report which ended up making 83 recommendations, many of them detailed improvements to recruitment, selection and appointment processes.

We wanted all posts to have a job description and person specification and to be advertised, usually externally. There should be more use of personality profiling, securing full employment histories and preliminary interviews to gauge people's suitability. Interview panels should be trained. No appointments should be made without full background and criminal record checks and verification of qualifications. We proposed a licensing system for those approved to work with children. We recommended making it a legal requirement to consult the central government lists of undesirables and for employers to notify those lists when dismissing people for misconduct with children. Probationary periods should be extended to a year; and the Government should fund a campaign to promote the status of work in children's homes.

Nearly a quarter of our recommendations focussed on improving the management of homes and their monitoring. Line managers of heads of homes should have residential care experience; and heads of homes should not be agency staff. Staff should be supervised regularly each fortnight and be able to raise any concerns about the welfare of children. There should be annual performance appraisals of all staff at which developmental issues should be raised and documented. Each home should have an up-to-date statement of its purpose and objectives; and receive regular visits by governing bodies and independent visitors. We wanted a more robust national system of regulation and inspection of all children's homes, with children having easy access to phones so they could raise concerns without being overheard. We proposed personal contracts for measuring individual child development.

We recommended that Government, employers and qualification bodies should devise a new work-based training system for more accreditation and portability of qualifications. There should be a new Personal Development Contract for all staff and managers working in children's homes. This was an alternative approach to requiring staff in children's homes having a Diploma in Social Work which some argued for but which we considered had little relevance to work in children's homes. We wanted the new Personal Development Contract to start within two years.

We wanted the Government to take the lead on securing and financing better training and development of staff for several years with earmarked money. They should produce a new Code of Employment Practice incorporating our recommendations and a set of national standards for children's homes. We urged the Government to ensure that health and education authorities gave more priority to the needs of children's homes and their staff for specialist services. We recommended that the Government establish a Development Action Group for three years to secure implementation of our recommendations.

On 2 November 1992 I sent our report entitled "Choosing with Care" to the new Health Secretary, Virginia Bottomley. She had been promoted after John Major's surprisingly comfortable Election victory over Neil Kinnock in April. On the 7 December the Government published what they now called the Warner Report and sent it to all local authorities urging them to respond to the key recommendations on the selection and appointment of staff and told them to report back on progress within three months. The report received prominent and positive media coverage with supportive editorials. The Daily Mail said: "In 200 terrifying pages Norman Warner reveals a pattern of complacency and official indifference going back years." I rarely agree with the Daily Mail, but this was spot on.

The Government expressed support for the report but 20% of Councils had not replied by the three-month deadline. No extra cash was made available to implement our training and development recommendations, improve police vetting or provide more support from the NHS. The social work professional bodies predictably supported their own social work Diploma despite its irrelevance to residential childcare. They were never challenged on this by the Government or local authorities. Civil libertarians disliked our probing people's backgrounds despite the dangers to children.

The guidance given to local authorities did improve the way that staff were selected and appointed, although criminal record checks continued to be slow and variable. Agency staff were still appointed to run homes. A Support Group chaired by one of the Committee's members did oversee some implementation of change for two years. I was kept well away from stirring up more trouble in a difficult area of public policy that Ministers wanted to close down. The Government's penny-pinching attitude to the Report's recommendations signalled clearly that it was not prepared to drive the fundamental change of attitude to residential childcare that was needed. Nothing much changed with the publication in February 1993 of Andrew Kirkwood's report on what had gone wrong in Leicestershire over Frank Beck – a tale of social services naivety and incompetence backed up by police failures. The Social Services Inspectorate continued to reveal poor practice in children's homes.

I continued giving interviews complaining about the Government's failure to drive real change or monitor what was happening to our recommendations. Fairly soon another scandal came to light in North Wales children's homes with hundreds of boys and young men sexually and physically abused over a decade without being stopped. This time it was failure by local councils, the Social Services Inspectorate, North Wales police and the Welsh Office. There appeared to be a national paedophile ring operating involving public figures. When the Waterhouse Inquiry was set up in 1996 to investigate this scandal

135

nobody in government could give a clear account of what had happened on implementation of our report.

Our recommendations did make some difference by preventing the worst consequences of poor recruitment processes; but they were not used to produce the systemic changes needed. There was no political or bureaucratic appetite to drive change. In an article I wrote for the Guardian in 1996 I acknowledged that I had failed to get children's residential care its place in the political and managerial sun that I was seeking. I said in terms that the responsible Ministers, Virginia Bottomley and Brian Mawhinney, were not prepared to give children's homes the high-level profile and commitment required or commit the money needed.

Beck himself died of a heart attack in Whitemoor Prison on 31 May 1994 but controversy continued. There were allegations that he had been poisoned by prisoners who had been his victims. At his trial a witness, Paul Winston, claimed he had been sexually abused in a home by the local MP, Greville Janner (later Lord Janner) who denied this in the House of Commons. The Director of Public Prosecutions decided not to prosecute. Many years later the allegations against Janner surfaced again in Theresa May's Inquiry into historical sex abuse but Janner died before these were examined. Our political system has totally failed the vulnerable children in residential care.

NHS Problems: East London and Essex

Before starting the Inquiry, I became Chairman of the City and East London Family Health Services Authority (FHSA) which covered three London Boroughs (Hackney, Newham and Tower Hamlets) and the City of London. I had accepted this job at the request of Tim Chessels, Chairman of North East Thames Regional Health Authority but on the basis of taking on a wider role in East London later. London's NHS was unstable financially and organisationally following Ken Clarke's 1990 reorganisation, with its purchaser/provider split and fundholding GPs. Three things were clear: the dominating teaching hospitals were not going to cede power or money without a fight; there were no strong commissioning bodies; and primary care and community services were weak and underfunded.

Sir Bernard Tomlinson had been appointed to review London's health services in the light of the Clarke reforms. His review was yet another attempt to sort out the perceived 'London problem' – too many individual specialist hospitals in the centre and too few people living there. Mergers of hospitals and other bodies were on the agenda, as was the idea of using commissioning bodies to rebalance services between hospitals and community services. Well before Tomlinson reported speculation was rife about re-organisations.

The FHSA I was to chair was a mess with little control over its finances and a well-meaning Chief Executive struggling to cope. The GPs of East London were a decidedly mixed bunch ranging from the innovative, high quality Bow group practice to single-handed alcoholics or incompetents whose patients queued along the Mile End Road in the rain waiting for their lock-up surgery to open. By the time I left in 1994 six of them were bad enough to be referred to the GMC – there could have been more. Fundholding might be Government policy, but it had little appeal to most East London GPs. After two years effort we had managed to persuade two practices to become fundholders. Shortly afterwards I went to a meeting of NHS Chairmen with the Minister, the late Brian Mawhinney. We went round the room telling him of progress on fundholding and I reported we had made a 100% increase, from one to two. I discovered that Mawhinney had little sense of humour. After lengthy negotiation 40 practices in Newham said they would form a multi-fund, but this collapsed when the GPs had to make firm financial commitments.

My first job was to find a Finance Director. After struggling to find applicants we appointed the least bad of two poor candidates. He produced a set of qualified accounts which were made less bad by the efforts of me and the Chief Executive; but he had to be replaced 18 months later after another set of qualified accounts. The place staggered from crisis to crisis. I came in one day to find a Nigerian GP asking for our help with the 300 African immigrants at his small surgery demanding to register with him because he was African. We sent staff to help him disperse the crowd. Apart from the Chief Executive there was little capability for meeting regional demands for strategic thinking. I ended up writing papers on integrating primary and community care services in an East London Care Development Agency.

By the end of 1992 Tomlinson had reported and the agenda changed. He identified that London's hospitals had a massive revenue overspend or funding shortfall, depending on your viewpoint. He wanted mergers of health authorities and hospitals and more investment in primary care and community services. In East London there was to be a single health authority supposedly combining hospitals and community services in the three boroughs and the City. Tim Chessels asked me to chair the combined authority providing Ministers approved and he involved me in choosing a Chief Executive. I was told by Tim's successor, Sir William Staveley, that he had put forward a number of candidates including me and that I had not been chosen by Ministers. I told Staveley what I thought of this duplicitous behaviour but wasn't sure if he or the humourless Mawhinney was the villain. I continued working on a primary and community care agency for East London; appointed a new Chief Executive for the FHSA; and resigned near the end of my term office in 1994.

Before leaving East London, I was asked in January 1994 to chair a short independent inquiry into complaints made about staff in South Ockendon Hospital and the community services to which patients with learning disabilities were being transferred before the hospital's closure in March 1994. The request came from the RHA and the Chairmen of South Essex Health Authority (responsible for the hospital to be closed) and of the Thameside Community Healthcare Trust (responsible for patients and staff transferred to the community).

There was great public concern about inadequate investigations of patient mistreatment in the hospital and about the transfer to community services of hospital staff thought to have mistreated patients. Families of patients, the two local MPs and the Community Health Council (CHC) were highly critical of the failure to act on available evidence. I knew this hospital's chequered history from my time working for Barbara Castle who had published in 1974 the report of a judicial inquiry into the hospital with a personal foreword. I agreed to investigate provided it was done quickly and I could question anyone, including doctors.

Three of us did the inquiry. There was not time to review the many investigations undertaken since 1974. So, I chose to take evidence on the six patients of most concern to the CHC and relatives. Five patients concerned the hospital and one community services. I was confident that this six would enable us to expose wider concerns. I persuaded relatives to let us tape interviews which would not go to the health authority or staff. When a senior consultant refused to give evidence, I told him I would make this public and report him to the GMC. He agreed to provide written evidence which damned him more than any oral evidence, so I printed extracts in our report. We took oral evidence from 22 people, all of whom remained anonymous in our report which we completed in four months.

For four patients we recommended no further investigation but that the authorities reviewed the files and made suitable apologies to the families. For one patient who had died in hospital in May 1993, a man aged 64, we were very concerned about the unexplained deterioration in his health before death and the allegation of sexual assault. We wanted this case re-opened for independent investigation with a view to disciplinary action. Another patient had been returned to the community in 1988 but in December 1992 he was re-admitted to hospital with bruising to his face, body and legs. I discovered appalling photos of his injuries in a hospital safe after an anonymous tip-off. He returned to the community but was re-admitted to hospital on 1 March 1993 under the Mental Health Act after highly disturbed behaviour. Later in March he told hospital staff that a member of staff at the community placement had been raping him. We recommended an urgent independent investigation of the allegations, with the patient having his own advocate to help him present information to the investigation. All these recommendations were accepted and acted upon.

There were a range of other concerns about which we made recommendations, especially about staff selection, skills and training. Many of these mirrored the concerns of my report on children's homes. The unsatisfactory values and lack of skills of many staff made them unsuitable for looking after people with learning disabilities. Neither we nor the families were convinced that vetting staff for criminal records was done properly. Many complaints by relatives were treated as staff disciplinary cases where a higher standard of proof was required than for complaints, thereby leading to dismissal of complaints. Evidence was often not preserved; and procedures were unclear. Too often patients did not have advocates to help them with complaints or the advocates were ignored. Investigators were often untrained. We said the Trust needed to be helped to produce a 3-year development plan; and to work out how to provide a more open climate for the management of learning disabilities.

We were particularly concerned about medical disregard of patients' physical health and the arrogance of a senior consultant who did not regard any senior managers as having the authority to question his judgements when complaints were made. This issue had been raised in the 1974 Report which stated: "No one person should be given or treated as having such power over the lives of the patients and be so free of any effective control." We made it clear that a complete overhaul was required of the role of doctors in multi-disciplinary working with people with learning disabilities, particularly the conduct of this senior consultant.

We made 18 recommendations. I insisted that the report's findings were made public at a press conference on 24 May 1994. Its findings were covered in the local media and the professional journals. The CHC and families felt vindicated. I was not asked to have any continuing involvement with South Essex learning disability services. Our report was called "Learning from the Past." I had little confidence the NHS would. The findings were similar to those of many future inquiries into the abuse of people with learning disability and autism in the care of the NHS.

Portfolio Man: Social Care, Charities and Social Research

I built a portfolio of activities mainly concerned with social care. I spoke at and chaired numerous conferences on community care and children's homes. I expressed a degree of scepticism about some of the hysterical claims of widespread satanic abuse and paedophilia. More prosaically I assisted Price Waterhouse with a 1992 review of Westminster City Council's social services department. Conservative councillors disagreed with their Director about subjecting inhouse adult services to market testing. Given this was Government policy and we could show how it could be done, the Director was bound to lose the argument. The project ended with a feisty public meeting and the departure of the Director. I was also asked to review the budget of

140

Havering's social services department where I persuaded the Director to accept some efficiency improvements if he wished to survive, which he did.

In 1991 the owner of Westminster Health Care asked me to become an adviser to his nursing home business. This was a rapidly growing company with an interesting management approach: its headquarters was kept slim and made to focus on supporting the matrons of homes. Regulation of care homes was still in its infancy but was bound to increase. Most homes had a mixture of residents: some paid for their own care while others received public funding. It was already clear that residents were becoming frailer and increasingly dependent. My job was to advise on what would happen to regulation and funding in this immature market as the company moved towards flotation as a public company. The big question was would public funding keep pace with the increasing dependency of residents. To date the answer has been a resounding 'no.'

By the mid-1990s there were about half a million places in registered residential care and nursing homes. Most of these homes were in the independent sector as local authorities and the NHS abandoned long-term care. This independent sector had an annual turnover then of about £8 billion but growth was slowing, as more people were supported to stay in their own homes. Although there were a few big providers of care homes, the sector was very fragmented with many small homes. There were increasing concerns about standards in homes and the training and qualifications of the care sector's workforce. In the summer of 1994, I became Chairman of a new body, the Residential Forum, which aimed to influence the growing debate about standards in care homes and how they should be regulated. To avoid any conflict of interest I stopped advising Westminster Health Care.

Over the next two years we published an authoritative guide to standards in homes called 'Creating a Home from Home.' This involved consulting over 100 organisations and dozens of individuals and experts. Alongside this guide we produced a document on 'Reforming the Regulatory Framework for Care Homes' in response to a Government consultation. Shortly after launching these two publications, I resigned to help the Labour Party (see below). The Forum continued to influence government and the content of the Care

Standards Act in 2000. It still exists as a website and in 2019 I hosted a House of Lords reception for it.

1994 saw growing activity on the registration of social workers and social care staff. Some regarded this as a means of protecting the public, while for others this was about social workers having their own regulatory body, like other professions. The difficult problem was which occupational groups working with children and adults to include in a regulatory system. A very inclusive approach to what was being called a General Social Services Council would involve registering nearly 250,000 people; while restricting it to those whose competence and conduct posed the greatest public risk, involved about 50,000 people. The Government hired Price Waterhouse to advise them on this problem and I joined their team.

In March 1995 we produced a report that proposed establishing a regulatory system in a phased way. The Conservatives were not really interested in this issue. It was a Labour Government that eventually established a General Social Services Council in 2001, following the Care Standards Act 2000. The Coalition Government unwisely scrapped the Council in 2012, in a bonfire of quangos; and transferred social work regulation to the Health Professions Council but excluded other social care staff. The 2015 Cameron Government returned to the issue by trying to regulate social work within the Department for Education. I led opposition to this when the Children and Social Work Bill was in the House of Lords; and a few of us persuaded Ministers to establish an independent body for social workers. Using regulations made under the Children and Social Work Act 2017, Social Work England was eventually established in December 2019 as the independent regulator for England's 100,000 social workers. It had taken 25 years to successfully complete this project.

I included in my portfolio a good deal of work with charities. I joined the Board of my local Leonard Cheshire Home and became Chairman of the Royal Philanthropic Society (RPS), set up in 1788 to take homeless boys off the streets of London. RPS sold a site to create a capital fund and we used the income to help care leavers and youngsters on the cusp of offending. They needed to expand their services and change their charitable purposes which were governed by an C18th royal charter. It took two year's negotiation with the Home Office and Charity Commission to achieve new charitable purposes and to expand services. Turnover was still too small. Despite nervous trustees, I pursued a merger with a larger organisation – Crime Concern. In 1996 the merged bodies became the Rainer Foundation and a decade later morphed into Catch 22. This was primarily an educational social business with an annual income of about £13 million and me as an honorary Vice President. This experience and another with a bankrupt educational charity, revealed what hard work it was keeping charities viable, especially when trustees and staff were incapable of facing financial realities.

My involvement with the Carers National Association was more rewarding when I helped them assess if the 1993 community care reforms had improved support for carers. Drawing on survey material from over 400 carers the result was disappointing given that local authorities had had over 3 years to prepare for the community care changes and had plenty of new money and guidance. The majority of carers had not noticed much change, and some said support had become worse and more expensive. Over half the carers who had experienced a community care assessment of their needs were dissatisfied with the outcome. I called my report 'Just a Fairy Tale' which was how one carer described the community care experience of her mentally ill husband. Roy Griffiths, who had championed the cause of carers, provided me with a foreword; but, sadly, died just before publication in March 1994.

I agreed we should undertake a larger national study and we persuaded Boots to fund it. I settled on four topics for the study First how much did carers know about the community care changes and what were their sources of information. Second to what extent had community care assessments met their own needs or those of the cared for person. Third what services were carers receiving, were they new services and what unmet needs remained. Last, what was the extent of charging for services and what were carers attitudes to paying for services. I organised four surveys: a telephone survey of those in our first survey; a postal survey of 1650 carers across UK, plus three small focus groups; a postal survey of the social services departments in England and Wales, with an 80% response rate; and a MORI survey of public attitudes to carers and funding their support.

In June 1995 I published my report entitled 'Better Tomorrows.' It received good coverage in the regional media and trade press, plus the

Guardian and Telegraph nationally. The title was more optimistic than the findings. The great majority of carers – over 60% - did not know they could receive an assessment of their needs; and most didn't know what services were available or that they could complain. Only about a quarter of carers had their needs assessed; only half of these assessments met their needs; and only a third had the assessment confirmed in writing. Only 10% of social services departments were providing carers with a weekly break; and only 20% of carers had a week's holiday each year.

Respite care was the overwhelming unmet need of carers. As a society we were then – and now – failing to provide basic support to most of the millions of primary carers: a regular weekly break, an annual holiday, access to a support group and a crisis helpline. There were huge variations in whether carers were charged for services and how much, with many of the charges probably illegal. The good news was that the public supported doing more for carers, with 90% wanting carers to have a minimum package of breaks free of charge and two-thirds rating them as more deserving of public support than any other group, including pensioners.

This carers report revealed the massive gap between the political rhetoric of supporting carers and the day-to-day reality of the help they actually received. Although legislation was passed soon after this report requiring assessment of carers' support needs, carers had to wait until the 2014 Care Act for coherent legislation on assessing their needs and meeting them. Even then it was left to individual local authorities to decide whether to make charges for support. However, this legislation did introduce direct payments to carers so that they could decide what support to purchase for themselves. I was a member of the Parliamentary Joint Select Committee that considered the draft 2014 Act and secured some improvements.

I had other research experience after becoming a Senior Research Fellow at the University of Kent where I helped them set up a European Institute of Social Services (EISS) and became Chairman of its management board. After the collapse of the USSR, the EU developed programmes to help newly independent Eastern European countries. In 1992 I was funded to advise the Hungarian Government on services for the elderly and mentally ill. It was depressing to see psychiatric hospitals where political prisoners had been detained. There was little interest in services for those released and little capability to deliver them. When I visited an old people's home the residents all stood to attention by their beds, reluctant to talk to me. There were no individual rooms and few day activities. I tried to interest people in day centres and transport to take elderly people to them, without much success. I discovered that the new Hungary had largely written off the older generation that had suffered under Communism and were concentrating on younger people and new technology. I wrote a report with projects the Government could consider but with little expectation they would.

An EU conference in London on commissioning services for the elderly was more successful. In 1994 I gave a paper on market-oriented public services in Copenhagen which enabled me to see some of the impressive Danish community services for people with disabilities. A 1995 seminar on social security that I conducted for some Albanian civil servants ended up with us stopping them coming to blows over welfare benefits entitlements. In 1996 I chaired an interesting conference on changing approaches to mental health in Barcelona which produced much common ground on treating mental illness in the community, although a few psychiatrists still wanted a lot of compulsory detention.

I used my academic status to secure funding for a study of US mentoring schemes aimed at keeping young people out of trouble. In the 1980s the US had turned away from public sector responses to social problems. The Kennedy/Johnson Great Society programmes were seen by the political right as failures because of the increase in school dropouts, teenage pregnancies, youth unemployment, juvenile crime and substance abuse. President George H Bush in 1989 was seeking "a thousand points of light" with schools, churches, business and civic society working to tackle social problems. I was unconvinced by his moral crusade but thought there was merit in the idea of older role models helping young offenders, drug users and truants.

My view was supported by the 8 projects I visited in New York, Washington DC, Philadelphia and Virginia. The Big Brothers/Big Sisters of America programme had started 80 years ago and by the 1990s was in 40 locations helping 40,000 children with adult mentors mainly through schools. This had inspired the I Have a Dream (IHAD) Foundation started in Harlem in 1981 by Eugene Lang. He promised to pay the college fees of a class of high schoolers in his old school,

75% of whom were likely to be dropouts. Using a lot of mentoring support, it was a great success; and within a decade over 100 millionaires in 40 cities across America had followed Lang's example. The IHAD Foundation helped these programmes to establish themselves and work with schools and education authorities. There are still many IHAD projects across the US today and even one in New Zealand.

At the other end of the spectrum were church mentoring schemes like the one I visited in Virginia where the black congregation provided the mentors. In New York, the YMCA was running a mentoring scheme for disabled women and girls; and the City University was mentoring high school students: both these projects relied on state funding. The same was true of Mentors Inc in Washington DC which was similar to the New York scheme. The most interesting project was the 'Linking Lifetimes' project run by the Centre for Intergenerational Learning in Philadelphia. This used mentors over 55 in its 11 youth at risk and young offender projects: the oldest mentor had just died aged 92 and several were in their 80s. Evaluation showed both mentors and mentees were lonely and formed relationships that benefited each other. The growing body of evaluation of US mentoring projects were positive about the benefits for mentors and mentees but made it clear that mentoring was not a panacea for a range of social ills, however much Republican politicians might wish it was.

In July 1993 I presented my US study at a London conference organised by New York's Commonwealth Fund. This was aimed at developing a UK mentoring network. It proved an influential event and helped create a steady growth in UK interest in mentoring during the 1990s, especially in business. Organisations like the Prince's Trust, Community Service Volunteers and NCVO have championed mentoring in social areas and set quality standards. Gradually, mentoring to help social inclusion among disenchanted young people has become more common in the UK, but not on the scale and with the flair as in the USA. I strongly encouraged the use of mentoring in the youth justice reforms described in Chapter 8).

Local Government Commission and Tackling Sleaze

In 1995 I decided to change direction. John Major's government had run out of steam. Neil Kinnock and John Smith had partially rebuilt

Labour's credibility. Smith's sudden death from a heart attack in May 1994 dramatically changed British politics. New Labour was born and was creating a political buzz under the leadership of Tony Blair and Gordon Brown. Blair's successor as Shadow Home Secretary was Jack Straw who I had known since my time with Barbara Castle. I talked to Jack about helping the Labour Party.

In June 1995 there were major changes in the Local Government Commission which since 1992 had been reviewing the case for splitting up counties, particularly in urban areas, into new unitary local authorities. Decisions had often been contentious with counties challenging decisions in the courts. Progress was slower than the new Secretary of State, John Gummer, wanted; and he revised the guidance in 1994 to make it clear that unitary authorities were the preferred solution. However, the Commission's chairman, John Banham, a committed Cornishman, kept serving up proposals that retained whole counties and made several public utterances that displeased Gummer further. In March 1995 Gummer referred cases back to the Commission and Banham resigned. Gummer then reconstituted the Commission in June under a new Chairman, Sir David Cooksey, to deal with about 20 contentious outstanding cases by the end of 1995. He consulted Labour about new members, and I was nominated.

The Cooksey Commission had about six months to complete its assessments and report back to Gummer. We had to rely on MORI polling for peoples' sense of identity with particular places. A judgement had to be made about the viability of new unitary councils and the impact on counties of separating larger towns. There was not time to collect new evidence, but we could test what had been collected by face-to-face meetings with key protagonists. We realised that in many areas longstanding grievances were being played out. Also that some questionable decisions had been made on the viability of new unitary authorities: Berkshire was the prime example where a high performing county had been turned into six small unitary authorities less capable of running equivalent quality education and social services. But the political direction had been set. Ministers wanted more unitary authorities and Labour didn't object – not least because they were rarely in power in the counties.

We divided the cases. I knew most about the Kent cases – the three Medway towns and Dartford and Gravesham – but was suspect because I had worked for the County Council. I still managed to get the least bad outcome, which was one new unitary, the three Medway towns. Two of us were despatched to assess the cases for Blackburn and Blackpool, both supported by local MPs. I thought the cases were not strong, but the lacklustre performance of Lancashire County Council got them over the line. I was asked to talk to Ken Clarke about his support for his constituency, Rushcliffe. This was one of three Nottingham suburbs – the others were Gedling and Broxtowe – that considered they should be unitary authorities. After his perfunctory outlining of Rushcliffe's case, I assured him that they didn't have a prayer and neither did the other two. His grin suggested he knew he'd been rumbled.

We were working two days a week reading an enormous amount of material and meeting twice a month. By the end of 1995 we had decided in favour of 8 new unitary authorities: Blackpool. Blackburn, Halton, Peterborough, Thurrock Warrington, The Wrekin and Medway (Rochester, Chatham and Gillingham combined). We turned down 12 others (including Norwich, Exeter and Gloucester) for a variety of reasons. This didn't please Ministers but the skills of David Cooksey enabled us to clear those hurdles. We handed in our report in January 1996. I resigned from the Commission shortly after when I assumed the role of policy adviser to Jack Straw.

The gloss of the 1992 Election victory soon wore off for John Major with the September eviction of sterling from the European Exchange Rate Mechanism on 'Black Wednesday.' His government became mired in sleaze with the cash for questions scandal in 1994. Major tried to head this off with the appointment of the Nolan Committee into Standards in Public Life which reported in 1995. Nolan couldn't say if standards in public life had deteriorated but thought most of those in public life adhered to high standards. He was struck by the variations in practice; and wanted all public bodies to have a code of conduct and a consistent legal framework. Nolan set out seven principles for public life: selflessness, integrity, objectivity, accountability, openness, honesty and leadership: these still operate today. He thought that public mistrust of politicians had not been helped by 30% of MPs having paid consultancies. The Commission recommended a raft of detailed changes for MPs, Ministers, civil servants and quangos which the Government broadly accepted.

Despite the Nolan Report, the cash for questions issue wouldn't go away. (A few MPs – all Conservatives – were still under investigation at the time of the 1997 Election.) Public distrust of politicians and the way public bodies were both appointed and run had become a pre-election issue. I thought the issue still needed more attention and worked with a new think tank DEMOS. I produced a pamphlet on 'Restoring Public Trust: A Governance Act for Public Bodies' published in December 1995. It proposed a legal framework for Nolan's recommendations (except those relating to MPs which were for Parliament). I wanted to establish an independent Commission of Public Governance with three main functions: oversight of public appointments through a Public Appointments Commissioner; ensuring compliance of public bodies with governance requirements; and adjudicating on allegations of serious governance breaches by a body or individual officeholders. The Commission should have sanctions, including re-constitution of public bodies and penalties for individuals, up to disqualification from public office for life.

My proposals were too strong meat for the Conservatives but had more resonance with Labour who committed in their 1997 Manifesto to making quangos "properly accountable to the people." They wanted to place the Nolan agenda in a wider governance of Britain context. This would involve funding of political parties, a new Code of Conduct for Ministers and civil servants, a more independent Government Statistical Service and better accountability of quangos. By the end of 1995 it was clear that the Labour agenda on constitutional reform was continuing to increase. I worked with the Association of District Councils (ADC) on whether local government should play a bigger role in the NHS by commissioning community health services alongside social care.; and a big article on this on this for the Guardian. I began to be drawn into Labour's growing interest in Regional Government; and was persuaded to speak at a conference on whether regional chambers could become NHS strategic planning bodies.

This re-awakening interest in the NHS had been stirred by a request in to go to Buenos Aires to give a lecture on the NHS to South

America's Health Ministers at their annual jamboree. This was noteworthy less for the health sessions but for the Tango evening in an alternative part of Buenos Aires; and a breakfast meeting the following day with Fernando Cardoso who later became President of Brazil and was interested in the NHS.

By early 1996 I realised that I would have to choose between being a jobbing consultant or devoting more time to helping Labour win an election whenever John Major called one – May 1997 at the latest. Although I continued with some consultancy projects, in February 1996 I agreed with Jack Straw that I would devote two days a week to acting as his senior policy adviser. I was accepting that I would probably move into the Home Office if Labour won the Election. But I made it clear that, whatever happened, I would be in Atlanta for the 1996 Olympic Games with my two sons.

Preparing for Government

I knew Jack had fallen out with John Smith in 1993 by publishing a pamphlet calling for modernisation of Clause IV of Labour's constitution which pledged "common ownership of the means of production, distribution and exchange." What had displeased Smith had the opposite effect on Tony Blair who was determined to modernise the Labour Party to make it electable. Blair had appointed Jack as his successor as Shadow Home Secretary, with the requirement to make law and order a Labour issue and not be outflanked on toughness by Michael Howard, the then Home Secretary. Hence the strapline, "Tough on crime, tough on the causes of crime." The second part of the mantra was more to my taste.

After such a long time out of government, Labour had few people with Ministerial experience: two to be precise, Jack Cunningham and Margaret Becket. In January 1995 I had raised the issue of preparing Labour for government in a letter I still have which included the following paragraph. "On day one, many new Labour Ministers will find a wave of paper, people and issues coming at them. They will not be used to the volume. Organising themselves to cope will not be easy unless they have thought about this beforehand. Setting up machinery that they have confidence in for Parliamentary, Departmental, Cabinet,

150

Media, Party and Constituency business will be difficult.........
Selecting the wrong people for particular jobs can cause medium-term
problems and even disaster."

This issue had clearly registered with Jonathan Powell, Tony
Blair's Chief of Staff. He organised two weekends at Templeton
College Oxford for groups of Shadow Ministerial teams to prepare for
government. These took place in April and May. I spoke at both and
participated in the May event as part of the Home Office team.
Anderson Consulting and former Ministers, senior civil servants and
quangocrats spoke at these events. There was also group work on
relevant projects. These events produced a degree of team bonding that
carried over into government. Blair's initial Ministerial appointments
changed few of the personnel from the Templeton participants.

My first task was to produce some order into the disparate range of
topics that had been accumulated by the Shadow Home Office (HO)
team. The topics went much wider than the traditional HO brief. Urgent
attention was required because on 22 January Tony Blair had asked all
Shadow Cabinet Ministers about proposed legislation, low cost/no cost
initiatives, changes in machinery of government and Europe. This
followed Blair agreeing with John Major that contact could begin
shortly between the Shadow Cabinet and senior civil servants. I collated
and edited a mass of policy and speech material and produced a reply to
Blair with two main enclosures.

One enclosure was a law-and-order programme for the first term in
government, drawing on commitments already made. There were two
big ticket items: a Crime and Disorder Reduction Bill focussed on
crime prevention and tackling neighbourhood anti-social behaviour,
together with reform of the youth justice system, especially tackling
persistent young offenders. The other main items were a review of the
failing Crown Prosecution Service (CPS); an overhaul of sentencing
for serious offences after a public consultation; a review of police
accountability and creation of a police authority for London instead of
the Home Secretary being responsible for the Metropolitan Police; a
review of the Prison Service, then being run as an Executive Agency
and with a population out of control; and several other items like
probation training and parenting issues. Tony Blair was comfortable
with this programme and it became the basis of HO legislation and
work in government.

The second paper outlined Labour's burgeoning constitutional agenda. Much of this agenda was also being worked on by the Constitution Unit at University College London. Legislation would be needed on Scottish and Welsh Assemblies; incorporation into British law of the European Convention on Human Rights (ECHR); Regional Chambers/Assemblies for England; Freedom of Information; and reform of the House of Lords. There were other possible issues such as electoral reform and referenda, together with a new assembly for Northern Ireland if there was a peace agreement. Only one of these – ECHR incorporation – was clearly for the Home Secretary but others could be handed to Jack on a personal basis. Constitutional legislation on the scale envisaged would have to be spread over several Parliamentary sessions. Blair needed to consider his priorities and who would handle them.

We also flagged up HO changes needed. These included transferring the Met to a new police authority; reviewing management of the Prison Service; strengthening medium-term planning and direction of programmes; and a new Electoral/ Constitution Unit. None of us realised the problems with the existing HO machinery. These only became apparent after my meeting with Richard Wilson, the HO Permanent Secretary on 23 May. In 1995 there had been a critical report on the HO's senior management. Richard sent us the report which included the statement that "the Department is seen as inward looking, resistant to new ideas, too negative in orientation, slow to deliver, remote from its services and insufficiently driven by outcomes or needs of client groups." The HO Management Board wasn't much good either.

Following the Wilson meeting I began working on a policy programme management system for managing change in the HO and integrating the criminal justice system. I knew how easy it was for governments to be blown off course by events or concentrating on eye-catching announcements instead of delivering commitments. I thought competent management of demonstrable improvements would produce political dividends. I wanted a system for managing the five key stages for policy success: policy review and development; public consultation on proposed changes; operational development of final policy; legislative preparation and passage; and operational implementation. The operational work would be where the HO would be weakest.

I designed a system for monthly monitoring of progress on key initiatives. I knew the difficult bit would be ensuring the Ministerial team paid attention to the monitoring and held civil service feet to the fire. That turned out to be the case.

The most important preparatory work was the legislative programme for the first Parliamentary session. The biggest Bill would be the Crime and Disorder Reduction Bill with several major strands. There was reform of the youth justice system with a new national board and multi-agency local youth offending teams; new duties on local government for community safety plans and crime prevention; testing and treatment orders to combat drug-related crime; various new orders including anti-social behaviour orders and parenting orders; action to ban handguns and possible action on stalking and constraining paedophiles. This would be a major Bill and more detailed work would be needed pre-election.

I prepared Labour's policy on youth justice reforms using a critical report, 'Misspent Youth,' by the Audit Commission. I set out our thinking on these reforms at a Ditchley Park weekend conference in December 1996. This was well received and alerted professionals to Labour's intentions. At this time there was much public concern about the lack of effective action to deal with persistent young offenders. Early in 1997 Labour decided to have a card with five pledges delivered to each household. At short notice, David Miliband asked for a pledge on tackling crime. Without fully realising what this involved, we suggested halving the time from arrest to sentence for persistent young offenders. (see Chapter 8.)

The other major piece of legislation was a Bill to incorporate into UK law the European Convention on Human Rights (ECHR). The ECHR had been largely drafted by British lawyers in 1945 but bizarrely had never been incorporated into UK law. If an issue involving the Convention was raised in UK courts, this could mean cases ended up in the Strasbourg Court for resolution. Only incorporation in UK law would give UK courts discretion – a 'margin of appreciation'- to take account of particular national circumstances in making their decisions. This situation had led to the Strasbourg Court taking decisions that were contentious in the UK. During 1996 I spent a lot of time in technical discussions with constitutional experts about how to legislate for incorporation.

153

MPs did not want ECHR incorporation to override Parliamentary sovereignty and allow courts to rule that an Act of Parliament contravened the ECHR. Although this excited politicians, from the citizens' point of view there was some merit in permitting this. Some constitutional experts took this view. In the end Parliamentary sovereignty triumphed. Jack Straw and Paul Boateng published a document which I helped draft in December 1996 with the politically appealing title of 'Bringing Rights Back Home.' This would require courts to construe all legislation consistently with the ECHR; require future derogations from the ECHR to be expressly authorised; and apply the ECHR to public bodies. A Human Rights Commission or Commissioner was proposed.

Other preparatory work was undertaken. I costed Labour's HO commitments and suggested ways of funding them. I prepared a work programme for the first Parliamentary session; and wrote a paper on integrating criminal justice budgets. One of the system's problems was the poor performance of the CPS in securing convictions. CPS morale was low and there was much internal dissatisfaction with its senior management. Staff representatives helped us produce an analysis of the problems, including the inability of CPS solicitors to prosecute cases in court. We included in the Manifesto a commitment to increase CPS effectiveness much to the annoyance of the Director of Public Prosecutions (DPP).

Police performance was also an area of concern. I could see no effective system for measuring operational performance. This was flagged up for early attention, as was the system for selecting Chief Constables. Labour was committed to removing the Metropolitan Police from direct HO management and creating a police authority instead – as happened elsewhere. The most controversial police issue was the mishandling of the murder inquiry into the death in 1993 of Stephen Lawrence, a young black student. The CPS had abandoned the charges against five white suspects on the grounds of insufficient evidence. There was a whiff of police corruption and racism around the police investigation.; but the Met Commissioner had assured the local MP the investigation was thorough. A private prosecution failed in 1996 with the acquittal of the five accused. This meant that under the double jeopardy rule then in force, once acquitted the accused could not be retried.

Stephen's mother met Jack in early February 1997 to press for an independent inquiry, but she couldn't be given any commitment because as Home Secretary he would be the Commissioner's boss and would have to make his own inquiries first. The game changer was the inquest into Stephen's death at which the five suspects refused to give evidence on the grounds that this might incriminate them. The jury returned a verdict of unlawful killing, the result of an unprovoked racist attack. The Daily Mail published front page pictures of the five suspects under the banner headline "Murderers," and challenged them to sue the paper.

The biggest problem a new Home Secretary would face was the Prison Service. Prisons had a near capacity population of 60,000 prisoners. The numbers were still rising and creating a serious overcrowding problem. The management of prisons had been passed, controversially, by Ken Clarke, to an Executive Agency under the leadership of a businessman, Derek Lewis. He had been sacked by Michael Howard after a prison escape and was thought to have been wrongfully dismissed. The situation was a muddle with a review being conducted that would not be available before the Election. I decided to do my own analysis and set out the key elements of a prisons' strategy for Labour in office.

Each month the Prison Service had a net intake of 500 a month and this would continue throughout 1997, taking the population over the capacity limit of 60,000. No new capacity was planned, and the revenue budget for the next two years was insufficient to fund new capacity. There was a growing revenue burden from PFI prisons and no obvious sources of savings or new money. Overcrowding was now inevitable, with all the dangers of serious disturbances. The warnings of prison governors should be taken seriously. Michael Howard, with his slogan of 'prison works,' and his prisons Minister, Ann Widdecombe, were leaving behind a mess. If prisons spiralled out of control, their successors would be blamed, not them.

I considered Labour should act quickly on taking up office. I wanted to publish the Lewis review and an audit of the HO's finances to show the mess inherited. This would pave the way to say that under the circumstances and to avoid damaging other vital services like police and fire, the new government was forced by their irresponsible

155

predecessors to take the exceptional step of establishing a ceiling on the prison population. This ceiling would be set at 60,000 and would last for at least two years while a full-scale review produced a longer-term solution. I then wanted the prison and probation service to identify for early release up to 5,000 prisoners with good disciplinary records and who presented little risk to the public. They would complete their sentences under strict community supervision. At the same time, urgent steps should be taken to reduce the number of prisoners on remand, especially 15 and 16-year-olds in adult prisons. I considered this politically feasible for a new government.

This firefighting needed to be accompanied by a more strategic overhaul of prison policy. The Conservatives were rushing through Parliament the Crime (Sentencing) Act which toughened up sentences and would increase the prison population: it received Royal Assent on 21 March. I wanted to halt commencement and ask the Court of Appeal to produce draft sentencing guidelines for securing more consistency and have a public consultation on these new guidelines. There should be an independent financial review of the prison estate (including PFI prisons) to produce a more cost-effective estate for up to 60,000 people.

I also proposed reviewing the merits of breaking up the monolithic Prison Service into separate functional units: high security, community prisons, women and young offender prisons but with common support services. Until this work was done, I suggested retaining the Executive Agency but with the Home Secretary answering to Parliamentary on prisons policy. I realised that I wouldn't know until we were in the HO whether Jack and Tony would be bold enough to follow this advice. I had my doubts but thought it worth setting out a plan.

At the end of January 1997, I met Richard Wilson in a Whitehall wine bar to discuss Labour's agenda for his Department using published documents. By then it was clear that the Election was Labour's to lose. We agreed to meet again when the Election was called. By March most of the preparatory work that could be done had been done. It would be for Tony to settle Jack's Ministerial team and approve his special advisers. 1st April saw a wonderful spoof scoop in the Independent claiming that the Powell brothers had persuaded Tony Blair to make Mrs Thatcher the UK Ambassador to the US. The news went round the world and wound up the Labour left before people realised the date of publication.

On 8 April John Major finally called an Election and the Shadow HO team left their Parliamentary offices to campaign. I decided to work from home and minimise my visits to the frenzied atmosphere of Labour Party HQ where most of the occupants were half my age.

6. Consigliere (Part 1): A Home Office Diary – 1997

The Election Campaign – April

Michael Howard tried to settle a few things with Jack Straw just before dissolution, including the prison ship the Tories had bought for £4 million and sailed across the Atlantic for another £1million. There was a planning dispute about its berthing in Dorset and Howard needed Jack's agreement to its use which was given reluctantly, and probably unwisely. The prison population had passed 60,000. Without the ship it would be police cells next at £120,000 a year per prisoner. I had warned Jack that prisons could be his BSE if he didn't move swiftly to implement my strategy: agreeing the ship made that more difficult. I told him he needed a better Prisons Minister than the person he was proposing.

On 15 April I had another meeting with Richard Wilson and then a further one at the HO on 23 April with a few senior staff. Although cordial, I sensed they would try to slow things down on prisons to avoid upsetting the Prison Service. They were looking forward to a change of Ministers, unsurprisingly. I handed over our briefing papers including the details of our Crime and Disorder Bill and notes on the other first session Bills so they could organise the Queen's Speech. I gave Richard our paper on HO organisational changes we wanted and one on CPS reform which I said was not just for the Attorney General because it was part of criminal justice reform, a Home Secretary responsibility. I agreed to meet his senior staff on 28 April but said I would not discuss prisons policy.

On 24 April I was at the funeral of my wife's mother of whom I was very fond. It was the day that Tony Blair decided he wanted a law and order initiative and press conference the next day. Somehow, we repackaged our stuff on youth justice reform, tackling disorder and community safety into a pamphlet called 'Time to Act.' When Tony launched this on 25 April Jack persuaded him to promise that all this would be in the first Queen's Speech, with Gordon Brown sitting beside him unable to challenge costs. This enhanced my Svengali reputation in the HO.

I spent the morning of 28 April in the HO meeting with all the Grades 2 and 3, chaired by Richard Wilson. This was to give them some 'feel' for what life would be like with Labour Ministers and Jack's wish to have a dialectic with them. Some seemed institutionalised and wary, but they gradually warmed up a bit. Richard told me the meeting had gone well and they saw me as someone who could help them. I remained sceptical. The trick was not to be taken over by the senior civil service and never tell them everything. They usually want to diffuse accountability and leave themselves bolt-holes.

Later I briefed Jack on the HO encounters and gave him an aide-memoire for his meeting with Tony when he was offered the Home Secretary job: keep gambling, get the voluntary sector, do ECHR in the first session and keep options open on House of Lords reform. I gave him a list of ten priorities for the first term and a distribution of Ministerial duties that was more coherent than Richard Wilson's, emphasising a preference for five junior Ministers because of workload. We agreed to meet in the HO on 2 May.

I had spent much of the Election campaign disentangling myself from my consultancy work and feeling sad about my mother-in-law's death. John Major seemed confident but rather detached from his Party. The Tory's 'New Labour, New Danger' campaign flopped. Their pension plans blew up in their face. Health and education played well for Labour, as did law and order on the local doorsteps. Euro divisions and sleaze continued to dog the Conservative campaign, with a journalist, Martin Bell, in his trademark white suit, contesting the Tatton seat held by Neil Hamilton, the MP at the centre of the cash for questions scandal. (I was consulted about a candidate to oppose Hamilton but had no credible suggestions.)

After a nervous start Blair campaigned well and harmoniously with Gordon. In the last week Tony looked tired but confident; and he was speaking increasingly without notes and with conviction. Major looked beaten but determined to stay on the pitch until the final whistle. The polls were steady at 47/48% for Labour; 31-33% for the Conservatives and 15% plus for the LibDems. No-one in the Shadow Cabinet believed them. I was confident of a 50-60 seat Labour overall majority, double Jack's forecast. The pollsters were twitching in case they had got it wrong. On the weekend before polling day Edwina Currie forecast a Labour landslide, blaming it all on John Major.

I had a domestic polling day, voting late and opting out of New Labour's youthful party at the Festival Hall. I'm not sure how New Labour I really am, with my 1960s liberal values and religious scepticism. By 2am it was a landslide with friends and my euphoric daughter calling that Portillo had gone, as had Waldegrave, Lang, Rifkind, Forsythe and Newton. All sorts of Labour candidates, unvetted by the New Labour casting department, were getting elected. Peter Snow was having fun with new BBC technology that enabled him to blow up Tory seats. Slightly numb I slipped into bed at 3.45am.

Settling into the Home Office – May

The next morning John Major made a dignified exit and went to the Oval for some cricket. Tony and Cherie Blair arrived in Downing Street through Union Jack waving crowds. There was the usual speech about trust and delivering promises; but a good phrase on "practical measures for noble causes." Teletext announced Jack was Home Secretary two hours before his meeting with Tony at 5pm. I agreed to meet him at the HO at 6pm.

Much civil service fussing and piles of briefing. Richard Wilson had acted on the papers I had given him, with a letter on the legislative programme ready. I was reminded of a remark about a Permanent Secretary with a season ticket on the line of least resistance. I gave Jack champagne and a framed cartoon showing politicians damned in hell for promising tax cuts and a balanced budget. We agreed to meet tomorrow after everyone had slept

We reassembled at lunch time on Saturday, 3 May. Civil servants all stood up when Jack came in as was their practice with Howard. I remained seated with my civil service sandwiches. The bids for the legislative programme were agreed: Crime and Disorder Bill, ECHR, handguns ban, and data protection with scope for adding freedom of information (FOI). I had worked on the latter with the FOI campaign and the IPPR think tank; but was not optimistic about FOI in the first session: the civil service would oppose it with arguments about damaging the frankness of their advice to Ministers. But it was worth a try. Jack made clear prisons were his most difficult issue: signalled the direction of travel I had proposed; and said the Sentences Act would not be implemented. Civil servants were told that all submissions to Jack should be copied to me so I could comment. We were in business.

Work began properly on 6 May when all the Ministers turned up in what looked like their best suits, ready for a team photo. Jack kept to the allocation of duties I had proposed with Joyce Quin combining prisons and probation and Europe, with her MEP experience. Nick Timmins had done a profile piece in the FT on me and Michael Barber under the heading that only Straw and Blunkett had appointed heavyweight advisers. I sorted out a room for my fellow SPAD, Ed Owen, who would deal with the media. There were rumblings of discontent from nearly 20 disappointed former Shadow Ministers who hadn't got jobs. The shortest Ministerial career also ended when Derek Foster, the new Cabinet Office Minister, resigned after 3 days because he was not in the Cabinet, which he claimed he was promised. His place was taken by Peter Mandelson who was to coordinate the presentation of Government policies and have a daily meeting with the PM.

The next day was wall to wall meetings – immigration, prisons, budgets, youth justice, Europe, police and constitutional policy. We started getting across signals and decisions to officials, especially on prisons. The Home Secretary would resume answering Parliamentary Questions on the Prison Service rather than pretending these were operational matters for the Executive Agency. The process of unpicking Howard's Sentences Act began with abandoning the repeat burglars' provisions which would have sent the prison population soaring. We started agreeing measures like tagging to ease the pressures on prisons. I did a letter for Jack to send Mandelson to get him involved in the public presentation of our prisons' strategy. We went to the HO canteen for lunch where staff were taken aback by the Home Secretary grabbing their hands to shake.

The public expenditure meeting was rugged. Officials had resurrected all their pet bids for 1997/98 and 1998/99. We scaled down the bids, which Howard should have dealt with, and concentrated on the needs of the Prison Service. A letter went to the Iron Chancellor setting out our stall. The Ministers went off to the first meeting of the enlarged Parliamentary Labour Party (PLP), now so big the Synod room in Church House had to be hired – appropriate given the evangelical tone of New Labour. The evening produced a cliff hanger over the ECHR Bill being in the Queen's Speech on the grounds of an overcrowded programme; but No.10 called me later to say it would be back in if it was ready by summer. I told Jack to make sure at Cabinet tomorrow that it was shown as a HO Bill. We needed some liberal measures.

8 May was the first Cabinet of the new Government. The big story was how Tony wanted Ministers to address each other by their Christian names. Officials were not sure what to do. Ann Widdecombe was said to have had a spat with Howard when she said officials could call her Ann because God did. Jack confirmed the ECHR Bill was in the Queen's Speech along with other HO Bills – but no FOI. Tony said leakers would be out on their ear and people should stay on message. Alistair Campbell wanted all media requests cleared with No.10 and lunches with journalists recorded. Rumblings of New Labour thought police.

Jack did a good piece on the Today programme about taking responsibility for the Prison Service and need for more community punishment. Told Richard Wilson Jack wanted a Directorate of Punishments Policy combining prisons and probation. We had first meetings with Paul Condon, Met Police Commissioner and David Ramsbotham, Chief Inspector of Prisons. Condon in a state about corruption and sacking corrupt officers. The police disciplinary rules required a criminal standard of proof which was difficult to achieve. Officers went sick and retired on enhanced pensions which were damaging police budgets. This looked like a fight with the Police Federation. Civil servants were nervous about Ramsbotham and his critical reports. Jack told them they could check reports for factual accuracy but otherwise not delay publication: Ramsbotham immediately handed over a giant report on women's prisons. I agreed to have a private meeting with him.

On Friday I went to No.10 for first gathering of SPADs chaired by David Miliband. There were 40-50 people there, mainly 30-somethings endlessly looking at their pagers and mobile phones: my only technology is a biro. Much earnest talk of networking, bringing in more technology, guarding the sacred text (the Manifesto) and delivering pledges. Big pre-occupation with 'staying on message' and coordination of announcements. Great suspicion of the civil service thwarting New Labour. I stay largely silent but point out that the civil servants have their own networks and were best handled by showing them your usefulness rather than by confrontation. These were clearly subversive thoughts, made worse by me telling the meeting they could not expect Departmental press officers to do Tory rebuttal.

Jack phoned me on Sunday about a huge submission on the Data Protection Bill. I promised to read the deathless HO prose, send him a two-page summary and move the submission on to Gareth Williams to deal with. Officials seem obsessed with getting the Home Secretary's fingerprints on everything. I tell the private office to stop simultaneous submissions to Jack, me and other Ministers: he should get them at the end of the process.

Monday, 12 May, was the first weekly Ministerial lunch, using the model adopted by Barbara Castle, whereby Ministers and advisers meet without officials to discuss how things were going and what was in prospect. We agreed I should design a system for tracking progress on manifesto pledges. There was a wider problem of tracking what the HO had promised to do and early warning of problem areas. The previous summer the Prison Service let out a lot of prisoners because they had miscalculated their sentences; and the first the HO knew was when an ITN reporter told them. Merseyside MPs were pressing for re-opening the Hillsborough Inquiry in the light of new video and medical evidence; but the original judge, Peter Taylor had died so a new judge would be needed. Another judge would be required for the Stephen Lawrence Inquiry. There were likely to be other inquiries in the HO woodwork and I was charged with finding what skeletons were in the cupboards.

Most of the next day was spent preparing for tomorrow's Queens Speech. Suddenly ECHR legislation was going to solve all the world's problems. Little do people realise the arguments going on in government about Parliamentary sovereignty and establishing a Human Rights Commission into which equal opportunity and race organisations would be absorbed. Robin Cook climbed on the human rights bandwagon with a razzmatazz announcement about an ethical foreign policy and restrictions on arms sales. Wilson is still not moving fast enough on setting up a new Corrections Policy Directorate so we can motor on a new prisons strategy.

May 14 was festive with Tony and Cherie Blair walking to the State Opening of Parliament. We briefed the media on the Queen's

163

Speech and enjoyed a gossipy day about Ann Widdicombe's wish to make a personal statement about Michael Howard lying to the House of Commons. In 1995 Howard sacked Derek Lewis as Director of the Prison Service after a series of escapes. Lewis sued the HO and won; and an independent inquiry had now said Howard was wrong to sack him. Widdecombe who was Prisons Minister at the time and opposed the sacking, now said Howard lied and was unfit to be Tory leader. HO officials were very nervous. Asked for comments, we said we did not wish to intrude into private grief. I went to the Constitution Unit's summer party and was feted by the liberal intelligentsia over the ECHR Bill but doubted this popularity would last long.

The next day brought positive media coverage of the Queen's Speech and a supportive bilateral meeting with Tony. He agreed that a quick start should be made on the youth crime agenda and promised support on tough measures. Jack was to meet the Lord Chief Justice about the Sentences Act. Tony wanted a full briefing on the scale of the prison problem. He didn't support executive release and didn't at this stage want to release longer term plans like merging prisons and probation. He was supportive of reforming the CPS quickly, but I didn't think he realised this could mean firing its top people.

I skipped a meeting with Mo Mowlam about returning IRA prisoners to Northern Ireland prisons; but there was no escape from the Irish sideshow of Roisin McAliskey's baby and its imminent birth in Holloway Prison. Martin McGuiness was given the usual MP's treatment of visiting her and made a speech to Holloway's Governor about her health and British intransigence. We hoped she would agree to have her baby in hospital.

We also had our first meeting with the Prison Officer's Association (POA) whose conference was the following week. They wanted to stop the privatisation of prisons and to have their right to strike restored. They claimed they were promised this by Tony and John Prescott; and were armed with an ill-judged letter from Tony. Jack had to leave the meeting and they made the same speeches to me and Joyce Quin. On Jack's return I suggested the civil servants left so they could tell us what they really wanted. After a lot of stuff about Labour loyalty they wanted something to tell their conference. Afterwards, I drafted a soothing letter and lined up George Howarth for their conference.

16 May required a 5.30am start so we could get to Winchester Prison (Jack's first prison visit) and then on to the prison ship at Portland. Arriving at Winchester we found a young man had hung himself three hours previously and not been on suicide watch. We went round the prison with a media circus. Jack's security officer got detached as Jack darted into cells and later had trainee hairdressers waving scissors at him. We did the 'World at One' in Weymouth police station and then went on to the prison ship. This was soon to be home to 600 prisoners. It was like a giant cross-channel ferry without the duty free. The cabins/cells were well kitted out, but it was very claustrophobic, with dodgy air-conditioning. If there was a fire it would be a disaster. We said any go ahead to its use must await clearance by health and safety. The weekend brought another mound of HO submissions, including a request from Australia to exhume the skull of an Aboriginal leader from a Liverpool grave.

On Monday morning I cleared my pager of messages for Rachel Whetstone, Howard's SPAD: one was a date with her boyfriend. More interestingly was an invitation to a meeting on Howard's leadership bid that I was tempted to accept. An announcement was made on Tony's idea of a drugs Czar and our new Treatment and Testing Order: I was still trying to work out the Czar's role. Spent morning on Jack's speech for the Queen's Speech debate.

No-one would be listening to Jack because he would be followed by Ann Widdecombe's attack on Howard who she claimed had "something of the night about him." There was something odd about a pro-hanging, anti-abortion, anti-divorce, anti-feminist and no sex before marriage protagonist becoming a heroine of the liberal press. She stood immediately behind a tense Howard and delivered a 40-minute onslaught on how he had lied to the House about not pressurising Lewis to sack the Parkhurst Prison governor. She laid out Lewis's track record in reforming the Prison Service and effectively killed Howard's leadership bid.

The next day's papers were full of Widdecombe versus Howard rather than New Labour's criminal justice reforms. We had been having our own spat with Derry Irvine (Lord Chancellor) over a letter I drafted for Jack to send youth court magistrates about our pledge to speed up the processing of persistent young offenders. Derry wrote a pompous letter saying only he could write to magistrates. More interesting was the lunch with HM Inspectorate of Constabulary and their concerns over police corruption and organised crime. They listened politely as I outlined our youth crime agenda; but I hadn't captured the interest of these giants from the days of police officer height requirements. I had a good meeting with the Refugee Council about how we could improve support for asylum seekers, not a popular subject with any Party. I encouraged them to write a proposal on voluntary sector hostels in London as an alternative to shipping people off to Merseyside.

On Wednesday Jack went to Police Federation Conference in Blackpool and announced the Task Force on Youth Crime I was to chair. Good coverage on evening TV. Unfortunately, Myra Hindley came out of the woodwork. She had appealed against Howard's ruling that she would never be freed; and the High Court had given her leave to seek to have this ruling subjected to judicial review. Jack and Ministers have to avoid comment and I persuaded them not to make public comments about life means life.

On 22nd Jack phoned after Cabinet wanting to have lunch to discuss an independent commission to devise a system of proportional representation to be put to a referendum before the next Election. This was an idea from the joint constitutional committee with the LibDems when Tony wasn't confident about Labour's majority. Robin Cook was the PR enthusiast while Jack was committed to first past the post. Nobody seemed to know Tony's mind but as far as I could judge he might settle for 500 or so constituency MPs plus 20% or so on top from a PR-based list. I pointed out the difficulties of choosing a commission which could vary from 3 wise men/women chosen by the three main parties to 20 constitutional experts who would never agree anything. Appointing on Nolan principles would not be quick. Later we met Bob McLennan of the LibDems who was dismissive of a Nolan approach. Said we thought LibDems were anti-sleaze. He wanted 8-10 members with a judge or businessman as chair and a mix of politicians and experts – a total male chauvinist. He wanted a proposal in writing. PR only benefited the LibDems and I couldn't see how this helped Labour at the next Election.

Later I dashed to St James' Palace for the launch of RPS's fundraising video with our patron, the Duke of Edinburgh. I decided not to tell him I was working on tightening gun laws. By the end of the week HO civil servants had calmed down over the Howard/ Widdecombe warfare. I thought it a macabre comedy, but they hated the personal confrontation. I went to my second SPADs meeting which was so dreary I vowed to absent myself in future.

After the Spring Bank Holiday, Jack returned from his first EU foray at the Joint Home Affairs Council. The aim was to secure a Treaty amendment that recognised the UK's (and Ireland's) right to enforce border controls because we were islands. This was a prize the Tories never achieved. It is striking how many Interior Ministries across the EU want to stop extension of Community competence while all the Justice Departments and Foreign Offices wanted to extend it. 28th May was a good day for Europe with NATO and Russia signing a mutual cooperation pact, formally ending the cold war.

I rehearsed Jack for the Devolution Cabinet Committee meeting on the Barnett formula which gave the Scots £1.5 billion a year more than they should have. Even Joel Barnett who invented the formula in the 1970s, thought it should be scrapped. We needed to get this reviewed in the comprehensive spending review, but the Iron Chancellor doesn't want to discuss it to protect his Scottish credentials. The Welsh are limp, so Jack had to be the hard man armed with a few Treasury titbits fed to me.

We had another ECHR meeting and won the argument in favour of a White Paper. I was losing the argument on the Bill providing for a Human Rights Commission into which the equal opportunities and race equality bodies could be incorporated. I vowed to keep plugging away. Daily Mail having a strop because we are implementing a manifesto pledge to abolish the daft 1980 'primary purpose' provision in the immigration rules. This enabled people to be turned away if they had married a UK national abroad but allowed people to settle if they had married an EU national. Tony and Mandelson nervous so abolition postponed.

On 29 May provided Jack with further thoughts on an independent PR commission. The least bad solution seemed to me a mix of politicians and technical experts chaired by a judge, with no rush to set it up and a Referendum Bill in 2000 or even after an Election. I was convinced the issue would divide the Cabinet because there was no obvious advantage to Labour.

Terrible meeting on a dire draft circular from officials on what police should do with information notifying them of the movement of sex offenders: it was all about protecting the back of police rather than protecting children, with no obvious consultation with Health or Education departments. Sent back for major re-write. I finished the day with a note to Jack and Joyce Quin on why we should give the new National Youth Justice Board a power to manage the whole under-18 secure estate, as happens in Sweden. This should wake up the Prison Service and local government if I could pull it off.

Increasing the Pressure for Change – June

June began with our first Ministerial awayday in the splendour of the National Liberal Club. The focus was on HO savings for the comprehensive spending review. Two big questions remained unresolved: the lack of appetite for tackling police inefficiency and reversing prison population growth. We also had to retool sentencing policy, revamp both probation and the prison service, modernise the criminal justice system and reduce its costs and reform youth justice. All without spending more money. This was without tackling immigration and asylum seekers where spending was demand-led with increasing numbers of people entering the UK. Ministers offered few sacrificial lambs. I was expected to turn water into wine.

Papers on 3 June were full of stories about special advisers and politicisation of the civil service. This had been brewing for a few weeks as senior civil servants saw their advice facing competition. The Independent published a full list of advisers, 'Blair's special team' as they called it. The Guardian called us a 'political army.;' and the FT talked about "muddy water lapping at the doorstep of No. 10." Alistair Campbell conducted what he called a 20-minute seminar with the Lobby. This probably meant nobody else spoke and explained the hostile media coverage. Fortunately, Nick Timmins showed me as a cut above the young apparatchiks: a kind of aging red guard capable of writing the thoughts of Chairman Tony.

There was a boring meeting with the Prison Governors Association who sounded rather like the POA but with better suits. They just moaned and groaned about all the people who shouldn't be in prison, so

168

Jack asked them to conduct an exercise to show in detail the categories of prisoners who shouldn't be there. Spoke to the Prison Service about the bail application by Roisin McAliskey who had post-natal depression. I reminded them there was a baby involved and they should get some decent psychiatric advice. Talked to Joyce Quin about Parole Board appointments and the lack of women and ethnic minorities: provided some alternative sources for candidates to the usual HO approach.

Yet another meeting on ECHR with Derry Irvine who conceded a White Paper and said he favoured a declaratory approach as in New Zealand, so the judges didn't look as though they were striking down Parliament's legislation. I suspected he had been got at by the senior judiciary feeling nervous about seeming to tell politicians what to do. Jack and I tidy up the minute to go to Tony on setting up an electoral commission to come up with a PR voting system; and I provided some names of politicians and experts. He accepted my advice that names should be cleared with LibDems before discussing terms of reference and they had to accept the alternative vote as a possibility. We needed to flush out what Tony really wanted.

The morning of 4 June was dominated by Inquiries; but started with news of a Judge (Mitchell) threatening to jail 20 detectives for contempt of court when a drug trial collapsed because they destroyed vital evidence. On Stephen Lawrence we moved to trying to find a Chair. On Hillsborough a new public Inquiry was looking inevitable with the level of Merseyside feeling that there was a police cover-up. Stories continued on the politicisation of the civil service but there were more features and letters saying special advisers prevented politicisation. I began thinking this angst was being stirred up by senior Mandarins who don't like the No.10 set-up, especially Jonathan Powell's appointment as Tony's Chief of Staff.

The next day the abolition of the primary purpose rule was finally announced. There were bizarre press stories about the HO extracting Ronnie Kray's brain. I knew how Ronnie must have felt after hours of grilling HO Directorates about their savings for the spending review. Richard Wilson and I acted as investigating magistrates. We focused on police efficiency or lack of it. I raised the idea of a cheaper uniformed public presences than PCs, more private security guards, cutting the cost of back-office services and more performance measures. Probation people were lacklustre. I told them if they couldn't raise their game, we might well look at training prison staff to do more community supervision, with Wilson's support. Continued interrogations of other HO Directorates on 6 June and reported situation to Jack. Have briefed Nick Timmins on law and order aspects of spending review for FT piece he is writing and encouraged him to write about the Barnett formula.

Uneventful Ministerial lunch on 9 June. These lunches were not working well – too many people. Meeting on sentence calculation after Prison Service errors forced Howard to free prisoners last year. Officials argue that the Courts changed the law and Prison Service was blameless. After the meeting I suggested that in implementing the Sentences Act, we should change the system and get courts to do sentence calculations. Jack agreed so I told officials to put this to Lord Chancellor. Published consultation paper on making bribery and corruption of MPs subject to criminal law. I had persuaded Jack to treat MPs the same as all other public office holders who misused office – in line with my 1995 DEMOS pamphlet.

The following day we had a good meeting with Louis Freeh, Director of the FBI. Good media coverage of the anti-bribery consultation document. Prepared plan for Jack's speeches for next 6 months so that our policy agenda could unfold. We had a preparatory discussion for the meeting with Derek Lewis. I thought his book, 'Hidden Agendas' was well-written and interesting but some of his unkind remarks about HO civil servants seem to have been taken excessively to heart – what sensitive souls they are. Lewis had called me to ask for a meeting with just Jack and me, so the distrust was two-way. Tory leadership first round results had Ken Clarke in the lead and Howard in last place – much mirth.

Frenetic EU activity by Tony to secure the borders control deal at the Amsterdam summit on 16 and 17 June. He flew off to see Chirac on 11 June. A protocol attached to the Treaty securing our borders eluded Thatcher and Major and might make it easier to sort out the messes we've inherited on immigration and asylum. The meeting with Derek Lewis went well with some good ideas on restructuring the Prison Service and linking it more to probation that I will follow up. Jack's proposal for sending MPs to jail for bribery is called a real vote winner by Auberon Waugh.

The civil service is at its nit-picking worst over pumping a little money into victim support schemes for an announcement by the PM in two days' time. I suggested that £1 million was added to their grant for more court support services. Jack accepted and closed the meeting: the civil servants are still arguing as I get them out of the room. I tell them if we spent this amount of time on every £1 million of HO expenditure we would never go home.

12 June was the day for the first 50 prisoners to go on the prison ship, even though it was still being fitted out: much media interest. A fire alarm caused evacuation but fortunately no-one escaped. Meeting with Mike O'Brien who had written a paper on putting a chief executive in charge of immigration instead of policy civil servants: pointed out errors in his text and told him it would be difficult to convince Jack but I'd come with him to a meeting. Stocktake meeting on Crime and Disorder Bill. Items kept being added, with the latest being luncheon vouchers for jurors from Derry. I secured firm decisions on a White Paper in December confined to youth justice reforms and an early announcement of the youth justice task force.

Times had big feature on the new HO team – 'Reformer Straw is on parole.' I received biggest mention after Jack, but my age was revealed causing my wife to call to speak to her 'golden oldie.' Alistair Darling announced a spending review, so I hold yet another meeting with Wilson and officials. HO savings are still inadequate and a dozen savings reviews are agreed for a Ministerial away day next week. HO see themselves as savings hawks but there is little top management grip. Their management culture and Departmental Board are poor. I stop a submission seeking more money for criminal injuries compensation.

Chirac threw his weight behind Tony on border controls and Scottish devolution was progressing. The list of subjects reserved to the Westminster Parliament was agreed and the Judicial Committee of the Privy Council would resolve disputes. Jack and I are devolution sceptics. The English politics of this was being overlooked because of the large number of Scots in senior Cabinet posts. Buck House was in a steamer about what would happen if the Queen was asked to read out a speech in Edinburgh that contradicted her speech in Westminster. Who would be a constitutional monarch under New Labour. The Bill to ban handguns passed the Commons by 200 votes.

The weekend was spent on paedophiles and trying to develop a custodial strategy that curbed the growth of the prison population, developed community punishment and changed sentencing policy. The discussions with the LCJ, Tom Bingham – a man with a bone-crushing handshake – had been useful. The judges seemed to have no idea of the impact of their sentencing practices on the prison population and cared less. Bingham was considering a guideline judgement on burglary and had been offered access to HO research and statistics – something never done before.

The issue of releasing paedophiles threatening to repeat offending was becoming a major problem. We had increasing numbers of sex offenders, obsessive stalkers and mentally disordered offenders leaving prison ready to offend, with psychiatrists saying they could not detain someone under the Mental Health Act if they had no treatment for the person. Danger to the public seemed not to count. To cap it all The Observer had a piece on a Kent nudist club with 11 convicted or suspected paedophiles who photographed child members. Wrote a paper on engaging with these issues.

The week of 16 June began with a morning in the opulence of Lancaster House discussing a clutch of HO reviews for cutting expenditure and linking probation and prison services. I had persuaded Jack to reduce the Prison Service's submission for five new private prisons to two plus a 3-year extension of Blakenhurst Prison. Suggested doubling up and in cell TV as alternative contingency plan to more prisons. Still await No.10 agreement to announcement. Difficult meeting the next day with Jack on using secure training centres for 12 to14 year-olds, which I oppose. The efficiency review of the CPS was announced, with their areas to be brought in line with police areas.

I presented to the Ministerial team my proposed policy and political management system. This started with a tracking system for delivery of Manifesto commitments with key milestones and target dates. There was a short watch list of danger zones or banana skins, which were in plentiful supply in the HO. I identified four key work areas that each Minister should focus on over the next 12- 18 months; and a set of inter-departmental relationships on key topics to which named Ministers should pay attention. This was later agreed and used during my time in HO. I suspect it fell into disuse after I left.

Good meeting with George Kelling, American author of 'Broken Windows' and 'Fixing Broken Windows.' New York police chief, Bill Bratton, was using Kelling's ideas on zero tolerance of low-level crime and disorder to stop areas becoming major crime problems. Kelling had a low opinion of the Association of Chief Police Officers who he saw as a vested interest resisting change and demanding extra resources without being held to account. Told him that was my view. Police efficiency and the Prison Service were our greatest challenges.

EU agreed the border controls protocol, something Thatcher failed to achieve. Pictures of Tony riding a bike to lunch in Amsterdam with Chirac and Kohl walking. The Scots were proving more difficult than the EU over Westminster's sovereignty. Spent much of 18th negotiating with No.10 a minute from Jack to Tony on the override. It was becoming Tony, Jack and Derry Irvine against the other Scots.

Equally difficult was keeping track of paedophiles on release with one arrested after appearing on daytime TV ('Kilroy') and saying there's nothing wrong with sex with children. I met with Gareth Williams and Alun Michael and we agreed officials needed to make much clearer in guidance what police should do on prisoner release. My view was they had to tell parents if children were at risk, whatever the liberal lobby said. This meeting turned out to be prescient as the next day the Mail ran a story that there were over 250,000 convicted sex offenders loose in the community.

Mike Foster decided to press on with his Private Members Bill to ban foxhunting. This came to the HO because Jack Cunningham and MAFF refused to handle it. It is a Manifesto commitment and highly contentious; but Jack seems uninterested in saving foxes. A deal was agreed with Mike to have a joint committee of MPs and Peers to consider the Bill as a means of easing its passage. The Tories are making the news with Ken Clarke and John Redwood joining forces for the final Leadership round against William Hague – all to no avail as Hague wins by 92 to 70. Jonathan Aitken was called back to the witness stand in his libel case because he has lied; and his wife has left him.

Office meeting on the rating of a computer game, 'Carmageddon.' Players are supposed to avoid killing pedestrians but can play it to do the opposite. BBFC, the regulator, eventually agrees to give it an age 18 certificate, but manufacturer argued the game was exempt. More of these violent games look likely to test the censorship rules. Cabinet decided to relaunch the Millennium Dome project at Greenwich, with Peter Mandelson charged with putting something interesting in the Dome.

Today (19 June) we had our first meeting with the Fire Service chiefs: my old Kent colleague, Jeremy Beech, had come to see me about how to present their ideas. I told him mergers were on the agenda and that we might want to think about merging control rooms for emergency services. This is difficult territory with an 'Old Labour' Fire Brigades Union. They had tried to stop a new fire station opening because the bedrooms were too small until it was pointed out to them the public didn't know they slept on the job. We were not in a good place for a lengthy dispute with the FBU because the Green Goddesses were reducing in numbers as were soldiers to drive them.

We briefed the POA and the Prison Governors Association in advance of our announcement today of two new private prisons – offset by the reduced length of contract for Blakenhurst. This took the sting out of their reaction. The POA even agreed to participate in a joint working party to see if they would reduce the public sector cost of running Blakenhurst if it was returned to public sector management.

Spent most of Friday (20 June) chairing first meeting of Youth Justice Task Force. We had our photos taken by Sky and photo libraries, so we were expected to endure. Good discussion on aims and objectives of youth justice system that provided material for legislation. This broke out of the sterile discussion of 'welfare' versus 'punishment' which tended to argue that no child should be punished no matter how serious the crime. Agreed to consider statutory time limits for all stages from arrest to sentence to speed up dealing with persistent offenders. Rejected Martin Narey's proposal for removing 17year-olds from youth courts: no good evidence and would increase prison population. Interesting discussion on not paying legal aid lawyers if client failed to turn up in court: shock horror from lawyers.

Weekend media dominated by how Jonathan Aitken lied and pulled the wool over Robin Butler's eyes in the investigation John Major asked him to conduct. Guardian portrayed the investigation as a couple of toffs from Eton and Harrow having a chat. Robin clearly should have told Major to make his own judgement. Jack and I had

174

already discussed splitting the Cabinet Secretary and Head of the Civil Service roles which I favour, and which Tony will have to decide.

Good Ministerial lunch on 23rd which decided to go ahead with a Hillsborough review of new evidence by a judge. Jack calmed down Ministers over a proposal I had written for two-tier policing, as an alternative to endlessly increasing bobbies on the beat. Uniformed civic guards employed by local authorities and properly regulated would be a cheaper alternative. I agreed we needed a better name, but Jack wanted the idea pursued. Ministerial joy at the appointment of Brian Mawhinney as Shadow Home Secretary. I recalled a story that when his Ministerial helicopter landed at Stormont his Private Office was told 'the ego has landed.'

Richard Wilson and I briefed Jack for his meeting with Barbara Mills, the DPP, who is resisting CPS reform. Ronnie Biggs had been found in Brazil and HO officials weren't keen on extraditing him. I suggested the 'Today' test should be applied. How would Jack explain to John Humphreys why he wasn't extraditing a convicted criminal who was making a fool of the criminal justice system? That settled matters.

Sad and inconclusive meeting on 24th with Lawrence family and their advisers. The police aided and abetted by the CPS had screwed up the criminal prosecution and the ill-advised civil case had collapsed. However unsavoury the accused, we could not set up an inquiry that was effectively a new trial. We were trying to persuade the family to accept a wider inquiry on the relationship between the black community and the police.

Today was the long plod through the Scottish and Welsh Devolution White Papers. I had written Jack a brief on the main shortcomings of the preferred Scottish version: no Westminster override; the Scottish Executive to be equivalent to the Government in London; Barnett Formula triumphalism; overblown role for Scots in EU negotiations. Good detailed briefing and amendments from officials. Robin Cook and LibDems pressing for progress on PR voting system for 1999 European Parliament Elections: but there was no Bill in the legislative programme and no-one knew Tony's views. I was tasked with finding out.

Met Tim Hornsby of National Lottery Charities Board to tee up applications for youth justice and community safety projects to start in 1998 when £160 million would be available. I duly recognised that lottery money was not to be substituted for public expenditure on statutory services; but there was no objection to me sending him a list of favoured topics and encouraging voluntary organisations to apply for funding in those areas. My HO minder seemed surprised by this creative budgetary approach I'd learned in local government.

On 25 June Jack spoke at police conference with my beefed-up speech on need for greater efficiency. Officials were reluctant to tell chief constables to be more efficient, with a lot of mumbo jumbo about operational independence. Yet some forces like Thames Valley were reducing crime without moaning about more money. HO would lose an ECHR case on age of homosexual consent – a manifesto commitment on a free vote. So, informal discussions with Stonewall were opened, with an amendment to the Crime and Disorder Bill a possibility. Families leaked Hillsborough Review and Lawrence Inquiry but no great problem apart from No.10 wish to manage the news.

Tony issued a firm statement to Sinn Fein/IRA about a ceasefire and opening talks. The response was a rocket attack on the police. Tom Bingham had called for a Royal Commission on crime and punishment: we were non-committal. His arguments seemed to be that judges were influenced by public opinion and only politicians could change that. I thought judges were supposed to be impervious to the mob's call for tougher punishment and to mete out fair sentences. We needed to keep talking to him about sentencing guidelines.

I spent Friday 27th producing papers for the next Youth Justice Taskforce meeting; and mapping out a statement for Jack that brought together prison, sentencing and community punishment. The management culture in the Home Office seemed non-existent; and I resolved to launch my Policy and Political Management System to exercise more grip. Over weekend I rewrote paper for No.10 on family-strengthening measures as basis for taking forward parenting initiatives. They wanted Jack in lead on this rather than Harriet Harman's new Women's Committee.

The week began with lots of Budget speculation: Jack went to see Gordon about more generosity towards the voluntary sector and disadvantaged groups in the Welfare to Work scheme. Stocktake meeting before Jack saw Derry on the overloaded Crime and Disorder Bill which had too much trivia from HO and Lord Chancellor cupboards. Today (30 June) was dominated by the Hillsborough statement. A dry old legal stick, Stuart-Smith, had been found to review the evidence to see if another public inquiry was needed. Victims' families were in London in droves to cheer Jack. Finished the day meeting Richard Wilson and HO brass to progress chase the Prison Audit and material for Jack's speech on prisons, sentencing and community punishment. I could see why Jack told Ed Owen that he needed me to boss the civil service about.

Papers full of pictures of Chris Patten wiping away a tear at one of the farewells to Hong Kong: much folding of union jacks. An unenthusiastic looking Tony was spending only 6 hours there, one of which was on the royal yacht with Charles. The No.10 Lobby briefing had only four lines on the HK visit which revealed Campbell's and Mandelson's views. I remained unconvinced about Patten's enthusiasm for promoting Hong Kong democracy during his 5-year tenure, when British Governments had ignored this for 150 colonial years.

Maximising First 100 Days Achievements – July

After a difficult meeting with Derry on the Crime and Disorder Bill, 1 July produced an even more difficult one with the HO top brass on Stephen Lawrence. I had reminded people we couldn't have an inquiry that reopened events on the night of Stephen's death because this would be tantamount to a new murder trial. Jack handled meeting well and got all views out on table. Mike O'Brien was sent away with officials to find a solution involving reviewing and publishing the current police complaints inquiry. I found out later that this inquiry would convince no-one because it was being conducted by a Kent police officer, where Condon had been the Chief Constable during my time in Kent.

The next day Joyce Quin and I visited the Colchester YOI run by the Army and only opened 4 months ago. This was one of two Tory boot camps being evaluated, with another one not run by the Army. We were welcomed by Army officers with swagger sticks and the Adjutant-General arrived by helicopter. We saw a video with lots of bayonetting and offenders doing drills. Young offenders were marched to lunch, holding their mugs and cutlery behind their backs. We were told the emphasis on drilling in the first 6 weeks was popular and achieved team

177

building: I kept a straight face. The inmates had no personal possessions in this period and slept in dormitories, with prizes for the best kept rooms. Cupboards were full of neatly folded clothes and I wondered about sending my sons here for a while.

There were good programmes teaching numeracy and literacy, together with vocational skills and team-based physical activities. These all had generous instructor/offender ratios; and the offender population seemed not to have difficult to manage individuals. Some youngsters preferred this regime to previous prisons; but all it really showed was that constructive regimes, a lot of space and generous staffing ratios were beneficial, irrespective of drilling.

On return Gordon was in full flow on the Budget, abolishing pension credits and cutting corporation tax. Jack was briefed for another round on the devolution White Papers and protecting the Westminster override. The rest of the day was spent dealing with press coverage of a HO study of 200 serious incidents in 1996 by prisoners under probation supervision. There were 69 murders, 32 attempted murders and 30 rapes. As one newspaper put it: "convicted criminals are being charged with murder at the rate of more than one a week while being supervised by probation officers." The Daily Mail congratulated Jack on open government; and the Probation Service was incandescent, suspecting a plot. In truth it turned out to be a giant cock-up by the HO press office, publishing without telling Ministers.

3 July began with a meeting with Mike O'Brien and Nick Hardwick of the Refugee Council who had done the work I'd asked for on an alternative to the shambolic system for supporting asylum seekers. Most of the proposals depended on restoring payment of social security to asylum seekers. I had never believed the savings the Tories claimed for benefit withdrawal, but the inflated claims were built into public expenditure assumptions. New Labour Ministers were unwilling to restore benefits which would have been the cheapest option. Nick produced some ideas for changing housing regulations so local authorities could use spare accommodation. The best option was to use the local voluntary sector more and restore benefits; but it looked as though politically we would carry on with local authorities paying private hotels and London shunting asylum seekers to cheaper Northern areas.

We decided to hang tough with the POA who were taking the Prison Service to court for transferring staff from London to Lancashire and East Anglia because of overcrowding. Officials came to see me about the Prison Service Audit which they had reworked as I suggested showing the lack of resources the Tories provided for their policy of 'prison works' and the serious consequences of overcrowding, prisoner unrest and lack of constructive regimes. Pictures of Gordon as Oliver Cromwell with his Budget for the long term. I thought the abolition of tax credits for pension funds would return to haunt him but extra money for health and education was popular, despite committing half the 1998/99 contingency reserve.

Chaired full day meeting of Youth Justice Task Force on 4 July. HO officials were nervous about attending meetings of a body whose advice the Home Secretary might reject. I told them to leave this to me. We agreed a main aim of reducing offending for the system and those working in it. Came up with a solution to the problem of repeated cautions: police reprimand for first offence, then a final warning before charge. We had a first shot at the problems of the secure estate for which I was planning a very interventionist approach by the new Youth Justice Board.

We announced using the Secure Training Centre Howard had signed a contract on just before the Election; but it and others would have their regimes reviewed as part of youth justice reforms. That announcement had been obliterated by Gordon Downey's 900-page report on cash for questions and its "compelling" evidence that Neil Hamilton had received cash direct from Al Fayed for his lobbying services.

Earlier Jack had phoned from Whitemoor Prison to say he was sitting next to Tony at PMQs when he said that Jack would be announcing shortly new measures to improve the treatment of victims in the court system. We hastily re-announced the measures to protect witnesses and the extra £1million for Victim Support that Tony had announced a month earlier. The press didn't seem to notice that this was the same material.

Evening spent at London Criminal Courts Solicitors' dinner as guest of CPS lawyers who gave me an ear bashing about Barbara Mills thwarting CPS reforms. The highlight of the evening was the hissing and booing of Tom Bingham, the LCJ, after he told an unsavoury joke about a Cambridge undergraduate raped in a punt. When the judge was asked what sentence the offender should get, he answered "a half blue I should think." Bingham sat down to modest applause, his reputation seriously damaged, particularly as journalists were present.

Weekend dominated by Drumcree march in Portadown by the Orangemen and the lockdown of the Catholic area by the RUC. Ronnie Flanagan's arguments that allowing the march stopped Catholics being murdered looked unconvincing.

The week of 7 July started with a visit by Peter Mandelson for a presentation on the prison population. On arrival he pointed out that the pictures of former Home Secretaries in the corridor leading to Jack's room had no picture of his grandfather, Herbert Morrison. Like a Roman Emperor, he remarked that this was an inauspicious start to his visit. Quick as flash Richard Wilson said the picture had been taken down for cleaning. This produced a Mandelson smile and a response that he supposed this was why Richard was a Permanent Secretary. This no doubt helped Richard's chances of becoming Cabinet Secretary.

Despite civil service uneasiness the Prison Audit had been revised in the way I proposed, showing that Howard did not fund prisons adequately and another £40 million or so was needed over this year and next. The discussion with Peter went well and he engaged with the issue. The upshot was agreement to send the Audit to the Treasury with a request for more money. We denied the Times claim that we would use tagging to release 4,000 prisoners because it required legislation and that tagging made more sense pre-prison.

The next day brought leaking of the security assessment on the Drumcree march, more tagging stories and an apology from Bingham for his poor taste in jokes. Nick Timmins had a piece about Permanent Secretaries and Wilson succeeding Robin Butler. I met some of them at the FDA summer party and wondered why I'd ever aspired to be one. We had an inconclusive meeting about changing the standard of proof for dismissing corrupt police officers to balance of probabilities – my strong view. Howard had left us an unworkable sliding scale for different offences and the tension between Chief Constables and the Police Federation was mounting.

9 July started with another grinding meeting on the Devolution White Papers. With Jack now described as the leading 'Devo sceptic.'

We had done the private minute to TB on the 'override' for a private meeting next week and No.10 had assured me Tony was 'on side.' I went to No.10 to discuss with David Miliband and the Policy Unit my paper on 'family-strengthening measures'. I might have blotted my copybook by my lack of enthusiasm for adding a section on strengthening marriage because Tony was keen on moral leadership. I told them it would be a political mistake to pontificate on marriage and asked if they knew enough about the private lives of Labour Ministers to risk this. Better not tell Tony that Suzanne and I co-habited for 12 years before marriage.

Grim meeting with HO officials about public expenditure, with their huge shopping list of items they wanted Jack to fight for. I had briefed him to concentrate just on more money for prisons this year and next. Richard Wilson supported; and a string of disappointed officials traipsed out. TB robust at PMQs about abolition of hunting but the Foster Bill could still be killed with smiles. A row was brewing over the creation of more Labour Peers: I had been sounded out but suspected I was more useful in HO. Nolan reported on corruption in local government, giving them a fairly clean bill of health. He supported my line on criminal convictions for all serious abuses of public office. My DEMOS pamphlet recommendations might happen.

Police corruption was grabbing headlines. One chief constable said his force had people who wouldn't be employed by Sainsbury's; but Police Federation said their members were like doctors and needed the same protection from malicious complaints. My recollection was that the GMC disciplinary procedures used the civilian standard of proof, not criminal standard like police. We put out a statement about our determination to root out corrupt cops and I asked HO officials to check out the standard of proof in disciplinary systems for doctors, lawyers, nurses and military officers. Chris Mullin had become chair of Home Affairs Select Committee and I suggested asking him to do an inquiry into the police disciplinary system.

10 July saw 100,000 pro-hunting rally uniting William Hague and David Bellamy. Massive police protection of HO and Home Secretary who was against a ban. Strange discussions with No.10 about homosexual age of consent. I wanted to do a deal with Stonewall under which they settled for a free vote; but Mandelson seemed to want us

181

pushed into a decision by the European Court of Human Rights and to use the Crime Disorder Bill to make the legal change. We don't want our flagship law and order Bill badged by gay sex so did another letter to No.10 explaining our position.

Bingham acknowledged that judges were filling up jails by responding to a more vengeful public mood. Media failed to cover the fact that when he went on circuit 6 months ago to hear appeals, he handed out tougher burglary sentences than trial judges. Still better a sinner who repents. Jack still muttering about a Minnesota sentencing grid for judges, but I suggested he didn't mention this to Bingham and Irvine. Press had picked up that the FOI White Paper was to be delayed and blamed the civil service: the truth was that the draft wasn't very good. The subject looked to be heading Jack's way. Approval given to arrest Ronnie Biggs when new extradition treaty came into force.

Spent much of 11 July wrestling with a turgid HO draft circular on implementation of the Sex Offenders Act. The text was all about police notification of information rather than what officials had been asked to do which was to agree across Whitehall a document setting out the roles of police, probation, education, health and social services. I sent the text to Alun Michael saying it should be downgraded to preliminary advice with a Government-wide circular by year end. Many HO officials live in a bubble sealed off from other Departments.

Weekend spent grappling with prison population now heading for 64,000: I had wanted to cap it at 60,000 before Election. No political support for early release. We would have to look at six Army sites for low security prisoners and this had been leaked. I was determined to stop another ship. Derek Lewis was telling me to release more women and young offenders, but this wouldn't provide accommodation for higher security males. The courts were dealing with cases faster and it was taking time to get across the message about tougher community punishments.

On Monday (14 July) Jack and I met to discuss voting systems and PR for the 1999 European elections. I thought Tony was going to do a bounce on PR for the 1999 elections. No.10 muttered to me about not circulating a letter from Jack seeking colleagues' agreement to preparing legislation on a regional list system, with registration of political parties. No.10 were making a pig's ear of age of consent for gay sex. We had a clear position with Stonewall for a free vote and legislation in 1999/2000 if vote was in favour of change. Now the Lobby was being told that there was no agreement with Stonewall – which was untrue – and that the law officers had said we would lose the ECHR case and have to settle out of court. While HO was handling reducing the age of consent for gay sex to 16, I discovered the Health Department was contemplating raising the age for sale of cigarettes to 18.

We had a scratchy meeting with the Magistrates Association who didn't like some of our youth court changes, especially using stipendiary magistrates to speed up cases. I pointed out they were taking longer to deal with fewer cases than they were 5 years ago. Stocktake on the Crime and Disorder Bill showed we were keeping to our timetable despite a ruckus with Derry Irvine about the volume of criminal justice changes we were making. Jack owned up to still wanting a single police final warning and wanted to discuss with me again. I later finally convinced him that this was impracticable; and he settled for my proposal of one reprimand before the final warning, as long as I emphasised no informal warnings. At last, a decision.

The next day saw the result of the No.10 Lobby briefing on the age of consent. – an Independent front-page headline, "Gays win key battles… but still they can't go to War." A quiet understanding with Stonewall had been turned into concessions wrested from the Government. Scottish devolution was coming to a conclusion with Jack getting a lot of credit for standing up to the Braveheart tendency. TB met the Loyalists to tell them about his meetings with Sinn Fein.

I agreed with Jack that the registration of political parties would be dealt with in the legislation on PR for the 1999 European elections, but Party funding would be separated. Derry seemed to have persuaded TB that he should handle Party funding; but No.10 sounded me out about Jack's views. We suggested Derry chaired a Committee, but policy stayed with Jack and the HO. This was just as well as next day Derry launched an attack on legal fat cats which presumably included Cherie Blair. Legal profession retaliated, with attention drawn to £650K spent on refurbishing his official residence and the price of his Pugin wallpaper.

July 16th saw good coverage of Jack's first speech on regulating the private security industry. I had told him and Alun Michael that speeches were fine, but legislation would have to consider what to do about electronic tagging and all types of security personnel, whether employed in the public or private sectors. We had to be clear if we were regulating for probity or competence, or both. The day also produced a wonderful equal opportunities letter from the Palace: "The Queen is content to place her prerogative and interests, in so far as they relate to the Succession to the Crown, at the disposal of Parliament, for the purposes of any measures providing for the removal of any distinction in (sic) the sexes in determining the succession." Too late for Anne I suspect.

Briefing meeting with ACPO was one long commercial for why the police needed more money with all the new kit coming along. DNA would soon replace fingerprinting and video evidence would be more acceptable for vulnerable witnesses like children. The forces outside London thought they were poor relations of the Met, which they were. No Government could cut the Met's budget without accusations of not protecting the capital. That meant 27,000 police officers in London, whatever formula was used. I thought there were too many small forces with unimpressive bosses and that we should pursue mergers and improve back-office efficiency. No HO appetite at all.

Jack went to see Tony before Cabinet to talk about the Westminster override before the Cabinet Committee settled Devolution White Papers. Tony was still trying to look as though he was above the override battle and let Jack and Derry be his rottweilers. Cabinet informed of PR decision for European elections which was announced by Jack later. He justified PR for European Parliament but not Westminster on grounds that the former was not an executive body. Nor was the Westminster Parliament, but he wasn't challenged.

Review of Prison and Probation announced (17 July). Advance briefing was well covered by press who understood that it would look at a merger. Predictable hostility from NAPO. HO policy capability on this subject was weak and I couldn't get Richard Wilson to move faster to strengthen it. I wanted to remove juveniles from Prison Service, shake up its HQ and set up day prisons outside their control. Rather uninspired meeting with Alun Michael and officials about police key objectives. HO officials had got the message that community safety and youth justice had to figure; but their lack of managerialism meant they struggled with setting key objectives and KPIs to measure progress.

18 July was yet another prisons day but began with an 8.30 meeting with HO officials who wanted my ideas on two-tier policing before a submission went to Jack. There was good coverage on Rambo's (David Ramsbotham) critical report on women's prisons. He wanted smaller units on the outskirts of towns. Like me he wanted to break up the Prison Service monolith. I had arranged to see Derek Lewis and Securicor privately outside HO to discuss prison initiatives. Briefing meeting with Jack and officials before he met Alistair Darling (Chief Secretary) on Monday about extra £43million this year and next for prisons. We had the Prison Audit in good shape which we were going to publish despite Treasury objections because it stopped them and No.10 leaving us high and dry on rising prison numbers. TB already twitchy about a statement linking sentencing to rising prison numbers.

Went to Youth Justice Taskforce late where there was good discussion on the roles of Youth Offending Teams (YOTs) and the National Youth Justice Board. I've already told Jack I would like to chair YJB. Scratchy discussion on YJB supervising the performance of youth courts: it was already clear the Magistrates Association and Lord Chancellor's Department would oppose this. Heather Mills of Observer called wanting brief on replacing lay magistrates with more stipendiaries – very timely.

Day ended with the good news that Gerry Adams had called on the IRA to declare a ceasefire. Also, a hilarious submission asking Jack to agree release of papers that included the 1967 Sexual Offences Act; the criminal case file of Lord Alfred Douglas dating from 1924; the conviction of the Wheeldon family for attempting to poison Lloyd George in 1916 and the banning of Radclyffe Hall's lesbian love story 'The Well of Loneliness.' It was a complete mystery why the HO had needed to withhold these papers for so long.

After a weekend being irritated by Derry's claims to be the architect of ECHR incorporation when Jack and I wrote the policy and I positioned it in the legislative programme, we had a real-world meeting with Alistair Darling on the Prison Audit and funding. This went well and I agreed with No.10 we would announce extra money this week and publish the Prison Audit. This cleared way to have a Parliamentary statement on sentencing and criminal justice changes on 30th. Regular meeting with Condon produced the argument I'd predicted that Met had to have 27,000 police officers. Senior cops seem unable to accept that policing was being changed by technology, civilianising posts and private security industry; and that there was plenty of scope for substitutability in policing, just as there was in medicine and law.

We had a tutorial with Derry about the Crime and Disorder Bill which had to provide for Manifesto commitments whatever Derry and his Department thought. Derry was becoming a roadblock we had to manoeuvre around. The Guardian and Times had a leaked version of the HO comprehensive spending review due to be released on Friday with me as the mastermind of the cuts. Despite being marked 'restricted' it had been sent to 90 people, many of whom had photocopied it: there's no security in the HO. Barbara Mills popped in to tell me how well the CPS reorganisation, she opposed, was going: I didn't dare tell her about the two submissions in my in-tray about concerns over CPS handling of deaths in police custody.

22 July saw the publication of the Welsh devolution white paper and no rumpus from Trimble after his meeting with Tony: the decision to return four IRA prisoners to NI went off quietly. I talked to No.10 about Herman Ouseley's Guardian front page remarks on black people losing out in Blair's new Britain. I told them that ethnic minority representation in appointments and honours was not as good as it should be, but the Commission on Race Equality had been difficult to engage with on a Bill to improve the Race Relations Act. CRE's ambivalence was matched by No.10's. Yet another tutorial with Derry, this time on youth justice and his opposition to a detention and training order. The HO had done nothing on this, so I wrote my own proposal for the weekend box.

The big news was TB's announcement of a new consultative Cabinet Committee of 11 with 5 LibDems and serviced by the Cabinet Office: Jack was a member with Blair, Cook, Brown, Prescott and Ann Taylor. This was to "usher in a new era of politics in which parties that agreed with each other should be able to say so and make an input to each other's ideas." Jack was convinced that Tony would not go for much PR at Westminster; but my No.10 sources had been talking about 500 first past the post seats, with the rest PR which would have produced a minute Labour majority in the 1997 Election.

Jack and I settled pre-Recess announcements and I agreed them with No.10. The prison ship had an open day with media. HO still arguing with the Birmingham 6 over their compensation for wrongful conviction in 1991. Went to see Derek Lewis privately at his flat to discuss his and Securicor's ideas for day prisons and using tagging to keep offenders in own homes.

Wall to wall coverage on 23 July for Blair/Ashdown concordat: it took media and Cabinet by surprise. Spent much of day discussing with Jack his statement on reshaping the criminal justice system. Rewrote HO text on community punishment to make it tougher and more coherent and with sections on youth justice and welfare to work. Sent it off to No.10 after another talk with Derry and Jack about squaring Mandelson.

Scottish Devolution White Paper published on 24 July with media casting Jack in role of battling Mel Gibson's Braveheart. Lawrence Inquiry which was to be announced next week leaked to Mail who covered it favourably. It turned out Neville Lawrence worked on Paul Dacre's house; and there were some strange NUS politics at work between Jack and Dacre. Jack's race relations speech to the Black Jewish Forum went down well, especially idea of Racial Advisory Forum. Wrote brief for Jack's meeting next week with Len Peach the Commissioner for Public Appointments bringing out unsatisfactory position on ethnic minorities and women, especially in HO. DPP admitted in court she was wrong not to prosecute two police officers who pinned down Shij Lapite who had 45 injuries with the police unscathed.

I was always going into Jack's office to find him pawing over orange and black folders marked 'Secret' and signing warrants. I now found he had to authorise the arming of foreign protection officers because of our new firearms legislation. We were taking Home Secretary accountability to absurd lengths. Good submission from officials on Irish prisoners. With the peace negotiations we were spending more time on these issues: the way prisoners were treated; their transfer to NI; and now repatriation to Irish Republic where I suspected they would be released early. Wars end with wrangles over prisoners so this might be good news.

The HO comprehensive spending review plans were published on 25 July. Making them happen would occupy much of next 12 months:

187

Jack wanted me to keep a close eye on the prisons/probation review and the probation efficiency review. I gave him a paper on day prisons using tagging, sleeping at home overnight with education and training programmes and behavioural change courses. I knew the HO would oppose it but told him this was a 'big idea' that could be floated at Party Conference.

John Major kicked up merry hell in the HO because it had announced the outcome of an inspection of Huntingdon Life Sciences – an animal experiments company – in his constituency without telling him. Two people were charged with cruelty. HO inspectors would have been within their rights to close the place down but had nowhere to transfer the animals there: 1000 dogs, 10 baboons, 200 marmosets, 450 macaques, 13,000 mice, 35,000 rats, 2000 rabbits, 4,000 guinea pigs, 3000 birds, 4,000 fish and various other creatures undergoing 'scientific procedures.' There was no HO policy for dealing with Noah's Ark.

I spent most of 25 July visiting four divisional police stations in South London. Good discussions on using technology to identify crime 'hotspots' and tracking known criminals. Watched this in use. Many of the prominent offenders were 14-16 years old, with drugs their main business, as I saw from filmed drug sales. Massive increases in domestic violence and big load of convicted paedophiles they were trying to keep track of using photo galleries in stations. Interesting discussion about policing of clubs where 1000 plus young men can be disgorged on to the streets at 2 to 3am. Agreed to discuss with HO charging proprietors for policing, as happened with football matches.

Weekend media go after Barbara Mills and deaths in police custody. Good coverage of Prison Audit and extra money for prisons which would not have happened without our Manifesto commitment. Interesting asylum application from Hong Kong Chinese journalist under threat of snatch by mainland government. Officials raised death penalty as part of ratification process when ECHR legislation passed. We need a debate on death penalty like a hole in the head and I agreed with Jack and Derry that some very long grass should be found.

On Monday (28 July) we met Len Peach about public appointments. I pointed out that magistrates had to declare their political allegiance so that local benches reflected their community; so why should the Major/Nolan definition of political activism be used, particularly as it didn't cover donations. The HO submission on this was hopeless and didn't cover improved gender and race balance: it was what HO would have served up for Howard. Peach was worked over by five Cabinet Ministers but said they needed to discuss this with Nolan. Jack asked me to rewrite HO policy and fix to see Nolan.

Ministerial lunches were good social glue but useless for discussing difficult issues. I agreed with Jack he needed more one-to-one meetings with Ministers to hold them to account. Meeting with officials on immigration and asylum issues was hopeless, with none of their proposals costed. They were sent away to produce a menu of costed proposals for half-day meeting with Jack. Grovelling apology sent to John Major about non-consultation. A furious John Morris (Attorney-General) told Barbara Mills he wanted to be consulted on decisions not to prosecute after deaths in police custody.

The next day ECHR policy was discussed at Cabinet Committee but little support for Bill to include establishment of a Human Rights Commission: we managed to keep open option of a Commission not funded by Government. Jack's evidence to Home Affairs Select Committee went well. I chaired fourth meeting of Youth Justice Taskforce. They supported my paper on new detention and training orders with incentives for early release to community supervision and community staff working with young offenders in custody. This would now to go to Cabinet Committee for legislative approval.

Lord Nolan resistant to changing his definition of political activism at meeting with him. Wonderful HO submission on how a female prisoner who married a male prisoner managed to get pregnant. It turned out that the part-time chaplain left them alone in the vestry. The HO promised that in future "governors would ensure risk assessment procedures would be carried out." I interpreted this to mean condoms would be issued.

Jack's statement on sentencing and community punishment (including tagging) went well on 30th after trailing on Today programme. By one of life's great ironies, we had to ask the Queen to exercise royal prerogative of mercy for all the prisoners Michael Howard released unlawfully. Lord Chancellor's Department insisted on a meeting of the Ministerial Group on Youth Justice to try to restrict the scope of changes in the Crime and Disorder Bill. With support from Alistair Darling, Paul Boateng and Estelle Morris they were seen off.

Up early on 31 July for meeting with Jack and officials who wanted the National Youth Justice Board to be based in HO (in other words neutered) and YOTs to be under probation service control. I got very rough and said Taskforce advice was local authority chief executives should chair a steering group for YOTs and the best candidate should be their manager. I insisted that the YJB should be an independent executive agency reporting direct to Home Secretary. I had agreed all this with Jack before Election and he duly overruled officials. Good coverage for Parliamentary statement on sentencing and community punishment with FT saying this showed prison wasn't working.

Stephen Lawrence Inquiry announced. Lawrences seemed content. Meeting on new definition of crime statistics which would show 20% increase. Agreed new and old stats should be published together for at least a year; and that in future stats should be published twice yearly on fixed dates in April and October so publication date wasn't politically controlled.

August started with a flurry of news before holidays. Labour lost the Uxbridge by-election with 3000 swing against Labour. Tony's intervention did little good and was made worse by No.10's crass decision to impose a candidate instead of the guy who nearly won in May. 31 working Peers announced. Richard Wilson had been made Cabinet Secretary and came to chat: we agreed to lunch after the holidays. Jack asked my views on a replacement and I told him it should not be anyone from a HO background: Richard seemed to have told him the same. Good coverage for the Stephen Lawrence Inquiry with only the Telegraph lukewarm. Barbara Mills criticised by High Court for failing to prosecute four West Midlands police. The end seemed nigh.

Discussed with Jack next steps on an Electoral Commission. Agreed we should slowdown George Howarth on setting up body to consider this and try to make this a topic for the new Lib-Lab Cabinet Committee. Reported my discussions with IPPR and Anthony Lester about foundation/private funded Human Rights Commission, with approving noises from Government but no financial commitment. LibDems won't play and want this to be raised in new Cabinet Committee.

Told Jack that Tony had put him in charge of scoping family policy issues, including parenting, with a small group of junior Ministers. This

190

followed some work I did with Geoff Mulgan at No.10. Told him I would prepare a response to Tony for his return. He left for holiday with prison numbers dropping; HO releasing documents dating from 1876 to 1914 about Irish Political Societies; and replying cautiously to Mo Mowlam about repatriation of Irish prisoners. As part of peace negotiations Mo wanted to downgrade security of some IRA prisoners, have more open visits and temporary release and repatriation of more to NI. The peace negotiations will inevitably mean some risky calls on Irish prisoners, but the English politics of this needed to be remembered.

I went for lunch with Melanie Phillips to brief her on youth justice changes. This was well received but produced a diatribe on why Tony should do more to support marriage. I later fended off a plea for a new definition of obscenity and the leisure industry wanting to amend the Sunday Observance Act 1780. Plenty of scope here for silly season media stories.

The media started examining the performance of the first Labour Government for 18 years. I assembled material for a piece in The Independent. I thought we had done well in the HO, after all the pre-Election talk of an inexperienced Government with few hard-edged policies. Within 3 weeks we had a free vote on a total handgun ban and introduced the Firearms Amendment Bill on 22 May. In the Queen's Speech we committed to a Crime and Disorder Bill in the first Parliamentary session to improve community safety and reform youth justice. We wrote to the Courts in May to press them to speed up dealing with persistent offenders as part of our fast-track pledge. On 8 May Jack announced that all Parliamentary Questions on prisons would be answered by HO Ministers in place of the Howard system of treating them as operational matters to be answered by the Prison Service.

We set up the Taskforce on Youth Justice on 17 June – a new approach to policy development with outside experts working with civil servants. I had chaired 4 meetings by the summer recess and crafted much of the material for a White Paper. The Manifesto pledge of a Prison Audit was published on 25 July revealing a funding situation worse than Howard claimed. We had secured an extra £43 million a year from the Treasury. We'd promoted community punishment as an alternative to prison and announced a range of alternatives including tagging, enhanced supervision, taking away passports and driving licences. We'd enabled young ex-offenders to benefit from the welfare to work initiative.

We had announced more attention and funding for the victims of crime. We set up a new inquiry into the Hillsborough disaster. There was a new Inquiry into the context of the Stephen Lawrence murder and an announcement on 19 May that the Crime and Disorder Bill would have new offences of racial harassment and racially motivated violence. Parts of the Crime Sentences Act were implemented with tougher sentences for repeat sex and violent offenders and drug dealers. We negotiated with the EU legal certainty for frontier controls which the Conservatives had failed to do. On 19 May we committed to legislate in this Parliamentary session to finally incorporate in UK law the ECHR which the UK had largely written in 1945. On 9 June a consultation paper was published on the prevention of corruption in public life, including making bribery of MPs a criminal offence.

On my count we had moved to implement 12 Manifesto pledges in 100 days. This had done much for Jack's standing when four Cabinet colleagues were being tipped for the chop. This progress would not have happened without the preparation before the Election and my pressurising the HO after it.

Death of Diana – August/September

With Jack and Tony away, August was largely political trivia. There were squabbles over who should pay for rescuing the victims of Montserrat's volcano eruptions and pictures of Princess Diana and Dodi Al Fayed on holiday. The firearms lobby wanted more compensation for our handguns ban. The Mail on Sunday published material from David Shayler, a former MI5 employee, alleging waste and communist paranoia in the security services. He revealed who they kept files on and bugged., including Peter Mandelson. (Jack knew they had files on him from his NUS days but seemed unbothered.)

Derry continued sniping about the youth justice changes which simply provoked criticism of him by the Sunday Telegraph. I used the work done by the Youth Justice Taskforce to convince the Ministerial Group that our policy was settled enough for legislation. I gave No.10 a brief for a law and order announcement strongly featuring the youth justice changes. I agreed with them a paper on family policy for the new Ministerial Group.

I was waiting for politics to restart when I woke up on 30 August to learn that Princess Diana and Dodi Al Fayed had been killed in a car crash in Paris, being chased by paparazzi. Tony badged Diana as the 'People's Princess' and No.10 were running the operation of her return to the UK and funeral. All the HO had to do was find a cooperative coroner so that Dodi could be buried as a Muslim within 24 hours.

On 1 September we met David Ramsbotham about his hard-hitting report on YOIs. I wanted to use this to wrest control of YOIs away from the Prison Service but was not getting much support. My fallback position was to make the YJB the purchaser of all secure accommodation for juveniles which had Jack's support. The Prison Service came to see me about deteriorating industrial relations and I agreed to talk to Jack about involving the TUC. No.10 had halted much Government business out of respect for Diana so publicity for Jack's regional tour was cancelled. Cold water was poured on the Welsh Secretary's proposal to make St David's Day a public holiday.

The next day the news broke that Diana's driver was three times over the alcohol limit. I suggested we sent a Met observer, but Jack was not keen. Funeral arrangements were being driven by No.10 who withdrew Jack's invitation – odd as HO had policy responsibility for the monarchy. He asked my advice and I encouraged seeking reconsideration, but this was unsuccessful. St James Park was full of queues to sign a book of condolences. A million people were likely to turn out for her funeral. Government had largely stopped although Mo Mowlam pressed on with reforming NI police to which we gave support. There was no interest in our start of registering released sex offenders that had excited so many recently.

On 4 September I spoke to a conference about our youth justice reforms and had a dust-up with a few academics and disgruntled probation officers who thought them too harsh. The HO Forensic Science Unit sent a team to Paris. The first vision of Diana was seen at St James' Palace. Alistair Campbell wrote an article for the Guardian explaining our injunction on further Shayler revelations because the Mail on Sunday would not let us see his text to check for risks to agents. The ECHR White Paper was agreed by the Cabinet Committee in terms of policy. After editing it would be published in mid-October.

I told Richard Wilson about my work with Derek Lewis and Securicor on pilot schemes for community day prisons and that Jack was positive. We would tag people 12 hours in their own homes and then tag them for 10 hours at a day centre providing intensive education, behavioural and employment training, with some fitness activity. These centres would be run by a not-for-profit community trust with local authority involvement and using short-life premises. There would be a management contract with Securicor for tagging and security at the centre, probably piloted in Manchester first. Richard was positive and I asked him to have this evaluated discreetly without involving the Prison or Probation Services who would leak it and try to kill it. Richard agreed to find a couple of officials.

Came back from long birthday weekend in Paris (9 September) to find normal government resuming. The High Court had upheld our Shayler gagging order. Proposals for transferring decisions on temporary release of Irish prisoners to NI Secretary and Irish Government but No10 trying to argue this is nothing to do with the peace process. This change is inevitable, but I warned Jack that the PM's fingerprints should be all over individual decisions because of future scrutiny. French continued to resist proper document checks at Gare du Nord to stop illegal immigrants boarding Eurostar.

In my paper pile I found a submission on armed perimeter security for prisons, prompted by an off the cuff remark by Jack. This was placed in the context of previous reports on the subject and armed escapes by Irish prisoners. The arguments against had been put fairly but it had been copied widely. If this had leaked it would have damaged the NI peace negotiations and caused general uproar over a proposition which had little support. I had no confidence the Prison Service could train a reliable cadre of staff to run armed perimeter security and that it would take only one trigger-happy prison guard to run amok to finish a Home Secretary's career. I scribbled a note to Jack proposing a rapid burial – which was achieved.

Jim Callaghan had picked up a whiff that the Government might reduce the 30-year rule on release of official papers. I was not surprised. This was the man who had thwarted the Wilson/Castle trades union reforms; failed to call a 1978 Election when ahead in the polls; and pursued an incomes policy against the advice of his Chancellor that produced the winter of discontent and 18 years in the political wilderness. I always thought his reputation for avuncular political wisdom much overrated. I hoped our FOI reforms would deliver earlier access to official papers, which, eventually, they did.

The MoD produced a collector's piece on opening up more Army posts to women with a 7-line gem. "In infantry and armoured units it is the current military judgement that introducing women into predominantly male units and in particular into very small teams forced to spend long periods in close proximity isolated from others, might fundamentally change the relationship between the team members in a way that would materially affect the team's cohesion in battle, so damaging its combat effectiveness." In other words, the boys might start fighting each other over the girls rather than fighting the enemy. I wondered how many drafts this had gone through before Cabinet circulation.

The Scots voted overwhelmingly (75%) for a Scottish Parliament, with nearly two-thirds wanting tax powers. I doubted this would stop calls for independence. An EU survey revealed UK had the worst problems of crime and vandalism which helped with Crime and Disorder Bill. Tony's speech to TUC about modernising or die was upstaged by the Archbishop of Canterbury's speech of support for trade unions' collective ideals. Our stocktake meeting on the Data Protection Bill failed to produce a privacy solution acceptable to both media and European Court of Justice. Fayed acknowledged driver was drunk. Angela Eagle was first Minister to come out as a lesbian. Tony appointed Stewart Sutherland to chair a Royal Commission on Long-term Care which would fail to produce a solution (see Chapter 13). Over weekend read HO staff survey showing racial discrimination, with lack of success at promotion boards. CRE needed to get involved.

Met with Jack on 15 September to discuss parenting and progressing Tony's initiative on family policy. He also agreed my idea of an external sounding board group he'd chair without HO present. I was getting a lot of pro-Judges lobbying from pressure groups as the ECHR debate on Parliamentary sovereignty intensified. The HO had failed to come up with any offensive remarks made by Irish Republicans in the Second World War, but Jack still decided Sinn Fein shouldn't be invited to Cenotaph ceremony. It turned out that HO Ministers had to authorise the use of several hundred animals each year for testing chemical effects of weapons on humans: Gareth Williams drew the short straw.

Broadcasting Standards Commission said two-thirds of adults worried about violence shown on TV and psychologists were reporting children worried by horror/violent images. We needed to find a different chair for the film censor – the BBFC – to the 67year-old Peer the HO were proposing. HO came up with compromise on 17 September of Lord Birkett for two years and appointing two new Vice Presidents. We rejected and fixed another meeting. The first Cabinet committee meeting was held with LibDems. No mention of an independent commission on voting systems but some support for a Human Rights Commission.

Jack was getting credit for a more sympathetic approach to rape victims in courts, with giving evidence behind screens and protection from prurient cross-examination. I discovered there were still over 500 outstanding 1994 asylum applications from Rwanda and Burundi. These people were never going back yet the HO made such a meal over dealing with them because of their obsession with so-called 'pull factors.' Sadly, Jack wrote to Jim Callaghan to tell him his secrets were safe with New Labour.

On 19 September I switched on TV to find that the Welsh had voted 50.3% to 49.7% in favour of a Welsh Assembly, with the Welsh Secretary, Ron Davies, talking about an emphatic victory. Went to Jack's house to work on his Conference speech. We gossiped about whether Alun Michael would be moved to Wales. Favourable coverage in Mail about speech on reforming probation. I left to chair Youth Justice Taskforce where we had a squabble between the magistrates and the justices' clerks about who should be responsible for managing youth courts more efficiently. All agreed that the YOIs needed better regimes and the YJB would need to commission these for the under-18s. ACOP – the probation bosses – were trying to take control of YOTs but I said they wouldn't succeed because I had agreed with Jack that all posts would be filled by open competition.

I had a good meeting on 22 September with Derek Lewis and Securicor on what we were now calling prison without walls. They had obtained a Counsel's opinion on what could be done without new legislation. Prescott was acting as peacemaker on freezing Ministerial pay. Jack took my advice on armed prison perimeter security and noted submission with no follow-up action. I had a meeting with Anna Coote about strong female opposition to Jack's role on family policy but made it clear this was Tony's decision, not Jack's. Yet another meeting on the spending review. Most parties had accepted there was no more money, apart from the police. I suggested the best line for them would be flat budgets with more functions. It looked as though a senior police officer would become drugs czar. Ramsbotham's report on Feltham YOI published on 23 September showed what a mess YOIs are.

Meeting with Condon on 24th about Met's funding in which HO tried to give him hard time but Jack kept to my line of level funding but requiring Met to improve efficiency. We helped Condon with costing Met's national security work; and I raised the issue of their reserves which annoyed officials. Jack briefed on following day's launch of youth justice consultation paper before flight to Cleveland for youth justice workshop and meeting with UK's 'Robocop', Ray Mallon and his zero tolerance of minor crime and disorder. Crime fell in Cleveland when Mallon retired dead wood in CID and concentrated on crime hotspots.

LibDems got very excited about PR at their annual conference. Tony was playing cards on PR very close to his chest while enjoying a 93% approval rating as PM. We were thinking of making it easier to transfer NI prisoners on a permanent basis; but papers on 25th full of Unionists walking out of their historic first meeting with Sinn Fein. Held press conference on youth justice consultation paper in Jack's room. This had not been done before and journos were impressed. They focussed on parenting orders and reparation to victims.

Back down to earth with yet another meeting with Derry on the Crime and Disorder Bill. The correspondence between him and Jack will provide a field day for historians. The papers were full of Derry's decision to take the full Ministerial pay award despite the hair shirt approach of the rest of the Cabinet. Reminded Richard Wilson I needed discreet help with evaluation of mounting material on 'prisons without walls' project.

Interesting visit to LSE with George Howarth to see INFORM computer system on cults and so-called new religious movements. Tories had pulled their grant – only £2000 – but Met and others still used them. I told George that cults continued to be a problem area and we should restore their grant. I still deeply distrusted the scientologists and wished we were more aggressive towards them like the Germans.

26 September produced positive media coverage of youth justice consultation paper. "Straw puts onus on parents to beat child crime." (Times); "Parents ordered back to class in youth crime war." (Telegraph)' "Straw to combat crime-breeding excuse culture." (Guardian). There was a complimentary Times editorial – headed 'Tough and Tender'- about Jack thriving "in the slow development of policy and legislative spadework" away from the limelight. I got a mention in this as the person who had helped him secure a better rapprochement with the civil service than his predecessor. People were noticing our different approach to making public policy.

Spent morning organising next chunk of work for Youth Justice Taskforce and afternoon in the Criminal System Review being chaired by the Treasury. I pushed hard on alignment of boundaries of criminal justice agencies and integrated budgets at regional and local levels. Predictable resistance from the Lord Chancellor's Dept and the Law officers. John Major was still pressing HO about losses of Huntingdon Life Sciences following a Channel 4 programme. A new certificate had been issued but we would not withdraw criticisms.

Trying to preserve the sovereignty of Parliament over any reintroduction of the death penalty was getting us into a terrible tangle on signing an international declaration calling for the abolition of the death penalty. Jack's convoluted proposition to Robin Cook supported the abolition but preserved Parliament's right to a free vote. I remained unconvinced we had to parade Parliamentary sovereignty like this.

Jack off to Party Conference on 29 September after telling Bar Council's annual dinner – chaired by Cherie Booth/Blair – that high fees from the public purse had to end. I read a disgracefully racist speech by the Chief Immigration Officer: sample quotes were Jamaicans are mainly involved in drug dealing, Nigerians and Ghanaians are mainly involved in credit-card fraud and the Irish come here to sponge. I supported complaint by Sussex police about it. Keith Hellawell approved by Tony as Drugs Czar.

Off to Brighton on 30th to hear Tony's triumphalist Conference Speech to the faithful. Little HO mention but he announced the new

Ministerial committee on the family Jack was to chair. Party Conference was never my scene. After a chat with Barbara Castle, I headed home. Back in the HO I found that the Albanian Ambassador and his family and chauffer had applied for asylum but our man in Tirana doubted he would be shot, as claimed. Head-masterly minute from PM telling Ministers how to behave during UK's EU Presidency.

Then back to Brighton on 2 October for Jack's Conference speech in the deathly post-lunch slot. The Ministerial team were all on parade and Tracey and Sharon had come down from Newark to tell Conference how Jack's crime-busting had improved their lives. Big cheers for youth crime changes and doing more for victims but biggest cheer was for ECHR incorporation. Jack got a standing ovation but seemed a bit uncertain how to respond – no armpit salute. Robin Cook who followed said fastest selling item in Conference shop was the 'Tough on crime, tough on the causes of crime' bilious green coffee mug. Did a bit of media briefing and went to Liberty's ECHR debate before sneaking off home.

Focussing on Policy Implementation – October/November

Spent much of 6 October preparing a note disentangling a web of issues concerned with the regulation of content in telecommunications, broadcasting, film, videos and other media industries. Much of this was outside the HO remit with a new regulatory body, OFCOM, in prospect for broadcasting and telecommunications – although even here content was to be hived off to another new body, the Broadcasting Standards Authority. Films and videos (including games) were to remain with the HO. The trouble had started with the BBFC allowing pornographic content in an R18 video that Customs and Excise deemed obscene and illegal. It was clear that the BBFC's Director could not be controlled by its Board.

The Board President post was vacant, and I had continued to advise against appointing the HO candidate, the Vice President, Lord Birkett. The next day we had a meeting with Birkett and another BBFC Board member. They couldn't explain why they had changed BBFC guidelines to allow material in a video Customs and Excise regarded as breaching the Obscenity Act. There were no minutes of meetings or

199

decisions. The Board seemed more concerned about allowing sufficient R18 videos to keep the sex shops in business. My advice not to appoint Birkett was vindicated and Jack decided both should be replaced.

7 October saw another meeting between Jack and Derry about including changes to custodial orders for juveniles in the Crime and Disorder Bill. I had advised Jack not to give ground and the orders stayed in the Bill. The press was full of Paul Condon's speech about "a significant minority" of corrupt officers in the Met. We supported Condon on tackling corrupt police officers at our meeting with him.

David Ramsbotham delivered his thematic study on young offenders on 8 October and it was as hard-hitting as I had encouraged him to be. Discussed with Jack candidates for new HO Permanent Secretary and encouraged him to reject two former HO candidates being pushed by Robin Butler. My advice was the same as Richard Wilson's, that the HO needed an outsider. Jack decided to see the boss of GCHQ. Came across sad letter from father of Rachel Nickell murdered 5 years ago and still awaiting payment from Criminal Injuries Board for his grandson: told officials I wanted a reply dealing with the claim for Jack to send. European Court of Human Rights delivered their ruling on reducing age of consent for gay sex to 16.

10 October spent on Youth Justice Taskforce and how we would implement change. At Strasbourg summit Tony announced date for White Paper on ECHR incorporation.

Much of morning of 13th was spent finding out for No.10 what went on in Rome over weekend between English football fans and Italian police when England drew with Italy. Huge number of complaints about Italian police. Much speculation on whether Tony would shake hands with Gerry Adams when they meet in Belfast.

On 14 October we met with Derry on cost of ECHR implementation, with him trying to get HO to pay for judicial training. I pointed out that his Department would have spent money on judicial training anyway, and it would just have to be spent on ECHR training: Derry was just trying it on. ECHR Bill's introduction was being held up because HO had failed to get Queen's agreement to placing her Prerogative and Interest at the disposal of Parliament. This was in case she refused to consent to the marriage of a descendant of George II under a 1772 Act, thereby denying the person the right to marry under the ECHR.

Briefed Jack on launch of first paper on youth crime reform. Also, on first meeting of the Ministerial Group on Family Policy. My paper had been circulated with its measured approach to marriage rather than the enthusiasm Tony was said to favour. Jack and I met the Prison Service over their so-called management review, an attempt to pre-empt some of the savings required under the spending review. I had briefed Jack to say all their ideas were provisional and they had to find the money for much-needed management training from their own resources. Typically, their IT broke down at the presentation. Jack sent a letter to Lord Birkett with a list of questions and action points following our meeting on 7 September.

The next day we launched in the FCO's Locarno Room the consultation paper on youth justice reform. There was an audience of 300 from press and various agencies. Six Ministers sat there and answered questions and Jack and Derry were matey and made solid speeches. Delegates over lunch told me they had never seen such Ministerial commitment. Much of the press conference was dominated by secure accommodation. The afternoon was taken up with two unproductive meetings: first with LibDems on the concordat; and the second with the Prisons Ombudsman who wanted to extend his remit and investigate suicides despite his underwhelming performance.

On 16 October we had a lively first meeting of the Ministerial Group on the Family punctuated by personal experiences. One Minister described it as an 'Encounter Group.' Lengthy discussion on marriage with Peter Mandelson suggesting we should describe it as an ideal state to which people might aspire. Female Ministers a bit tight-lipped at this point. The majority supported the formulation of Government policy on marriage in my paper. Jack took my advice and set all the junior Ministers to produce topic papers for the next meeting. NAPO had written in to complain about Jack's unparliamentary language of putting a rocket up the backside of uncooperative probation officers. I checked that he had indeed said this both on the BBC and ITN, but he was unrepentant and disinclined to retreat.

The same day Lord Nolan's successor, Patrick Neill, was introduced by No.10 and Jack to the media as the new 'Sleaze-buster.' Neill had a wider remit than Nolan, having been asked by Tony to look at Party funding. Despite this Tony had also said he wanted legislation

201

this session to ban foreign donations and disclose donations over £5000. So, Jack also briefed the media on this, without them seeming to notice the contradiction. I had tried to persuade Jack to open up the issue of public funding for political Parties, without success; and I was hoping Neill might venture into this territory, using the argument that it was the price of democracy.

Jack despatched me to a meeting on the regions to be used for PR in the EU Parliamentary elections with Nick Brown, the Chief Whip, and Labour Party apparatchiks. They all wanted to construct regions that produced Party advantage and Brown had wound up Tony on this. I reminded Brown that in the discussions with the LibDems they had been promised that Government Regions would be used, apart from merging Merseyside with North-Western Region. These were the regions we would be putting in the legislation. There was much huffing and puffing as I found myself in a minority of one. Jack wanted to go to Tony, but I suggested he waited until we saw the Party's alternative.

Chief Press Officers had recently left six Government Departments and decided to do a bit of spin doctoring on their own behalf on 17 October: they had formed the Tumbril Club with a tie and a scarf with a guillotine on them. We had a good relationship with HO Director of Communications, Mike Granatt, who was also conducting a service-wide review of these roles. Politicisation was on everyone's lips, but I suspected competence was as much of an issue. Interestingly No.10 briefed the media on Derry Irvine's shake-up of legal aid which they said they were handling because it was an example of the Government's ability to make hard choices. Nothing to do with Departmental competence of course.

We had suffered a few defeats on the Firearms Bill in the Lords when hereditary Peers turned out in force to vote. One amendment was to allow registered disabled to own small calibre pistols. The idea of wheelchair – bound gunslingers toting firearms caused a few raised eyebrows. This would only hasten Lords reform.

At meetings with the Irish Government on repatriation of terrorist prisoners, they accepted that remission arrangements in Ireland were more generous than in UK and that the integrity of British courts' sentences had to be recognised. They seemed to accept there would be no release in Ireland without consultation with the UK Government.

Some of the first to go would be people involved in high profile bombings. Jack was willing to let the Irish say this issue had been discussed and the UK government was considering the matter. My advice to Jack continued to be not to repatriate anyone without the written approval of Tony.

Weekend media full of stories of Cabinet reshuffle. Handled a call from Kent about hundreds of Slovaks besieging Dover. A film had been shown on Czech TV showing New Labour Britain as a land of milk and honey. Gordon Brown working hard to show how expensive it would be to join European Monetary Union with his spin doctor Charlie Whelan telling media a different story to Alistair Campbell. Result was Brown/Blair split stories.

On 20 October there was an early meeting of the Ministerial Group on youth justice, mainly about our paper on youth court reform. Jack had supported my idea of a panel to which offenders pleading guilty could be referred for an action plan of change for up to a year. This would have the incentive of no conviction if they kept to the plan and didn't reoffend. Much Group support for the idea but strong opposition from Lord Chancellor and Treasury. Jack summed up as support for putting this in the forthcoming White Paper but not including it in this session's Crime and Disorder Bill.

Jack rushed to Paris for meeting with French Interior Minister on lack of immigration controls at entry to Eurostar and at Calais. We were considering action against SNCF for allowing inadequately documented people on their trains. The French answer was armed men in black at Gare du Nord and Calais. We wanted better joint working and liaison officers at Calais and Paris. A new front was opening up with Czechs and Slovaks being allowed to sail to Dover from Calais and my old Kent colleagues being overrun.

I went to see Nick Brown again about regions for the European elections PR system. Party apparatchiks argued over computer systems and wanted to leave this to the Boundary Commission to decide. I kept to Government Regions and after talking to Jack told Nick that these regions would go in the Bill.

Next day Jack announced he had agreed with French a seminar on football hooliganism in Blackburn during UK Presidency to help them prepare for hosting the World Cup. Then a tranche of meetings on the spending review to show officials that Ministers were sticking to an efficiency agenda. This was taking up a lot of time, but I was making progress on a common criminal justice budget: Treasury and HO supported, with Lord Chancellor predictably opposing. Dashed to Canterbury to deliver lecture on youth justice changes. Spoke to police officers from Nottingham sent by their Chief Constable to find out what this inter-agency cooperation was all about because the Home Secretary kept talking about it.

On 22nd we held a big office meeting on the HO budget for 1998/99. You knew there was a lot of infighting because all the top brass turned up. I had briefed Jack privately on danger zones and we did a double act on dubious proposals. We protected research and youth justice pilots, pushed police efficiency and threw out barmy proposals for cutting immigration expenditure given the backlog of cases. HO civil servants only seemed to receive messages if they kept hearing them from Ministers. Had private meeting with Jack to try to soften the custodial provisions for 10 and 11-year-olds. We agreed to keep current proposals based on seriousness of offences and persistence but not implement them. The best I could do.

Held meeting on tagging where we only had two suppliers: Securicor and small new market entrant, Geografix. Danger of big monopoly supplier was considerable; and we needed to make a market. Decided to meet Geografix boss to assess their capacity to expand. Tagging had to be sold as alternative deprivation of liberty to custody for some offenders. Bingham warming to idea of panel of experts advising judiciary on sentencing but nervous about issuing binding guidelines. We now had a relationship with him, without Derry interfering.

Czechs and Slovaks continued pouring in. I thought best option to stem flow would be to impose visa requirements so that ferries liable for any non-visa people they brought in but FCO reluctant. Threatening gypsies with detention caused many to waive asylum claims and return to France which hardly suggested much fear. This would be on agenda for Havel's visit in November. I accompanied Mike O'Brien to see delegation from Kent about Dover's problems with Roma.

Discussion with HO civil servant who had agreed to watch three of the R18 videos whose classification BBFC had approved. In Bat Babe there was the first oral sex scene and penetration in full focus.

In another cunnilingus. Whatever the rights and wrongs, this represented a step like change in BBFC policy, without any liaison with Customs and Excise. Officials reported BBFC chastened and expected changes. Our mauling of Birkett justified.

Report received on dangerous released paedophile Robert Oliver. Probation had assessed him and found him still associating with other paedophiles and "still very dangerous to children." He was being assessed by a forensic psychiatrist in a regional secure unit. Everyone agreed he was dangerous, but he was under no form of post-release licence or restriction. I was clear that we would have to consider reviewable sentences and stronger post-release supervision for people like Oliver.

Held meeting with interest groups on 23 October to brief them on forthcoming ECHR White Paper. I had been reducing their expectations on a Human Rights Commission. Text was duly leaked to FT but no great harm as Jack launched White Paper and Bill the next day. Our title of "Rights Brought Home" had survived. Cabinet committee had agreed FOI legislation would only exempt policy advice if it could be shown that substantial damage would be caused by release. Civil service wanted more restrictive provision.

I had told Jack that Tony wanted a stocktake meeting on criminal justice. We met to agree items for agenda: improving police efficiency; reform of probation service; more work on youth courts; single budget for criminal justice system; and funding for Prison Service. Officials despatched to work up briefing. I left for a few days with Suzanne in New York.

On return on 29 October, I went straight from the airport to a conference on restorative justice where Jack committed the government to RJ in youth justice reforms. Then to HO for first 'Think Tank' lunch where we invited outsiders to give us their views on criminal justice changes. Launch of ECHR White paper and Bill had gone well. Gordon Brown had committed UK in principle to joining single currency if economic circumstances right but not likely to take decision in this Parliament. Tony had not supported visa regime to deal with Czech and Slovak influx, so we cut time for putting case to stay to 5 days. Jack wrote to Cabinet colleagues for agreement to policy on registration and funding of political parties. Briefed Jack for launch of PR for European elections because Tony decided not to do launch.

Started next day with 8am breakfast meeting on reforming youth courts and secured agreement to my scheme for referring first-time guilty pleas to panel for an agreed reform programme which avoided conviction if completed. This would go to other Ministers for agreement. Prevention of Terrorism statement went well, with Jeremy Corbin complimenting Jack on ending exclusion orders. Not sure he realised that the Prevention of Terrorism Act would be renewed next March, with the possibility of a new comprehensive anti- terrorism measure to follow. Left early on 31st for weekend conference at Ditchley Park on preventing youth crime chaired by former Tory HO Minister. This gave me the chance to explain our youth justice reforms to an informed criminal justice audience.

Spent Monday morning (3 November) at Ministerial Awayday focussed on spending review, the agenda for the next year and preliminary thinking about future legislation bids. We would go for bills on criminal justice, immigration and race relations: I argued strongly for race relations. Jack signalled his intention to overhaul probation and integrate it more with the Prison Service; and his commitment to a single criminal justice budget and improving police efficiency. Had useful discussion with officials about progressing my ideas on day prisons and they agreed to produce a draft submission. Briefed Jack with officials for next day meeting of joint committee with LibDems.

Robert Fellowes was trying to use ECHR to develop gagging orders on press over royal household matters: HO officials seemed more sympathetic than I was. Suspected attempts would be made to use FOI discussions to claim more protection for Royals. Press were now claiming ECHR and the new data protection legislation threatened press freedom. Praise from Guardian unusually for allowing Mail on Sunday to publish Shayler's criticisms of MI5. Jack told Irish Government he was repatriating three Irish prisoners.

Meeting next day with Jack and Nick Ross who hosted BBC's Crimewatch programme. Ross wanted to be appointed as a crime prevention supremo. After 30 minutes he was passed to me for an hour in which I listened sympathetically to his ideas without any commitment. Meeting with LibDems discussed ECHR, European elections UK's EU presidency. But independent voting commission was left to a Blair/Ashdown meeting, but it looked as though Roy Jenkins would chair it.

Afternoon of 4th spent on Steering Committee for delivering HO spending review commitments. Pressed reluctant HO for more robust approach to Prison Service and police efficiency; and injected a greater sense of urgency into review of prison health service for which I want Department of Health to be made responsible. Prisoners are citizens and should get NHS treatment like everybody else. Mike Foster's foxhunting ban Bill was published with no Government commitment on Parliamentary time. Commons overturned Lords' amendments to Firearms Bill with 140 majority.

Busy 5 November. Ministerial Group on Youth Justice supported my proposal for youth courts transferring first-time guilty pleas to panel for contract with offender. Lord Chancellor's objections outvoted, so it could be included in White Paper. Then had two-hour discussion with the Administration Group of Prison Service HQ. They were an old-style policy division who confirmed my view that HO needed a new policy capability to advise the Home Secretary on community and custodial policy as a counterweight to the Prison Service operational Leviathan. Told them courts not Prison Service should do sentence calculations.

Enjoyable private lunch on same table as Matthew Paris and Virginia Bottomley. Latter launched an attack that the Government didn't make themselves available to interest groups. I countered with a long list of groups we had consulted before and after Election, most of whom told us Howard and Co. had ignored them and wouldn't even let some of them into the HO. Rest of table thought this was just sour grapes by the dispossessed.

Jack spent most of day in ceremonials: rehearsal for Cenotaph ceremony; police funeral; meeting with Duchess of Kent; and black-tie dinner with Met. I spent rest of it wrestling with Lord Mancroft's determination to install Pronto gambling machines in pubs when they were clearly addictive; and Czech/Slovak arrivals in Dover. We had only returned to Calais a 100 of the over 400 arrivals in last two weeks of October. French using Dublin Convention to be difficult about returns and P&O ferries were not complying with our legal directions to return people direct to Czech Republic and Slovakia. Day ended with

207

good news for UK animals: completion of negotiations with 3 companies to end testing of cosmetic products on animals.

Spent 6 November with George Howarth at Thorn Cross YOI in Warrington. 44 of the 240 inmates were on the High Intensity Programme (HIT) being evaluated along with Colchester YOI (visited on 2 July) as part of the so-called boot camp programme. HIT provided an accredited enhanced thinking course to stop impulsive behaviour; a lot of attention to anger management; and drug awareness. As in Colchester there was daily drill, PE and regular room inspection, with a lot of emphasis on good health and cleanliness. HIT was nearly a third cheaper than the Army, had better outside links and accredited training completions. Youngsters were positive about HIT and less cowed than at Colchester.

Returned for briefing meeting with Jack on Freemasons because Derry trying to back track on commitment for all in criminal justice system, including judges, to declare their membership. I said we must stand firm and tell judges we would legislate if necessary. Officials looked nervous. Papers full of stories of links between Tessa Jowell's husband, David Mills, and Formula 1 lobbying to abort tobacco advertising ban.

On 7 November discussions continued with DETR about who appointed the Met Police Commissioner when there was a London Mayor. Jack unwilling to give up job but I thought we had to give Mayor some say in the appointment. Read summary of report on prisoner who had escaped from Belmarsh High Security Prison. He assumed identity of another prisoner due for release that day and over 4 hours managed to pass through a variety of checks without his identity being detected. He was still at large. It turned out he had escaped before and the prison governor was called Duff.

Jack had decided to appoint David Omand from GCHQ as new HO Permanent Secretary, Robin Butler's preferred candidates didn't meet criteria of HO outsider with credible management experience and being comfortable with new technology. Weekend media carried announcement. Spent Saturday at research conference on crime reduction to help provide an intellectual framework for shifting resources to prevention. Sunday papers covered our initiative to release prisoners to home detention with curfews enforced by tagging.

Week beginning 10 November started with half-day seminar on parenting with Jack and six junior Ministers. This was a Ministerial confidence-building exercise. I had set things up for 30-40 experts to strut their stuff. There was still some Ministerial nervousness about government involvement in parenting but also increasing public support for government playing a role in parenting education and support.

Held office meeting with nervous officials about our ideas for reforming the probation service. I wanted at least a national probation service, probably regionalised and possibly with a new name. They were terrified of merging probation with prison service and had been slow to understand that probation changes were essential if community punishment was to become an acceptable alternative to prison for courts and public. It was made clear to them that there was going to be a prison-probation review. Separately, the immigration service fessed up to the fact that they had 33 Bahraini and 11 Saudi applications for asylum 'stockpiled' at the request of the FCO, some from 1990. They didn't want any Ministerial action and I suspected their submission was so they could say Ministers had been informed.

Jack had to write to colleagues about legislating to prevent frequent draw lotteries in pubs and clubs because Mancroft would not give in without legislation. A former Tory MP was oiling up to senior officials about the wealthy and well-connected investors behind Interlotto who owned Mancroft's Pronto game and how embarrassed they would be if they found themselves at odds with the Government. It was clear to me that they were nervous about losing their investment – allegedly £30 million. Ministers and officials gave no ground. I launched merger of Rainer and RPS in evening with Alun Michael.

The next day Jack announced the new arrangements for setting tariffs for Thompson and Venables of the Jamie Bulger case, following the House of Lords judgement. He had accepted my advice that in setting tariffs in such cases he would listen to independent advice on the development of juveniles, despite HO opposition to such a panel. Media coverage was balanced. Candidates for President of the BBFC were interviewed and it was clear that Andreas Whittam-Smith, first editor of The Independent, would be appointed. At an office meeting it was made clear to officials that we were going to act on a register of Freemasons across the criminal justice system and that included judges.

209

They were nervous about the Lord Chancellor who Jack agreed to speak to.

Much of 12 November was spent at HO meetings on Jack's behalf on YOTs, mentoring, and Parentline funding. I was spending more time acting as his eyes and ears and effectively deciding things. The first bit of the jigsaw on tagging was put in place with an announcement of the success of the trials in Manchester and Norfolk, with more in the pipeline for early prison release. I wanted a bolder announcement on the research and the new Home Detention Curfew, but Jack and officials were more cautious. I thought we needed to be much more bullish on alternatives to prison if we were to change sentencing behaviour. Progressing day prisons was proving hard work, with the HO and Prison Service very opposed.

Interesting meetings with Condon and about a new Met Deputy. Finding good candidates had been a struggle; and I thought John Stevens was by far the best. Also struggling on FOI, with civil service digging in about release of policy advice. Jack told officials he was content to give reasons for refusal of British citizenship applications which would scupper Al Fayed's appeal to House of Lords about his citizenship rejection. Officials in a bit of a state.

Coverage of yesterday's tagging announcements was positive. By a lucky coincidence Bingham made a speech to judges and magistrates telling them not to hand out prison sentences unnecessarily. Brazilian high court has rejected our extradition request for Ronnie Biggs – at least we tried. Alun Michael and I met private security industry about regulation. Alun wanted a quango but that needed legislation, not easily available. I tried to persuade him to give a bigger role to police but he's not keen. I needed to get Jack more involved before this unregulated and growing industry had a scandal.

Meeting with junior HO and Health Ministers and officials about personality disordered offenders on 13 November. Health officials very reluctant to act but Paul Boateng could see the serious public safety issues. Officials sent away to work on defining conditions to be captured and how court's sentencing powers needed reshaping so that release and supervision could be conditioned by the danger to the public that an individual represented. I thought these people would need specialist assessment at a residential centre but DH officials very

210

nervous about being drawn into HO orbit. It was clear that for this issue and for prison health services and mentally disordered offenders HO and Health needed to work more closely. But both lots of officials preferred staying in their own silos. I had told Richard Wilson that these issues needed to be settled as a package between the two departments.

Started 14 November with good meeting with Jack on tagging and home detention curfew. Agreed it should be announced in Parliament the following week. After risk assessment this allowed early prison release of 3000 to 4000 prisoners a year. Political nervousness about being soft on crime but we had to be bolder on community punishment. Czech and Slovak gypsies descended on Westminster to protest over being denied asylum. We were poor at separating out economic migrants from genuine asylum seekers. Joel Barnett came out against his own 1970s funding formula that favoured the Scots.

The row over Bernie Ecclestone's £1 million donation to Labour before the Election had rumbled on for weeks, with unconvincing denials this had anything to do with Tessa Jowell aborting the ban on cigarette advertising at Formula One events. This complicated our legislation on funding political parties. We were proceeding with a Bill to prevent foreign donations and to make public all donations over £5000, even though Tony had also asked the Committee on Standards in Public Life to consider the issue. Ecclestone had made things worse, first by saying he'd offered another million after the Election – which fortunately had been rejected. He was now asking if he could have his £1million back. Finally, over the weekend Tony apologised on TV for his handling of the Formula One issue and admitted it was a blunder. At the same time, he said he might meet Gerry Adams before Christmas. I thought there were too many wealthy, untrustworthy characters congregating around Tony and too few people telling him to keep away from them.

After a meeting to protect the HO research budget on 17 November, we briefed Jack for his meeting with Tony on reforms to the criminal justice system and their funding, especially community punishments. Also briefed him for our meeting with Tony on the draft paper on family policy I had sent No.10. The case for extradition of Roisin McAliskey was dragging on but thankfully officials had followed my

211

advice and transferred her to the Maudsley Hospital where the care would be better than in prison.

Evening spent in seminar with review team on asylum system who seemed keen on establishing a network of reception centres. I was sceptical that this would speed up decision-making. Then I learned of the massacre of 70 tourists at Luxor's Hatshepsut's Temple which Suzanne and I had visited earlier in the year. We abandoned plans to visit Egypt that winter.

18 November began with George Howarth and I visiting a Lewisham citizenship project for 10/11year-olds – danger of drugs, keeping off railway tracks, how to make 999 calls and other aspects of C20th urban reality. Then lunch with No.10 colleagues about establishing a Social Exclusion Unit. Encouraged them to go for limited number of measurable changes and put a Minister in charge who'd make something happen. Legal status of transsexuals was bobbing about in government with No.10 nervousness. Review looking increasingly likely.

Good meeting with Tony and Jack on family policy. Blair still looking for a big idea but was thankfully cautious about promoting marriage, with my neutral wording seeming acceptable. He liked what he called the 'soft stuff' like parenting education and support. We encouraged him to engage more with Gordon on tax and benefit issues which produced rueful smiles. But he agreed he and Jack needed a private meeting with Gordon. Tony didn't want to commit to a Green Paper yet but was content for Ministerial Group to work up a further report. Later had a drink with Pat Hollis to discuss withdrawal of child benefit for non-school attendance. I agreed this not a good idea and would try to convince Jack.

Went to Birmingham on 19 November to deliver keynote speech on youth justice changes at NACRO conference. Went down well apart from tiff over my description of government policy as 'colour blind.' Speech given piquancy by publication same day of Bill Utting's report on children in care ('People like Us') in which he recommended the application to all institutions looking after children of my 1992 report 'Choosing with Care.' Returned to HO for stocktake meeting with Jack on Crime and Disorder Bill: everything was up to speed.

The Barbara Mills saga continued with her roasting at the Home Affairs Select Committee. It emerged that the CPS hadn't secured a single police conviction in any miscarriage of justice cases. The Attorney General had decided that the public interest would not be served by prosecuting Chris Patten for breaches of the Official Secrets Act in his book, "The Last Governor." I told Jack that after this he could hardly prosecute David Shayler. He decided to set the tariffs at whole life for the four Irish terrorist prisoners (the Balcombe Street gang) convicted of six murders in 1977. If he hadn't, he would be vulnerable to judicial review by other lifers like Myra Hindley who was already trying to mount a challenge.

20 November started with 8am meeting of Ministerial Group on Family Policy. Jack was late which provided time for much mirth about the Duke of Edinburgh's remarks on his success as a parent when praising his children for having done "rather well in very difficult circumstances." Lots of plaudits for health visitors and support for doing more on parenting education and support. DTI very nervous about family-friendly employment policies and more generous parental leave. We now had enough material for strong report to Tony aimed at working towards a Green Paper on Family Policy.

Media full of Utting's report that children in care still being abused and Rambo's highly critical report on YOIs. Prison Service now said they wanted to separate under-18s from YOIs. This helped my policy push to separate them completely, with the YJB commissioning all juvenile secure facilities. Jack made statement on home detention curfews which would release up to 6,000 tagged prisoners two-months early after risk assessment. I wanted this extended to 3 or 4 months later. Statement went well and in media next day. Another Friday was spent grinding through HO submissions looking for political booby traps.

Good start to week of 24th with FT article on how Jack was moving crime and punishment away from Tory senseless crusade to fill prisons. We were top for oral questions but there was little nervousness among Ministerial team because Mawhinney and the Shadow team were hopeless. Our lot were hardly Parliamentary giants, but they looked it compared to the Opposition. Jack had introductory meeting with David Omand, the new Permanent Secretary who wanted to have lunch with me asap.

Preparatory meeting on European Elections Bill which was straightforward apart from the unresolved issue of whether the lists of candidates should be open or closed. The Labour Party's apparatchiks all wanted closed lists so they could control existing MEPs. I suspected the LibDems would move amendments for open lists to give voters some say on individual candidates. We agreed to publish a consultation paper. Political journalists were more concerned about Humphrey, the missing No.10 cat, than the Chancellor's warnings of a tough budget. They seemed worried that Cherie Blair had bumped him off, Humphrey not Gordon.

Meeting with Joyce Quin and Prison Service on prison suicides which had increased to 64 in past year. I thought the Prison Service were rather complacent so flourished possibility of Prison Ombudsman investigating all suicides with published reports. A wake-up call for more work on this. Jack announced using Crime and Disorder Bill to set up panel to advise Court of Appeal on sentencing which produced a surprisingly muted response.

25 November was Budget Day. Corporation tax cut and advance corporation tax abolished; £300 million for a 5-year childcare plan to help a million children; and cold weather payments for pensioners, plus homilies on pay and public expenditure restraints. Commons emptied after Budget when Jack moved Second Reading of European Elections Bill.

Spent time with Nottingham MPs and local agencies discussing the youth justice changes and whether their areas could be pilots for the YOT system. These changes were attracting a lot of local interest and support. This was a lot more productive than British football hooliganism and the World Cup in France which was causing much angst in No.10. It was too late for legislation to restrict potential troublemakers travelling abroad and few restriction orders had been used. We were relying a lot on joint police seminars with French and other Europeans. Sent No.10 unconvincing minute that we had everything under control.

Jack had tried to help transsexuals by letting them have free birth certificates in their new approved gender. All this had done was to unleash a full-scale Whitehall review, fortunately not public. The road to hell is paved with good intentions.

Next day started with briefing Jack on Cabinet Committee on FOI White Paper. This was getting into a tangled mess over security and defence issues and the relationship of a confidentiality classification to the Official Secrets Act. I could see Tony changing the Minister responsible for this and it being moved to HO. Foxhunting Bill would take place on Friday with George Howarth drawing the short straw of HO Minister in attendance amidst growing political hysteria. Carefully crafted wording for him to use if massive vote in favour to the effect that amendments could possibly be moved to a suitable Government Bill.

Briefing meeting at No.10 on Ministerial Group on Family Policy followed by Ministerial meeting. Got them to agree a non-judgemental passage on marriage that I hoped would pass muster with Tony. Pat Hollis and I scotched the idea of stopping child benefit for school absenteeism: I explained that the Child Benefit Centre could end up stopping the benefit when a child had returned to school. Basis of a Green Paper could now be put to Tony.

Day ended with discussion with Jack about Freemasons. Derry did not want to compel judges to register and there were difficulties over compelling police officers to register because of existing contracts. The Masons were becoming stroppy, and the press was forecasting a Straw climbdown. I thought we had to stand firm. We agreed that Jack would write to Derry proposing a voluntary register for existing judges, but compulsory one for new judges. A similar approach would be used for police, prison staff and probation officers. But legislation would be held in reserve for non-compliance.

27 November was my big day with the launch of the White Paper on youth justice reform – "No More Excuses." This was the culmination of 18 months' work as I had written the first policy paper in March 1996. The statement to the House went well with lots of cross-party support. Tony showed full support by going with Jack to the Dalston youth project to mark publication and being late for Cabinet because of the traffic.

The Mountfield Report was published on the alleged politicisation of the Government Information Service. It found that the real issue was getting policy civil servants to be more aware of presentation issues. Mike Granatt as Head of GIS had spent a lot of time away from the HO on this issue. Alistair Campbell was now given the grand title of the "Prime Minister's Official Spokesman." As such he now seemed to be saying categorically no Government time would be found for a

215

Foxhunting Bill. A real tangle on the treatment of civil service policy advice developed at the Cabinet committee on the FOI Bill. Tony, Derry and Mandelson all seemed to be arguing different positions, with one option meaning that even papers marked 'confidential' might have to be released.

The next day, Friday, revealed excellent coverage of the White Paper. "Sweeping youth justice reform" (FT); "Straw goes to war on crime by young" (Guardian); and "Carrot and stick approach to youth crime" (Independent). We had won the public argument and now had to deliver change. Jack had asked to see a week's diaries of ten probation officers across the country to see how they spent their time. The free vote on the Foxhunting Bill produced a 260 majority for banning foxhunting. I realised Jack would have to change his tune on foxes as Suzanne and I enjoyed the musical Chicago.

A Not So Merry Christmas – December

I began December with my regular informal meeting with immigration interest groups. Also managed to agree my personal contract with HO seven months after being in post. Story had leaked of Derry wrongly advising that the Press Complaints Commission would be unaffected by Human Rights Bill. Undeterred he had given interview to Times comparing himself to Cardinal Wolsey, rather forgetting what happened to Wolsey. Predictable press hilarity and lobbying for Press Complaints Commission not to be treated as a public body. Tony finally decided not to give government time to Foxhunting Bill and announced establishment of Jenkins Commission on Electoral Reform.

Meeting on 2 December about mentally disordered offenders. Hard work getting health to accept public protection issues and securing a more rational allocation of responsibility between HO and DH. Briefed Jack for our meeting with the All-Party Parliamentary Group on Parenting. Meeting on Party Funding Bill revealed how difficult it was to define foreign contributions and what a nightmare this was for Northern Ireland parties where making public contributions would cause them to dry up. Jack wrote next day to Tony proposing simplifying the Bill on funding and leaving the detail on this to Patrick Neill's Committee on Standards in Public Life.

Modest coverage for our announcement of more money in 1998/99 for extra 600 police: good news is no news. We had a good lunch discussion on criminal justice with think tank outsiders. Jack is unusual among Ministers in exposing himself to alternative and critical views. Tedious meeting with No.10 on European Elections Bill and their obsession with closed lists that they control: we remained sceptical. Met with Jack to counsel against accepting HO advice to decant from Queen Anne's Gate and move temporarily to Marsham Street, refurbished at great expense. I suggested cheaper partial decant and phased upgrade of QAG. Gordon announced membership of Diana Memorial Committee he was to chair. So her legacy was to be in Treasury hands.

On 3 December we published the Crime and Disorder Bill with its raft of new orders: anti-social behaviour; sex offenders, lasting up to 5 years; parenting orders; child safety orders for out of control under-10s, along with curfew restrictions. It also introduced racially aggravated offences; drug testing and treatment orders for addicts over 16; and introduced up to 10-year supervision orders for sex and violent criminals leaving prison. There was early release from prison under curfews enforced by electronic tags for up to 6000 prisoners.

A large part of the Bill provided for our youth justice reforms with a single aim of preventing children offending. It also provided for time limits to halve the time taken by courts to deal with young offenders and for police final warnings and reparations for victims. The architecture for the youth reforms of a Youth Justice Board and local YOTs was provided for. The following day I went to Hertfordshire County Council to discuss their plans for implementing the youth justice reforms.

8 December was the last day before Jack went to Washington for G8 meeting on organised crime. Lots of tidying up. Letter sent to PM saying Royal Household should not be listed as a public body covered by FOI legislation in forthcoming White Paper. Letter to Derry that Scotland Bill should prohibit legislation on referendums that did not specifically relate to a devolved matter: in other words no referendum on independence. Regular meeting with Met Commissioner was concerned with police corruption and Police Complaints Authority's report criticising Met handling of the Stephen Lawrence case. Tony had commissioned work under Mandelson's direction for production of

Government's First Annual Report around Easter. He also launched the Social Exclusion Unit based in the Cabinet Office and with a network of Ministers supervising it.

Quiet couple of days catching up with people and paper in Jack's absence. Sadly, Joe Ashton's 10-minute Rule Bill amending 1961 Suicide Act to permit assisted dying was defeated on 10 December by 234 to 89. Tony approved the appointment of Gary Hart, an Islington solicitor, as Derry's special adviser/minder. He also shook hands with Gerry Adams and Martin McGuiness at the meeting in the Cabinet Room where an IRA rocket had been fired in John Major's time – as Mo Mowlam reminded everybody in colourful language.

Jack returned on 11th when HO was first order for oral questions which went off smoothly. He chaired a productive meeting of Ministerial Group on Family Policy. We agreed a progress report to go to Tony before Christmas. But were still some way from a Green Paper. This meeting coincided with the humiliating defeat of Government's proposed cut in lone parents' benefit by 457 to 107.

I started week of 15 December with a meeting at No.10 to update them on our efforts to improve the Immigration Service's performance on asylum claims, an uphill task. This was followed by a meeting with Ian Blair, Chief Constable of Surrey about the interface between public and private policing. There was the usual collection of weekend leaks: Andreas Whittam Smith to be the BBFC President; and the PCA report on the Met's screw up of the Stephen Lawrence investigation. More significant was the problem of accommodating a dangerous paedophile released from prison and now housed in a police cell costing £25,000 every two months. The psychiatrists had ruled he was unsuitable for Rampton special hospital and was evil rather than mad. It took us another two weeks to house him with 24-hour security, costing £65,000 a year. Department of Health were of no help.

Briefing meeting for session with No.10 on privacy and the Data Protection Bill.: they had suddenly woken up to the fact the Bill was about to go into the House of Lords. I cleared the Second Reading speech for Gareth Williams to use the next day for introducing the Crime and Disorder Bill, again in the Lords. Day ended with first two Christmas parties.

Morning of 16th spent in HO Steering Group to ensure our efficiency agenda was being progressed. Meeting with Joyce Quin and officials on improving quality of probation officer training. LCJ concerned about media driving longer sentences. Conciliatory letter sent to Bingham telling him about HO research on this we had now agreed to publish in January. Brian Mawhinney on warpath about prostitutes' cards in phone boxes. This was a genuine problem in Westminster where there was clearly a market. HO had overlooked a letter on this from Westminster Council. Soothing letters sent to Mawhinney and HO set to work on using criminal law to prosecute 'carders.'.

Pre-Christmas release of six IRA prisoners was being sought by the Irish Government. But they needed to change their law which capped at 20 years the sentences for the offences concerned. They agreed to do this and give assurances that repatriated prisoners would complete UK sentences. A nervous No. 10 had to agree and didn't want the likely media backlash before Christmas. Our proposal was to tell prisoners of repatriation before Christmas, but to delay a move to New Year. Irregular financial regulation in the Channel Islands and Isle of Man were causing concern, in US as well as UK. More Christmas parties.

Next day I attended a meeting of the Crime Prevention Board which Jack and Alun Michael wanted to use to drive the crime prevention agenda through better police and local government cooperation and more engagement with the voluntary sector. Difficult conversation with Nick Ross about whether we are going to give him a crime prevention role – prevaricated, not terribly well. Lunch with Crime Concern. Patrick Neill wrote to say he was launching today his consultation on funding of political parties. He drew attention to the fact this was bound to overlap with our Bill so we might want to remove funding aspects from it. No surprise there given the No.10 muddle. Another Christmas reception.

18 December brought a letter from Irish Government telling us that the legislative changes for repatriation had been made and giving assurances on no diminution of UK sentences. Unfortunately, the Irish Prime Minister announced the same day the early release of nine other IRA terrorists on condition of no more IRA involvement. This was to help the peace process but inevitably inflamed the media. After a lot of back and forth between us and Dublin and No.10 we decided not to compress the usual timescale for repatriation – usually about two weeks – and repatriate in New Year. Dublin was not pleased.

We announced Andreas Whittam Smith as the new BBFC President who immediately established a review of the guidelines for judging films, videos and games and their impact on children. Donald Dewar published the Scotland Bill and the SNP duly focused on Westminster's retention of powers. The LCJ sitting in the Divisional Court rejected Myra Hindley's appeal against Jack's decision that the Moors murderer should die in prison. More Christmas parties.

Friday was taken up with the Cross-Departmental Review of the criminal justice system that I sat on as Jack's representative. Much Departmental protectionism. Weekend papers full of Tony's announcement of the Cabinet Committee on Lords Reform to be chaired by Derry with Jack as a member. The Manifesto commitment was limited to removing the speaking and voting rights of hereditary peers. But some Minsters wanted wider reform while some leading Peers wanted to retain 100 hereditary Peers. The scene was set for a major bust-up.

On 23 December a story broke in the Mirror of a Cabinet Minster's son caught drug dealing. Nobody named the Minister or son because he was too young to be identified in a court case. A tough new Press Complaints Commission code of practice was also about to come into force banning stories about the children of famous people, unless in the public interest. Two female Mirror reporters, pretending to be trainee estate agents, had taped a conversation with the son in a Clapham pub. The son allegedly offered to get £10 of cannabis resin from a friend and shortly after handed over a plastic bag saying it was good strong hash. A lab test confirmed the reporters had bought about two grammes of cannabis resin. The son was said to have gone to a police station, confessed, been arrested and then released on police bail.

The Cabinet Minister remained anonymous. Tony said on Christmas Day there was no question of the Minister resigning. I was down in our Welsh cottage, as a legal battle ensued over whether the Minister and son could be named without being in contempt of court. The plot thickened when a Mirror reporter went to a police station on 29 December, handed over the plastic bag and was promptly arrested and released without charge. On 30th the Attorney-General secured an injunction preventing the naming of the son. I had my suspicions, which were soon confirmed. On New Year's Eve Jack was named on the internet; the next day in a French newspaper; and on 2 January in the Scottish Daily Mail because the injunction did not extend to Scotland. I rushed back from Wales to be with Jack at his HO press conference late on Friday when he explained what had happened. It was clear that the Mirror's editor had told him before Christmas about the 'sting' and a couple of days later he had gone with his son to a local police station where William made a statement.

At the press conference Jack was frank, made it clear he still opposed the legalisation of cannabis and that he had not contemplated resigning. The PM had given him his full support. The subsequent press coverage made little criticism of the way he had handled his son or his own conduct and was mostly sympathetic. A Daily Telegraph Gallup poll showed that 82% thought he had handled the situation with his son very or fairly well. 69% thought he was doing a good job as Home Secretary, with only 15% dissenting. The CPS decided there was insufficient evidence to prosecute; and William was cautioned on 12 January.

Debate continued for a while about legalisation of cannabis but there was no political outcry for Jack to resign. Tony emphasised how well Jack had handled the situation. Jack effectively terminated public discussion with a short press notice on 12 January saying William was learning lessons from the episode and thanking the media for their restraint.

7. Consigliere (Part 2): Home Office Life – 1998

The Third Way – January/February

I kept no diary after January 1998. This chapter is based on daily calendars and personal papers. When I returned to the HO on 5 January normal business was resumed with a meeting with Met Police Commissioner. Unfortunately, the FT had carried a briefing on family policy given before the William episode with the headline 'Straw plans classes in parenthood.' The seven IRA prisoners were repatriated to Northern Ireland without fuss. We even told No.10 that we didn't agree with Mo Mowlam that time spent by an IRA prisoner in a foreign jail awaiting extradition should have the time deducted from their sentence. I spent much of 9 January with those handling asylum seeker claims and with the Prison Service discussing their business plans.

On 12 January we had the normal Ministerial lunch and my weekly meeting with Jack. The following day we met the Audit Commission to discuss their critical report on police performance. At the time I was developing a standardised system for measuring performance at borough commander level, with the information to be made public. I was also discussing with the HO research unit how we could measure police value for money. These projects would improve police accountability and public knowledge but I began to realise I had few supporters for them, either officially or politically.

I went to yet another meeting of the inter-departmental group trying to streamline the criminal justice system. I met David Omand to settle the structure of an Immigration Awayday we would hold in February. No Government time would be made available for the Foxhunting Bill after all; and if it was filibustered in the Lords that could be dealt with by the using the Parliament Act. Finally, a clear decision.

Much of 14 January was spent writing a speech on youth justice reform for Gareth Williams to give to Labour lawyers, as civil servants weren't allowed to do it. Then a meeting with David Omand on developing a standards' programme for the prison and probation services. Tony had agreed a review of financial regulation in the

Channel Islands and Isle of Man. Terms of reference, person to do it and announcement were all settled. Exposing money laundering this close to home would not be popular. Andreas Whittam Smith wrote showing he had got the bit between his teeth and was sorting out the chaotic processes of the BBFC. He was warming up to removing the Director.

15 January started with meeting Patrick Neill who made it clear he was going to deal with funding political parties in his own way and time. I prepared for the all-day meeting of the Youth Justice Taskforce the following day. My papers for the rest of January have been lost but much of this period was spent preparing for Tony's visit to Washington in February. Blair had forged a strong personal relationship with Bill Clinton, now in his second term. They had both presented themselves as pursuing a political 'Third Way' between market-driven economic laissez-faire and left-wing socialist collectivism.

Reforms of unconditional welfare payments and being tough on crime and its causes were features of their policy approaches. Clinton had been much tougher than Tony on crime, with his misguided 'three strikes and you are out' sentencing policy that had driven up the US prison population. The Clinton welfare to work programme was harsher than New Labour's welfare reforms and reflected America's strong commitment to individualism. Tony's strong personal faith seemed to me to place him much more in the communitarian camp whereby individuals were more moulded by community norms than individualism. This was much more consistent with Labour's historical collectivism and helped challenge the Thatcher nostrum that there was no such thing as society. At the time and still, I thought the Blairites were struggling to convert the 'Third Way' from a slogan to a coherent political philosophy.

Tony had hosted a 'Third Way' event with the Clintons in the UK and Clinton wanted to reciprocate at a Washington event planned for 4-7 February. This was to be a political event without civil servants. It was organised by David Miliband and Sidney Blumenthal, Clinton's special adviser and a former journalist. Being on the plane with Tony was a 'must have' New Labour ticket and I had no expectations of getting one. To my surprise, not only did I end up on Concorde with Jack and Tony, but I was to attend the seminar with Clinton.

I spent the morning of 4 February with Jack at a criminal justice seminar before we flew to Andrews Air Force Base where we landed on the wrong part of the base. Eventually the welcoming party found us; and a motorcade took 16 of us to Blair House, the President's guest house opposite the White House. Jack and I left for a dinner at the British Embassy with senior US criminal justice personnel where I exercised restraint about the insanity of Clinton's three strikes prison policy.

The next day for me started with Tony's breakfast meeting with the Congressional Irish Lobby. This was to give them an update on the peace process. It was also for Tony to discourage them from fundraising for the IRA who we saw as terrorists, but some Democrat politicians regarded as freedom fighters. We went to the welcoming ceremony at the White House followed by lunch with the Deputy National Security Adviser. Jack and I then went to Baltimore and at City Hall had an interesting discussion on juvenile justice with some judges. My sense was that too many US youngsters ended up in the courts and custody who would have been given a police caution or community sentence in the UK. We then went to see a Baltimore preventative community project run by the City's police. I wasn't invited to the black-tie official dinner so a few of us explored DC which I knew well.

During this period all hell was being let loose by the US media on Clinton's alleged relationship with Monica Lewinsky. This was the front-page news in the Washington Post on 6 February with Tony's visit on page 18. It dominated the Clinton-Blair press conference. After Tony and Jack's breakfast with Al Gore, Jack and I went off to Capitol Hill for a short tour and a meeting with Minority staff on the work of the Judiciary Committee. More interesting was the lunch at the Justice Department with Janet Reno, the Attorney General, and her staff. She had a special interest in juvenile justice and prevention, so we had a good discussion about our youth justice changes. She seemed to me Clinton's liberal conscience.

The afternoon was devoted to the 'Third Way' seminar in a large blue and gold upper room in the White House. This was scheduled to last four hours with a three-part agenda: the new economy; one nation/ one America; and the Third Way – defining a new social majority. I had no idea what would happen given what was going on in the media and that Hilary Clinton was a participant. The event was set up as a square with Clinton and Jack facing Tony, flanked by Hilary and Al Gore. There were 11 Americans and 9 Brits with some of each around the table and lesser mortals like me off to the side by a large window with a magnificent view of the Washington and Jefferson Monuments.

The strongest voices on the British side were Tony and Gavin Davies of Goldman Sachs; and on the US side, were the Clintons, Larry Summers, Assistant Secretary at the Treasury and Andrew Cuomo, Secretary of Housing and Urban Development. Gore looked a little over-awed by the occasion; and perhaps this was a foretaste of why he lost to George Bush in the 2000 Election. Everybody round the table recognised that globalisation and new technology were going to change society dramatically. There was much common ground on the social problems of loss of jobs for manual labour, the job destruction of technology and growing inequality in society. There was agreement on the need for investment in education and upskilling the workforce, with more family friendly workplaces.

What was lacking for the most part in this seminar was any coherent centre-left economic solutions that could be delivered without big budget deficits. My notes from the time show that it was only Gavyn Davies who mapped out a programme to tackle these problems: expand in-work welfare; design a minimum income guarantee (negative income tax); subsidise low paid jobs; stem the flow of unskilled workers with education and training programmes; tighten eligibility and time-limits for benefits. Politicians would have to accept that such a programme would not save money initially and explain this to the electorate. This was not a ball anybody seemed keen to run with.

Before the seminar I had been wandering around the White House with one of Jack's protection officers. We were stopped by two Secret Service agents who after checking our passes asked the protection officer if he was carrying a weapon and if it was loaded. When he said yes to both, they looked a bit non-plussed but let us go on our way. In a David Baldacci thriller, I thought we would have been wrestled to the ground. After a farewell dinner in Blair House, it was home next day on Concorde. The journalists on board were more interested in Tony's views on what Clinton got up to with Lewinski than with the Third Way seminar. Tony was suitably Delphic.

Routine Government – February/March

It was back to normal on 9 February with a Ministerial Awayday. This was more of a stocktake than consideration of new initiatives. We discussed a Home Affairs Select Committee report on police discipline and complaints. Tony had accepted our advice that we should use Parliamentary Counsel to technically improve the Foxhunting Bill without showing any support for it. A modest Green Paper was launched on local government reform, with elected mayors, weekend elections, polling stations in shopping centres and more Cabinet-style governance. I was disappointed by its absence of anything on reducing the number of local authorities or English devolution using city regions or regional assemblies. A missed opportunity in my view.

The weekend had further stories of a Straw-Irvine feud. Derry had fed the media a story about him taking over a new super-Ministry in charge of criminal justice and courts. He had also antagonised everybody by giving an interview saying there was to be a new privacy law to gag the press on private life revelations. This had produced rebuttal from Tony and Jack in Washington and from Robin Cook who said he had not complained about press coverage of his private life. The press wanted Tony to slap down Derry. Jack and Gareth were briefed for a meeting with Tony on privacy and the forthcoming passage of the Human Rights Bill in the Lords when this issue would be raised.

Tuesday morning was spent at the Cross-Departmental Review of the criminal justice system. Progress was slow with departmental protectionism well to the fore. I had a meeting with the Cabinet Office about Tony's response to the report on family policy sent him in December. He had engaged with the issue and set out three principles: the family as an essential unit of social stability; modern families continually evolving as women gained a more equal position; and Government's primary concern being the stability of relationships where children were involved. He set out what he saw as the main elements of a modern family policy and some specific policy proposals he wanted worked up. We discussed Tony's structure and the detailed policies that now needed work across Whitehall.

11 February started with a Parenting Education and Support Conference where Jack delivered a speech I'd written. Met with Jack and his private secretary to discuss future speeches and his role as a

government big hitter on wider policy issues outside the HO brief such as family policy, welfare reform or rights and responsibilities. He also needed to make more visits outside London. We were trying to establish whether Jack really wanted to expand his remit and how he wanted to spend his time. Later that day there were meetings with the Drugs Czar, Keith Hellawell; discussion of future prisons and probation policy; and briefing for the Cabinet Committee on Lords Reform.

Jack and I had been concerned for some time at the lack of a talent pool for Chief Constable appointments, particularly with several of them suspended for various misdemeanours. He had asked me to discuss this with the head of HMIC who acted as a talent scout and tried to ensure that those with potential had the right job experience. David O'Dowd had confirmed we were right to be concerned about the shrinking talent pool. As a result, on 12 May I went to North Yorkshire to join John Stevens of HMIC on his inspection of that police force.

This was ostensibly because of my role in trying to improve police efficiency but I also wanted to see John in action. It was clear to me that he was a potential Met Commissioner, a job likely to fall vacant soon. I sat in on all the meetings and saw how John pushed his senior colleagues without losing their respect. It was interesting to see how police forces disliked criticism by their peers and took more notice of that than directions from the HO. There was little doubt in my mind that John was a strong leader who could also handle politicians.

Suzanne and I celebrated our wedding anniversary with Jack and Alice. Jack had been at Heathrow negotiating with Lord Wakeham, Chairman of the Press Complaints Commission (PCC) an amendment to the Human Rights Bill to protect press freedom before Monday's Second Reading in the Commons.

The weekend media had stories on whether we would axe juries for fraud trials; and Jack ruling out another Hillsborough inquiry. There was a thoughtful article by Peter Riddell about the possible impact of Lords reform on the House of Commons. The broadsheets were preoccupied with the Human Rights Bill and privacy. Thanks to Derry saying that the PCC would be treated as a public body, the papers were on the warpath about the Bill giving a right to privacy and damaging press freedom. The papers were unaware of the private negotiations with John Wakeham.

Monday started with a seminar I'd commissioned on measuring interagency performance in reducing youth crime. Jack started it off and I chaired it. After the Ministerial lunch I had a word with officials about the likely London Fire Brigade strike over budget issues – to stiffen their resolve. We finally had a response from Tony about Lord Archer's Private Member's Bill that provided on the death of a Monarch for the eldest child to succeed regardless of gender. He agreed that it was difficult to oppose this in principle but doubted this was the right vehicle. Interestingly he revealed that No.10 understood the Queen would be sympathetic to the Government using this Bill for addressing the issue of the succession.

The Human Rights Bill Second Reading went off well. Jack revealed the outcome of his discussions with John Wakeham on a 'public interest' defence. Amendments were promised that would mean newspapers couldn't be prevented from publishing material provided it was in the public interest and a paper had observed the industry's code of practice. The PCC was not exempted from the ECHR. He also said the Government had not decided whether to overturn a Lords amendment exempting church organisations from the Convention. The amendment I had slipped in at introduction, with Gareth Williams' help, had survived. This meant that when a Bill was introduced into Parliament a Government Minister had to certify on the face of the Bill that it complied with the Human Rights Act. That is still the law today.

The next day's papers had Jack as hero of the hour who had defeated Derry's backdoor privacy law. We issued our consultation paper on alternatives to a normal jury trial for complex fraud cases. The 1000th offender had been tagged and another 6000 were likely to get early release with tagging, which could also be used as a bail condition. We were pushing on with tagging as an alternative to custody without the adverse response predicted.

Tuesday was very relaxed with a routine meeting with immigration interest groups; a meeting with my Canadian opposite number; a HO discussion on working up Tony's family policy ideas; lunch with a journalist; a seminar on dealing with offending behaviour; and listening to a HO official telling me how good he'd be at running the Prison Service. I treated myself to avoiding Jack's meeting with the HO trade unions.

Wednesday started with a meeting to discuss strengthening the family life section of the Government's first annual report. Jack met Hillsborough families and broke the news to them that the new evidence didn't justify another inquiry and made his statement to Parliament. I wasn't convinced this issue would go away because on the evidence available I thought the police had mishandled crowd control. But the judge's review saw it differently. Letter fired off to John Prescott about the growing number of undocumented passengers arriving at Waterloo on Eurostar – nearly 500 a month. We could consider amending the 1987 Channel Tunnel Act to require the French to enforce document checks on SNCF. We also announced the system for new judges, police and prison officers, magistrates and probation officers to register freemasonry membership – against Derry's wishes on judges.

Went to Wales for a few days returning on 24 February. I started with a meeting with an official doing a review of the Cabinet Office for Richard Wilson, as the new Cabinet Secretary and Head of the Civil Service. Richard had asked me to participate. I suggested they should be more energetic about coordinating cross-departmental issues; should focus much more on implementation of policy; service more Minister-led groups with officials and experts; and reshape regional and local government. These ideas were all solemnly recorded but I doubted much would change.

Meeting with Richard Tilt about POA who were on the warpath over our refusal to rescind Tory ban on strike action by prison officers, claiming this was promised by Tony before election. Discussion with Alun Michael about speeding up criminal record checks. Briefing meeting with Jack on the European Elections Bill which was in Commons Committee. Found time to write speech I was giving next day on long-term policy on law and order. BA board were still refusing to fly Salman Rushdie. Mo Mowlam wanted to exclude registration of freemasons in NI because of Loyalist Orders and numbers in RUC. David Omand was trying valiantly to get HO to write shorter Home Secretary minutes to PM.

The rest of the week was very quiet with routine meetings and catching up with paper. February ended with the final phase of surrendering handguns and Jack speaking at the EU Presidency seminar showing off our experience in policing football hooliganism. Gareth

Williams used Jeffrey Archer's Private Members Bill in the Lords to announce that the Queen had no objections to giving daughters equal rights to the succeed to the throne, but this Bill would not be the vehicle for doing it.

March began with meetings with the Met Commissioner, the usual Ministerial lunch and a meeting with the Police Federation about the disciplinary procedure. There was HO Questions and a meeting with Prison Service about the POA's discontent. I had another informal meeting with the Chief Inspector of Constabulary about the talent pool for promotion to Chief Constable. I told him I thought this could only be tackled by pulling through the system more younger people, including more women. I discussed progress on the youth justice Manifesto commitments with David Miliband at No.10; and gave a talk to the Social Exclusion Unit about our family policy work. We were working up the idea of establishing a National Family and Parenting Institute to lead this work. Helped Jack prepare for Times interview on parenting that went well

The media were full of stories about the two independent judge reviews into the CPS. The Glidewell review would show a culture of mismanagement – as we had been saying – which caused thousands of prosecutions to be lost each year. The Butler review would show that the CPS was soft on rogue cops who mistreated suspects in custody. Barbara Mills looked to be for the chop.

On 4 March I chaired a meeting on the Youth Justice Board having a development fund to undertake research and to jump start innovations. I met with Jack on European elections and with him and the TUC about the POA and their pursuit of being allowed to take industrial action. We had meetings with the Police Superintendents and ACPO about police disciplinary procedures following the critical report by the Home Affairs Select Committee. I realised how much time we spent on process meetings but wasn't sure what to do about it.

I spent the morning of 5 March at a conference on staffing children's residential care and giving a speech on my 1992 report, 'Choosing with Care.' (That Spring I found myself giving more and more speeches on the Government's criminal justice policies, family policy and human rights.) Later that day I met with David Omand to discuss implementation of the youth justice changes. The week ended with lots of media stories about secret talks with Tories about Lords reform and whether it would go wider than simply removing hereditary peers which was all the Manifesto had promised. The Freemasons gave in and agreed to reveal police links. Silly tiff in the Lords about whether Gareth Williams was right to reveal Queen's view on abolition of male crown succession.

The week of 9 March was a quiet one for me with many routine meetings of no great consequence, apart from those concerned with progressing the youth justice reforms. There was a political spat over Jack's decision on medical grounds not to extradite Roisin McAliskey to Germany: she was still in the Maudsley Hospital with her baby which I kept a watch on. Tony met Gerry Adams to discuss Sinn Fein's return to peace talks. The Labour row continued over the Government's refusal to provide time for the Foxhunting Bill.

It looked as though there would be no major reform of House of Lords, just removal of hereditary peers. A closed list system was announced for European elections. David Ramsbotham told the Home Affairs Select Committee that prisons were gripped by an underworld drugs culture. This provoked the HO to raise the issue of who set his mandate and how much freedom he had to report to Parliament: I was in the more freedom camp, which was probably a niche market.

Good press and public reaction to Gordon Brown's budget on 17 March. Over 50,000 asylum seekers had to be given permanent leave to remain because the Immigration Service could not sort out their claims. The row continued with Conservatives over Lords reform, with Lord Cranbourne trying to delay and save some hereditary peers including himself. Work was going on in the Cabinet Office on 'People's Peers' replacing some hereditary peers. The Scots continued trying to narrow the scope of Westminster reserved powers in the Devolution Bill, but Jack and Derry were resisting. Churches lobbied to amend the Human Rights Bill to ensure they could appoint only teachers of their faith in their schools.

The second half of March was taken up with completion of the Crime and Disorder Bill in the House of Lords. An amendment was moved to abolish the death penalty for treason and piracy and subject them to a maximum of life. I spent a lot of time on the processes and timing of implementation of the youth justice changes. Police efficiency and the spending review of prison and probation services also took up a lot of time. Ronnie Kray failed to secure his release or transfer to open prison. Wormwood Scrubs was described as a torture prison because of beatings by staff, with prisoners threatening to sue the Prison Service. Further Irish prisoners were transferred to Irish prisons on condition of no early release.

The BBFC gave 'Lolita' an 18 classification; and its Director finally resigned. After much argument Jack announced on 23 March changes to the police disciplinary system for corrupt or incompetent police officers. They would be dealt with using the civil standard of proof – the balance of probabilities – instead of the criminal standard – beyond all reasonable doubt. This had taken a huge amount of time and effort but was an important change. The Lawrence family kicked up a lot of dust over Sir William MacPherson as chairman of the Stephen Lawrence Inquiry, but Jack gave him his support. Judges continued to complain about registering freemason membership; but Lord Bingham came out in favour of weekend prisons. Began discussions within HO on strengthening senior police officer training.

Work continued on a Green Paper on Family Policy and the Ministerial Group on the Family met on 26 March. On the same day I discussed improving diversity in HO with David Omand. First meeting with the Black Police Association took place on 30 March and I made myself available to them for informal contact. Met Commissioner wanted Macpherson inquiry to be able to cross-examine Lawrences to help protect Met's reputation. We told him this was a bad idea and if he had concerns over their evidence the Met's counsel should pursue these with the Inquiry's chairman. Mo Mowlam asked for time in the legislative programme for settlement in NI as all sides were inching towards an agreement.

The Good Friday Agreement and Spring Fever – April/May

April began with Jack launching the new National Crime Squad (NCS) which was a 'poor man's' FBI with whom we had had discussions. It would take over the National Criminal Intelligence Service (NCIS) from the HO; and focus on the 200 top criminals thought to be controlling the main organised crime gangs. Nearly 1500 specially selected and vetted detectives would be seconded to the NCS for up to 5 years.

Releasing paedophiles at the end of sentence continued to attract much public and media concern. The public wanted these characters locked up permanently and the media were pre-occupied with the police costs of protecting paedophiles on release from vigilantes. Although Jack talked tough to the Daily Mail and we tried to reassure people, we had no criminal justice powers to contain them. I was getting nowhere with the Department of Health on persuading them these people had a personality disorder and should be supervised under mental health legislation.

In the run-up to the Easter break a huge number of office meetings were crammed in, including briefing Jack for the Commons Second Reading of the Crime and Disorder Bill on 8 April. Most of these meetings were on HO funding problems and Parliamentary matters. I had also committed to an in-depth BBC interview on youth justice. We had fixed the date for the release of the annual crime statistics to avoid political manipulation and as luck would have it, the date fell on 7 April. Fortunately, overall crime in England and Wales fell by nearly10% although violent crime was edging up by nearly 2%. There was then the predictable argument as to which Party could take the credit for the drop.

Jack and Derry decided to reverse their opposition to Donald Dewar's list of specific subjects reserved to the Westminster Parliament in favour of a broad-brush reservation and Derry wrote to the Cabinet on 7 April explaining the change. I wasn't convinced we'd heard the last of this issue. Yet another Inquiry into abuse in children's homes – this time in Wales – ended their public hearings on 8 April. I duly reminded anybody listening what I had said about staff recruitment in my 1992 report 'Choosing with Care.'

Excitement and tension mounted about whether a NI peace agreement would be reached by Easter, with Tony in Belfast doing bi-lateral meetings on 8 April and exuding optimism. The Belfast Agreement – or Good Friday Agreement as it became known – was reached on 10 April. For most of the Easter break this agreement was the main political news, with predictable Daily Mail outrage at the prospect of early release of terrorist prisoners in the Irish republic.

I went on holiday until 20 April and avoided reading about HO matters. However, I did pick up the news, released in my absence, that the Medway Secure Training Centre – a private sector contract authorised by Michael Howard – would be opened before my return for 12 to 14-year-olds. I had advised against this because I wanted to consider its use as part of a review of all juvenile custodial provision but had been over-ruled by Jack. The media criticism was predictable and could have been avoided.

My return on 20 April brought a flow of briefing meetings on HO and criminal justice funding problems for the next Cabinet Committee meeting on public expenditure. Jack had to be briefed for the Commons Second Reading that day of the Data Protection Bill and another canter round the track on personal privacy versus press freedom of speech. Ministerial lunches were by now a bit lacklustre, but they did help to keep the political team informed.

I had more and more meetings, which I usually chaired, about the work of the Ministerial Group on Family Policy, funding for the charity, Parentline and establishing and funding a National Family Policy Institute. Family policy was now getting a lot of public airtime. Ted Wragg at Exeter University published a study on boys' literacy problems being worse than girls and Dads not reading to their sons. Jack weighed in with crime research showing boys who offended in their teens carried on doing so into their twenties; and started blaming Murdoch's Sun for promoting a laddish culture. The Sunday Times joined in, encouraged by No.10 I suspected, with articles on "The Trouble with Boys" and how Tony was demanding action. What had started as a supporting act to youth justice reform now had star billing.

The Met Commissioner took to the air waves claiming the Stephen Lawrence Inquiry was proving unfair to the police because of the way they were cross-examined at hearings. Later in the week he was predicting the end of bobbies on the beat because of funding shortages. He didn't seem to know about the work we were doing on two-tier policing on which we had another meeting on 22 April. Retirement beckoned.

There was real momentum behind the Good Friday Agreement. Mo Mowlam had produced a draft Bill providing for the elections to the new NI Assembly and its operation, together with an Order authorising a referendum on the Agreement. Jack agreed the transfer of five more terrorist prisoners to the Irish Republic to serve out the rest of their life sentences. William Hague supported the Government's action despite opposition to the transfers in his party, including from Baroness Thatcher.

Much of 23 April was spent at a conference and a meeting on the prison health service which is poor. I had been raising the fundamental issue of who should be responsible for prisoners' health services – the HO or the NHS. I argued that being in prison should not mean lack of access to the NHS and wanted the HO to transfer the responsibility and funding to the Department of Health. Unsurprisingly DH were opposed to the idea because they knew they would need to spend more. However, I had achieved political engagement with the issue.

Probation had drawn public attention to cuts in Prison Service programmes for treating sex offenders. Local police and probation services were struggling to supervise some dangerous paedophiles with inadequate powers and funding for the costly supervised housing needed. Vigilantes were now posing serious threats to released offenders and the media were demanding Government action. We were trying to quell the vigilantes and hold things together until the new Sex Offender Orders in the Crime and Disorder Bill came into force. The police could then apply for an order if a released offender posed a threat to children. If the order was breached a five-year prison sentence could be imposed plus unlimited fines.

The last week of April produced a classic avoidable HO storm. This concerned Mary Bell who as an 11-year-old had killed two young children in 1968 and served 12 years in prison for manslaughter – not murder. She was now 41 and herself a mother, living anonymously in Northern England. She had received payment for her cooperation with a journalist, Gita Sereny – biographer of Albert Speer – who had written a book about her, 'Cries Unheard.' This book had revealed Mary's mistreatment by her mother at an early age and was being serialised in the Times. This produced outrage in most other newspapers – especially the Telegraph – because of the payment, said to be £50,000.

No.10 wanted a robust response. Jack duly expressed concern and promised a review of whether the proceeds of crime legislation applied. I picked up office rumours that the HO knew all about this and that

235

officials had approved Sereny's interviews with Mary Bell. An urgent meeting was called with the Permanent Secretary present. Two officials, who I had never seen before, sat quietly at one end of the table with some bulky files. After a desultory discussion, I sensed we didn't know the full story and suggested we heard from the officials with files. Documents were produced showing the probation service had thought it beneficial for Mary to talk to Sereny about her childhood. No-one had thought to tell Michael Howard, as Home Secretary.

Jack rapidly announced an Inquiry after the media discovered that officials had known about Mary Bell's cooperation with the book all along. The media pursued Mary Bell and her teenage daughter who knew nothing of her mother's past. There was an abundance of tabloid outrage over the £50,000 payment but the Attorney General said this was not illegal. The Press Complaints Commission investigated whether the Times had breached their Code of Conduct by serialising the Sereny book. Predictably by mid-May everybody had lost interest, having caused unnecessary hurt to Mary Bell's daughter.

April closed with the media rating the performance of the Government after a year in office. The Blair bubble had not burst, with even the Daily Telegraph saying over 70% of people were satisfied with his performance. Brown, Straw and Mowlam were seen as the star Cabinet performers, but several Cabinet Ministers continued to be ready for the chop. Tony said there was no room for complacency; more change was promised; and an annual report would be published – eventually in July.

May 1998 started with me applying to become Chairman of the Youth Justice Board to be set up under the Crime and Disorder Act. Transfer of Irish prisoners to the Irish Republic continued. The Tories argued against Lords' reform, with Crossbench Peers pressing for more fundamental change than just removing hereditary Peers. Agitation for another Hillsborough Inquiry continued. A new HO group was set up to give more attention to the release of dangerous paedophiles; and I tried to persuade No.10 to focus more on offenders with severe personality disorders. On 21 May Jack announced the establishment of a Race Relations Forum he would chair to give ethnic minorities a voice at the heart of Government.

We had arcane arguments about how to apply the Human Rights Bill to the Channel Islands and Isle of Man without forcing their hand by putting it in the Bill. Even more angels were counted dancing on a pin head over Lords amendments to the Bill exempting churches from the provisions applying to public authorities. They claimed the Bill gave the courts rights to exercise jurisdiction over spiritual matters which it didn't. We rejected the Lords' amendments but added some reassuring vague wording about courts having regard to a church's rights as representatives of their members.

Police issues continued to occupy a lot of time, along with money and prisons. Met corruption issues continued to surface but few police officers seemed to be prosecuted. A No.10 taskforce started daft stories about the police being used to round up truants without, as I pointed out, any idea what they would do with them. Bizarre suggestions emerged that parents should be jailed if their children truanted. The media soon realised this story was not going anywhere. We went to see the Chief Secretary about the state of the HO budget without much joy. Londoners voted in favour of an elected Mayor which would enable us to hand over running the Met.

Tony's visit to Saudi Arabia and Egypt raised concerns about London harbouring terrorist dissidents. We had excluded 14 foreign nationals in the past year for terrorist activities; but had to explain to No.10 the need to strengthen legislation on UK fundraising for overseas terrorist activity and the absence of a legislative slot. Towards the end of May I was shown the Labour Party's evidence to the Jenkins Commission on voting systems, setting out its opposition to PR. This wouldn't please Tony.

The most dramatic event for me in May was a secret meeting with Daniel Machover, a lawyer, who had called me privately about Wormwood Scrubs Prison. At lunch he handed over a disturbing dossier about assaults and intimidation of prisoners and staff at the prison. There were some graphic photos of injuries to prisoners but also claims that some parts of the prison were effectively run by violent prisoners with the collusion of prison officers. I discussed the dossier with Jack. We agreed I would hand it over to the police and inform the Prison Service. Which I did.

This led to an unannounced inspection by the Chief Inspector of Prisons. He found that "more than 160 prison officers were involved in inflicting and covering up a regime of torture which saw savage beatings, death threats and sexual assaults inflicted on inmates." His report was published eventually with a Parliamentary statement on 28 June 1999. Before that statement the CPS had announced on 15 June that 25 prison officers had been charged with assaults on prisoners. Then a further 27 were prosecuted in a series of trials spread over 14 months. By September 2001 six had been jailed for their sadistic attacks. At that time the police were still investigating another 36 allegations and there were 41 civil claims against the Prison Service for alleged assaults.

The Chief Inspector and I both thought the place should be shut; but there was bi-partisan political support for keeping it open because of the shortage of places. I lost track of what happened after 2001 when there were still cases outstanding and big question marks over the prison's future. Yet at the end of 2020 'The Scrubs' remained open, still with Inspectorate reports citing above average drug taking and a culture of assaults on staff and prisoners. Despite this, no Minister has been able to close it and replace it with a modern prison.

The Long Goodbye to the Home Office – June to September

On 8 June, an independent selection panel submitted my name to Jack as the most suitable candidate to chair the Youth Justice Board. After securing Tony's approval my appointment was announced on 30 June to Parliament. There were predictable accusations of cronyism, but they seemed half-hearted. I was to take up my appointment on 1 October when the Board came into existence but would then have to resign as senior policy adviser. In the meantime, I sat on the appointment Board for YJB members and looked for an office outside the HO and a chief executive.

There was still a lot of HO business to deal with before I left. July started with a row with Alistair Darling (Chief Secretary) over the Prison Service budget for the next three years, with the Treasury seeking fantasy efficiency savings and making the maintenance backlog even greater. I used back channels with No.10 to reduce the efficiency

238

savings, restore the maintenance budget and protect extra funding for the juvenile secure estate – in my new role. The Comprehensive Spending Review settlement for the next three years was announced before the summer recess and the HO now had a reasonable settlement for the rest of this Parliament. Peace had broken out with Paul Condon over corruption and he thanked us for the support we had given him. Work started on building a new relationship with the Irish Government following the success of the Good Friday agreement.

On 29 July I was made a Peer and a little later had to meet Garter King of Arms at the College of Heralds to choose my title. I had decided to be Lord Warner of Brockley because it was where I grew up and I thought it would have pleased my late father. The title didn't enthuse Garter, but I gave no ground. He then did his pitch to sell me a coat of arms, a bit like a double-glazing salesman. I declined but as I went to leave, he told me a story about his meeting with Cherokee Indians to discuss a possible coat of arms. I didn't invite him to my lunch with family and friends when I was introduced into the Lords on 12 October by Barbara Castle and Gareth Williams, with the three of us dressed in ermine.

The Crime and Disorder Act received Royal Assent on 31 July. The work done before the 1997 Election enabled this large Bill to reach the statute book in 15 months. Work had also begun on a new White Paper on how the Government would continue to tackle crime. No.10 had begun a private discussion with me about my thoughts on a medium-term agenda for law and order. I provided a longer paper for them to put into Tony's summer reading box. He in turn made clear to Jack in a minute at the end of July that he would be coming back to this medium-term agenda in the autumn. Before we all went on holiday a Ministerial awayday was set up for October and Jack took my No.10 paper for his holiday reading. I took a thriller to Italy.

We all re-assembled at the beginning of September. The feed-back from No.10 on my medium-term paper was that the PM thought I'd outlined a good agenda but he "hankered for something a bit more in the blue skies category." David Miliband's interpretation of this was we needed a symbolic idea like 'zero tolerance; Tony set great store by the experience of New York and he "aches for a view of what an ideal criminal justice system would be like." The next stocktake meeting

239

would discuss the paper and the shape of a radical agenda; he was interested in some specific crime targets; and he wanted papers on links between drugs and crime and on how indirect Government action like family policy would impact on crime. The problem with Tony was that when he engaged with an issue he tended to ask good questions, to which few of us knew the answer.

I still had a month of routine HO business like the Met and Prison Service, accelerated release of Irish terrorist prisoners and stopping the flow of Czech and Slovak asylum seekers. There was also some strategic business to attend to before I left. I needed to produce a note for Jack setting out the future law and order agenda for a political Cabinet on 10 September. This outlined our criminal justice change agenda; what we were doing on indirect causes of crime; how we would target police activity on the most prolific criminals and crime hotspots; and the development of community punishment as an alternative to prison. I emphasised the danger of promising to reduce crime given that it rose on average by 5% a year historically. This was without any expectation any elected politician would take notice.

The stocktake meeting with the PM on 14 September was a bit trickier. We had a well-written draft crime White Paper with few new ideas. I agreed with No.10 that it would be best to focus on Tony's response to my summer paper; and discuss three things: the merits and limitations of the zero-tolerance approach to low level crime; domestic violence which was a big part of violent crime but had received little attention; and police efficiency and community patrolling alternatives to 'bobbies on the beat.' That is what we did but I didn't have time to liven up the White Paper before my departure. The bids for the legislative programme for the rest of this Parliament was another piece of unfinished business awaiting my successor, Justin Russell – now the Chief Inspector of Probation.

I visited the new Medway Secure Training Centre on 3 September to see what it was like. I insisted on lunching alone with a group of the inmates which made the managers nervous. The young offenders were quite complimentary about the regime and one said it was better than his children's home. It was clear the custodial estate would be a major challenge, especially improving the quality of education and training.

240

I spent much of September preparing for the YJB to open for business on 1 October. My chief executive had found an office close to the HO; and we had appointed a Board with me sitting on the appointment panel. Our first meeting had been arranged; I had agreed a provisional budget with the HO prior to a later discussion with Jack; and I had recruited a secretary. I gave a lot of media interviews and spoke at conferences to explain my approach. I rounded this off by drafting a press notice for the HO to use announcing our establishment and the focus of our early work.

During the summer Jack had raised the issue of me being an unpaid adviser. This met serious resistance from the Commissioner for Public Appointments and Richard Wilson, the Cabinet Secretary. To avoid a row and difficulties for Tony I identified topics I could advise on without a conflict of interest with my YJB appointment and put these to David Omand, the HO Permanent Secretary. We ended up with me becoming a co-opted member of the Ministerial Group on Family Policy and being able to attend meetings with Jack and Tony and give advice when it was sought. Nobody was going to tell the PM or Home Secretary that they couldn't seek advice from whoever they liked.

After a farewell party in which I was described, somewhat unhelpfully I thought, as the Deputy Home Secretary, I left to run the Youth Justice Board, secure in the knowledge I could get into No.10 or the HO when necessary. I put these access arrangements to the test on 12 October when, after being introduced into the House of Lords, I attended the Ministerial Awayday and did a presentation on the medium-term agenda for law and order with the HO Permanent Secretary present. For another year or so I continued with the work I had started on family policy in early 1997.

Crafting a Durable Government Family Policy: 1997–1999

Focus on family policy started with a Labour discussion paper on parenting published in November 1996. It concluded that the "roots of criminal and delinquent behaviour are planted in childhood. Research has shown that parental supervision and discipline is the key to its prevention. Despite the difficulty of parenting, little attention was given to helping people acquire the skills to cope with bringing up children

241

in today's world." It called for better parental education and support; a wider acceptance that having a child was not a totally private matter; a better work/home balance with more family friendly policies; and a higher priority for children in care. I thought it wasn't a bad starting point.

Labour had gone into the 1997 Election with a Manifesto commitment to strengthen family life but had tended to link parenting policy to the criminal justice agenda under the mantra of "tough on crime and tough on the causes of crime." Initially all the attention to parenting was linked to the youth justice reforms and the Crime and Disorder Bill. I wasn't comfortable with this narrow approach. But in September 1997 Tony decided he wanted an initiative on family policy led by Jack, not the Minister for Women, Harriet Harman. This did not please the sisterhood. I came up with the idea of a Ministerial Group on the Family chaired by Jack and this was announced by Tony at the Labour Party Conference on 30 September. The first meeting of the Group took place on 16 October to discuss a paper I had prepared and agreed with No.10. This was restrained on the virtues of marriage.

I set up a seminar on 10 November for all the Ministerial Group to hear the views of about 30 external experts. They were pleased that the Government was giving more attention to parenting, although the Ministers remained nervous about discussing this subject in public. We followed this event with a note I drafted for discussion with Tony on 18 November. This meeting went well but Tony wanted a big idea and wasn't ready to contemplate a Green Paper. No.10 staff were developing ideas on the tax issues relevant to family policy, but we encouraged Tony to engage with Gordon on taxation (see Chapter 6 entry for 18 November).

I reworked a Cabinet Office Paper, now headed 'Strong Families, Healthy Children,' for the next meeting of the Ministerial Group on 26 November. This set out a range of problems and a possible approach. The key areas for attention were parenting support, work/life balance, supporting marriage, domestic violence, teenage pregnancies and tax/ benefit issues. The Ministerial Group supported the approach and agreed some wording on marriage. The aim now was to get a fuller document to Tony by Christmas in order to maintain momentum and to find a way of engaging the Chancellor on the tax/benefit issues.

On 22 December Jack sent to Tony and the Cabinet a report from the Ministerial Group headed 'Supporting Families.' That text had a statement of the Government's position on the family to which Tony's specific agreement was sought to ensure the whole Cabinet got behind the document. We asked if the Group should head for a Green or White Paper on the Family in the Spring. The following day Jack sent Tony and Gordon a minute I'd drafted about bringing tax and benefit issues into the exercise. Christmas and the William episode paused matters. No.10 staff told me Tony didn't want to respond until he and Jack had discussed the text with Gordon. That meeting took place on 27 January with little Treasury comment other than that the text seemed "too socially authoritarian."

On 3 February 1998 the PM finally surfaced with a response to the December document. He wanted more clarity on the principles guiding Government policy and more detailed policy proposals. He wasn't hostile to people such as gay couples choosing lifestyles different from traditional families; but the Government's primary concern should be with the stability of relationships where children were involved. Here two parents offered the best prospect of stability and that was often most easily found within marriage. This was going to be a drafting challenge. There were several specific policy proposals for consideration. Tony wasn't ready to decide on a Green Paper but wanted to maintain momentum, with a further report by Easter. Members of the Ministerial Group were set to work on the specific items on the Blair agenda, with a further meeting of the Group set for the end of March.

In the meantime, I had been working up the idea of establishing a national body to oversee the development of family policy independent of Government. There was already a Family Policy Institute which undertook research, but it lacked impact and funding. I wanted to replace it with an independent National Family and Parenting Institute with its funding underwritten by government. I chaired a meeting of voluntary organisations and professional bodies on 22 April to assess reaction to this idea. There was considerable support for a national body provided it was at arms-length from Government; and for a national helpline building on the work of the charity Parentline. I secured the support of the Ministerial Group to a national body and helpline; and worked with No.10 and the Cabinet Office on a report for discussion with the PM.

Before anything could be sent to Tony, on 30 April he sent Jack a minute setting out clearly what he wanted to see in the document. He wanted "a comprehensive package of policy proposals, with particular emphasis on measures to encourage stability in family life" and to "minimise the risks of break-up." This package was to include economic support; choices about balancing work and home; access to parenting education and cutting teenage pregnancies; modernising services supporting families such as health visitors; better support for stability in relationships and marriage. It was clear that a busy PM was now devoting serious thought to this project. I worked up a document with Geoff Mulgan at No.10 for Jack and me to discuss with Tony on 12 May.

At that meeting we'd hoped to get Tony's agreement to moving to a Green Paper. We failed because he still wanted something "harder edged" on promoting marriage and stable relationships than I had produced. I tried to persuade him that that there were two potential points of intervention by government – when couples were thinking of getting married and when they were thinking of getting divorced. But Tony wanted changes to the tax and benefits system to encourage marriage which would inevitably mean a row with Gordon. Eventually we secured his agreement to more work by the Ministerial Group and working up a possible Green Paper. We had to pause and regroup.

I spent the next month putting a revised document to the Ministerial Group and working with No. 10 on how we could convince Tony of the merits of a Green Paper. I agreed with them and Jack a short snappy summary for Tony on "Strengthening Family Life by Modernising Family Policy" which was well-received. I also used this time to progress the idea of a National Family and Parenting Institute after securing the agreement of the Ministerial Group to a non-statutory body as a charity The Cabinet Office were persuaded to bring together an inter-departmental group to agree funding and terms of reference for the Institute. I convinced Jack he should meet a group of people I identified as possible trustees of an Institute; and he gave an interview to the Daily Mail on 16 June trailing an announcement on an Institute.

Geoff Mulgan and I spent time talking privately to Tony about the political downsides of financial incentives for marriage, particularly how it would alienate the many stable cohabitees (then including myself.) with children who simply didn't want to marry. By the end of

June, I had agreed with No.10 a timetable for next steps. First there would be a major speech by Jack in July setting out the case for a new approach to family policy. Then a consultation document would be launched in September. Finally, we would aim for a Green Paper in the first quarter of 1999. The launch on 23 July of an All-party Parliamentary Group report on "Family Matters" was used as a non-partisan platform for Jack's major speech.

We followed this with another Ministerial Group report to Tony and secured his agreement to a consultation document in October. We spent the summer polishing a consultation document titled "Supporting Families" setting out the Government's ideas which included setting up a National Family Policy Institute. This was successfully launched on 30 October. By this time, I had left the HO but had ensured the establishment of a Family Policy Unit within the HO. This Unit handled the comments on the consultation – over a thousand responses as it turned out – and set up the Institute. It organised a new Family Support Grant scheme for voluntary organisations to help families and extra money for Parentline which provided freephone help.

I remained an unpaid adviser to Tony and Jack on family policy as a member of the Ministerial Group and continued to keep an eye on setting up the Institute and the production of a response to the consultation. I sounded out the late Tony Newton, a Conservative ex-Cabinet Minister, as Chairman of the Institute to avoid it being too New Labour, but this was vetoed by Ministers sadly. In the Spring of 1999, the Government launched its response to the consultation, reporting what it had done so far and its future plans. There were five strands of continuing work: better services and support to parents; better financial support to families; helping families balance work and home; strengthening marriage; and better support for serious family problems.

The Ministerial Group continued with a programme of work, including for teenage boys, young men and fathers. The Institute was established with a budget, a Board of Trustees and a programme of work. I decided that I had done my bit to develop and promote family policy. I detached myself from this work at the end of 1999, hoping the initiative would survive. It was time to pay more attention to youth justice reform.

The Institute has survived, although it dropped 'National' from its title in 2006. It has run Parents' Week annually since 1999. In 2011 it launched a Family Friendly Scheme under which organisations joining the scheme take a 'Family Friendly' pledge. Since 2010 it has produced a report on the UK's progress towards becoming a family friendly society – never higher than C. It has produced several research reports on families in the age of austerity. It has explored the use of social media to engage with families. It continues to do interesting work on family issues. I am glad I persisted with the Institute's establishment – at the time not a totally welcomed idea.

8. Tough on Crime, Tough on the Causes: 1996-2003

Creating a new Youth Justice System: 1996-1998

New Labour's reform of youth justice began with two 1996 documents. First was the Audit Commission Report 'Misspent Youth' which was highly critical of the youth justice system for its lack of interventions when young people offended and the absence of reparation to victims. The result was repeated court appearances by persistent young offenders and no effective action to stop them reoffending. The second document was a Labour consultation paper, 'Tackling Youth Crime: Reforming Youth Justice.' This echoed the Audit Commission criticisms but set out two ideas of mine: new multi-agency youth offender teams (YOTs) locally and a National Youth Justice Board.

The first of these ideas was similar to the teams I used in Kent Social Services in the 1980s (see Chapter 4). These had more than halved the number of juveniles taken into care or placed in custody; and Kent had re-offending rates half the national average. The second idea was because I considered little would change without an independent national body to drive change with a link to a Minister. Reform of the youth justice system became a major plank of Labour's election offer.

By early 1997 a Crime and Disorder Bill was likely to be first session legislation for a Labour Government with youth justice reform as part of it. I wrote a paper on reform in February 1997 setting out the main items for a White Paper to precede this legislation: changes to court administration and powers, bail supervision (a major problem then); final warnings; community interventions; YOTs; and a National Youth Justice Board. I proposed setting up a national taskforce with outside experts that I would chair to help produce the White Paper and legislation. I didn't trust the HO to do this work at pace and I wanted to control the agenda. We framed a manifesto pledge to halve the time for courts to deal with persistent young offenders. This was one of 5 pledges on a small card sent to all households in the 1997 Election campaign. This ensured priority after the Election.

As described in chapter 6 the Youth Justice Taskforce met frequently and fed ideas into the White Paper on youth justice reform, 'No More Excuses,' published in November 1997. The taskforce continued making proposals for the Crime and Disorder Bill which had its Second Reading in the Commons in April 1998. We issued our final report in July when the Bill received Royal Assent. We then disbanded, with some members joining the Youth Justice Board for England and Wales (YJB), as it was now called. I became chair of the YJB in June 1998 and it came into operation on 1 October.

The YJB had 12 members (including me) from a range of backgrounds, as required in the legislation. I had secured a small Board chosen for personal qualities rather than a large one representative of vested interests – the HO approach. The YJB had 4 female and two BAME members including a black paediatric forensic psychiatrist. We were a more diverse body than HO quangos of the time. The Board met monthly to review progress and agree policy and procedures. Each Board member took an interest in a particular region and reported back to the Board on visits. I managed the interface between the YJB and government departments (especially the HO) and Ministers. I handled external relations with interest groups and publicity. Using my relations with the media was key to securing support for change, not least because I continued to be involved with the Government's law and order agenda.

In October 1998 the YJB had a big remit to deliver under its new statutory duty of preventing offending (including reoffending). It had to set up 155 local multi-agency YOTs by April 2000. They needed to be operating with approved youth justice plans and budgets agreed by the local contributing agencies. The YOTs had to be ready to handle all the young offenders coming from both magistrate and crown courts under a raft of new orders made under the Crime and Disorder Act. The police would be using a totally new cautioning system with a final warning and a form of restorative justice for victims. This required a big recruitment, training and guidance programme to be delivered in 18 months from scratch.

Guidance on new orders was largely produced by the HO, with the YJB turning this into procedures for local use. Local authorities set up steering committees chaired by their chief executives, to put in place YOTs, youth justice plans and budgets, with YJB support and direction.

248

We had to recruit our own staff and ensure local areas kept up to speed. We set up pilot schemes for YOTs and disseminated information for them. Simultaneously we helped the HO on new legislation for the scheme I had devised for youth offender panels. These panels would give young offenders appearing in court for the first time the chance to agree a contract to stop offending under the terms of a new court order, a referral order. Successful completion of the contract avoided a conviction. These referral orders were provided for in the Youth Justice and Criminal Evidence Bill which received Royal Assent on 27 July 1999.

In October 1998 I agreed privately with Jack and David Omand a YJB Development Fund budget for 1999/2000 of £30 million and for 2000/01 of £35million: later £20 million was added for 2001/2. This money was used to establish local schemes to cut offending. We wanted to develop 20,000 bail supervision places to stop spree offending on bail and no shows in court. There would be intervention programmes to stop offending after final warnings: parenting and mentoring programmes; reparation schemes: cognitive thinking programmes; drug and alcohol programmes; and youth inclusion programmes in crime hotspots. We let local areas choose the most appropriate schemes likely to prevent offending in their areas, provided they put in matching money. The only other condition was that all schemes would be evaluated as part of the research capability the YJB was developing.

Putting the Reforms into Practice: 1998-2000

A year after the YJB's establishment about 90% of YOT managers had been appointed. We had worked with local areas to help them produce credible youth justice plans; and to explain our information requirements and the IT they would need. This had meant resolving local disputes over information sharing. There was a lot of local haggling over budgets, where the lion's share was coming from social services budgets. The NHS and education were often slow to come to the party. We declined to lay down a formula but said we would be critical of youth justice plans that lacked credible funding. The YJB funded a national management development programme for YOT managers provided by the Office of Public Management. At the end of 1999 we started a 'training the trainers' programme to train practitioners working with young offenders.

The current system of youth justice lacked any consistent and structured way of assessing the needs of young people and the degree of risk they presented to themselves and others as they entered and left the youth justice system. We worked with Oxford University's Centre for Criminological Research and a panel of YOT managers and others to develop an assessment tool we called ASSET. This would help practitioners to assess and score on a consistent basis all the areas of a young person's life most linked to offending. This in turn would help YOTs match young offenders to the most appropriate programmes. The aim was to use this tool at the beginning and end of a young person's contact with a YOT or custodial facility. After piloting and training staff we planned to introduce ASSET in April 2000.

Probably our most difficult task was building by April 2000 a system for commissioning secure accommodation for young offenders sentenced to custody. We had also to create a central placement scheme to make it easier for YOTs to find suitable places. We inherited a motley bunch of facilities. These were 13 Prison Service YOIs for under 18s, now managed separately from the 18-21 YOIs; 31 local authority secure units; and 3 secure training centres run by the private sector.

The local authority units were the most expensive and had children who were not offenders. The YOIs were the largest and cheapest but had been heavily criticised by the Prisons Inspectorate which led to the separation of the under-18s. The secure training centres were inherited from Michael Howard contracts that I had wanted cancelled, without success. We lacked information on the condition of the estate we inherited and its suitability for our needs. We spent a year reviewing the secure estate and putting in place new commissioning and placement systems.

The HO and Prison Service were strongly opposed to the idea of a purchaser/provider split. I had argued for it based on my local government experience and convinced Jack. I had made it clear that the YJB would set national standards and introduce service specifications to deliver those standards. Our commissioning strategy would use service level agreements that set out the number of places we would fund by geographical location. There would be monitoring arrangements that gave us routine access to ensure compliance and a range of sanctions and measures to encourage good performance and penalise bad. I said I would use contracts and the power of the purse to drive regime changes. This worried the top of the HO and Prison Service, although many juvenile YOI managers supported this approach. There was an element of bluff in this as I wasn't sure of the support I'd get when it came to withholding money from the Prison Service.

At the centre of our new system was a placement scheme to stop the stories of young people being bussed round the M25 for hours searching for a custodial place. We tracked each placement from the provisional booking through to admission, transfer and discharge using new IT and a team of placement officers. This enabled us to verify payment and help with demand forecasting, as well as providing a better experience for nervous young offenders. I put a nurse manager in charge of this new commissioning, purchasing and placement system, supported by a head of contracting and head of placement. They inherited a budget of about £150 million a year from the HO and Prison Service from which they had to buy places for about 3300 children then occupying this non-system. I made it clear from the outset that YJB policy was to reduce the use of custody and to shrink this sector, with redeployment of funding into community sentences.

A key part of the shift from custody to community was to be the new Detention and Training Order (DTO) that would come into operation in April 2000. I had been a strong supporter of giving courts the option of a custodial sentence that could be served partly in the community. This had been tried before with a Secure Training Order but without adequate funding for the community part of the sentence. That order would be replaced by the DTO with much greater investment in the community half of the sentence; and with a YOT supervising officer involved in the planning and delivery of the sentence from the beginning. The new national standards for youth justice would prescribe the role of YOTs in the DTO.

In the build up to D-Day (1 April 2000) when the new youth justice system went live, public attention focussed on community rather than custodial changes. The highest profile of these changes was the Anti-Social Behaviour Order (ASBO) which was not simply for juveniles. The term ASBO had entered the national language as a response to young people causing mayhem on council estates; but it had broadened into a mechanism for dealing with 'neighbours from hell' some of

251

whom might be juveniles. The purpose of ASBOs was to target activities that disrupted the lives of individuals, families or communities, whoever was causing the disruption. New Labour had successfully badged ownership of ASBOs as part of convincing the public that they could be trusted on law and order.

ASBOs were made by magistrates on application by a local authority or the police. Typically for a young offender the order would prevent him frequenting certain areas, possibly at certain times or taking part in particular activities. It was a civil order but breaching it was a criminal offence, arrestable and recordable. YOTs were notified of ASBOs for juveniles and had to bring home to them the seriousness of their conduct. Sometimes they failed as with the Nottingham 14-year-old who in 2000 became the then youngest recipient of an ASBO and shortly after the first to receive a custodial sentence after a hundred arrests. Jack asked me to chair an Action Group on ASBOs which produced in the summer of 2000 a protocol showing how police, local authorities and others could work together to protect local communities.

Alongside ASBOs the other community order that attracted a lot of attention was the Parenting Order. As already described, New Labour had been very effective at linking parenting competence to youth offending and raising in the public mind the importance of parenting and family policy. As part of this agenda courts could use Parenting Orders to require parents of young offenders to attend parenting classes. The public response to this initially was mixed, but YOTs tried to put in place courses that were very practical. In time they trained people who had been on courses to teach skills and techniques to other parents. Men tended to be reluctant to complete courses, but many mothers found them useful and said so. The people I spoke to who had been on courses were usually positive about courses even when they had been hostile at first.

Another big community change in the reforms was that to police cautioning. The new final warning scheme was a complete break with the past culture of repeat cautions where nothing much was done to change behaviour. That culture was epitomised for me by a letter from a magistrate in early 1997 to say that a 15-year-old had stood up in the youth court and said he couldn't be convicted because he hadn't received his five cautions. I had persuaded Jack that we should allow the police to use one reprimand before issuing a final warning but that it should be accompanied by an intervention with an emphasis on reparation to a community or victim. Repeated reprimands were not acceptable even though some forces were not keen on interventions with final warnings. The big exception was Thames Valley Police whose Chief Constable, Charles Pollard, was a YJB member.

Before the 1997 Election Thames Valley Police had looked at experience with restorative justice in the US, Australia and New Zealand and how this had produced behavioural change in offenders. They had been using restorative conferencing linked to a caution whereby the victim and perpetrator met with a trained facilitator to discuss the impact of the offence on the victim and whether the perpetrator considered they should make some amends. Both Jack and I had attended conferences. It was clear that they could have a beneficial effect on both parties, particularly those offenders who had convinced themselves that their offence harmed nobody. Four years' experience of restorative conferencing in Thames Valley convinced the YJB to invest in restorative justice projects linked to the new final warnings. Gradually other police forces became convinced of the cost-effectiveness of restorative conferencing and trained their officers in the restorative justice approach.

The YJB continued to advocate and fund 'RJ' as it became known and its use with final warnings and Reparation Orders. Sir Charles Pollard (as he became) continued to work with the wider criminal justice system to spread its influence with adult offenders. A research study in 2007 by Lawrence Sherman and Helen Strang found that RJ had a higher rate of victim satisfaction and offender accountability than traditional methods of justice delivery. There is now a Restorative Justice Council, and the Ministry of Justice supports the approach. There is even an international restorative justice week celebrated in many countries. I did my best at the YJB and later to spread the RJ gospel whenever I could.

By the end of March 2000, 155 YOTs had been established with agreed budgets and youth justice plans, trained staff and about 450 new intervention programmes, partly funded by the YJB. This had been achieved not by civil servants but by local staff, many of whom were on secondment to the YJB. The only two people with central government experience were me and the YJB chief executive, Mark Perfect, who had lived up to his name despite having a Treasury background. The YOTs came into operation on 1 April, with Final Warnings and the community orders operating from 1 June. The two-month gap was to enable YOTs to finalise their working arrangements with police and courts. The new juvenile secure estate operated under its YJB contracts from 1 April when the DTOs also started. We began piloting the new Youth Offender Panels in 7 areas on the same day.

To mark this significant achievement, we organised the first of what became an annual conference at Westminster for 600 delegates, virtually all from local areas. I had assembled a posse of Ministers to speak including Jack Straw, Estelle Morris (Education Secretary), Mo Mowlam (Cabinet Office) and John Hutton (Health). This was to demonstrate to local people that there was cross-government working. I also had as speakers the Drugs Czar, Keith Hellawell, and Trevor Brooking, the Chairman of Sport England, who made a great speech about how sport could build self-esteem and provide an alternative to anti-social behaviour.

We also had YOTs, parents and young people speaking at the two-day event, with extensive TV and print media coverage. Perhaps the most courageous speech was from a mother who had been the subject of a Parenting Order telling the conference how the experience had improved her relationship with her sons and helped her get them back into school. But as I told the Conference this was only the end of the beginning.

Delivering the Persistent Young Offenders Pledge: 1997-2001

As YJB Chair, I continued to have oversight of the work I had begun in the HO on delivering the Government's Election pledge to halve the time for persistent young offenders between arrest and sentence. Delivery required the cooperation of the police, the CPS and the Courts, plus their respective government departments. A definition of a persistent young offender had taken some time before being agreed eventually by Ministers. The target was to reduce the time from arrest to sentence from 142 days in 1996 to 71 days before the next election.

254

I had secured approval to employing consultants, PA Consulting, to help align the different organisational procedures, identify the main bottlenecks and sort out many local problem areas. This work involved grinding away at the details of local processes that had been causing inter-agency problems for years. Without PA Consulting and someone in charge close to a powerful Cabinet Minister, performance would not have improved. People simply couldn't be bothered to change their working practices. When we started there were about 20,000 cases a year going to magistrates' courts, taking about 100 days; and another 2,000 or so going to crown courts, taking over 200 days. So, a good deal of improvement was needed.

Despite the objections of the Lord Chancellor, in 1999 we started publishing individual court performance figures on speed through the system. There was a big improvement in the magistrates' courts but no change in the crown courts. Magistrates became much more committed to the youth justice changes than the crown courts where judges showed little interest. We drove down the numbers in the magistrates' courts to 83 days in 2000, 68 days in 2001, 63 days in 2002 and 58 days in 2003 when I left the YJB. But in the crown courts the 212 days in 1999 had reduced only to 188 days in 2003. We just reached the target of 71 days by the 2001 Election, but no thanks to the crown courts. When the Ministry of Justice discontinued these statistics in 2008, the crown courts were back over 200 days. Despite an increase in their caseload the magistrates' courts continued to perform well and were at 50 days in early 2008.

Embedding Reform and New Initiatives: 2000-2001

A major reason why we had this new operational system up and running across England and Wales in 18 months, was the attention we paid to communications. I was determined to cultivate the national media and tell them what we were doing. But I also wanted YOTs and others to do the same with local media. To help them and other local staff we needed to provide timely and attractive material. That is why I appointed a Director of Communications with a budget and staff to do this. We also had a former Editor of the Times, Charlie Wilson, on the YJB.

We organised events/seminars to explain and promote the work of YOTs and the new intervention programmes. At the end of 1999 we started publishing a glossy and illustrated bi-monthly broadsheet of 8-12 pages. This was for youth justice professionals, policy makers, teachers and others like MPs and journalists interested in our work. We encouraged articles from practitioners and other agencies and even opened our pages to journalists. We set up a website within gov.uk that was well used. This had a special section on delivering the pledge on persistent young offenders and one for YOT managers – the Yot Club. Other sections were added over time. A video was made on the new final warning scheme for all those involved with delivering it.

To make a noise about the new system we organised a youth justice week at the end of March 2000 culminating in our two-day conference. This brash approach didn't please everybody, particularly the staider parts of the HO and Lord Chancellor's Department. I was even accused of a cult of personality. But I always kept Jack in the picture on what I was doing; and made sure regular detailed reports were sent to him and the HO about progress om implementing the new system. Each year we published our accounts and an annual review with the first one issued in June 2000. This transparent approach won us supporters and made it easier to work with other agencies to secure money and support for activities aimed at preventing offending. The YJB and YOTs were never going to be funded adequately by the HO for preventative work. We had to build alliances quickly before Jack and I left the scene.

The first area where I sought alliances was sport, so I started with a lunch with Trevor Brooking, then a Match of the Day pundit and Chairman of Sport England. I knew, and said at the time, many young people were faced with a lack of good opportunities to be involved with sport and drifted into drug misuse and crime. Sport was an effective way to divert young people, particularly boys, away from crime; but it was in decline in schools. We needed many more sports projects outside school hours across the country. Trevor shared my view, so the YJB worked with Sport England and the Cabinet Office's 'Positive Futures' programme to set up sports projects, initially using confiscated drugs money to pay for coaches and hire of equipment. Trevor and I launched a London project with Kevin Keegan, then the England manager, with good media coverage. I declined to compete with Trevor and Kevin in a heading contest for the TV cameras.

By mid-2001 we had over 20 of these projects running. They started to capture the attention of football clubs who were looking for community projects that they and their young players could become involved with. Over the next few years many of the leading clubs – and indeed some in the lower leagues like Leyton Orient – started community schemes for more deprived young people, some excluded from school. Many of these schemes had an educational element as well as sport. Marcus Rashford had predecessors willing to become more involved in less fortunate lives, albeit not on the same scale as his achievement.

These preventative programmes became an increasing part of YJB priorities, as we focussed on our statutory duty of reducing offending. We had started in 2000 with 70 Youth Inclusion Programmes (YIPs) on some of the most deprived estates across England and Wales. These worked with the 50-60 most at risk youngsters providing structured and supervised activities outside school. They taught life skills, provided sex and drugs education and used activities to teach relationship skills. Team sports, debating societies and creative classes taught the value of working together, listening, cooperating with others and building self-esteem. The early experience of YIPs indicated that when young people were occupied constructively crime rates fell. An estate in Derby reported crime reducing by a quarter after YIP started. Crimes largely committed by young people like shoplifting and thefts from cars, halved. I bid for more money in the next spending round to expand YIPs.

School holidays were prime times for young people to become involved in anti-social and criminal behaviour. I secured some money from Tessa Jowell at DCMS for what we called 'Splash' schemes in the Easter and Summer school holiday in 2000. These attracted some matching local money and were modelled on the YIP schemes. We put in place 150 schemes. Estate schemes in Gateshead and Birmingham reported a drop of a third in youth crime. Liverpool who ran a city-wide scheme reported the quietest summer they could recall. The YJB were convinced that more YIP, Splash and Positive Future targeted schemes were needed with sustained funding. We could show they were working but we still had to take the begging bowl round Whitehall to fund future

257

schemes, despite our success and our statutory duty of reducing crime. The HO didn't see it as their job to fund these schemes.

As we approached April 2001, we reviewed the second round of annual youth justice plans from YOTs. The overwhelming majority were good or satisfactory with about 10% needing improvement. We had secured extra funding for YOTs from the HO for 2001/2 and held back the allocation of that for the YOTs whose plans needed most improvement. In most local areas extra money had been allocated to YOTs, so 2001/2 budgets were about 25% higher than the first year. But the contributions from education and health was still low at 12% combined. I criticised publicly these low contributions which annoyed some Ministers.

Overall, the first year of operation had been a success. In that year YOTs took decisions on about 150,000 juvenile offenders. About half these were reprimands or final warnings, with the rest court sentences. About 55% of final warnings received an intervention and we pressured YOTs to do better. A good start had been made with Reparation Orders, with about 15,000 used in the first year. Restorative justice approaches were beginning to take hold although some police forces remained sceptical. Bail Supervision Schemes needed more attention, so we issued new national standards. The ASSET documentation was not being used everywhere and we increased funding to secure 100% use.

Over a thousand Parenting Orders were issued in the first year; and YJB itself had funded over 40 parenting programmes in local areas. These orders were beginning to attract more public attention and approval, being seen more as constructive rather than punitive. Even with these programmes many young people lacked a stable adult in their lives. There was a particular problem with boys and the lack of good male role models. I pushed hard for more attention and money for mentoring programmes. We had funded over 40 mentoring programmes in the first year which helped about 1500 young people. We then set up a three-year programme to fund 750 new mentors in about 30 areas, with the emphasis on hard to reach ethnic minority young offenders. I visited a number of the programmes with black mentors – including some ex-offenders – who impressed me enormously with the way they placed structures around some chaotic black youngsters. I was also very proud of the fact that about 12% of YOT staff were from ethnic minorities.

The YJB placed a lot of emphasis on data collection so that we could account for our work and expenditure and that of YOTs. This increased our credibility with politicians, media and public. We were also doing annual MORI surveys of the thoughts and experiences of young people. In the first two months of 2001 MORI quizzed over 5000 schoolchildren aged 11-16 and 500 young people excluded from school but in educational programmes. This showed that criminal activity and drink and drug abuse was significantly higher among those excluded from school. 60% of excluded children admitted committing a criminal offence in the past year compared with a quarter of those in school. However, there was also a worrying increase in crime and anti-social behaviour within schools with 60% or so of youngsters being afraid of physical assault and being robbed. Only half excluded children lived with a father or stepfather, compared with 80% of those in school. The YJB's surveys of children showed clearly that tackling juvenile crime could not be left to the criminal justice system.

YJB data also revealed that we needed a programme for tackling the most persistent young offenders. Three per cent of juvenile offenders were committing 25% of the crime. After a good deal of research and argument we introduced in April 2001 a totally new approach – the Intensive Supervision and Surveillance Programme (ISSP) with funding of £45 million over 3 years. This was an expensive programme costing about £6,000 a year per place to deliver. It was to be used only for the most persistent offenders who committed imprisonable offences on four occasions in a year and had received at least one custodial or community penalty. ISSPs were highly structured and based on the latest research evidence. It had an intensive programme of education and training that tackled the needs of these young offenders. This was combined with robust community surveillance.

For the first 3 months of an ISSP at least 5 hours supervision a day was provided with monitoring during evenings and weekends. Surveillance was provided by a mix of tagging, voice verification, tracking or policing. The whereabouts of all ISSP offenders was checked at least twice daily with a facility for 24/7 surveillance if necessary. Predictably some people challenged the surveillance aspects on civil liberty grounds. My public response was: "For those who are nervous about civil liberties, all I would say is that the alternative for these youngsters is custody." ISSPs could be used for bail, community orders or the community part of a DTO. Initially we approved 28 ISSP programmes – some city or county wide – and later, another 10 or so.

The YJB's biggest headache was the unwieldy and underperforming secure estate that we had inherited. In our review we found we had 2870 places in discrete juvenile units in YOIs run by the Prison Service; 100 places for girls in adult prisons which was totally unacceptable; 300 places in local authority secure units, most of which I suspected we didn't need; and 130 places in 3 private sector secure training centres (STCs), our only new facilities. There were more places than needed, given our intention to reduce use of custody with more community interventions. The situation was complicated, however, by the huge geographical variation in court use of custody. Work we did between October 2000 and September 2001 showed the ratio of custodial to community sentences ranged from 1 to 3 in some places to 1 to 26 in others. This justice by geography could not be explained by gravity of offence.

By March 2001 we had conducted a thorough review of the secure estate and drawn up a reform plan for the next 4 years. We were confident that the YOTs and community penalties would reduce custodial sentences. The use of ISSPs would add to that reduction We had shown that the new bail supervision and support schemes we funded had reduced remands to custody by over 20% by early 2001 and would continue to do so. We wanted to shrink the secure estate and reconfigure it in three ways. First to increase the provision for young women outside the Prison Service, so none were placed with adult offenders. Second to have more appropriate provision for vulnerable 15 and 16-year-olds – especially those with challenging behaviour – outside the Prison Service. Third to better match places to geographical demand in order to reduce distance from families and YOTs.

Our plan was to build about 400 new places in the independent sector. There would be two new 32-place units for young women at two of the existing STCs and another small unit for young mothers and mothers to be. In addition, we proposed three new mixed units in Milton Keynes, Brentwood and the North-West, mainly for 15-16 -year-old boys, but with a few places for girls. New places would go in areas of shortfall like London, South-East, North-West and Wales, which had no unit for juveniles. The areas of surplus were the Midlands and the South-West. To make clear our intentions we gave notice that we would not fund places in Portland in a year's time and would open negotiations for a juvenile YOI in Wales. The whole upgrading programme would cost about £250 million over 3 to 4 years, with most of the money coming from the HO. The YJB also committed to spend more money each year on education and training programmes on the secure estate.

The 2001 Election

In late April I made a short visit to Florida's juvenile justice system. I had heard good reports of their preventative programmes and that they commissioned services rather than running them directly. I started off at the State Juvenile Justice Department in Tallahassee, Florida's capital. I arrived on the last day when Florida's Congress was in session. I observed the massed ranks of lobbyists seeking some pork in the barrel of US politics. I also met the Florida Secretary of State, Katherine Harris, who had certified Florida's controversial Electoral College votes for George Bush in the 2000 Election that secured him the Presidency. George's brother Jeb was Florida's Governor at the time and Katherine's boss. Nobody seemed to think this significant.

I drove myself round Florida for four days visiting three custodial facilities (somewhat misleadingly called academies), two community programmes and an assessment centre. Everyone was very professional and many of the staff were well qualified. The community programmes were very similar to ours. I had doubts about aspects of the custodial commissioning processes but the most striking thing for me was how low-level offences could produce a custodial penalty. There seemed to be no equivalent to our cautioning and final warning system by the police and nothing like our range of options for community punishment. I left Florida thinking we had little to learn from their juvenile justice system and wondering about what their electoral processes had delivered to the world.

Back home the polls suggested that Tony would call an Election soon. This could mean Jack being moved but for now things were going my way. A report by the Council of Europe recommended that its

261

members set up a range of early intervention programmes to stop offending, drawing on the UK's youth justice reforms. More significantly, I had persuaded Jack that the youth justice approaches should be applied to young adults. A White Paper published in February 2001, 'Criminal Justice – the Way Ahead,' announced that the YJB in partnership with the National Probation Service and the Prison Service would draw up a plan for dealing with offending by 18-21-year-olds. We knew that 100,000 hardcore persistent offenders committed 50% of crime and half these were under 21. The White Paper argued that tackling this group required targeting them with intensive and coordinated programmes that stopped offending, not simply locking them up. I had secured a commitment to apply the youth justice lessons to other groups of offenders.

Sure enough, in mid-May an Election on 7 June was announced with purdah stopping any further announcements. By then I had secured the funding needed for the next two years; the policy commitment on 18 to 21s; and a national roll out of Youth Offender Panels and Referral Orders in April 2002. The Election Manifesto included a commitment to build on the youth justice reforms "to improve the standard of accommodation and offending programmes for 18 to 20-year-old offenders." The only small set back was postponement of the next Youth Justice Conference until November.

I managed to take over a speaking commitment from Jack in a personal capacity on 23 May and gave a speech on 'Criminal Justice Tasks for a New Parliament.' This enabled me to push the applicability of the youth justice reforms to other groups of offenders and giving sentencers a wider range of options. I made the mistake of showing Jack a draft who promptly cut out my more radical ideas for commissioning from a wider group of programme providers than the prison and probation services; and breaking up the monolithic prison service. I wanted to separate out the less serious offenders from the hardcore and provide a more bespoke response to offending for three groups – 18 to 24-year-olds, women and older men with sentences under 4 years.

My concern was a new Home Secretary who wanted to be a hard man and turn back the clock. David Blunkett had been openly seeking the job and hinting that he'd be much tougher on criminals than Jack

Straw. The 2001 Election was almost a re-run of 1997 with a lower turnout and Labour winning 413 seats, 5 fewer than previously. The Tories under William Hague were hopelessly divided over Europe, with two future Prime Ministers who symbolised that division, David Cameron and Boris Johnson being elected to Parliament for the first time. Tony could not persuade Gordon to move to the FCO. Jack ended up as Foreign Secretary, inheriting 9/11 a few months later, rather than taking over John Prescott's portfolio of housing, local government and transport. David Blunkett came to the HO. I knew life would change, probably not for the better.

Reform Becomes More Challenging: 2001-2002

Throughout the summer life carried on much as before. In July a new system of community payback was attached to Reparation Orders for cases where there was no individual victim. Tony launched this scheme with a local YOT and plenty of pictures of him watching graffiti being removed from walls. Then came a tap up with David at the end of August when he complained about my independent approach to issuing press notices. I was trying to reduce the use of custody, not least because there was a wide geographical variation in custodial sentencing of juveniles. We had collected all the data on youth court community and custodial sentences for October 2000 to March 2001. At the end of August, I published it as part of the YJB's statutory responsibility to monitor the operation of the youth justice system.

I had kept the head of the Magistrates Association informed and he supported my approach. He and I appeared on the Today programme with John Humphreys who failed to get the bust up he expected. I was not surprised I'd irritated Derry Irvine and his department by publishing data on the judiciary's performance. I pointed out that the YJB was an independent body with a statutory power to publish information in the public interest. This information revealed that many courts, particularly in the North, were much more punitive for the same crimes than others. I promised, however, to keep him informed with the data which I would be publishing every 6 months. David Blunkett joined in the criticism because I had published this data without his approval. (I thought the criticism was more to do with the good media coverage we'd received.)

I apologised for not informing the HO press office earlier, promised to look into our processes on return from holiday and invited him to meet the Board. No promises were given on future conduct.

I decided to carry on as if nothing had happened. I knew I had to shield the Board and YOTs from Ministerial egos and protect what we had achieved. I published a full year's data on youth courts excessive use of custodial sentences, especially short ones. I asked YOTs and courts to work together on using the range of more effective community sentences now available. To his credit David supported the launch of ISSPs and was as critical as me of short sentences. I thought he was beginning to see the advantage of me taking on courts rather than him.

We standardised rewards and sanctions across the secure estate to ensure greater consistency in the treatment of young offenders. The Prisons Inspectorate gave a positive report to the separate Feltham YOI for 15 to 17-year-olds and credit to the YJB for the improvement. I set up a Health Steering Committee with the Department of Health that I chaired to try to improve access of young offenders to CAMHS services. There were very high levels of mental health and behaviour disorders in the youth justice system, with suicide and self-harm the most prominent. The YJB wanted to see the NHS honour its obligations to this group of disenfranchised children. To help this process we produced a checklist for YOTs to use to ensure the health needs of young offenders were met and piloted an assessment tool linked to ASSET, with new training programmes on health needs for YOT staff. We also kept reminding everybody that it was the YJB that had delivered the Government's 1997 pledge to speed up the system for dealing with persistent young offenders.

In November 2001 the Board held its second annual convention in Westminster with 700 delegates and chaired by Trevor Phillips. The speakers included the Attorney General, the HO Minister responsible for youth justice, the Lord Chief Justice, Lord Woolf, and the Met Deputy Commissioner speaking about the huge growth of street crime in London where both perpetrators and victims were often juveniles, many of them first-time offenders. This was a new challenge for YOTs in London's crime hotspots to share intelligence with their neighbours. Lord Woolf was very positive about our ISSPs and community sentences and gave strong encouragement to courts to minimise custodial sentences. The YJB messages were getting through to key decision makers and spreading around the country. In part that was because we were commissioning independent research.

Our research had shown the 3 key factors in a child's life likely to cause offending were low school achievement, family problems and peer behaviour. Sending young offenders to prison wouldn't tackle these problems. Independent research on the 70 YIPs we had set up in 2000 revealed they had been even more successful. YIPs had reached about 8000 young people aged 13-16 in the most deprived areas. They had cut offending by up to a third in some areas and school exclusions had been reduced by a third. We also funded independent research into the huge variation in the use of custody where ratios of custodial to community sentences now varied between 1 to 1 and 1 to 42.

We measured the impact of Splash schemes in school holidays in 2001 (including half-terms). Around 35,000 young people took part in 11,000 innovative programmes from Samba dancing to web design and journalism, with the average daily cost of £3 per youngster. The result was motor crime down by 11% in Splash areas, compared with 39% increase in other high crime areas. Juvenile nuisance and drug offences down by even larger percentages. In the 24 sport Positive Future programmes for 4,000 youngsters living in deprived housing areas, independent research showed up to a 77% reduction in recorded crime. We entered into discussions with the Arts Council about the arts being integrated into offending behaviour programmes. With funding from the Paul Hamlyn Foundation, we launched a scheme to do this at Tate Modern in March 2002.

By the end of 2001, 3000 parents had completed parenting programmes, two-thirds voluntarily and a third as a result of Parenting Orders. These had produced a reduction of a third in the number of offences by children whose parents were on the programme; and over 90% of parents said they would recommend the programmes to others. About 60% of victims participating in restorative justice said they would recommend it to others and offenders reduced further offending. None of this was earth-shattering but it represented solid progress and achievement by YOTs across the country.

In early 2002 an event occurred that destabilised my position at the YJB. In October 2001 the job of Chair of the Audit Commission was advertised. I was attracted by its wide remit across the NHS and local government. It was only one and a half days a week, so I could combine it with the YJB which increasingly required less time. The independent selection process chose me as the most suitable candidate and recommended my appointment to Stephen Byers the appointing Secretary of State. He confirmed my appointment, as did the PM. The job required political independence, so I was asked to resign from the Labour Party. I did this before flying to India on holiday in mid -February.

Few people knew what was afoot, including David Blunkett, because I had been sworn to secrecy. Early in the morning before flying home our bedside phone rang in the lodge in Ranthambore National Park. With my mind on the final tiger safari, I found myself talking to No.10, with a private secretary telling me to report to Downing Street the following day. On the evening of 6 March, I met at No.10 with an embarrassed Nick Raynsford, the Minister for Local Government, who told me the Government had decided not to proceed with my appointment. even though I was the most suitable candidate. This was because the Local Government Association had objected to my appointment. I noted that Byers was allowing an interested party, the LGA, to veto a public appointment approved by the PM after an independent selection process and he lacked the courage to tell me personally.

The LGA arguments that I would not act in an independent and non-partisan way were insulting to both me and the Commission. It inferred that somehow a part-time Chairman could manipulate 18 other Commission members and the Comptroller and his staff. I reminded Nick that his Department asked me to resign from the Labour Party (which I had done) and had agreed a press notice and media handling plan before I went on holiday. Byers' action would cause problems for David Blunkett over whether I was sufficiently independent to chair the YJB. I told Nick that Byers could expect a robust response.

The Byers announcement late on a Friday went down badly. The following day the FT carried a big article with the headline "Byers faces fury for allowing veto of top appointment." I had told its public policy editor, Nick Timmins, exactly what had happened. This had been confirmed by his other sources. Professor Tony Travers told the FT, "it is a tragedy that someone who is extremely well fitted for the job is ruled out because of weakness and other problems in government." LGA Conservatives told me privately that the moving force of opposition to me was a Labour Peer from the North-East and a friend of Byers. A few in the media tried to present this either as a Tony crony story or me sulking by resigning from the Labour Party. But they quickly chose to publish my correcting letters.

I wrote to Byers on 11 March telling him what I thought of his decision; and separately to Tony, David Blunkett and Alan Milburn, explaining that I had left the Labour Party because Byers' Department had asked me to and that I could not go back on that without causing problems for the YJB. I apologised to David for the secrecy I had been asked to keep. I had an extremely friendly and apologetic personal letter from Tony. The pressure was building on Byers over his SPADs' conduct and other matters. He resigned on 29 May, never to return to government or the frontbench. I had been collateral damage from a failing Cabinet Minister with poor political judgement.

As it turned out this unsavoury episode had no adverse effect on my personal reputation or my YJB role. By mid-2002 the YJB was able to demonstrate that the new community orders and final warnings were working. Interventions with final warnings were showing reduced offending. The 129 Bail Supervision and Support Schemes we funded for 17-year-olds was improving court attendance in over 90% of cases. These offenders had committed serious crimes (mainly burglary, violence and handling stolen goods) but 54% complied, reoffending on bail reduced and nearly 80% received non-custodial sentences. In the first half of 2020 we completed rollout of all our 41 ISSP programmes. We finished building the first new custodial unit for girls near Rugby in the summer of 2002 and began the process of removing all 15 and 16-year-old girls from adult prisons.

Not everything was going our way. Throughout 2001 street robbery and knife crime, increased significantly, especially in London and with juveniles as significant perpetrators. The stabbing and death of 10-year-old Damilola Taylor in South-East London in late 2000 symbolised the issue. Matters were heightened when four youths (including two 16-year-olds) went on trial for his murder at the Old Bailey in June 2001 and were later acquitted. Tony was under pressure to respond to public and police outrage. In March 2002 he set up a Street Crime

Action Group that he chaired in the Cabinet Office. The Group had several Cabinet Ministers including David Blunkett, a trio of Chief Constables who acted like prosecuting counsel, a few senior civil servants and me.

Some participants were in Action Man mode trying to impress the PM. The mood was that something had to be done. The 'something' was taking these kids off the streets, especially in the 10 high street crime areas. The problem was the police were not very good at catching the street robbers: YJB research showed only about 10% got caught by the Met. Our research also showed that if young offenders were caught, we had a growing range of effective programmes to put them on. I had to remind the 'lock them up brigade' that if we placed in custody a lot of 12 to 16-year-olds – either on remand or after sentence – then many of them would be too young or too vulnerable to be placed in YOIs. This would mean using very expensive LA secure units that would bust the YJB's budget. My lone supporter was Alan Milburn, the Health Secretary, but I had done enough to prevent over-reaction.

We ended up agreeing that the police had to be more visible on the streets; offenders had to be processed faster through the courts and those remanded or sentenced would not walk freely on the streets. I was to get money for more ISSP schemes and preventative Splash schemes; and the police had to have more presence in schools. The bad news for the YJB was that the courts could send more 12 to 16-year-olds to secure accommodation if they were committing imprisonable offences when on bail. This in large part resulted from the Lord Chief Justice pronouncing in January on custody for mobile phone street robbery, despite his support for our community orders.

David and John Stevens showed public harmony and we quickly organised a joint YJB/Met Police conference in April. David announced the expansion of ISSPs to all London Boroughs, the West Midlands and three other police forces as well as making them sound as tough as possible. I used the extra money to expand Splash schemes to 300 more estates in the highest street crime areas, for use in half-term breaks and to extend them to 9-12-year-olds in the summer holidays. More emphasis was given by John Stevens to police and schools working together to spot likely offenders. The YJB opened discussions with the Premier League about extending the work clubs like Arsenal were doing working with schools in deprived areas and to extend this to working with YOTs. Some YOTs and a few YJB members didn't like the tougher tone, but I explained political reality and told them it could have been much worse.

In the summer we published our second annual report 'Building on Success.' This set out the evidence that the reforms were working, although we had not been able to reduce the use of custody as much as we wanted. I used the report to question the claims that youth crime was spiralling out of control. I pointed out that the British Crime Survey and police reported crime statistics didn't provide any data on the age of perpetrators. Whereas HO statistics on cautions and sentences and the YJB's annual MORI survey categorise on the basis of age. This data showed either a decline in youth crime or little overall change. I suggested in articles and interviews that what we were seeing was moral panic. Street robbery and anti-social behaviour made youth crime more visible, but it wasn't increasing overall. My take on this issue was different from much of the media, public and elected political class of the time.

Throughout 2002 we kept pushing out the data on what was working and what wasn't. The success stories were clear. The youth courts were speeding up; the ASSET tool worked; the ISSPs were effective provided they lasted long enough; short custodial sentences were useless; with good supervision you could stop offending on bail; final warnings were much better than the old cautioning system; and school holiday schemes reduced youth crime, as did YIPs in high crime areas. The jury was still out on parenting programmes, restorative justice and Referral Orders but they were worth persevering with. DTOs looked as though they needed rethinking. It was clear that low detection rates by police were a serious problem in some high crime areas. If the police didn't catch young offenders, they couldn't be placed on our effective programmes to stop offending.

Two new HO Ministers arrived in June 2002 sympathetic to the youth justice reforms – Charlie Falconer and Hilary Benn. Hilary made it clear that he saw the youth justice reforms as the flagship for criminal justice reform. In the school summer holidays we had another successful and larger Splash programme, but I had to work hard and use political connections to winkle money for it out of Whitehall.

269

Despite its success and No.10 support I could not get the money for this preventative work integrated in the YJB budget. However, Gordon Brown announced that 25% of his Children's Fund allocation would go on youth crime prevention.

New Zealand committed itself to YOTs and the Tory and Lib Dem shadow teams were making supportive noises about them. It was starting to look as though we might be able to secure cross-party support for the youth justice reforms rather than them being a political football. I was still unsure about David Blunkett's support, particularly after a spat I had with him over a BBC interview I gave. He thought I should have obtained HO approval, but I disagreed and declined to clear every interview with the HO. I wasn't sure what would happen next but decided to test matters by inviting David to give the keynote speech at the YJB's third national conference in November 2002, which he accepted.

The conference was chaired by Fiona Bruce of BBC News and Crimewatch. It was quite low key compared with the first two. I brought everybody up to date and outlined the agenda for the next year – more of the same, as we could show a big drop in reoffending. David made a speech about prevention and working together to save children from dysfunctional families. There were good practitioner and young people contributions and we launched 10 effective practice guides. By the end of 2002 we had also established a secure email service between YOTs, police, courts and the secure estate. We were also trying to build a workforce of skilled youth justice professionals and piloting a Professional Certificate in Effective Practice for both new and experienced practitioners. The YJB ended 2002 having fought hard to avoid moral panic and to protect the staff of YOTs.

Continuing Progress and Missed Opportunities: 2003

2003 started with the YJB announcing that by January 2004 ISSPs would be available to every YOT. Research had shown that six-month ISSPs provided more supervision and activities that challenged hardcore offending behaviour than short prison sentences. It was already in 119 YOT areas and would be established in the remaining 36 areas. The evidence suggested it would be even more effective if extended to 12 months. The key seemed to have been the effectiveness of tagging in curfew hours. ISSPs were proving more effective than the DTO because the time spent on rigorous community programmes was longer. I was beginning to think that the community part of the DTO needed to be lengthened but without a longer period in custody.

In 2005 there was a comprehensive research evaluation of ISSPs. This revealed that they had reduced custody by just over 2% when custody was rising for every other age group. Frequency of offending by these frequent offenders was down by 40% after one year and 39% after two. Seriousness of offending was down by 13% after both one and two years. The cost-benefit analysis showed average savings of £80,000 per start of each ISSP.

Reducing custody for juveniles remained the hardest part of our job. By mid-2003 we had reduced the number of 16-year-old girls in adult prisons to a handful and would achieve removal by our target date of the end of 2003. We had committed ourselves to reducing the number of juveniles in custody by 10% by March 2005 and by July 2003, the juvenile population had reduced by 12.6%, compared with October 2002. In the same period the adult prison population had increased by 2%. It would take a decade to see big reductions in the use of custody, but we had stopped the rise.

In 2003 I also announced that we would pilot a new approach to stopping young people getting involved in crime at an early age. This would involve setting up 14 Youth Inclusion and Support Panels (YISPs) in the ten highest street crime areas. The panels would be made up of members of the community and a range of agencies including YOTs, teachers, police, health and social workers. They would identify 8 to 13-year-olds showing the sort of behaviour that research suggested could lead to crime. If the young person and family agreed their details could be shared with the panel, they would help the young person and their family to access mainstream services and have key workers.

March 2003 brought a big breakthrough with HO research comparing reconviction rates of juvenile offenders dealt by the police and courts in the first 3 months of 1997 and 2001. This showed that 26.4% were reconvicted in 2001 compared with 34.1% in 1997. This was a 22.5% reduction that could be attributed to the youth justice reforms when we had only promised a 5% reduction by 2004. This data was reliable and striking enough for No.10 to get the PM involved. The April edition of YJB News had a big spread featuring Tony thanking YOTs for what they had achieved.

The YJB's third annual report was published in June 2003, just as I left. It demonstrated that we had put in place a coherent youth justice system in three years. We were reducing offending and reoffending. There were still too many juveniles in custody but ISSPs had shown they reduced the use of custody. There was still too much geographical variation in the range and quality of services, the behaviour of courts and the outcomes for young people. We knew much more about the characteristics of young offenders from ASSET and our research. This showed that many started offending at 11 or 12, with truanting, unmet special educational needs and living in single-parent households. Prevention programmes, like Splash and YIPs, worked if Government took the trouble to invest in them on a regular and reliable basis. (The report even had a picture of Prince Harry supporting such a programme at West Ham football club.) We had trained a cadre of good and committed staff and managers.

Despite the success of the reforms, I still sensed that David Blunkett found it difficult to own the youth justice agenda. I kept trying to engage with him over the issue of applying the lessons of the youth justice reforms to the 18 to 21-year-olds, as promised in the 2001 Election Manifesto. The HO Permanent Secretary, John Gieve, and one of David's SPADs also tried to help me, as did Hilary Benn; but David simply wouldn't meet me to discuss the issue. He made little secret that he wanted to be seen as tougher than Jack. It seemed as though my card was marked as part of the wimpish former regime.

I kept plugging away on the YJB taking more responsibility for 18 to 21-year-olds, given the poor condition of their YOIs. The Board agreed a paper setting out the case for remodelling the 18-21 system on the same basis as the youth justice changes. This suggested a pilot scheme on how this might be tested. It did at least produce some movement with some 17-year-olds being allowed to remain in the juvenile YOI when they reached their 18th birthday. That was as far as I could progress matters.

David had effectively abandoned the work Jack and I had started on alternatives to custody and other forms of liberty deprivation for non-violent offenders and for women. It was unclear what his longer-term strategy for prisons was, other than to seek more funding. Tony wanted a longer-term strategy and decided to hold meetings with David to work up such a strategy before agreeing extra funding. He asked me to attend these meetings, apparently without telling David. This did not help my relationship with David. After a couple of meetings, he wanted to see me privately to ask if I was on his side or not. All I could say was that I couldn't decline to attend meetings to which the PM had invited me. I escaped from these meetings before any prison strategy was agreed.

I had been running the YJB for nearly 5 years and was getting restless. I had been Chairman of the National Council of Voluntary Organisations since 2001; and in 2003 I became Chairman of a new London Regional Sports Board, as part of Sport England. I began looking at other options including a move to social housing which interested me. I wasn't sure if I wanted to be re-appointed to the YJB if the 18-21 age group were off-limits. Slightly to my surprise David did re-appoint me as YJB Chairman but three weeks later came a bigger surprise. Alan Milburn left the Cabinet abruptly causing a Cabinet reshuffle. John "oh fuck, not health" Reid became Health Secretary on 13 June, with me joining his Ministerial team.

Postscript: Youth Justice Success but Prison Policy Failure

I had a lot of personal respect for David Blunkett. His blindness required him to work much harder than a sighted person, but it also seemed to make him suspicious of people outside his personal circle. He had been an effective Education Secretary and he did some good things in the HO including taking a better grip on the asylum system. But the quest for toughness effectively ended serious work on alternatives to custody and using prisons differently. It was a missed opportunity not to apply the lessons of the youth justice reforms to 18-21s and women, given the supportive text in the 2001 Election manifesto. 18-21-year-olds in custody continued to get a much worse deal than under-18s.

From the Department of Health, I watched with disbelief the introduction of indeterminate sentences under the 2003 Criminal Justice Act. Instead of the extra 900 extra prison places it was supposed

273

to require, a decade later there were over 6000 extra people in prison for longer than the sentences a judge would have handed down for their offences. The adult prison population in England and Wales had grown by about 3000 between 1997 and 2003 to nearly 64,000. But by 2010, when Labour left office, it had soared to 84,000. It rose even higher and stayed above 80,000 until Covid19. This need not have happened because alternative approaches were being developed and could have been taken to scale.

Fortunately, the youth justice reforms carried on much as I left them but with continuing improvements in performance. The YOTs and YJB are still operating today, much as before. The only threat to them came from the Coalition Government after the 2010 Election. In a bonfire of quangos an attempt was made to abolish the YJB. I managed to assemble enough support in the House of Lords from Labour, LibDems and Crossbenchers to thwart abolition. In March 2020, prior to Covid lockdown, Lord Tom McNally and I hosted a 20-year celebration for YOTs, with all previous YJB chairs and Jack Straw present.

The number of juveniles in custody did not follow the same path as for adult offenders. The numbers stayed fairly steady until 2008 and then started dropping significantly as ISSPs and DTOs continued to be used by courts. In 2009/10 DTOs accounted for 90% of custodial sentences for juveniles. In March 2020 YJB statistics show only 780 juveniles in custody on average in any one day, a fall of nearly 70% compared with 10 years previously. This was thanks to the policy consistency of my YJB successors. Reoffending rates continued to drop and were down 25% between 2000 and 2008.

I still feel immensely proud of what was achieved with the youth justice reforms. We had shown public sector reforms could work and stay the course. YOTs are a local multi-agency model that could be copied for other complex social problems. A missed opportunity was not applying the reforms to 18-21-year-old offenders and probably women. The failure to break up the monolithic Prison Service and redesign punishment and rehabilitation policies for less dangerous offenders remains an area of public policy failure.

9. Yes Minister - Drugs, Bugs and Bureaucracy: 2003-2005

Life as a Minister

One afternoon in June 2003 my home telephone rang. No.10 asked me to speak to the Prime Minister. Tony Blair wanted me to become a Health Minister. I reminded him I was no longer a member of the Labour Party to which he replied, 're-join'. By 6 pm that evening I was a Health Minister and found myself back in the Department of Health (DH), twenty years after leaving it as a civil servant. This was the start of a chaotic, absorbing and often frustrating experience at a time of great change and turmoil for a national icon – the NHS. Suddenly riches beyond its wildest dreams had become available after years of penury. But the cash was accompanied by an avalanche of change driven by the Prime Minister, special advisers and a small cadre of Ministers and civil servants. The NHS liked the money but wasn't keen on the 'change' part of the deal.

My time as a Minister was one of political controversy. The events of 9/11 had led to a war in Iraq driven from the other side of the Atlantic. A British Prime Minister had decided to support an unpopular US President. In doing so he spent much of his political capital. The Labour Party, like the country, was divided over the Iraq war. I was uneasy without a new UN resolution which was ruled out by Chirac's last-minute change of heart. At the time I thought it reasonable to believe that Saddam Hussein still had chemical weapons that he was willing to use. The Chilcot Inquiry eventually revealed we were wrong. At the time few realised how inept the US would be at replacing Saddam and securing the peace. I realised I was a Blair appointee when his political share price was falling. On a personal level I liked Tony Blair and supported his public service reform agenda.

Unlike my elected colleagues I had no electorate or trade union links to worry about, so it was easy for me to keep my foot on the reform accelerator. Unlike them I had managed big organisations and taken them through periods of change. As a former senior civil servant, I was well-versed in mandarin behaviour and knew how government departments and their client organisations could thwart reform. I never thought the British civil service was the Rolls-Royce machine that many liked to claim. As a former Cabinet Secretary, Lord Butler, said in an interview in May 2010: "the job of a civil servant is being a mercenary." They were there to be listened to but ultimately to be directed.

My experience provided me with a healthy scepticism about some of the advice I received and the confidence to reject it and find alternative ideas. This experience and perspective made it easier to be a reforming Minister. But even as a politically-savvy manager rather than an ideological politician, I couldn't escape the fetters and distractions of Ministerial life. These impose considerable constraints on all Ministers, whatever their political party, and are little understood by much of the public and commentariat.

There is a lot of routine in the life of a Minister which has little to do with changing the world: correspondence, Parliamentary business, speeches, duty Minister rosters, voting, Cabinet committees, EU business and dealing with the media. Elected Ministers also have to nurture their constituencies and manage their small Parliamentary constituency offices. As an unelected Lords Minister, I had many of these distractions but also some different ones – namely the business and preoccupations of an unmodernised House of Lords.

Most people, including elected Ministers, do not understand the role and workings of the House of Lords as an antiquated and over-large scrutiny and revising second Chamber. They have little sympathy with the fact that as a Minister you cannot rely on a whipped majority, as in the House of Commons, to get the Government's business through. In the Lords no government usually has a majority. With the Foundation Trust legislation in 2003 John Reid – who liked to refer to the Lords as the 'Eastern Front' – had to accept me negotiating with the opposition parties to secure the legislation. Commons Ministers don't realise how much time Lords Ministers spend on House of Lords business.

As Lords Health Minister, I covered all aspects of DH (and Food Standards Agency) work in the Lords as well as handling my own portfolio of responsibilities. This meant appearing regularly to answer oral questions, signing off all written health answers in the Lords, dealing with frequent debates and taking all DH legislation through the Lords. These duties did not exempt me from my share of the normal Ministerial slog of signing hundreds of replies to MPs a month (including 150 unsigned letters to MPs my colleagues had dumped in my room); being a duty Minister over weekends and in Parliamentary Recesses; and covering for other Ministers when they were overseas. My own portfolio produced its share of Cabinet Committees, media appearances, overseas visits and speeches to conferences.

Looking back over my time as a Minister I find I gave about 60 conference speeches and averaged one or two media appearances a week; signed the best part of 10,000 letters; undertook EU Ministerial meetings and about five or six other overseas representational visits; and acted as Duty Minister for about 40 weekends and 15-20 weeks of Parliamentary recesses. As the only Minister who lived in London and had no constituency, I was a sitting duck for the Duty Minister roster. All this took time away from policy work, thinking and implementing change. Admittedly some of these diversions (such as a visit to China to sign health agreements) were not without their interest and fun.

As Duty Minister in November 2006, I found myself in COBR meetings dealing with the poisoning of Alexander Litvinenko with Polonium 210. This had all the ingredients for a TV drama – foreign agents using a radioactive substance to poison someone on UK soil in a public place; FCO diplomacy with a powerful foreign country in a state of denial; a police investigation fraught with intelligence implications and new scientific challenges. On top of this was handling concerns about public and NHS staff exposure to radioactive dosages. A bemused public and hyperactive media had to be kept informed in a fast-changing drama.

This is when you learn what Government is all about – "events, dear boy, events" as Harold Macmillan said. As the responsible Minister you have to take decisions with imperfect information and try to keep people informed without raising public anxieties or jeopardising a criminal prosecution. Events like this were not much to do with my day job but it was what you turned your hand to as a duty Minister.

Whatever else a Minister does, keeping your boss informed is critical. John Reid was easy to work with even though I lacked his Labour Party background and some backbenchers found me too managerial. Keeping the Prime Minister on side was even more important. This was never a problem with Tony Blair providing he was convinced that you were driving reform as fast as possible. He was accessible, unlike his next-door neighbour cocooned in the Treasury. Blair was skilled at keeping himself sufficiently informed through his staff without becoming submerged in detailed documents. This meant keeping No.10 apparatchiks on side.

The biggest distraction from my main Ministerial portfolio was the House of Lords. Apart from my role as a Health Minister I was part of the Government's payroll vote for all its legislation in a Second Chamber in which it had no majority. If the Liberal Democrats and Conservatives joined forces – as they regularly did - they could defeat the Government on its legislation unless the Crossbenchers sided with the Government, which back then they often didn't. This meant that for parts of the year either I based myself in the Lords or I abandoned Departmental meetings, jumped in a Ministerial car and sprinted up the Lords' stairs to get into the division lobby in the 8 minutes then allowed to me.

One of the greatest problems was oral questions. Unlike the Commons the Lords has no set days for particular Departments' oral questions. It started each sitting day with four oral questions (which could be on anything) lasting 8 minutes each. This meant, as happened to me on occasion, you could end up having three or even four questions on totally different topics on the same day on matters outside your main portfolio – and sometimes with little notice. For me this meant spending the morning before questions becoming an instant expert on anything from avian 'flu or contaminated blood to obscure cancers or mixed-sex hospital wards. Fragments of briefings for oral questions could be dredged up from my memory in media interviews to slow down a tormentor like Paxman or Humphreys even if it didn't totally distract them from Ministerial pursuit.

By 2003 the Lords had become more politically confrontational following the removal of most hereditary peers and the realisation by many campaigning organisations that the best place to sandbag the Government was in the Lords where there was no Government majority. Sometimes civil service accuracy failed. On 25 October 2006 I was asked an oral question about the cost of tattoo removals under the NHS. This followed a Commons answer that said the NHS removed 187,000 tattoos a year. I didn't believe these figures and asked the DH statisticians to check them. Silence reigned until just before I went into the Chamber to answer the question when I was told that the correct figure was not 187,000 but about half a dozen. I had to acknowledge the figures were wrong; use jokes about a surgeon on the Conservative benches having to use his skill to remove 'I love William', 'I love Iain' and 'I love Michael' tattoos from Conservative MPs because of their frequent change of Leader. I was also able to be rude to Lord Tebbit which always went down well on Labour benches.

Debates and legislation in the Lords took up a lot of time. Apart from many Orders and Regulations, I piloted through five major Health Bills: the Health and Social Care Act 2003 (which set up Foundation Trusts and new inspectorates/regulators); the Human Tissue Act 2004 (which reformed the law on the removal, storage and use of human organs and other tissues following scandals over the widespread misuse of children's organs at Alder Hey Children's Hospital); the Health Protection Agency Act 2003 (which provided a statutory basis for the agency); the NHS Redress Act 2006 (which reformed the Clinical Negligence Scheme); and the Health Act 2006 (which banned smoking in work and public places).

Three of these were very controversial and occupied a lot of time on the floor of the House, sometimes until late into the night or even early morning. We finished the Foundation Trusts legislation at 5am with me negotiating amendments with John Reid and the Opposition benches through the night. The parents of Merseyside dead children sat watching my every utterance during the Human Tissues Bill. The civil libertarians were out in force for the Bill banning smoking in public places and workplaces – not to mention the House of Lords cigar and pipe club. I even had to persuade my colleagues to amend the Bill to allow smoking on stage in plays where this was artistically required by the play.

Your quality of life as a Minister depended a great deal on your Private office. I chose the Private Secretaries I wanted, not always what I was offered. Ministers have only themselves to blame if they put up with Private Office personnel who are unsuitable. If you cannot trust your Private Secretaries – and I have been one – you are in trouble. The frenetic lifestyle makes a sense of humour important. Your Private Office have to be able to cope with you applying to official submissions a stamp which reads "I haven't got time to read this CRAP"; and accept that your gym and theatre engagements are very high priority diary commitments.

Health was a 'hot' issue in my time as a Minister, with many debates requiring me to sit on the front bench for hours at a time. My attention would wander. During one interminable speech by an opponent of a smoking ban in public places I was in a private reverie and was accused of not paying attention. Rather ill-advisedly I told him his endless repetition must have caused me to doze off. There was an uproar but business speeded up. My personal record was 8½ hours on the front bench for the Second Reading of Lord Joffé's Assisted Dying Bill in 2006. I had to pretend to be neutral (the Government's position usually on private members bills) even though many people knew I strongly supported the Bill.

This sketch of Ministerial life in the Lords is not intended to excuse my mistakes – which I acknowledge freely – but to demonstrate how much time is taken away from a Minister's main job and priorities. In terms of Ministerial accountability this may be important, but it comes at a price in terms of tiredness, rushed decision-making and distraction from implementing change. The more we tie up Ministerial time in Parliamentary and media activity – important though they are – the less time Ministers have to think through the policy, legislation and implementation implications of changes they are trying to make.

Modernising the Regulation of Medicines

When I became the Pharmaceuticals and Life Sciences Minister in 2003 many people had a different attitude to science and medicines to today's Covid dominated world. Politicians rarely claimed they were following the science. Little attention was paid to the processes for producing lifesaving medicines. When it was, the public didn't always like what it saw, with the tragedies of Thalidomide and infected blood still present in the public consciousness. Media stories were often negative about drugs causing adverse effects; about a research-based industry making hefty profits; and about animals being used for testing drugs before they were tried in humans. Scientists were criticised – especially by faith-based communities – for tampering with nature. Personal privacy was often seen as in conflict with research needs, especially with the advances in genomic medicine.

Those producing new drugs sometimes felt hard done by. One of Pfizer's top managers told me in early 2005 that he thought the public regarded the pharmaceutical industry as no better than the tobacco industry. Big Pharma often felt misunderstood over their obligations to shareholders and the need to fund a research base that could not produce Derby winners every time. Yet the day-to-day reality of our healthcare system was very different. Diseases that used to kill no longer did so, largely because of modern medicines. Infectious diseases that caused so many childhood deaths 60-70 years ago were curbed significantly by antibiotics and other new drugs. As we create new ways of killing ourselves through bad lifestyle choices, scientists and the pharmaceutical industry keep coming to our rescue. To fight a modern pandemic we need new vaccines and anti-retrovirals, as Covid19 has demonstrated so dramatically.

No healthcare system can operate without ready access to new drugs or old drugs re-purposed. Modern electorates now expect governments to provide the latest drugs for keeping them alive and maintaining their quality of life, whatever their bad lifestyle choices. That is why medicines, vaccines and devices are a growing part of the non-labour costs of the NHS. Back in 2003 about 10% of its budget went on medicines – somewhat more if medical devices and vaccines were included. With coronavirus it will be a lot more. Then, as now, much of the population rely on pills to keep themselves alive and believe they have a right to access those drugs, irrespective of cost or personal behaviour. This attitude is fed by a media awash with news of the latest wonder drug for saving lives.

I found myself in a world with conflicting views of Big Pharma and with conflicted roles of my own. I was expected to regulate the safety and efficacy of the UK pharmaceutical and devices industries. But at the same time, I was to be a tough negotiator of the prices the NHS paid for these drugs and devices. Alongside these two roles I was expected to promote a research-based UK pharmaceutical industry which provided high-quality, well paid jobs and supported Britain's science and research base. I was reminded regularly, inside and outside Parliament, that I had conflicted roles but no-one had a better alternative.

To regulate the pharmaceutical and medical devices industries a new DH Executive Agency had been established in April 2003 called the Medicines Healthcare products Regulatory Agency (MHRA). This was the result of a merger of the Medicines Control Agency and the Medical Devices Agency. The former had been established in response to the thalidomide scandal in the 1960s. Devices were the poor relation of pharmaceuticals and were less rigorously regulated. When I arrived the MHRA was still finding its feet under its new Chairman, Sir Alasdair Breckenridge and did not have a Chief Executive. There were concerns that the regulator was in the pocket of 'Big Pharma'. This view was fed to some extent by the MHRA who considered only knowledgeable scientists could regulate the industry. This meant recruiting people from Big Pharma. The DH claim was that poachers could become effective gamekeepers; but the MHRA's predecessors had a poor record on transparency and involving patients.

This was a tricky time for a new Minister and a new Regulator. The MHRA's main role was assessing the safety, quality and efficacy of medicines and authorising their sale or supply in the UK for human use. It also audited the bodies that approved devices. In these roles it had to operate a post-licensing surveillance function; sample and test medicines for quality defects in their manufacture; monitor the safety of unlicensed imported products; regulate clinical trials; promote good practice in the use of medicines and control their labelling. There was plenty of scope for things to go wrong with a public hungry for new cures and an industry eager to provide them but with healthy profits. The Minister's job was to be 'hands off' on the MHRA's technical work but ensure a flourishing and safe drugs and devices industry that could generate wealth for UK plc without bankrupting the NHS. The trick was to keep well-informed, avoid detailed interference but make sure my presence was felt selectively. If there was serious trouble Ministers would have to intervene, whatever the MHRA thought.

In 2003 the role of national regulators across Europe was being increasingly absorbed by the European Medicines Agency (EMEA) as the harmonisation of pharmaceutical regulation gained pace. The European research-based pharmaceutical industry was struggling, although the UK was doing better than mainland Europe. Clinical trials for drugs were cheaper to conduct in Asia and the power of the US drugs market tended to suck research talent across the Atlantic. The US Food and Drugs Administration (FDA) was effectively the dominant regulator in pharmaceuticals; and the increasing European emphasis on controlling drug prices did not endear US 'Big Pharma' to European governments. Nor did the UK's veto on direct marketing to the public of prescription drugs. A significant body of controversial EU legislation was also in the pipeline on clinical trials, use of human tissue, traditional herbal remedies and medical devices.

I supported Alasdair Breckenridge in bedding down the new Agency and appointing a Chief Executive. But I thought the MHRA needed to improve its communications and to involve patients more; and should overhaul its system for collecting information on adverse drug reactions (the yellow card scheme). I required them to develop a 5-year corporate plan which would cover the period when the EU Presidency was held by the UK. I was looking for innovation in three areas: taking medicines off prescription; allowing prescriptions to be issued by health professionals other than doctors; and giving patients a bigger say on adverse reactions to medicines.

There was much professional angst about taking medicines off prescription. I agreed a 3-month consultation beginning in November 2003 to allow a low dose statin, Simvastatin 10mg, to be purchased over the counter by patients. The result was a third of consultees in favour, a third against and a third not against but with some questions. Doctors were divided, with the BMA and the Royal College of GPs opposed but with other medical royal colleges either supportive in principle or not opposed. After considering the arguments the MHRA's Committee on the Safety of Medicines (CSM) advised Ministers that the 10mg Simvastatin could be made available without a prescription through pharmacies to people with a moderate risk of a heart attack (ie.10%-15% risk of myocardial infarction over ten years).

I wanted to implement the scientific advice but realised that accepting it would put us out of line with other countries: the FDA, for example, would not approve statins off prescription. Already nearly 2 million people a year in the UK were taking statins and these were thought to be saving 6,000-7,000 lives a year. By extending patient choice over access to low dose statins through pharmacies we would empower people to take more responsibility for their health. The pharmacists' professional body supported the move and provided guidance to all pharmacies. On 12 May 2004 John Reid announced that the UK would be the first country to provide statins over the counter without a prescription. The statins controversy continued in the medical journals but we continued cautiously with a case-by-case approach on taking other medicines off prescription. The statins decision did not open the floodgates, but did establish a process, using the Committee on the Safety of Medicines and public consultation, for selectively taking medicines off prescription.

Alongside this issue was allowing health staff other than doctors to issue prescriptions. This would reduce the work of doctors and improve patient access to medicines, but the idea was viewed with suspicion by many doctors. Progress had been slow since initiatives started in 1999 but in April 2003 it was agreed that supplementary prescribers could prescribe in accordance with a diagnosis and treatment plan agreed by a doctor. I wanted to go further and move to a system whereby at least trained and approved nurses and pharmacists could prescribe an agreed list of medicines. Initially nurses were trained and restricted to a limited formulary with about 250 prescription medicines; but slowly this list was extended.

Gradually I authorised physiotherapists, chiropodists/podiatrists and radiographers to become supplementary prescribers after appropriate training. Trained nurses and pharmacists in secondary care were then allowed to prescribe controlled drugs and unlicensed drugs. From these beginnings we now have a system in which a wide range of trained health professionals are approved as independent prescribers to prescribe any medicine for any medical condition. As the NICE website makes clear, these independent prescribers include nurses, pharmacists, physiotherapists, therapeutic radiographers, optometrists and podiatrists. There are now thousands of approved independent prescribers, mainly nurses and pharmacists. Yet an over-cautious NHS has too often been slow to apply this innovation.

The Thalidomide tragedy highlighted the need for routine post-marketing surveillance of medicines; and the Yellow Card Scheme was set up in 1964 to help secure this. By 2003 approaching half a million reports of adverse drug reactions (ADRs) had been reported to the MHRA or their predecessor bodies. In 2003 about 18,000 ADRs were coming in under this early warning system, although a Yellow Card notification did not necessarily mean an adverse reaction was caused by the drug. But Yellow Cards could only be sent in by health professionals and it was difficult for researchers to access Yellow Card data on specific drugs. The limited access and restrictions on patients notifying ADRs direct were justified sources of complaint but MHRA professionals were very reluctant to change the scheme.

After several discussions with the MHRA chairman I announced on 21 July 2003 an independent review on these issues by Dr Jeremy Metters, a former Deputy Chief Medical Officer. After public consultation, Metters produced a report published on 4 May 2004, the 40th Anniversary of the Yellow Card scheme. His report recommended improving access to data by researchers and regular publication of anonymised aggregated data on the MHRA website. I put these recommendations out for wider consultation; but I accepted with immediate effect his recommendation for direct patient reporting of ADRs through the Yellow Card scheme. This caused consternation in the MHRA, but I instructed them to produce a system for patients to register ADRs and to raise public awareness of the scheme. I then released a private secretary on promotion to take forward this work. It was heavy going.

It took me until January 2005 to announce that the MHRA would publish anonymised data on ADRs on their website; and that researchers could access detailed data subject to approval by an independent committee that the research was ethically and scientifically sound. It took even longer to set up pilot schemes for patients to directly report ADRs to the regulator. Forms to report ADRs were eventually made available in 4,000 GP surgeries across the UK; and patients were also able to report online. Progress slowed further after my job change in 2005. It was early 2008 before the MHRA established a full-scale patient reporting system as part of the Yellow Card scheme. By early 2009 the MHRA reported receiving about 25,000 ADRs a year under the scheme. It took 5 years for the MHRA to fully accept direct patient notification of ADRs.

The Seroxat Episode and Prosecuting GSK

During this heavy lifting on the Yellow Card scheme, I had a further struggle with the MHRA. This was over the anti-depressant Seroxat, then being taken by half a million people. A 2003 BBC Panorama programme had revealed that many people taking higher doses of Seroxat were experiencing side effects of nervousness, aggression, irrational thoughts and in some cases feelings of suicide. There had been cases of suicide among young people that had attracted media attention. GSK, Seroxat's manufacturer, had sought to reassure the public ever since the drug was licensed around 1991. The MHRA was aware of the concerns and in January 2003 had launched their own review of Seroxat and other similar SSRIs (Selective Serotonin Reuptake Inhibitors).

This review included a small subset of patients for whom Seroxat was not licensed but was being prescribed by doctors. These were young people under the age of 18. An estimated 8,000 young people a year were being prescribed Seroxat at the time. For some of these young people the results were disturbing. A report from the CSM stated that children taking the antidepressant were more likely to self-harm or have suicidal thoughts. The CSM report was based on information that had suddenly been provided by GSK; and was published on 10 June. Doctors were discouraged from prescribing Seroxat for young people under 18. This information went to regulators in Europe and the US while the MHRA review continued.

Mind, the mental health charity, had demonstrated outside MHRA's offices over Seroxat. As a result, MHRA had invited MIND's Chief Executive, Richard Brook, to join the expert panel conducting the review. So far so good. However, in October 2003 MHRA reviewed data from the earliest trials of Seroxat and Brook claimed that MHRA's predecessor body had failed to pick up an important point. This was that Seroxat doses above 20mg a day worked no better than a lower dosage; but significantly increased adverse side effects causing serious problems for the 17,000 people a year taking the higher dosage. Brook fell out with MHRA in March 2004 and asked to see me. I was advised not to see him but did.

Brook told me that MHRA wanted to kick the whole issue into the long grass by referring matters to the EMEA, the European regulator. What really incensed him was that MHRA's Chief Executive had said he faced a criminal prosecution if he revealed anything that was commercially in confidence that he had learnt from his time on the

Expert Group. He felt seriously compromised as a patients' representative and wanted to resign to tell the truth as he saw it. I sympathised with Brook but asked for a few days to talk to the MHRA. Some robust discussions with MHRA staff followed in which I made it clear that threatening Brook was neither appropriate nor smart. I told the MHRA that Brook would resign and tell his story and made it clear that I would not sanction a criminal prosecution.

The Expert Working Group had not completed its work but it was clear there were serious concerns about excessively high dosages of Seroxat, even if it was suitable for use with some adults. If the UK acted against Seroxat the EMEA might not support this and there could be a legal challenge by GSK. I settled for a compromise in which the Chairman of the CSM told prescribers that the 20mg daily dosage of Seroxat was the recommended dosage for the treatment of adults with depression, social or generalised anxiety disorder and post traumatic-stress disorder. It was made clear that the 40mg dosage was only for adults with obsessive compulsive disorder and panic disorder and that increasing dosages above the recommended levels would not improve treatment efficacy. This letter was issued a few days after my meeting with Richard Brook.

I talked to Brook again and tried to persuade him to stay on the Expert Working Group. He declined to do so and on 23 March 2004 wrote a Daily Mail article that was very critical of the MHRA but did indicate that I had taken action. I remained puzzled by GSK's sudden production of data on the impact of Seroxat on children. In November I received a final report from the MHRA along with some NICE guidelines on the treatment and care of people with depression and anxiety. I insisted on publishing the report and NICE guidelines together on 6 December 2004. The report was not particularly critical of most SSRIs but was hardly a ringing endorsement and wanted dosages kept low. The advice was for careful and frequent monitoring, especially in the early stages of treatment and avoiding rapid withdrawal from SSRIs. The findings satisfied the drug companies by saying that SSRIs were effective in treating depression and anxiety, but they left me and others feeling uneasy.

A further Panorama programme on Seroxat in October 2004 had given a roasting to GSK and the MHRA. It surfaced publicly the concerns I had been pursuing about whether GSK had acted promptly enough early on in handing over to the MHRA crucial safety information about Seroxat's effect on young people under 18. A convoluted and unconvincing explanation had been provided to me about why GSK had mysteriously and suddenly handed over this material in June, just before my appointment. The early clinical trials data on the use of Seroxat with under-18s had clearly cast doubt on its efficacy and had revealed concerns about adverse reactions. However, this data had been merged with adult data into a meta-analysis and the significance of the findings for young people under 18 was lost in the bigger adult numbers. Allegedly, this only became clear after the first Panorama programme on the 11 May 2003; and this caused GSK to disaggregate the data and provide it to the MHRA.

I considered there was a strong case for prosecuting GSK for failure to inform the MHRA in a timely fashion of adverse reactions in juveniles. This started a full-scale investigation which sank into a bureaucratic and legal quagmire when I changed Ministerial jobs in 2005. It became the largest investigation of its kind in the UK and generated over 1 million pages of evidence as GSK challenged everything. The case limped on for another three years until in March 2008 government prosecutors finally decided not to prosecute GSK because they considered there was no realistic prospect of a conviction, given the then state of enforcement legislation. All GSK received was a slap on the wrist, with the MHRA Chief Executive, Kent Woods, saying: "I remain concerned that GSK could and should have reported this information earlier than they did."

The Seroxat episode fuelled a public debate about the MHRA being in the pocket of Big Pharma and the Government being too weak to intervene. The critics pointed out that the industry funded MHRA through fees; its staff came predominantly from industry and MHRA didn't publish the information to support its decisions or require industry to disclose adverse reactions promptly. There was also the argument that patients did not play a big enough role in MHRA decisions. The industry's only counter view seemed to be that the Government didn't do enough to support it as part of UK plc. I tried to tackle these systemic problems and bring MHRA's committee structure in line with the EU's new legislative requirements on topics such as clinical trials and homeopathic and herbal medicines.

Declarations of industry interest were strengthened; committee chairs were prevented from having any personal interest in the industry; and more lay members were appointed to committees. The MHRA Chairman realised change was needed and helped me quell internal resistance. In February 2004 I launched a consultation document proposing expansion of expert groups in line with EU changes, more involvement of lay people in committees and more rigorous arrangements over declarations of interest and avoiding conflicts of interest. I agreed reforms that became fully operational in October 2005, including more lay people om committees.

Abandoning industry fees to fund the MHRA was more difficult. This had been tried when the Medicines Commission was established in the 1960s and funded by government grant. Successive governments failed to increase grants sufficiently to keep pace with the growth of new drug applications. The result had been an enormous backlog of applications awaiting decision, with delays of up to 3 years before new drugs became available to patients. The Conservatives changed the system in 1989 so that the regulator charged applicants fees. I was challenged on this issue in February 2005 when I gave evidence to the Health Select Committee's Inquiry into the influence of the pharmaceutical industry. I explained that other countries such as Sweden and the Netherlands funded their pharmaceutical industries by fees and that government grants had not kept pace with the level of applications. This was not the answer that some Committee members wanted to hear but it sufficed.

The Select Committee quizzed me about being the Minister regulating the pharmaceutical industry, sponsoring it and controlling NHS drug prices. I accepted that these roles could be seen as in conflict but said I had never found it a problem in practice. I was able to be tough with the industry on issues like Seroxat, putting lay representatives on the MHRA and enabling patients to register adverse drug reactions but at the same time promote the interests of the UK-based industry in Europe and fight their corner on illegal activities by animal rights activists. I doubted the industry saw me as a soft touch in price negotiations. I didn't convince all Select Committee members but had managed to let my record speak for itself.

Medicines for Children

Big. Pharma was reluctant to invest in treatments for children because they considered the market too small and of little commercial interest. Studies for paediatric medicines could be long, difficult and expensive. Formulating on an industrial scale a precise dosage of a medicine for a diverse child population was technically difficult and expensive. Drug companies found it difficult to make paediatric medicine pay so they had largely disengaged. The result was that children – 20% plus of the population – lacked the same regulatory system for their medicines that adults had. Over 50% of the medicines used by children had not been studied in the age groups for which they were used. Drugs for children were often prescribed for use "off label" or were unauthorised products with no evidence-base.

The practical consequences of this were brought home to me on a visit to Great Ormond Street Hospital for Children. There I saw a child who had received leading-edge surgery to save his life. On discharge his parents were taught how to cut up an adult tablet into four or six dosages, crush them with a mortar and pestle and then try to dissolve them in some liquid as a basis for getting the mixture into the child. I thought this situation was both ludicrous and scandalous and decided to do something about it.

The situation was worse than I realised. There was no British National Formulary for paediatric medicine. Some committed doctors led by Sir Alan Craft, President of the Royal College of Paediatricians were trying to rectify the situation but DH civil servants claimed there was no money to complete the work, publish it and distribute it. The sums involved were £1 to 2million. I lost patience with the bureaucratic haggling and I instructed a DH budget-holder to fund the project. The first British National Formulary for Paediatric Medicine was published in 2005.

That was the easy bit. Harder was engaging with the drug companies, which had to be done on a Europe-wide basis for both licensing and commercial purposes, such as length of patent protection. I had a bit of luck because the UK was due to take over the EU Presidency in the first half of 2004. It could identify a few priority areas during its Presidency. With help from senior female doctors in the

290

MHRA and support from John Reid I managed to infiltrate the Whitehall bidding process for UK priority areas and make paediatric medicine one of the two UK Presidency priorities. I was helped by a changing mood in the industry where some leaders could see that resisting change in this area was indefensible and didn't help their somewhat tarnished social responsibility reputation.

At EU Ministerial meetings I found a surprising amount of support across Europe for progress on this issue. There was some tension with the industry over the length of patent protection, with the industry wanting 10 years and most countries' politicians not willing to go beyond 6 years. We secured the establishment of a Council Working Group in October 2004 to take forward paediatric medicine change on a Europe-wide basis. During the UK Presidency we progressed the drafting of an EU regulation on Paediatric Medicine and secured approval in principle to the regulation. Progressing this work required further meetings with European counterparts when Italy took over the EU Presidency.

This enabled me to sample the Berlusconi approach to government. On one visit to Rome I was met at the airport and swept through immigration into a huge limousine and given a large motorcycle escort to my hotel. Furious Italian motorists were swept aside as we hurtled into Rome. This was the life I thought, compared with my government car service Ford Mondeo with iffy suspension. Berlusconi might have his faults but he knew how to look after visitors. When I described my experience to a colleague he said I was just lucky. I had been used as the rehearsal for Tony Blair's visit a week later – which turned out to be true.

During the UK Presidency we established three main objectives. These were increasing (a) the availability of medicines licensed for use with children; (b) the information to doctors, patients and parents (including clinical trials data) about these medicines; and (c) research into medicines for children. It took until December 2005 for political agreement to be reached by the Council of Ministers on the text of a new Regulation and then agreement had to be reached between the Council, the Commission and the European Parliament which was finally achieved in 2006. Then the whole of Europe had a binding regulation on paediatric medicines. I was assured that achieving this in 2 years was remarkable by the normal timescales for EU legislation.

291

This regulation established a Paediatric Committee within the EMEA; set out the rules for new products, the marketing and authorisation of existing products and for orphan drugs and off-label products. It created a European database of paediatric clinical trials, some of which were available to the public; and created a symbol for packages of products authorised for use in children. There were many other detailed changes that took time to introduce but from that decision to make paediatric medicines a UK Presidency priority in 2004 children across Europe became protected by licensing of their medicines. All this from a hospital visit.

Paying for NHS Drugs

While progressing these changes I also had to renegotiate the prices the NHS paid for its drugs. There were essentially two payment systems: one for generic medicines; and a more elaborate scheme for funding new branded drugs – the Pharmaceutical Price Regulation Scheme (PPRS). The PPRS had been around since the 1960s. It had its critics but so far government and industry had been unable to agree on an alternative scheme. So every five years a reluctant set of combatants strapped on their armour for another round of jousting. As the responsible Minister I had to pursue two conflicting objectives: protect a strong efficient and profitable UK research-based pharmaceutical industry and secure NHS access to new drugs at affordable prices.

The UK industry was going through a difficult period with clinical trials becoming cheaper in Asia where regulatory systems were said to be less robust. Across Europe governments, pushed by Finance Ministers, were cutting drug prices and mainland Europe was losing its research-based pharmaceutical industry. The UK still had a lot of good science which attracted the research-based industry but the NHS was relatively slow to take up innovative medicines. Many existing patents would be running out in the next few years; and more new drugs were found to have adverse effects when used in large populations. The pipeline of new drugs was getting smaller, the cost of bringing them to market was increasing and potential new blockbusters were likely to be far fewer.

The NHS had been one of the fastest replacers of off-patent branded drugs with cheaper generics. In the UK generic drugs were responsible for about two thirds of drug volume and the proportion would increase as many named branded drugs lost their patent protection. Over 80% of NHS prescriptions were written generically and we were moving towards letting pharmacists substitute generics for branded drugs unless the prescriber specified otherwise. I had also imposed a price cut of £400 million a year on the generic sector – they barely blinked which made me think I should have been tougher. We also broke up a generics cartel, catching them in the act at a Heathrow hotel. All this was a useful signal about our approach to the research-based sector.

To make matters worse for the industry, the new National Institute for Clinical Excellence (NICE) was carrying out cost effectiveness assessments before a new drug became available in the NHS. Most but not all were approved by NICE but their processes meant new drugs came to market more slowly in the UK. Big Pharma was feeling sorry for itself when it came to the negotiating table. It had two main objectives – a price increase and protection of their right to fix the price of new drugs when these came to market. If they could push up the R and D tax allowance that would be even better. Their opening bid was a 3% price increase; and ours was a 10% price cut.

In the opening stages negotiations were conducted by DH officials and the ABPI negotiators on behalf of the industry led by a senior GSK executive. Ministers and the ABPI President – then Vincent Lawson of Merck, Sharp and Dohme – stayed in the background, although I was regularly consulted and tracked progress. The first months were leisurely and technical with discussions about allocation of costs and capital, returns on capital and sales, transfer prices from overseas affiliates, research and development allowances for incentivising innovation and, something dear to the industry, marketing allowances. My job on these issues was to avoid detail but ensure momentum without too many concessions. Growth of the marketing allowance needed restraint; return on capital needed to be kept around 20%; and the R and D allowance could be increased only if it produced a healthy price cut. My objective was a substantial price cut and a new agreement by the end of 2004.

The ABPI negotiators had a difficult job because they had to keep well over 50 companies – with considerable diversity in size - engaged in the process. Many were overseas companies; and the two UK giants – GSK and Astra Zeneca - tended to dominate the negotiations. The PPRS agreement was theoretically a voluntary one for each company; but if they did not participate in the agreement they would be subject to a price control order under Section 34 of the 1999 Health Act. I made it clear that we would apply price control for those who did not agree changes. Periodically the top brass of the big companies went to see the Prime Minister or the Chancellor to complain about the way negotiations were going – i.e. no price increase. Fortunately both Tony Blair and Gordon Brown made no rash promises to them.

Negotiations had formally started in November 2003 and by Easter 2004 little progress had been made. I told the industry that we had to complete an agreement by November 2004 for introduction on 1 January 2005. Otherwise we would make a price control order on expiry of the old agreement. This captured people's attention and increased momentum. As we approached the summer Recess the industry shifted from its no price cut position, subject to lots of safeguards around marketing spend, the R and D allowance and their right to fix the price of new products. I let it be known we would move a little from our 10% price cut position.

Further lobbying followed of Tony Blair, Gordon Brown and Patricia Hewitt at the Department of Trade and Industry. The message was that somebody needed to get a grip on these Health Ministers or there would be no UK research-based pharmaceutical industry. Foreign firms would leave in droves. Neither John Reid nor I were much moved by this sabre-rattling but Ministerial letters flowed into DH seeking a substantial move away from a 10% cut. I wanted to go to an 8% cut, which John supported, and that was our first move. This only encouraged the industry's big hitters to continue lobbying the Prime Minister etc. Pressure to settle for a 6% price cut came from DTI; the Chancellor was less precise but wanted less than 8%; and Tony Blair supported John Reid and me but wanted a deal struck. I thought from my talks with the industry leaders that they would settle for a 7.5% price reduction but in the end John and I agreed on 7%.

By this time we were into the summer holidays. I managed to track down the President of the ABPI, Vincent Lawton, in the South of France where he was on holiday. Somewhere in the French countryside, through a dodgy mobile phone connection, we agreed the 7% price cut. There followed an intensive two months of detailed negotiations with the final PPRS agreement published in November and coming into effect on 1 January 2005. Apart from the 7% price cut, the main features were an increased R and D allowance; and for the first time an allowance for developing paediatric medicines, which I had kept alive in the negotiations.

I thought we had reached a reasonable deal with the industry but some companies continued moaning. They were not best pleased when the Office of Fair Trading (OFT) announced in September 2005 that they were launching a market study into the PPRS aimed at assessing whether the scheme was the most effective way of securing value for money for the NHS and appropriate incentives for new medicines. By then I had moved Ministerial jobs; but not before I had gone on a "peace mission" to American pharmaceutical companies, with the Chairman of NICE. US companies did not like the PPRS settlement any more after our visit but I doubted they would stop selling to the NHS. They clearly used NICE endorsements to help market their products in other countries – seemingly on the principle that if the mean NHS used their products then everybody else should see them as value for money.

The 2005 PPRS settlement didn't last five years. OFT produced a report in 2007 that suggested replacing PPRS with what it called 'value-pricing'. This was aimed at stimulating innovative drugs that could be taken up quicker by patients. There followed some short-term price reductions in mid-2007 and a bad-tempered renegotiation of PPRS leading to a new settlement that began in January 2009. It is unclear that this agreement delivered any bigger savings. There was another PPRS in 2014 at a time of austerity.

In 2018 the 50-year-old system changed fundamentally and became the 'Voluntary Scheme for Branded Medicines Pricing and Access.' The new scheme was intended to improve innovation and speed up NHS access to new medicines within an affordability mechanism. It involved a bigger role for NICE in appraising all new medicines under a faster versions of their cost-effectiveness processes, starting in 2020. It remains to be seen how this works in the post-Covid19 world.

The Expanding Role of NICE

My 2003 portfolio included NICE, established in 1999 by Alan Milburn to assess the value for money of new medicines. Initially NICE had been a bête noir for Big Pharma who feared it would reject new drugs it had spent money developing or would slow down NHS market entry. By the time I arrived as a Minister the early hostilities had largely ceased. NICE had become part of the NHS landscape for pharmaceutical companies, with some even seeing benefits to NICE. A successful NICE appraisal helped with marketing new drugs outside the UK. NICE had established an international reputation for its evidence-based procedures and its appraisal findings were freely available on its website. It used independent committees that included industry and health experts as well as patients. Much of NICE's success had been down to its Chairman, Mike Rawlins and Andrew Dillon, the Chief Executive

NICE had started with a single programme producing recommendations on the value for money of existing and new medicines and other treatments within the NHS using what were called 'technology appraisals'. One or two waves of new technology appraisals started each year so that there could be a proper pipeline for the evaluation process. My job as Minister was to approve what was included in each wave to ensure maximum likely benefit to the NHS. I was also to ensure that if drugs were approved NHS budgets could accommodate the costs because often new drugs cost more.

Critics suggested that Ministerial involvement caused delay but I usually responded to submissions within 48 hours. My involvement prevented wasting time on evaluating drugs that were too far away from being licenced by the MHRA. I occasionally deleted a drug or shifted the balance in a list but never added totally new drugs. Nor was I put under pressure to do so by the industry. My involvement led me to ask questions about the system and this led to useful changes. I thought it would add value if NICE produced guidance on whole treatment pathways for particular conditions, rather than just appraising individual drugs. We began a programme of clinical guidelines that proved useful. NICE also began clustering the appraisal of groups of drugs for particular conditions so that there was more comparative information about their respective merits. These changes led us to separate technology appraisals of individual drugs from clinical guidelines.

There were areas where I thought NICE could do better. One of these was NHS delays in implementing NICE's recommendations which were supposed to be implemented within 3 months of Ministerial approval. NHS implementation was inconsistent and produced the very postcode lottery NICE was supposed to stop. I asked NICE to give more attention to implementation. They set up a team to help the NHS implementation, using 'tools' produced for managers and professionals to help them assess implementation costs, particularly when new drugs were very expensive – as with some cancer drugs. A 2009 report by Professor Sir Mike Richards, the National Cancer Director, showed a year on year increase of usage in 13 of the 14 NICE approved cancer drugs, with 7 increasing by 50% or more.

Another complaint to me by the drug companies was slow NICE processes. I asked the Chairman to try to make improvements. In 2005 they introduced a new speedier appraisal process which resulted in some new drugs being approved within 6 months of MHRA licensing. Later this fast tracking approach was applied to clinical guidelines. Delay remains an industry concern but credible assessment processes mean some delay is inevitable. Where I made little progress was my nagging attempts to get NICE to identify clinical practices or treatments that were out of date or poor value for money

By the time I ceased to be responsible for NICE, the original single technology appraisals programme had expanded into three programmes: technology appraisals; clinical guidelines on treating and caring for people with specific diseases and conditions; and guidance on the safety of interventional procedures, tests and treatments that involve entering the body through the skin or a vein, artery, muscle or body cavity. All these activities were to grow apace in the future. By the time NICE celebrated its tenth birthday in 2009 it had produced nearly 600 pieces of guidance ranging from cancer and coronary heart disease to the prevention of sexually transmitted diseases and the promotion of physical activity.

These last two pieces of work arose from another of my decisions. When I conducted the Arms Length Bodies Review(see below), one of the bodies that under-whelmed me was the Health Development

Agency (HDA) that was responsible for preventing ill-health and promoting good health. I thought it would benefit from NICE's more structured and evidence-based approach. So the HDA was merged with NICE in 2005. This led to NICE being renamed as the National Institute for Health and Clinical Excellence, although the established 'brand' of NICE was retained. The result was nearly 20 pieces of new guidance on public health being produced in 4 years, an output the HDA was incapable of achieving.

NICE grew in size, scope and reputation but not everything went smoothly. Most people accept in principle using NHS money efficiently, but if NICE or Ministers reject particular treatments it can be a different story. The conflicts then play out in public. One of the noisiest and longest conflicts was over relatively cheap drugs for Alzheimer's. In 2001 NICE had said that Aricept and similar drugs could be used for patients with mild to moderate disease but in 2005 it changed its mind and ruled these drugs were only cost-effective for people with moderate disease, not mild. Over 30 campaigning organisations came out against NICE's change of mind, supported by the Daily Mail.

My responsibility for NICE did not extend to the disease conditions in their appraisals. Some Ministers wanted to overturn NICE's decision but I argued that if we rejected NICE advice in this case we could expect more campaigns against NICE recommendations, especially where expensive life-saving drugs were involved. With John Reid's agreement I tried to diffuse matters by asking NICE to see if their calculations took sufficient account of the benefit to carers but with no success. There then ensued a series of legal challenges by patient groups and a drug company about NICE's processes before concluding in 2009 with the issue of a new version of the guidance which looked remarkably similar to their original one.

In 2004 NICE's IVF guidance raised different issues with its recommendation of 3 treatment cycles on the NHS. This was more likely to produce a pregnancy for infertile couples but multiple births might be involved and it was very costly. Scotland with its more generous NHS funding under the Barnett Formula provided 3 cycles as did a few English PCTs. I had my doubts about whether it was even the job of the NHS to provide IVF treatment and favoured limiting our commitment to one cycle. That was the line that John Reid took despite clamour from within the Ministerial team but PCTs could offer more if they could afford it. Interestingly the public noise level was far less than over the Alzheimers drugs.

Public battles continued over some NICE recommendations on expensive life saving drugs, especially for breast and kidney cancers. Some of these drugs only provided a small postponement of death at great expense. This later caused rule changes to the NICE cost-effectiveness threshold and longevity of life requirements before some of these expensive new drugs could be approved. The issue of bringing many of these new expensive life-saving drugs into NHS use continues to be a difficult public policy issue for NHS England and the research-based pharmaceutical industry in the UK. There are no easy answers to how to absorb these scientific discoveries into a tax-funded and inevitably cash-limited NHS.

Overall NICE has received relatively few challenges. The Health Select Committee has endorsed its work. Lord Darzi's Next Stage Review's final report in 2008 expanded NICE's role further as part of increasing an evidence-based approach to improving quality in the NHS. Darzi also wanted NICE to speed up its appraisals process and for patients to be guaranteed access to NICE approved drugs and treatments. Successive governments have supported the work of NICE, especially in an era when healthcare systems are financially challenged. Some would say it has become the most powerful quality determiner in the NHS.

Healthcare Industries Taskforce

A regular complaint from industry has been that the NHS and healthcare industries didn't work well together in the best interests of UKplc. We saw examples of this at the start of the coronavirus pandemic. During my time as a Minister the medical devices industry criticised the NHS's low take-up of innovative devices - often invented by NHS staff – and its opaque purchasing system. I responded by establishing the Healthcare Industries Task Force (HITF) composed of government and industry leaders. I co-chaired it with Sir Chris O'Donnell, then Chief Executive of Smith and Nephew. HITF brought together 200 experts from across industry and government, working in four groups, with Chris and me chairing alternate meetings of the main taskforce.

There was a lot of frustration within industry at the unwieldy structures and decision-making processes of the public sector. The DH/ NHS purchasing machinery was thought to be too preoccupied with price rather than value for money. I had a good deal of sympathy with this view but had to tell industry representatives that they had to reduce their margins on their old staple products like mattresses if they wanted the NHS to have the money to pay for innovative products. My co-Chair and I managed to hold the disparate interests together for nearly 18 months and to produce an agreed HITF report that we jointly launched at Imperial College London in November 2005.

Our report recognised the changing global and domestic business environment with huge technological advances transforming healthcare. NHS intelligence-gathering and purchasing had to change to reflect this. More focus on inventors and inventions within purchasing decisions was required and the NHS needed to be more commercially savvy about helping its own inventors so they could develop commercial products in the UK rather than moving across the Atlantic to do so. The HITF report had five main proposals:

- A new Devices Evaluation Service to make it easier to identify new devices and accelerate their take-up across the UK.
- A new Innovation Centre to be established to spread best practice in promoting and supporting the development of new healthcare technologies.
- Incorporating devices into the work of the new UK Clinical Research Collaboration with a focus on particular disease categories like diabetes so there would be more rapid take-up of innovative inventions.
- Maximising the UK's ability to influence international regulatory activity to prevent damage to the UK devices industry; and concentrating marketing efforts for these products on the USA, Germany, Japan, France and China markets.
- Improving training of NHS staff in the benefits of new technologies and strengthening industry involvement in NHS procurement processes.

Although the HITF report did not resolve all the problems it produced for a time a better relationship between industry and government. The Association of British Healthcare Industries continued for a while to describe on its website the HITF work as "a substantial success." However Covid19 has shown there is still a long way to go with improving working relationships between the NHS supplies system and industry.

Animal Rights: Activists or Terrorists?

The pharmaceutical industry was also displeased with another issue I found myself responsible for – attacks by animal rights activists. For some time these activists around the world had been taking direct action against scientists, research laboratories and drug companies. In the UK the focus of these activities was the Stop Huntingdon Animal Cruelty (SHAC) which campaigned to close down the company Huntingdon Life Sciences (HLS), Europe's largest contract animal-testing laboratory (see Chapter 6). HLS had been operating tests on about 75,000 animals a year from rats to primates. SHAC had been founded in 1999 and was bankrolled by wealthy anti-vivisectionists. Its founders had been involved in earlier campaigns against animal laboratories. The UK had a long history of animal experimentation because of its tradition of biomedical research and discovery.

Research in laboratories using animals had been licensed by the Home Office for many years and since the mid-1980s there had been an annual audit of animal experiments. In 2003 these experiments were running at about 3 million a year and growing. This growth reflected an expansion in biomedical research in the UK which governments had encouraged. Advances in genetics and the development of new drugs inevitably meant increased animal testing and some use of monkeys before drugs are given to humans. The importance of this testing was demonstrated by the serious immune reaction in 6 students participating in drug trials at Northwick Park Hospital in 2006. SHAC and others wanted to stop all use of animal experiments, not just to reduce the numbers; and were prepared to take extreme measures.

The activists were getting the better of the police by committing offences in one police force area then skipping over the border to another. The police were slow to learn the lessons from tackling football hooliganism – as I regularly told them – and coordinate information, share it between forces and take concerted action. The pharmaceutical industry was up in arms and demanding that the Government became more active. None more so than the Japanese pharmaceutical industry on behalf of whom the Japanese ambassador wrote to me – in a very polite way – requesting more urgent action. A Ministerial Committee, chaired by the Attorney General, Peter Goldsmith, was established to improve the police and government response, with me as a member.

The Committee realised the police response was inadequate but initially underestimated how well organised and informed SHAC activists were and what they would do. They were prepared to intimidate anyone doing business with HLS, including smashing home windows. They wrote to the neighbours of businessmen making false allegations of rape. They even approached small investors in GSK telling them to sell their shares or else. Rape alarms were thrown in roof gutters to keep people awake at night; cars were wrecked; and houses daubed with paint. University and pharmaceutical company staff were intimidated and new buildings attacked. The grave of a person whose company provided guinea pigs for HLS was dug up and the body removed. In the US SHAC and Animal Liberation Front (ALF) activists fire bombed property and began doing the same in the UK, with ALF detonating a device at the home of a GSK executive with his wife and children inside.

For the Ministerial Committee this was like a war and activists had to be stopped. When I called activists terrorists in a speech to the annual ABPI dinner in 2004, with over 1,000 people present, I captured the mood in the industry. More disturbing though was that a few people were so upset by my remarks that they walked out in mid-speech. I knew then that activists had penetrated the industry. SHAC and their supporters were using encrypted messages to orchestrate their actions across the country and seemed able to access personal information from industry records.

Under pressure from Ministers the police started to get their act together with improved information exchanges, a coordination unit and eventually penetration of SHAC with undercover officers. They discovered that there were clear links between SHAC and ALF, despite SHAC claiming otherwise. The police asserted that there were a relatively small number of activists but I had the uneasy feeling that SHAC had wider public support than the police realised. HLS secured injunctions under the Protection from Harassment Act but in 2004 failed to make these permanent. They tried suing for damages without success.

The police said that they were hampered in their activities by legislative shortcomings so we agreed to strengthen the law. This led to the passage of Sections 145–149 of the Serious Organised Crime and Police Act 2005 which aimed at protecting animal research. The new legislation prohibited criminal acts or threats designed to harm an animal research organisation and created an offence of intimidating any person connected to an animal research organisation (including employees and their families, research students, investors, suppliers and landlords). Sentences up to five years could be imposed for offences. In 2006 a molecular biologist became the first person convicted under the Act for attacking the property of a company supplying kit to HLS.

After my Ministerial move in 2005 the heat was turned up on SHAC on both sides of the Atlantic. In the US the so-called SHAC 7 were sentenced to a combined 24 years in prison and ordered to pay $1million in restitution. In Europe the police launched Operation Achilles against SHAC in 2007 with raids involving 700 police officers in England, Belgium and the Netherlands. Thirty two people were arrested, including Greg and Natasha Avery the co-founders of SHAC. They were found guilty of blackmail and eventually sentenced in 2008 to 9 years in prison, along with other SHAC activists who also received long sentences. ASBOs were imposed also to restrict contact with the targeted companies.

By 2010 the police estimated that three-quarters of the most violent activists were jailed. SHAC largely moved their activities to mainland Europe but there continued to be protests against HLS, Novartis, GSK and other drug companies. The terror tactics stopped in the UK and in 2014 SHAC's founders announced cessation of their operations because of the Government's "repressive actions." However, the public mood was changing against using so many animals in experiments; and some scientists argued for replacing animals with new techniques. Although the UK has a longstanding ban on using great apes such as gorillas and chimpanzees in medical research, we still use macaques. Animal rights issues around medical research have calmed down but the issue still surfaces occasionally. There are also other tricky ethical issues in the nexus between science, faith and politics.

The Clash of Science and Religion in Ministerial Life

A week into life as a Minister I found myself in No.10 with Tony Blair and John Reid launching the first government White Paper on genetics to an audience of distinguished scientists. (I suspected Tony's and John's grasp of the human genome was probably as sketchy as mine.) Not long after, I opened the new £40 million Biobank laying down genetic lines for future research before an even more distinguished scientific audience. Soon I found myself answering Parliamentary Questions, speaking in debates, piloting legislation and talking to the media on a range of controversial scientific topics: stem cells, genetics, use of human tissue, human fertilisation, contaminated food, variant CJD, animal experiments, alternative therapies, MMR immunisation among others.

I was in a world where there was a constant interplay between science, faith, politics and public concerns in an age of rapid scientific discovery. There was no escape because science and innovation were critical to making the UK economy a knowledge-based and high-value one if we were to compete with lower-cost emerging countries. Like other health Ministers, I usually backed the scientists, even if they weren't always the greatest communicators. I subdued my humanist instincts and tried to listen patiently to the concerns of those with strong religious beliefs. Even without the overlay of religion, issues like nuclear power and GM foods had shown how science and politics could have an uneasy relationship. Public suspicion of vaccines is another contentious research issue and has reared its head again with Covid19 vaccines. It was alive and well when I was a Minister with media hysteria over the MMR vaccine, despite the scientific evidence showing it did not cause autism.

One of the trickiest issues to handle was stem cell research. I was a strong supporter of the benefits this research could bring but it had powerful opponents. In 2004 I found myself confronted with a US-backed UN motion seeking to restrict the world-wide use of

304

embryonic stem cells in medical research. Despite an overtly Christian Prime Minister and a Health Secretary with a large Catholic population in his constituency, I was allowed to pursue the best interests of scientific research and patients. Working with DH officials and a good link-up with the FCO and our man in New York at the UN, I helped to ensure that the UK voted with the opposition to the US-backed motion – even though this meant voting with Iran. John Reid and No.10 were kept in the picture but the UK was not rolled over by a George Bush backed policy. The best interests of UK science and patients were protected.

A 2003 survey showed that 70% of the UK public supported the use of embryos for health research. But this didn't convince those whose religious beliefs claimed that human life began when an egg was fertilised. Telling them that the regulatory system for research with embryos ensured destruction of the embryos at 14 days, did nothing to reassure the devout. Things got worse when scientists in Newcastle became the first group in the UK to generate a human embryo by nuclear replacement. It was the wish of researchers to generate stem cells by cell nuclear transfer using cow eggs with human nuclei that pushed hybrid embryos into the political and religious spotlight. Somewhat reluctantly, the Government decided to review the 1990 Human Fertilisation and Embryology Act, itself a world regulatory first. This only encouraged those opposed in principle to hybrid embryos – many of them in the Lords – to campaign for a ban. Successfully, as it turned out. Just before I ceased being a Minister a White Paper was issued in December 2006 proposing, unwisely, to ban creating hybrid embryos in vitro on ethical grounds. I would not have been able to justify that.

Fortunately the scientists regrouped and pressured the House of Commons Science and Technology Select Committee. In early 2007 that Committee reported disagreeing with the Government, saying that outlawing the creation of embryos which are part-human, part-animal was unacceptable and would undermine the UK's leading position in stem cell research. They called for legislation which would regulate research using animal-human hybrid and chimera embryos through licensing. It would be illegal for all such embryos to be implanted and they should be destroyed after 14 days. The Government climbed down in the face of this onslaught from scientists, patient groups and many politicians. I watched the aftermath from the backbenches as new legislation was introduced at the end of 2007 for the regulatory body to license hybrid and chimera embryos.

This was debated in both Houses of Parliament, with further attacks from the Catholic Church hierarchy Around Easter 2007 Catholic sermons across the country condemned the proposed revising legislation. The Head of the Catholic Church in England and Wales and other church leaders lobbied the Prime Minister to change tack. Catholic government Ministers said they could not support the Government's own legislation and were given personal dispensations not to vote. The Prime Minister to his credit put his personal reputation behind the legislation and backed science against organised religion. As did the public, with 223 medical charities and patient groups signing a letter to the Prime Minister supporting the Government's change of heart. People weren't going to let a few bishops and cardinals get in the way of scientists finding cures to disease.

Another contested area was research use of human tissue. The ownership, storage and consent for usage of this tissue were all the subject of new UK and European legislation. The UK political focus on this issue arose from the way parts of dead children had been stored unceremoniously in Alder Hey, a Liverpool children's hospital, instead of being returned to parents for burial. Following an inquiry the Government had decided to legislate to introduce more safeguards; and use this legislation to incorporate into UK law new EU legislation. The 2004 Human Tissue Act required consent for research use of tissue consisting of or including human cells from living people (apart from embryos, hair and nails). Patients had the right to give their consent and to be sure their identity was not revealed; the material had to be stored correctly; and the research required ethical approval. Ministers were on the side of individual right to control access to their human tissue, much to the annoyance of some senior scientists.

Throughout the Bill's passage scientists continued moaning about bureaucratic barriers to scientific research that would damage the UK's science-based industries. I had a number of meetings with medical scientific leaders with a Ministerial colleague who had policy responsibility for the legislation. We were told that research and scientists would leave the UK for other countries where controls were less onerous. Pressure built up in the Lords but there was not much room for manoeuvre within the EU Directive. I also had bereaved parents keeping a beady on me in the Lords. Apart from tea and sympathy and a few modest amendments little of substance was conceded. Scientists continued to complain about the European Clinical Trials Directive incorporated in the Human Tissue Act but I had little sympathy with what I thought was overblown and insensitive lobbying.

Periodically the science - or lack of it - surrounding alternative therapies was raised with me. My position on the issue with the Prince of Wales and anybody else, was that homeopathic medicines needed randomised trials to prove their clinical worth like any other licensed drug. This wasn't received well by enthusiasts but nor was the absence of such trials by the scientists. My approach as a Minister was to act on any evidence of real harm caused by particular products – as happened with some Chinese products; shelter behind medicines regulation; and try to avoid well-connected advocates of alternative therapies. I did have to behave politely when discussing traditional Chinese medicine on a visit to Beijing and Shanghai in 2005 to sign health agreements. Finally NHS England grasped the nettle in 2017 and ceased funding homeopathic medicines under the NHS because they were no better than a placebo. This decision was supported by the High Court in 2018.

Reforming NHS Research and Development

The more I saw of DH and NHS handling of research and development, the more unsatisfactory it seemed. In 2003 DH didn't know how much the NHS spent on R and D because historically money labelled "research" could be spent by the NHS on other things, including balancing the books. Even money spent on R and D often went on researchers' special interests rather than national priorities. The UK lacked any system similar to that I'd seen in the US where identified centres of excellence were funded through federal national institutes who concentrated research money on those centres.

I supported the head of NHS R and D in DH, Dr Sally Davies, to begin bringing order to this chaos. The first step was to stop the random distribution of money to the NHS; and to refocus research effort on a smaller number of places pursuing clearer national priorities on the basis of competitive tendering for grants. Predictably this produced major upset in the NHS as some prestigious institutions saw their budgets cut and were forced to compete for funds. NHS R and D was rebranded as the National Institute for Health Research (NIHR) copying the US; but it took 2-3 years to work through all the reforms by which time I had moved on.

The second part of the reforms was improving coordination of research money between the different funding streams for medical research: the new NIHR; the Medical Research Council (MRC) which received its money from another government department; industry – mainly the pharmaceutical industry; and the large medical charities, particularly the Wellcome Foundation and Cancer UK, who funded a large part of UK medical research. I asked Sir John Pattison, the former DH head of R and D to see if he could find a way of bringing these various interests together in some kind of forum. His diplomatic skills were impeccable and he recommended the establishment of a UK Clinical Research Collaboration. I accepted his recommendation as a step forward within DH. But it did not go far enough, as I agreed later with Lord Sainsbury, then the Minister for Science.

Just before leaving this Ministerial job in 2005, Sir David Cooksey, a former Chairman of the Audit Commission and venture capitalist, began a review of all UK health research funding. It looked at the long-standing problem of translating UK scientists' world-class basic scientific discoveries into treatments for patients – the so-called 'lab to bedside problem.' Too many UK discoveries were turned into profitable treatments by others to the detriment of NHS patients and UK plc. When he reported in 2006 Cooksey made it clear that the UK needed to tackle the cultural, institutional and financial barriers to the translation of publicly-funded research into clinical practice. Unless it did, the UK would fail to reap the full economic, health and social benefits that should flow from its investment in basic research.

Cooksey wanted better coordination of health research and improved funding to support translation. He recommended a new Office for the Strategic Coordination of Health Research (OSCHR) to coordinate research between NIHR and the MRC and to monitor progress; the inclusion of additional but ring-fenced funding streams for DH research; and additional funding, including for Health

Technology Assessments, to support the take up of new ideas and technologies. In 2007 after I had left government OSCHR was finally established. It was the logical completion of the reforms that Sally Davies and I had started in 2003 but it had taken 4 years to achieve. By 2010 OSCHR was coordinating a public sector health research budget of about £1.7 billion a year.

Much of the overlap between DH and the MRC was eliminated but serious continuing challenges on translation were highlighted both by OSCHR in its first progress report and by others. In January 2009 a report by the Bioscience Innovation and Growth Team said that despite all the work done to improve translation of health research into clinical application "the adoption of new therapies, drugs and procedures in the NHS remains painfully slow... and the translation of these improvements into patient benefit has not materialised." Translation has remained a problem as was brought out in evidence given in 2014 to the House of Lords Select Committee on Genomic Medicine, of which I was a member.

Healthcare Acquired Infections and Dirty Hospitals

Tucked away in my 2003 portfolio were two subjects to which I paid little attention initially: cross-infection and hospital cleaning. Things changed dramatically in autumn 2003 when media stories a of 'super-bugs' felling swathes of NHS patients began appearing with increasing frequency. Front pages carried stories of MRSA (Methicillin-resistant Staphylococcus Aureus) and dirty hospitals. Vigilante visitors reported bloodstained and soiled linen, filthy toilets and unclean wards. Energetic reporters forged in the public mind a clear link between dirty hospitals and HCAIs. The public spotlight then was on MRSA, although it was soon to be joined in the dock by other superbugs, especially Clostridium Difficile or – C.diff to the cognoscenti.

Understanding causes and linkages in infection pathways took time, something in short supply in a media frenzy. Few reporters understood that staphylococcus aureus was everywhere; was usually harmless; and had been recognised as a common cause of infections since late Victorian times. No-one had bothered much while doctors could deal with the bacteria, first with penicillin and then with methicillin. But between 1993 and 1997, up to 30% of staphylococcus aureus became resistant to methicillin. MRSA became endemic in the NHS in these years when the number of reported cases rose steeply from less than 1,000 a year to about 9,000. One of my cheap shots was that MRSA took up residence in NHS acute hospitals under the Conservatives. With drug resistance rising, we had to change NHS behaviour on cross-infection and cleanliness.

Alan Milburn had made compulsory the collection of MRSA bacteraemia data from hospital trusts because the previous voluntary system (in place since the 1970s) led to underreporting. This change revealed that, despite some hospitals reducing MRSA, the total number of cases were increasing by nearly 4% a year. I began publishing data six-monthly rather than annually and later moved to quarterly publication. We started collecting data internally on a monthly basis to provide more up-to-date information; and local hospitals began analysing data by department. It was clear that local practices in acute hospitals varied enormously and I decided more central direction was needed.

By the end of 2003 the Chief Medical Officer had issued a report 'Winning Ways' to outline to hospital trusts the steps they should take to improve hygiene and infection control. All acute trusts were required to have a Director of Infection Prevention and Control to provide specialist advice, to require compliance with local guidelines and to start producing published reports on local progress. I decided we should have a 'clean your hands' national campaign because the scientific evidence strongly suggested that better hand hygiene was vital to stopping MRSA transmission. The National Patient Safety Agency had been piloting this idea and I put them in charge of the campaign and making sure that alcohol-based hand sanitising equipment was available near every patient in acute hospital wards.

A competition was held for firms to supply the NHS with these new alcohol rubs. We collected data on how many hospitals were pressing on with the hand hygiene campaign because the NHS response was mixed. The National Audit Office reported later in 2004 that 'there continues to be non-compliance with infection control practice'. They wanted to see all hospitals adopting the practices set out in 'Winning Ways'. It was to be the spring of 2005 before we could say with confidence that all acute hospitals had implemented the 'clean your hands' campaign. Even then urinary catheter care which accounted for nearly 25% of HCAIs was still a major cause for concern. Parts of the NHS are slow learners or just non-compliant.

Improving infection control in NHS acute hospitals was seriously hard work, with far too many doctors, nurses, managers and trust boards not paying attention to the danger to patients. Only through unrelenting political and management pressure did we see cases of MRSA levelling off and slightly dropping in 2004. In the period April – September 2004 MRSA bacteraemia in NHS acute trusts went down over 6%, compared with the same period the previous year. But the variation between regions was considerable. London with its many teaching hospitals was by far the worst; and the North East and East Midlands were much better than other regions. It was clear from the visits I made and conferences I spoke at that attitudes and attention to improvement varied enormously across the NHS. In most acute hospitals doctors and nurses were in charge of infection control but too often seemed unable to ensure their professional colleagues complied with good practice.

We launched a new onslaught on MRSA in 2004 by announcing a reduction in the number of targets but adding a new one of reducing the number of MRSA bacteraemia in hospitals by 50% by March 2008. Each NHS acute trust was set an individual target and this was to be monitored by Strategic Health Authorities (SHAs). The media promptly moved on from MRSA to other superbugs that the NHS was killing patients with. They had plenty to choose from because the Heath Protection Agency was collecting data that showed virtually all these infections increasing during the 1990s. Cases of Escherichia Coli doubled in the decade and was one of the most rapidly increasing bugs emerging in resistant form. More significant were the hyper-virulent new strains of the bacteria C.diff which colonised sites left free by the effects of antibiotics. C.diff spoors lingered indefinitely and caused acute diarrhoea in elderly patients, leading to more death certificates blaming this bug.

Public anxiety over superbugs rose faster than the NHS could respond. In too many hospitals there was a fatalistic acceptance of the inevitability of HCAIs and a reluctance to enforce better clinical practice. We extended mandatory surveillance to new HCAIs including C.diff in patients over 65 years which was later extended in 2008 to all patients over 2 years old. Unfortunately C.diff is spread by ingesting the bacterial spoors which then grow in the colon, so hand washing didn't solve the problem and other hygiene measures were required. Many acute hospitals continued struggling to contain a widening range of HCAIs and had to spend more money and effort to tackling them. Despite these efforts the number of people dying with HCAIs as a contributory or main cause of death on their death certificate increased. MRSA received more public attention but C.diff cases became more numerous and lethal, including for my 90 year-old mother.

Despite the lack of scientific evidence the media and the public were convinced that cleaner hospitals would eliminate HCAIs. Trade unions like Unison claimed that contracting out hospital cleaning services was at the root of the problem. I accepted a challenge to debate this with Unison in January 2005. I acknowledged that the number of NHS cleaning staff had reduced in the 1980s and 1990s but so had the size of the hospital estate – by 20%. Even if one disagreed with contracting out cleaning to the private sector, the evidence suggested that it mattered little whether cleaning was done in-house or by contractors. It was the quality of management at individual hospitals that counted. Independent inspections of hospital cleanliness by Patient Environment Action Teams (PEATs) revealed as many good - and bad - hospitals cleaned by contractors as those cleaned by the NHS in-house. NHS hospitals have shown the same variability in the way they tackle hospital cleaning as they have with controlling cross-infection. I suspect history may reveal a similar NHS inconsistency to hygiene during the Covid19 pandemic.

Nevertheless a clean hospital was probably the best starting point for tackling HCAIs and increasing patient and visitor confidence in a hospital. A wide range of commercial products were being promoted for cleaning up the NHS and boosting share prices in the financial pages. To introduce some rational basis for choosing products I introduced a Rapid Review Panel in 2004 run by the Health Protection Agency (HPA) to assess the scientific worth of products. The HPA produced a rating scale to help the NHS decide what products to use and to deal with inflated claims. This mechanism had mixed success and did not live up to the 'Rapid' part of its title. I also raised hospital cleaning standards; let the Heathcare Commission toughen up the PEAT system; and commissioned a new NHS cleaning manual.

As the 2005 Election approached, public anxiety about HCAIs did not abate, as new superbugs surfaced. I became entangled in a debate with the NHS about whether infection was being imported into hospitals by elderly people admitted from care homes – the reverse of the situation in Covid19. There was evidence suggesting that about 5% of patients were bringing MRSA into hospital and passing it on to other sick people whose immune systems were weak. At that time testing for HCAIs was a lengthy business with NHS path labs so I looked at new tests producing quicker results that were being used in the US. These were expensive but I arranged pilots of two-hour MRSA swabbing tests in three hospitals to see if this could control imported infection. This led later to the Darzi Report in 2007 proposing screening of all elective surgery patients for MRSA by March 2009 and for it to be extended to emergency admissions thereafter. Swabbing seems to have reduced HCAIs.

I was told the NHS lacked sufficient single rooms to isolate patients and reduce cross-infection. At that time the average number of single rooms per acute hospital was about 15% but in some older hospitals it was much less. As I was also responsible for hospital design I went to look at some French hospitals and changed the recommended standard for building our new hospitals. These were to be built with 50% of rooms being single rooms but this change would only help in the longer term.

Ideas poured in for the causes of infection: doctors' ties and shirt cuffs; nurses' uniforms and nurses taking their uniforms home to launder; hospital visitors, who needed to be stopped or restricted; visitors and staff wearing face masks. The cry went up to bring back matrons à la Hattie Jacques; and to put nurses more in charge of cleaning. We should sack contract cleaners and increase the cleaners pay. We were clear that hand hygiene was critical and so was measuring performance on HCAIs, department by department. Authoritative doctors or nurses at Board level needed to drive the infection control agenda and enable clinical staff to improve cleaning and hygiene. Without these cultural changes patients would continue to die from

313

HCAIs in NHS hospitals. We had to do more to get hospitals to pay adequate attention to cross-infection. John Reid wanted to introduce fines but I had my doubts.

We settled for a new hygiene practice code monitored by the regulator, the Healthcare Commission. They could issue 'improvement notices' requiring trusts to make improvements within a certain period. This code was eventually given a statutory basis in the 2006 Health Act which I piloted through the House of Lords. The new Code outlined how organisations should work to ensure that patients were cared for in a clean and safe environment. It told trusts what their duties were in terms of systems and how they should assess and manage risks, implement clinical protocols and provide training to staff. Boards and Chief Executives were told clearly that they would be held accountable for cutting HCAIs and preventing cross-infection.

All this effort did eventually drive down MRSA infections in acute hospitals. The March 2008 target of halving MRSA cases from the 2003/4 level of 7,700 cases was achieved and number of cases continued to fall. However in mid-2008 the Healthcare Commission warned that a quarter of NHS trusts in England were still breaching the statutory hygiene code. The problem had shifted in many hospitals from MRSA to the spread of C.diff which had a seasonal profile peaking in winter. In the winter quarter (January to March) of 2005, 2006 and 2007 C.diff cases remained at about 15,000 cases. The Healthcare Commission reported the scandal in Maidstone and Tunbridge Wells Trust where 90 patients had died from C.diff between 2004 and 2006. C.diff deaths started to fall and were said to be under 2,000 in in the winter of 2012.

However, the roll call of HCAIs continued to increase along with the length of their names: Norovirus, Escherichia Coli, Enterobactor, Glycopeptide-resistant Enterococcal Bacteraemia. Surgical sites, catheters and wards in NHS acute hospitals all created dangerous situations that could turn cure and care to danger and disaster. A UK shortage of microbiologists didn't help. Nor did the propensity of our doctors to over-prescribe antibiotics compared to their German, Swedish, Danish and Dutch counterparts. These countries had lower rates of MRSA than the UK; and made more determined efforts to root out HCAIs in their acute hospitals.

Death rates from HCAIs remain a global problem but there seem few up to date UK studies. The National Audit Office estimated in a 2009 report that HCAIs caused 5000 deaths annually and contributed to 15,000 other deaths. More scary was a modelling study by Almetric. com that I found. This estimated that in 2016/17 there were 653,000 HCAIs among 13.8 million adult inpatients in NHS hospitals in England; and that 22,800 people died as a result of their infections. Additionally there were an estimated 13,900 HCAIs among 810,000 frontline health care professionals. This report did not include infections in A&E, or in outpatient and paediatric departments. The modelling suggested HCAIs cost the NHS over £2 billion a year, including replacement for sick staff.

With or without Covid19, acute hospitals remain dangerous places. It's not so much a matter of saving our NHS, as saving us from it. All the 2004 furore about HCAIs in NHS hospitals may have died down, but I suspect the bugs haven't gone away. The NHS has been allowed to live with the problem and the consequences for patients. HCAIs are so yesterday.

Reducing NHS Bureaucracy

Another thing that never goes away is NHS bureaucracy. Even at the height of the Covid19 pandemic when volunteers were sought to help the NHS, it managed to produce an off-putting lengthy form and fail to take on many people. Back in 2003 questions were being asked about whether too much of the extra NHS money was going on 'bureaucracy.' The ill-conceived 2002 NHS reorganisation had proved expensive and added many more managers to the NHS payroll. Demands for local data were causing frontline resentment. Opposition MPs were landing telling blows about wasting money on bureaucrats rather than patients.

In Opposition, Labour had promised to save money on bureaucracy and "men in grey suits;" so more attention had to be paid to management costs and overheads. The Government needed to reduce NHS bureaucracy as part of its public service reform agenda. When John Reid discovered I had been a Thatcher efficiency scrutineer, he made me the DH 'bureaucracy buster.' None of my Ministerial colleagues had auditioned for the Clark Kent part so I donned my super hero outfit and started on DH and NHS bureaucracy.

In DH I had two aims. The first was curbing its insatiable demands on the local NHS for information; and the second was reducing the local impact of a growing number of inspectors and regulators. Earlier attempts to restrain demands on the local NHS had achieved little but I pressed on with a new programme called "Reducing the burdens on the NHS." After tedious discussions with statisticians, I established a system of Ministerial approvals (by me and the responsible Minister) for all new information requests placed on the NHS. I reviewed all existing returns to reduce their frequency and number. The periods for which returns were made, often lacked common definitions: for example, there were several ways of defining a month. This drove the NHS mad, so I started standardising definitions.

Then, much to the irritation of the civil service, I set up a system of 'man years' budgets. Officials had to show how many 'man years' it would cost the NHS to produce a particular return. The Department had to keep within a 'man years' budget I set and that reduced over time. Statisticians tend to have obsessive qualities, so I put a statistician in charge of this budget. Gradually the volume of returns started to decline in 'man year' terms, with most of my Ministerial colleagues supporting the exercise. The NHS noticed the change and a 2005 review of NHS data collections showed that DH had reduced the number of data requests. But there were still on average 600 collections a year and most of these were by SHAs who filled space left by DH statisticians. Bureaucracy, like weeds, needs constant attention.

I brought inspectors/regulators together to discuss coordinating their information demands and visits more effectively. Different inspectorates made similar information demands with little regard for the costs of those demands. Visits to hospitals were organised with a total disregard for the cumulative effect of these visits on the luckless hospital and its staff. These demands tied up a lot of senior management and staff time. These discussions under my chairmanship produced predictable prickliness about regulatory independence and deep suspicion of this interfering Minister who was already suggesting fewer organisations and smaller budgets. Was he now going to tell them how to run their affairs? (Listening to some of them, the temptation was enormous.)

The prevailing culture paid little regard to the cost and burden of demands on those being inspected. 'Independence of judgement' justified almost anything inspectorates/regulators chose to do. After several meetings, some hard work by officials and leadership from the Chairman of the Healthcare Commission, Sir Ian Kennedy, we managed to get a 'Concordat' agreed by the inspectorates. This would ensure that they worked more closely together in coordinating their demands on and visits to organisations. This was a small step on a long road to curb the growth and cost-inefficiency of public sector regulation.

Flushed with a degree of success, I herded DH statisticians into a new Information Centre with a new governing Board and a brief to make the mass of statistics collected more relevant and useful to NHS users. DH and the NHS collected a huge amount of data but this databank was mainly used for answering Parliamentary questions and Ministerial briefings, speeches and press notices. The NHS had been programmed to 'feed the beast' at the centre, which they often did resentfully. Little attempt had been made to convert this data into useful material for the NHS to use for improving its management and performance. I thought this expensive statistical resource required a change of focus.

A savvy ex-Sunday Times journalist, Tim Kelsey, had spotted a commercial opportunity for using this NHS information to benefit patients. He had set up a company called Dr. Foster Intelligence that converted NHS data into useful management information and sold it back to the NHS. In 2001 he had started publishing a Guide to NHS hospitals using a methodology developed by Professor Brian Jarman at Imperial College. I thought the Information Centre would provide a better service to the NHS and patients if it worked in partnership with Dr Foster. Tim also saw advantages to him of a partnership. Inevitably, the civil service was nervous, particularly when I proposed constructing a joint venture company between Dr. Foster and the Information Centre. There was resistance from the Centre's head and we had to secure Treasury agreement. Nevertheless we pressed on and in 2006 DH finally purchased a half share in Dr Foster for about £12 million with the agreement of the new DH Permanent Secretary. I launched the new joint venture but sadly we didn't all live happily ever after.

The Information Centre head resigned and seems to have turned whistleblower about the way the deal was done. This led to an NAO inquiry and a critical PAC report in June 2007 about the process.

Despite this the annual hospital guide continued and Dr Foster provided the first 'NHS Choices' website in 2006. That website helped provide the public with usable NHS information for exercising personal choices over where they received treatment and care. Dr Foster was turning into a very successful health analytics company and the joint venture needed money to expand. As DH owned half the company it needed to put in its share and this required Treasury approval. This became a stumbling block and DH withdrew from this successful public/private partnership.

I should never have underestimated the capacity of the public sector to foul up an enterprising public/private joint venture once a guardian angel moves on. The DH withdrawal caused problems but it didn't stop Dr Foster and it Intelligence Unit at Imperial College. They expanded their range and the annual hospital guide continued with the last one published in 2019. In 2015 Dr Foster was sold to an Australian communications company, Telestra, from where, as far as I can see, it is a successful health analytics company. If DH had stuck with its investment it could have made a tidy profit on the sale to Telestra.

Culling Quangos

The ALB review was the largest item on the 'bureaucracy busting' agenda and its origins had an amusing side. As part of its Gershon Efficiency Review, the Government was trying to cut Whitehall overheads and running costs. DH top management committed to cutting DH staff by about 38% through 'new ways of working.' The Permanent Secretary had sought to impress his new Secretary of State with this figure when John Reid arrived in June 2003. John had made me responsible for DH management issues so I explained to him that this figure was something of a Sir Humphrey manoeuvre. DH staff reductions looked less impressive when one realised that about a half were achieved by simply transferring people to arms-length bodies. This produced a colourful Glaswegian response from John, especially when he realised how much these bodies were spending. On 30 October 2003 John Reid announced the ALB Review as a centrepiece of an anti-bureaucracy strategy when he gave evidence to the House of Commons Health Select Committee.

The Review took longer than expected, with many bodies and parts of DH fighting to minimise its impact. They usually started by reminding me that Labour had set up many of the bodies I now wished to cull. This tune was sung joyfully by the Opposition in the Lords who cast me as Herod smothering Labour's creations soon after birth. All this had little impact because John Reid was totally supportive and often wanted to go further and faster. The first thing was to decide which bodies to include in the review.

The definition I used was stand-alone national organisations sponsored by the DH that undertook executive functions. This excluded numerous advisory bodies and tribunals with small budgets and few staff. About 40 bodies would be involved including seven due for abolition anyway. Some of this seven were to be replaced by new bodies, two of which were already operational (the Healthcare Commission and the Commission for Social Care Inspection) or about to become so (Dental Special Health Authority and the Human Tissue Authority). There were many overlapping and duplicated functions, with some functions of questionable regulatory and policy value. ALBs had set up their own human resources, finance, IT and facilities management departments at considerable cost. Consolidating these services offered worthwhile savings.

By Easter 2004 I had established that the review covered 40 existing or new bodies spending nearly £5billion a year with operating costs approaching £2billion. They employed about 22,000 staff. There was little doubt in my mind that we didn't need this scale of presence centrally to deliver good health and care services locally. Without change these ALBs were likely to grow and employ nearly ten times the staff of DH. Many had an accountability that was obscure or non-existent.

There were virtually no volunteers for change, so I went to see John Reid with a power point presentation on my proposals and just a private secretary present. I suggested we conclude the first stage of the review by announcing a 50% reduction in the number of ALBs; an administrative savings target of £0.5billion; and a reduction of 25% in the number of people employed by ALBs. This was to be achieved by the beginning of financial year 2007/8. John readily agreed. I returned to my room to inform officials of the outcome. They were relieved there were ALB levers to pull but nervous about what had been agreed. There was no point in delaying an announcement because the decision would leak.

John's announcement on 20 May committed us to consulting individual bodies on a set of proposals for merger, rationalisation or abolition to be concluded by end of June and announced by the summer Recess. I settled on four functional categories into which all bodies would fit: regulation; standard setting; safety and public protection; and central services for the NHS. If future needs arose, they would be fitted into an existing body rather than set up new one. On 22 July I published the results of our handiwork showing how the 42 bodies involved would be slimmed down to 20 between 2005 and 2008. This would produce savings in operating costs of at least £0.5billion from a base line of £1.8billion spent in 2003/4 and within a total expenditure of £4.8billion. It would reduce by about 25% the number of ALB staff.

Bureaucratic infighting with the ALBs resumed with greater intensity. This focussed on the size of the 2005/6 budget and the timetable for establishing the 20 new bodies, some of which required primary legislation. To concentrate minds, I offered meetings with John Reid if dissidents preferred dealing with him rather than me. This usually secured agreement. On 30 November 2004 John published our implementation plan with the supporting strapline of "Redistributing resources to the NHS frontline" This document set the parameters for 20 ALB change projects, saying what would happen to each body and when, with completion by April 2008. The 2005/6 budgets for the ALB sector were to be £100million less than baseline year 2003/4, with a further £200 million reduction in each of the following two years.

Predictably people continued to argue with DH civil servants about their savings. After the Christmas recess I sat down and simply cut the figures presented to me by officials so that the 2005/6 budget saved the £100million promised. I also indicated what they should expect for the next two years. Without clear Ministerial decisions on budget cuts, the DH review civil servants could not make the savings targets stick because individual ALBs appealed to powerful sponsors inside and outside DH. Arguments continued over the timetables for change and budgets long after I handed over responsibility for this area after the May 2005 election. There was some dilution but most of what I decided stuck.

I checked progress on the ALB review with a Parliamentary Question answered on 15 June 2009. Despite some delays, ALBs had been reduced to 20 on 1 April 2009, with 3 transferred into the new Care Quality Commission and the merger of the Health Protection Agency and the National Institute of Biological Standards and Control. One new ALB had been transferred from the Home Office to DH – the Alcohol Education and Research Council, so there were now 21. In 2008/9 ALB running costs were about £900 million (£800 million or so at 2003/4 prices) – a reduction of over 50% since the review started in 2003. Civilisation had not ended with this bonfire of quangos.

The whole 'bureaucracy busting' exercise was a classic example of public sector resistance to change. Once established in a fit of political enthusiasm, quangos are difficult to change, let alone abolish. They acquire Departmental sponsors who lack the appetite for contested change. Ministers should think carefully before setting up ALBs because not only do they develop a life of their own, they have a healthy appetite for limited resources. Covid19 experience suggests there is still much Ministerial appetite for creating new ALBs without too much thought. The Health and Care Bill will produce further organisational change and the opportunity to reduce the number of NHS bodies.

10. Financial Meltdown and Recovery: 2005-2006

The 2005 Election and New Ministerial Job

During the 2005 Election campaign I was left to mind the DH shop. When the election starting gun was fired Ministers ditched their red boxes and fled to their constituencies or to whichever marginal seat Party HQ dispatched them. Government was still governing after a fashion, so unelected Ministers had their uses in election campaigns. They can deal with unanswered Parliamentary questions and correspondence and handle urgent matters that crop up. They can go to broadcasting studios and convey a sense that government is still working.

The civil service kept an eye on me to make sure I didn't use the Department's press office inappropriately. I wanted to make sure DH didn't suddenly publish something lurking in their cupboards for months that would cause an electoral ruckus. I did manage to organise rebuttal of a bizarre round-robin letter Michael Howard sent to hospital trust chairs telling them their hospitals were killing patients with MRSA. I thought this an odd way to capture the NHS vote, particularly as I could point out a lot of hospital MRSA came in from the community.

Sitting in Richmond House it felt as though Labour would win – more because of the other parties' inadequacies than enthusiasm for another New Labour Government. The Tories were on their third leader since the previous election and still trying to convince the electorate they were likeable. Tony Blair and Gordon Brown had patched up their differences and were seen eating ice-creams in a comradely manner. Before the election, No. 10 asked me if I would take on NHS reform as a Minister of State. This seemed to have percolated through to the mandarins because they treated me as though I would still be around.

'Bureaucracy' continued to be a political issue with a government review by a businessman, Peter Gershon. The Opposition had set up their own review proposing savings from abolishing various health bodies and cutting DH staff. The 2005 Manifesto – entitled 'Forward Not Back' - reassured voters that new NHS investment was not being squandered. Staff in DH were being reduced by a third, with health

322

quangos halved: this freed up £500million for frontline staff. The electorate were promised that "further streamlining measures will allow us to release an additional £250 million a year for frontline services by 2007."

DH top brass were nervous about NHS streamlining and suspected I would be asked to deliver it. They began talking to me about their concerns, unaware I was no fan of Alan Milburn's 2002 NHS reorganisation. My steer to Nigel Crisp and his deputy John Bacon was that they should reduce the 28 SHAs significantly and align their areas with the nine Government regions. I told them I wanted to see far fewer PCTs focussed on commissioning acute hospital services more effectively, protecting community services and public health budgets and no longer running community health services themselves. I didn't think this was what these acute hospital veterans wanted to hear, especially about SHA cuts.

After a low turnout and some casualties, Labour claimed its historic third election victory on 12 May 2005. John Reid secured his release from DH and was piped aboard as Defence Secretary in the building next door; and Patricia Hewitt became Health Secretary with three new Ministers. The gender balance of the Health Ministerial team switched from 4:2 in favour of men to 4:2 in favour of women. (At the Labour Party Conference in September the women were all on stage like Girls Aloud receiving the Party's acclaim, with Liam Byrne and me kept below the platform like boy band warm-ups.). John Hutton went into the Cabinet and I inherited his portfolio on promotion to Minister of State, with the title of Minister for NHS delivery – later changed to Minister for NHS Reform.

The Prime Minister's brief for my portfolio was to increase patient choice, implement a new tariff system for paying hospitals; ensure existing targets were met and implement by 2008 the new commitment of no-one waiting more than 18 weeks from GP referral to hospital treatment; establish a better system for commissioning NHS services; implement the National Programme for IT; improve access to primary care and produce a White Paper for services outside hospitals; deal with all workforce issues (including pay and pensions); monitor NHS and DH financial performance, including PFI schemes and the capital programmes; and expand the private sector's role in diagnostics and elective surgery to increase NHS capacity and competition with NHS providers. I remained the Minister for all Lords' health business.

I thought the NHS delivery component of my job had four key elements: (a) reducing the number of NHS organisations (streamlining); (b) controlling the budget and improving financial management; (c) handling a range of outstanding workforce issues that were inflating the pay bill; and (d) improving the quantity (targets) and quality (regulation) of NHS services. I knew what I needed to do would be opposed by some Ministerial colleagues, many Labour MPs and the trade unions. The NHS had been given far too much money too quickly after a long period of underfunding and had spent much of it unwisely. I knew the NHS and some Ministers wouldn't like the cultural shifts Tony Blair wanted me to pursue, of more competition and patient choice (see Chapter 12).

Appropriately, my wife and I went to see "The Cosmonaut's Last Message" at the Donmar Theatre on the night of my appointment. The next day my relationship with Patricia Hewitt hardly got off to a good start. She came into my room and told me I wasn't her choice. All I could do was remind her it was Tony's decision and he expected change.

Streamlining the NHS

'Streamlining' was the word used to avoid saying we were reorganising the NHS again only three years after the last time. We fooled nobody. The NHS knew it meant big reductions in the number of SHAs and PCTs. I saw little point in pretending otherwise. DH senior management had taken some notice of my pre-election steer but were still a long way from what was needed in their briefing for incoming ministers. They seemed ever hopeful of saving some of their chums from the Ministerial axe. This briefing said there were 304 PCTs in England but they were looking to reduce this number to around 200 by April 2006; and that there were 28 SHAs with "plans to significantly reduce this number by April 2007."

The first 'streamlining' paper in May proposed "an orderly 'fit for purpose' process which identifies weakness in organisation and puts in place changes – some of which could be mergers – and development". The bureaucracy wanted to suck me into a process of slow evolutionary change. It seemed to have little understanding of what a commissioning-led NHS meant or that you needed far fewer PCTs if we removed provider services from them and boosted practice-based commissioning by GPs. I was reassured everything would be fine because there was a draft 'Strategy Risk Review Plan' – which was written in a unique form of English known only in DH/NHS management circles. Translated this said over the next three years the 28 SHAs - who were going to be reduced - would project manage everything and be accountable. It was time to turn the screw. In a series of meetings involving Ministers, special advisers, No. 10 and civil servants we shifted to a different position.

During June officials moved to halving the number of SHAs and saving £70million instead of £40million and completing the changes by 2007. Their front runner for PCTs was to reduce them to 200 which didn't save enough. They wanted the savings shortfall to come from PCT commissioning, despite the fact that Ministers wanted to strengthen PCT commissioning. I pushed for larger PCTs of at least half a million population with provider services hived off. I was making progress on SHA boundaries being based on the 9 government regions. By end of June, commissioning, far fewer PCTs and SHAs and the impact of more FTs, were being joined together by officials as a policy. I told them I also wanted to reduce the number of ambulance trusts; and decided to publish on 30 June the National Ambulance Adviser's proposals for halving the number of ambulance trusts.

To close the debate, I told Nigel Crisp in early July that we needed an agreed set of "givens" to communicate to the NHS by the summer recess and that we should complete all the organisational changes by April 2007. Patricia Hewitt supported closure of debate. What we didn't foresee was the decision by a group of British Islamic terrorists to blow up parts of London's transport system on 7 and 21 July and kill 50 people. This was not the best time to announce NHS streamlining. As Ministers we had to focus on supporting and thanking NHS staff and emergency services, especially the London ambulance service who were first on the scene deep in the underground stations.

After a burst of frenetic activity, a 7-page document with a timetable emerged, entitled "Commissioning a Patient-led NHS." This announced that practice-based commissioning would be rolled out everywhere by the end of 2006; asked SHAs to conduct an exercise by mid-October on the number of PCTs in their area against certain criteria; explained that there would be a later White Paper on services outside hospitals indicating new models of care; and said PCTs would become commissioning-led organisations with their role in service provision reduced to a minimum by the end of 2008. SHAs were told they would have to make the case for not being aligned with Government Office regions. Public consultation was promised later on PCT changes; but organisational changes were to be completed by April 2007; and changes to PCT service provision by the end of 2008.

The letter also stated that the number of ambulance trusts would be reduced substantially. It announced a rigorous development programme for more hospital trusts to become foundation trusts (FTs) by April 2008; and that there would "be a progressive move towards greater use of other providers, including those from the independent sector." I had achieved most of what I wanted except a much greater reduction in PCTs. Jane Kennedy, who was the Minister for London, would not reduce the number of PCTs in London at all. This was a major mistake, but I had no political support for over-ruling Kennedy and cutting numbers below 150 PCTs. For some elected Labour Ministers saving jobs was more important than NHS efficiency.

The release of this document on 28 July 2005 by Nigel Crisp was a public relations disaster, even though most of it was consistent with the 2005 Election Manifesto. The wording on PCTs divesting themselves of their provider services became more dirigiste than the draft I'd agreed. It changed from wanting PCTs to concentrate on commissioning and moved to compelling them to divest their provider services by the end of 2008. The result was we de-stabilised 250,000 community staff who thought their jobs were now at risk. I never found out who made the changes. Mentioning greater use of the independent sector inflamed the trade unions but that was inevitable. The main problem was DH top management ignoring Ministerial requests for a communications plan before issue to the NHS, with Crisp deciding to brief the 75-strong NHS Leadership Forum - allegedly in confidence. The story leaked, with media coverage of Labour splits over privatisation.

During the summer Unison and the Royal College of Nursing led opposition to compulsory PCT provider change. MPs joined in as they returned from holidays to prepare for the Party Conferences season and

Parliament's return in October. The campaign broadened into opposition to any NHS organisational change. Initially Patricia Hewitt recanted on PCTs being compelled to divest themselves of their provider services but in September tried to row back. I said we could not retreat and was supported by No.10. We insisted on completing the SHA-led provision of local plans for PCT changes by mid-October. At the end of September, I established an Expert Panel to help produce options for PCT change in each SHA area as a basis for statutory consultation. This independent element reduced the temperature. SHAs were encouraged to involve MPs in devising their local plans and MPs calmed down. Most of the Parliamentary noise was in Labour constituencies where the real issue was job cuts.

In mid-December I agreed publication of proposals for re-configuration (and reduction) of SHAs and PCTs for a 14-week statutory local consultation. A commitment was given that no decisions on re-configurations would be taken until local consultations had been completed and SHA recommendations had been considered by the Expert Panel. Strong guidance was given to SHAs about holding public meetings and continuing to involve local MPs. At the same time, I launched a consultation document for the same period setting out reductions in the number of ambulance service trusts from 31 to 11 (including London which remained unchanged). My reductions were much greater than those in the June review, with larger trust areas on the same boundaries as the new SHAs.

Throughout the consultation period I met frequently with officials to monitor progress and to ensure assistance was given in any hotspots of unrest. For the most part – whether from the reassurance or sheer exhaustion – the consultation on SHAs and PCTs went smoothly with little Ministerial involvement with MPs. With one exception, the consultation on ambulance trust mergers was reasonably peaceful. The exception was West Midlands where a large ambulance service in Birmingham was to merge with three smaller ones. The resistance was led by Staffordshire and its Chief Ambulance Officer, Roger Thayne. Threats were made to stand against MPs (nearly all Labour) at the next Election if they supported merger.

The colourful Thayne campaigned openly in opposition to the merger in the media including going head-to-head with me on the

Today programme. Unfortunately for him he got involved in an accident when driving an ambulance that he was not authorised to drive and colliding with a car driven by a police officer's wife. He resigned to go and advise the Welsh Assembly on ambulance services but quickly left that position. The Staffordshire saga was time-consuming but not without entertainment. I negotiated a settlement with local Labour MPs for Staffordshire to remain a separate trust for a while working in partnership with the new enlarged West Midlands Ambulance Service and merging later.

In April 2006 Patricia Hewitt announced the number of SHAs would be reduced to 10 on the 1 July; 302 PCTs would be reduced to 152 on the 1 October and the 31 ambulance trusts would be reduced to 12 on the 1 July, later reduced to 11 when Staffordshire merged. We had eliminated 190 unnecessary NHS bodies and rectified most of the botched 2002 reorganisation. With more Ministerial steel we could have abolished even more unnecessary PCTs. I regret not arguing more vociferously with political colleagues to reduce the number of PCTs to around 50-60. That was the most commissioners the NHS really needed and was capable of staffing with competent people. We were wrong to retreat so hastily on separating commissioning from provision in PCTs.

Niall Dixon, then Chief Executive of the King's Fund, put it very well in the Health Services Journal on 12 July 2007:

> *"The strategy itself... had much to commend it. The PCTs and strategic health authorities created by Alan Milburn were too small and numerous to be effective or to attract the quality of senior management required. Commissioning was clearly not working as it should, or as it would need to do in a reformed system, and it made sense for PCTs to concentrate on that rather than be distracted by the conflicting demands of being a significant provider of community services."*

The Audit Commission later found that £90million was saved in 2006/7 with a one-off cost of a £192million in redundancy and severance payments but with increased savings to follow in 2007/8 and subsequent years. New boards and management teams were recruited and in post in 2006. The new SHAs were a considerable improvement on their predecessors; and would have been a great help in handling the

Covid19 pandemic if Andrew Lansley hadn't mistakenly abolished them in 2012. The larger ambulance services improved planning, vehicle management and coping with emergencies. (Mistakenly, the Home Office abandoned similar plans to reduce police force numbers because of opposition by Chief Constables.)

Financial Meltdown and Regaining Financial Control

The Annual Report by the NHS Chief Executive at the end of May 2005 was totally reassuring, as were briefings for incoming Ministers. The NHS was improving performance steadily and the workforce was growing with 300,000 more better paid staff than in 1997. Staff recruitment and retention were good; and there seemed few problems with the National Programme for IT. Only as Ministers went round the NHS was this Panglossian view called into doubt. DH financial management systems seemed unable to forecast accurately the unfunded commitments building up: three new pay deals; rapid growth of NHS staff and their pay and pension costs; and the increasing NHS management and overhead costs. The unfunded financial overhang for 2005/6 looked to me well over £1billion.

On 17 May I sent Patricia Hewitt and Nigel Crisp a five-page memorandum on my first thoughts. This included my serious concerns about NHS finances, including the absence of any DH contingency reserve. Crisp never replied or engaged with me but preferred reassuring Patricia in their one-to-one meetings that the NHS would achieve financial balance in 2005/6. It became increasingly clear that we lacked reliable monthly data on NHS spending. Financial data was not consistent with that on workforce growth and higher activity levels. It was taking a month after the end of each monthly accounting period for the NHS figures to be collected and shown to Ministers. In motoring terms, we were driving a car with an unreliable speedometer and, as we discovered, not much of a braking system.

DH management did virtually nothing on NHS finances through the summer while I was dealing with 'streamlining' and performance targets. On return from holiday in September it became clear that NHS finances were heading over a cliff with a likely deficit of over £1 billion. Exploring the longstanding DH budget-balancing system was not reassuring. It involved some trusts 'volunteering' to underspend to offset other trusts overspending. This cosy NHS system rewarded poor financial management and was starting to fall apart in 2005/6 as those 'volunteering' underspends began to object.

DH had to find over £1 billion to repay the 2004/5 over-spend and cover a Treasury raid of £800million. They needed at least another £1billion for unbudgeted higher NHS staffing costs; and the DH central budget was over committed without knowing by how much. DH senior management's response was to require SHAs – 18 of whom were to be abolished – to enforce repayment of local debt. This exposed the fact that many trusts had been rolling forward debt for years and an increasing number of them were now incapable of repaying historic debt. This became known as the 'double whammy' - a forced reduction of income in a single financial year and a need to repay accumulated debts from this reduced income.

DH management had allowed large historic debts to build up across the NHS: many are still there today. There was no systematic NHS scheme of repayable loans over a longer period. What was happening made a mockery of the resource allocation system because many of the areas with the greatest health needs were forced to transfer their extra allocations back to over-spending areas with lesser health needs. Money was transferring from the needy North to the wealthier South. Local protests increased and became public. Ministers now faced a complex NHS financial mess with little useful or timely data. The Jumbo jet to be landed on a postage stamp had the instruments of a 1940s Lancaster bomber.

Patricia Hewitt called a meeting in October to review the 2005/6 NHS expenditure figures. The gross deficit looked to be heading over £2 billion despite the large budget increase. Officials could not reconcile finance figures with workforce or activity data; or say whether the position was worsening significantly. I could see no evidence for Crisp's optimistic view that the NHS would deliver financial balance. Patricia asked for ideas on action we should take. I thought the situation was worsening and, in my experience as a manager, there were only a few ways that the NHS could cut expenditure at this stage of a financial year. These were a recruitment freeze; cutting maintenance; and reducing the training and education budget. I recognised that winter was a difficult time for the NHS but given how rapidly its workforce had increased I thought we should freeze recruitment of selected staff groups.

This was strongly opposed by DH top management who said that at most such a freeze would delay the recruitment of 75,000 staff and would take time to implement. Political anxieties were skilfully played on by suggesting that this would look like a panic measure and would damage target achievement. I pressed the case for a recruitment freeze but had no support. If we had imposed a freeze from November (which was possible) and the average pay and on-costs of the staff affected was £30,000 a year in the remaining five months of the year nearly £1 billion could have been saved, more than the eventual deficit. Decisive action in October 2005 to impose a partial recruitment freeze and a package of economy measures around maintenance and training could have prevented much of the ruckus that followed.

The decision was taken to improve monitoring of financial performance through the 28 SHAs, two-thirds of whom disappeared the following July. Turnaround teams were brought in from the private sector, with a Turnaround Director from one of the big accounting firms. 175 PCTs were visited and a large number of hospital trusts. What the teams found was a horrifying picture of poor financial management and inadequate control systems across the NHS and particularly in the PCTs. In many trusts there turned out to be poor engagement with doctors over a trust's financial problems and hopelessly optimistic planning and income projections. Some trusts seemed literally unable to stop cash going out of the door. There was a huge contrast between the financial management of Foundation Trusts (FTs) and other trusts – later confirmed by Healthcare Commission's assessments. The FT regulator had better and more up-to-date financial data than DH Ministers had.

It was made brutally clear to senior officials that getting NHS finances back into balance was a top political priority. Although this probably stopped further deterioration, I doubted we could get the NHS deficit below £1 billion. Patricia met the Chancellor to try to reduce the amount repaid to the Treasury, but Gordon gave no ground and £800million was removed from DH coffers. I turned my attention to reducing DH central budgets, allegedly under our direct control. By pressurising officials, we were getting financial reports 10 days after the end of each month. Using this information, a meeting took place on 12 January 2006 between Patricia, me and Jane Kennedy with Nigel Crisp, John Bacon, Richard Douglas and other key officials. It was not a happy occasion.

Three quarters of the way through the financial year the NHS deficit looked to be about £1billion even after all the work done to control spend. I exposed that far from being a source of comfort, the DH central budgets were another problem, not only for the current year but for the following year as well. The DH management team had created some 500 budget-holders, many of whom acted like patrons of various NHS special interests. The top management seemed incapable of controlling these budget-holders. For the next financial year (2006/7), only two months away, the DH central budgets were over-committed by about £2.5billion, against an allocation of £12.7billion. The Chief Medical Officer and his staff were the main culprits; and the DH Accounting Officer seemed unable to require him to adhere to budgetary constraints. The DH civil service corporate management had collapsed. It was left to Ministers to impose financial discipline on Whitehall's top management of the second highest spending department.

At the 12 January meeting we agreed that I would work with the Finance Director, Richard Douglas, to lop some £400 million from the 2005/6 central budgets. I pressed for a £600 million cut which was the goal I pursued. Liam Byrne, with his McKinsey experience, helped me scrutinise and cut the central budgets for both 2005/6 and 2006/7. All members of the Ministerial team were required to cooperate with this exercise by not approving submissions from the multiplicity of DH budget-holders for new expenditure commitments. This stopped the culture of separate submissions to individual Ministers racking up expenditure with no effective corporate financial control. I didn't achieve my £600million saving, but its threat secured close to £400million savings in the last 3 months of the 2005/6 financial year.

Patricia Hewitt and I met Crisp, Douglas and other key officials weekly to scrutinise a schedule of NHS deficits and surpluses and to interrogate them on stemming the outflow of money, drawing on information from turnaround teams out in the NHS. This relentless political scrutiny – which should not have been necessary in a well-managed Department – paid dividends. With help from the reduced central budgets, the eventual deficit for 2005/6 was kept to £550 million, less than 1% of the total budget. If the Treasury had not removed £800 million there would have been a small surplus. But the political and managerial effort involved had been excessive; and we could not continue running DH and the NHS in this way. New corporate and financial management was required.

I regarded Nigel Crisp's position as untenable and either he or I had to go. Ministers had been forced to take over the financial management of DH when he was the Accounting Officer. I wrote Patricia Hewitt a personal letter on 3 February making it clear I had lost confidence in Crisp and did not believe he would set up and run a new DH Management Board effectively. His system for managing central budgets was totally unsatisfactory and DH top management had been slow to recognize NHS loss of financial control. There was a longstanding problem with the working relationship with a powerful CMO who effectively ran a separate financial fiefdom. Combining the posts of DH Permanent Secretary and NHS Chief Executive hadn't worked and we should revert to separate posts.

At the time I suspected Patricia Hewitt thought I was rather harsh; but rereading my letter now I regard it as an accurate if brutal assessment. To her credit Patricia didn't duck the issue and raised matters with the Prime Minister. Crisp resigned and left quietly, if unusually, with a peerage. Many people within the NHS approached me privately to congratulate Ministers on biting this particular bullet. Balancing budgets was not the only NHS financial problem.

The Private Finance Initiative and Excess

Alongside the 2005/6 expenditure crisis I wrestled with the problems of the Private Finance Initiative (PFI) used to build new hospitals. Labour had embraced the PFI system initiated by John Major as an off-balance sheet way of having new hospitals after a long period of NHS under investment. The money borrowed under PFI was not counted as public borrowing and enabled the Iron Chancellor to keep to his 'golden rule' of public debt not exceeding 40% of GDP. PFI was hire purchase and the money borrowed had to be repaid – usually over 30 years – by local NHS trusts. Many were hopelessly optimistic about their ability to make repayments from their annual allocations. DH and the Treasury allowed early PFI enthusiasts to agree one-sided deals in favour of lenders. Larger revenue budgets fuelled over-optimism by NHS trusts and an appetite for inflexible and costly repayment contracts.

By 2005/6 PFI had become a problem for DH because of the large number of new schemes being approved with hefty repayment revenue commitments. I became concerned about the affordability of prospective PFI schemes and obtained a list of their costs. I found that DH was on a trajectory to build a further £12 billion worth of PFI hospitals. Looking at the DH revenue income projections to 2012, the NHS could not afford a shopping list of PFI schemes of more than £7-8billion. I decided we needed to cut the size of the PFI programme by about a third. even though this meant dropping some high-profile projects. There was a proposed rebuilding of the Barts' and Royal London hospitals, estimated to cost over £1billion: and a totally unaffordable PFI project for Leicester hospitals in Patricia Hewitt's constituency.

I discovered a complete fantasy scheme in Westminster for rebuilding the Royal Brompton, St Mary's and Hammersmith hospitals and a new academic medical campus at Paddington Basin. Leaving aside the planning problems - such as a bridge over the Regent's canal – the projected costs were already over £1billion and well on the way to £2 billion. Despite the expenditure of £13 million on consultants' fees, I instructed officials to kill off the Paddington Basin project through the SHA. This was done eventually to the relief of most local NHS people, albeit with some political flak over wasting public money on consultants.

The Treasury became very agitated about the effect on 'the market' of my PFI retrenchment. I held a meeting in my room with DH and Treasury officials and Gordon Brown's special adviser Shriti (now Baroness) Vadera). There was a grudging acceptance that the programme had to be cut and that many of these projects would not pass HMT value for money tests. But I was told the market had to be prepared for an announcement and we needed an appraisal process for pruning the projects. After some bluster about consulting the Chancellor, there were no real arguments against slimming down the £12 billion programme to about £7billion because the revenue unaffordability arithmetic was unambiguous. It was agreed that the PFI programme had to be reduced to manageable proportions, but I had exposed several high-profile projects for the axe. The Barts and Royal London scheme became the subject of an Evening Standard campaign, with a stream of celebrities telling us how their lives had been saved by the hospital. Unwisely No.10 intervened and saved this project.

The PFI row coincided with a ruckus in the Labour Party in October 2005 about my proposals for reducing the number of PCTs and removing their provider services. There was huge opposition from the unions over jobs, especially Unison, and a backlash from a growing number of Northern Labour MPs. A Parliamentary Labour Party meeting addressed by Patricia produced the view that unelected Lords Ministers should not be allowed to decide contentious issues. One of my fellow Ministers, Jane Kennedy, a Liverpool MP wanted to take over some of my job and I was softened up for a change of roles.

I resisted on the grounds that I should finish the job Tony Blair had given me and we should not kow-tow to the prejudices of Labour backwoodsmen. I made some concessions by handing over areas short on popularity - cutting the PFI programme, approving local service reconfigurations and not becoming the Minister for efficiency and productivity on a new Cabinet Committee. I insisted on retaining responsibility for NHS finances and the resource allocation system because these were integral to NHS reform. I made it clear this was the basis on which I would continue as a Minister. Patricia wisely accepted my proposals.

This episode exposed the limited appetite among many elected Labour politicians for taking unpopular decisions to improve NHS efficiency and performance. Delivering uncomfortable messages to her colleagues wasn't Jane Kennedy's forte and she resigned under Tony Blair, only to pop up again as a Minister under Gordon Brown. The PFI programme was cut back but the Barts scheme went ahead without adequate pruning and this caused continuing financial problems for the trust. In the meantime, there was NHS 'streamlining to finish; NHS finances to stabilise; and DH's top management to overhaul.

Replacing Top Management and the NHS Financial System

Rapid changes were made for the new financial year – 2006/7. McKinsey reviewed and helped reconstruct DH corporate management which reverted to a separate Permanent Secretary and NHS Chief

Executive. Sir Ian Carruthers, an experienced SHA Chief Executive, became Acting NHS Chief Executive; and Hugh Taylor acted up as Permanent Secretary and was later appointed substantively. A single DH Management Board with wider membership replaced the dis-functional two-tier system.

We accelerated the appointment of the ten Chairs and Chief Executives of the streamlined SHA structure so these could be in place by July 2006. Patricia Hewitt and I started meeting them with the new DH Management Board, with separate monthly meetings with the ten SHA Chairs on their own. A greater sense of corporateness across the DH and the new regional tier was created. Patricia did a good job of creating a sense that politicians and managers were engaged in a common endeavour of running the NHS – an approach rather lost by our successors.

The financial crisis of 2005/6 exposed major systemic problems with the way the NHS allocated money and held recipients to account. The Treasury ran public expenditure on the basis that any over-spending in one part of DH/NHS had to be offset in the same year by under-spending elsewhere. Unfortunately, DH had created a system that limited their ability to exercise control once they had released money. The situation would worsen with a market system whereby hospitals were reimbursed on the basis of their activity through Payment by Results (PbR) and there was a growing number of Foundation Trusts (FTs) outside Ministerial control (see Chapter 12). Creating an internal NHS market with greater patient choice meant those choices determined where money was actually spent, not necessarily where it was allocated.

The 2005/6 system made no provision for repaying the mounting level of historic NHS debt that had been exposed, nor the further debt held under so-called SHA 'planned support' (a euphemism for bungs). There were growing calls to write off historic debt. This would have punished the under-spenders who had loaned about half the debt and rewarded irresponsible over-spenders, thereby encouraging repeated bad behaviour. Write-offs would also have disrupted planned service developments of the financially responsible parts of the NHS and made a nonsense of the resource allocation system. Instead, as Ministers, we took the more difficult decision not to write off NHS debt but to create a better NHS banking system.

Unfortunately, this was supposed to be consistent with the government's Resource Accounting and Budgeting (RAB) system which imposed a statutory duty to break even over three years and rolling forward deficits year on year. This made it virtually impossible for an NHS trust with a significant deficit to get back into balance. We asked Sir Michael Lyons (then Acting Chairman of the Audit Commission) to review the effect of RAB on the NHS. In June 2006 his report was published recommending a more transparent system of loans and borrowing and ceasing to apply RAB at NHS trust level.

In 2006/7 we implemented these proposals in stages. Nearly £800 million of loans (top sliced from SHAs and PCTs) were issued to over 50 hospital trusts and PCTs, with a requirement to pay interest and to repay the principal from surpluses they had to generate. Repayment periods varied from 1 to 25 years. For 2007/8 the capital allocations for NHS trusts were replaced by new borrowing regimes. Capital funding for trusts became determined solely by the affordability of proposed investments, with borrowing subject to a prudential borrowing regime similar to that for FTs. This was to stop poorly managed hospital trusts 'splurging' on new facilities that they couldn't afford.

We accepted the Lyons proposal to remove RAB from NHS trusts incurring deficits but it would remain in place for SHAs and PCTs so NHS books could be balanced nationally. We delayed implementing this change until March 2007 to encourage profligate spenders to balance their books. We imposed for that year a growth figure of £4.5billion and a 2.5% increase in productivity. Given about £4billion was required for pay and another £1.7billion for reducing waiting times and existing service improvements, this was a tough but fair challenge for the NHS. To make this happen we handed over about £7billion from the DH budget to the new SHAs but held back £500million as a contingency reserve.

We left SHAs to make cuts to previous central programmes as they thought fit and allowed them to build up reserves by holding back up to 4% of PCT allocations. We used the regional tier to constrain NHS spend locally because history had shown so many local trusts declined to live within their budgets. Andrew Lansley abolished this control

337

mechanism despite some of us telling him it was a mistake to remove the NHS regional tier.

Unsurprisingly these budgetary control measures were unpopular, especially with the trade unions who opposed cuts in training, redundancies and a recruitment slow-down. We also imposed a tougher pay policy centrally of no more than 2% a year pay increases. We made clear this robust financial regime was necessary to bring the NHS into financial balance and move to a transparent system of loans and repayments. Ministers repeated to the point of boredom that the NHS had to improve financial management; that we were not going to write off deficits; and that we intended stopping the efficient bailing out the inefficient.

Some Labour MPs opposed the recruitment slow-down and cut-backs in services by inefficient trusts; and disliked the forced levy on PCTs and abolishing 50% of PCTs. Despite the criticism we stuck to our guns and were supported by Tony Blair as we put the NHS back on financial track. Despite the political trauma the NHS achieved a surplus of over £500million in 2006/7, a turnaround of over £1billion in a single financial year. Nearly 80% of NHS bodies achieved financial balance in 2006/7, compared to about two-thirds in 2005/6.

In their review of 2006/7, the Audit Commission reported a big improvement in NHS bodies performing satisfactorily in the management of resources compared to the previous year, although there was a long way to go before this could be said of all NHS bodies. Before I resigned at the end of 2006 work was well advanced on creating a new system that would enable an NHS Bank to oversee arrangements for repayable loans (with interest). Alongside this SHAs, could create regional contingency reserves, providing the integrity of the resource allocation system was preserved. Although the new system improved NHS financial discipline, it didn't produce good financial management in all PCTs and NHS trusts.

This financial turnaround was achieved primarily by political will. It made Patricia Hewitt politically unpopular; and she left the government when Gordon Brown became Prime Minister in 2007. Her successor Alan Johnson benefited from our work and acknowledged it. On 29 November 2007 Alan told Parliament: "financial projections at the end of September 2007 show that the NHS is forecasting a healthy

338

£1.8billion surplus for 2007/8 with only 25 Trusts forecasting a deficit."
Yet progress on improving NHS financial management was slow. The
Care Quality Commission's performance ratings of NHS trusts in
2008/9 showed only 103 out of 392 trusts were scored 'excellent' for
financial management, with 113 trusts rated 'fair' or 'weak.' Nearly
half PCTs, who allocated budgets were 'fair' or 'weak.'.

A reply to a Parliamentary question I asked in July 2009, said that
only 45 NHS hospital trusts had cumulative historic deficits, although
one – Barking, Havering and Redbridge – had a deficit of over
£100million. But the situation has deteriorated again over the past
decade. Many weaker trusts have had to merge with stronger trusts.
According to the Kings Fund nearly half – 46% - of the 225 provider
NHS trusts and FTs still ended 2018/19 with financial deficits. In total
these seem to have amounted to about £3 billion. At the end of 2019/20
the Kings Fund found that NHS providers held £13.4 billion in loans
from DH - nearly 10% of the then NHS budget. Deficits will be even
higher when the true cost of the Covid19 pandemic is known; and we
have calculated the cost of treating the backlog of millions of patients
whose treatment has been delayed by Covid19. There is now a danger
that governments give up on financial discipline in the NHS.

Yet we know competent financial management is consistent with
good patient care. The Audit Commission made clear in October 2007
that "managing money well goes hand in hand with providing better
patient care." The CQC have found the same thing in their performance
ratings. The Trusts with the best patient care usually have a top financial
management rating. Even so this fact is still often not accepted in the
NHS or Parliament, to this day. The public has too often been fed the
notion that the NHS can only improve with more money being thrown
at it. The political temptation to throw money at the NHS, with few
questions asked, will be great in the recovery from Covid19. It should
be resisted if the lessons of history are to be learned (see Chapter 13).

Curbing the Pay Bill and Workforce Conflict

Where did all the extra NHS money in the noughties go? The short
answer is on people who account for about two-thirds of the
NHS budget. It is the largest UK employer and one of the biggest

globally – in the league of McDonalds and Walmart. Back in 2005/6 the problem was the too rapid increase in staff numbers with too few questions asked about how they were used. Between 1996 and 2006 the number of NHS staff (FTEs -full-time equivalents), increased from 1.057million to 1.339million - or 2.5% each year. Many staff worked part-time so the number actually employed was much greater. These figures also excluded agency staff. At any one time 10% of NHS nurses – the biggest group of NHS staff – were employed through agencies. In 2005/6 the NHS was spending about £1billion a year on agency staff not in NHS head counts.

The largest staff increases were those for doctors, scientific, therapeutic and technical staff and managerial and central functions staff. The increase in the number of doctors employed in the NHS in ten years is staggering. From a base of about 86,600 doctors in 1996 the numbers increased to 126,250 in 2006 – a nearly 50% increase. Consultant numbers increased by some 60% at an annual rate of about 5%, as did hospital registrars. The GP increases were much more modest at a little over 20% or about 2% a year. The highest earning professionals were increasing the most rapidly and their pay was also increasing under new employment contracts. This had a major impact on the NHS pay bill.

Doctors were not the only group increasing rapidly in number. The scientists, therapists and technical staff employed by the NHS zoomed up from 94,300 FTEs in 1996 to about 134,500 in 2006, an annual rate of increase of 3.8%. This group also have a large number of agency staff not included in these numbers. Support to all these clinical staff also increased in the decade to 2006 by about 25% to nearly 360,000.

This huge increase in NHS staff was concentrated in the years 2000 to 2005 when the number of NHS staff increased by 250,000. This was an unprecedented level of continuing increase and well beyond the capability of the NHS to cope with, both financially and in terms of sensible deployment. Large parts of the NHS – Boards, management and clinicians – had no idea of the financial hole they had dug for themselves through their recruitment policies. In addition, DH senior management could also not reconcile their workforce data with financial data. They seemed not to comprehend the damage done to NHS finances by rapid staff increases and poorly costed pay deals. I am sceptical that much has changed.

NHS staff increases are rarely criticised. Indeed, Ministers continue to brag about the increased number of doctors and nurses recruited to the NHS as though it was a self-evident truth this would improve performance. For Conservatives and much of the media in 2005 and 2006 it was managers who were bringing the NHS to its financial knees. In reality administrative staff had increased by under 2% a year, in the decade to 2006, even with the misguided 2002 NHS reorganisation which had been reversed. No political party can significantly cut the NHS pay bill by slashing manager numbers because NHS administrative costs are relatively low at around 4% of the budget. The NHS's managerial problems are more to do with quality, not numbers, especially in finance, human resources and IT, and often with a lack of quality leadership.

Alongside increased staff numbers, there were generous new pay deals that I inherited back in 2005: a new consultant contract, a new GP contract (nGMS) and Agenda for Change which brought nursing and other NHS staff into a new system of grading and harmonisation of terms and conditions of service. The new GP contract was an attempt to change the way GPs worked, with more emphasis on ill-health prevention. The trouble was it cost much more than was anticipated. NHS finances took a further knock from the new consultants' contract that came into effect in 2005/6.

In negotiating that contract Alan Milburn had attempted to identify more precisely the NHS work done by consultants who mixed NHS work and private practice. An impasse over productivity for the NHS by these consultants had been reached in the negotiations with the BMA when Alan departed in June 2003. It was left to John Reid, the new Health Secretary, to head off a major conflict by agreeing a new deal that left productivity improvements to be settled locally between trusts and consultants. In practice the new contract's potential productivity gains were all too rarely realised. Instead, a clock-watching culture developed in some places that disadvantaged the NHS. Specialties with little scope for private practice gained unexpectedly large pay increases. The new contract cost over £100million a year more than estimated, with little evidence it led to consultants working longer for the NHS by doing more evening or weekend sessions.

341

New contracts for other NHS staff caused even greater pay bill problems. Agenda for Change affected nurses, physiotherapists, ambulance officers and many other NHS staff. It was meant to achieve greater fairness in pay and relativities. Negotiations had been going on for 3 to 4 years on a new national pay structure into which individuals would be slotted on pay spines through local union/employer job evaluation. A complex harmonisation process was to take place on local conditions of service which were many and varied. The grinding contested reality of Agenda for Change negotiations was very different from my benign civil service briefing. I learned more about arcane aspects of local ambulance trusts' meal breaks policies than I ever wished, as disputes and strikes threats surfaced nationally.

There are always winners and losers in job evaluation exercises: the winners stay silent, and losers make a lot of noise. Here the local disputes were usually settled by levelling up, rather than the reverse. Agenda for Change produced a warm trade union glow in the run up to the 2005 Election, but by the end of 2005 it was clear this new deal would cost £300million a year more than expected and provided for in budgets. These pay deals and the rapid staff recruitment created an unaffordable pay bill and its inevitable consequence, union conflict.

The NHS had to reduce recruitment as we tried to balance the 2005/6 budget. For the first time in a decade NHS staff numbers reduced between September 2005 and September 2006 - by about 30,000. This brought a chorus of union complaints and forecasts of doom. Labour's trade union comrades exhibited little sympathy for our predicament; and the years of rapid staff growth were conveniently forgotten as unions campaigned against job cuts and alleged redundancies. They were unmoved by earnings data I produced from Income Data Services (leading analysts of public and private sector pay). This showed that in the Spring of 2006 gross earnings for full-time staff averaged about £514 a week in the private sector, compared with £531 in the public sector: for women the gap was even wider - £406 a week in the private sector and £480 in the public sector.

A pivotal moment came with Patricia Hewitt's appearance at the Royal College of Nursing's Annual Conference on 26 April. I was due to speak at the Conference and thought it best that I went; but Patricia was nervous about a non-elected Minister speaking so she went. Things

342

went badly wrong when the RCN leadership lost control of a jeering, slow-handclapping audience. Patricia stopped her speech - although she later answered questions. All this was televised and the image of nurses booing and silencing a Labour Health Secretary did huge political damage, not only to Patricia but to the Government. If I had kept the engagement, it probably wouldn't have been televised and I would just have ploughed on with my speech. When I spoke at the BMA's GP conference six weeks later, catcalls and boos started. I just asked them to do it a bit louder as I couldn't hear them. This prompted the Chair to ask people to let the Minister speak even if they disagreed with him. We continued with good- humoured banter and I completed my speech and answered questions.

Despite subsequent RCN apologies for their Conference behaviour – which I thought was planned - our relationship with the RCN never recovered under their American General Secretary, Beverley Malone. I had a one-to-one meeting with her to explain in words of one syllable that it was difficult to have a relationship of trust with trade unions if the trust came in only one direction – from Ministers. Despite many disagreements with the BMA, I had good working relationships with the BMA Chairman, Jim Johnson, and GP Chairman, Hamish Meldrum. We could discuss matters privately without confidences being broken.

In May 2006 I wrote to all MPs refuting allegations of widespread job cuts. In June the Royal College of Nursing (RCN) issued a dossier claiming that "15,000 NHS jobs now at risk". In July I had another go at explaining that the NHS had to balance its books and the fact that some trusts had announced job cuts did not "translate as some reports have claimed, into widespread compulsory redundancies." I pointed out that the NHS Jobs electronic recruitment service advertised over 8,000 vacancies in May which suggested that there were still many jobs available.

In the summer I set up better data collection on jobs and redundancies from the new SHAs in order to refute the increasingly wild stories about slashing NHS jobs and redundancies. The RCN, Unison and other unions continued campaigning under the title of NHS Together (which included the BMA). They issued documents blaming privatisation and the government for job cuts. Not filling vacancies was casually equated with redundancies. There was no acceptance that the

343

NHS had to balance its books. It was almost impossible to engage in rational discussion with NHS unions as the Party conference season approached. A group hysteria had taken over, with many Labour MPs in a funk about losing NHS support. As things got rougher in the autumn, I agreed with the Home Office removal of nursing posts from the shortage occupation lists that justified work permits for overseas nurses. This cut competition for jobs from overseas nurses.

On 30 October I wrote a five-page letter to all MPs pointing out that in the normal course of events about 10% of NHS staff – 130,000 people – left their jobs each year: for new jobs, retirement or maternity leave. Some vacancies couldn't be filled immediately and claiming huge numbers of redundancies was simply untrue. Our evidence showed 900 redundancies in the six months to September 2006 - virtually all voluntary and far fewer than the 20,000 claimed. I put the jobs slowdown in the context of the extra 300,000 NHS jobs Labour had created, including 85,000 extra nursing posts. Supply and demand were now in better balance in the NHS job market; and "we should not be apologetic about asking the NHS to offer better value for money to the taxpayer". I explained what we were doing to help displaced people find jobs and to place newly qualified staff. Things calmed down a bit after this letter.

The increase in the pay bill meant I gave firm evidence to the nurses pay review body about controlling pay levels for 2006/7. My evidence to the DDRB on pay for 2007/8, was much tougher and upset the BMA because I said pay increases should be limited to 1.5%, by then the Government's public sector pay policy. I explained that this was all the NHS could afford and that consultants pay in 2006/7 had increased in percentage terms more than that across the economy as a whole. We had no real medical recruitment or retention problems and the number of NHS doctors had increased substantially since 1997. I pointed out in oral evidence that asking the NHS to implement unaffordable pay increases would lead to job losses. The BMA criticised my evidence and the DDRB were clearly uncomfortable with being asked to take account of affordability. I took the view that it was time for a dose of financial reality.

Alongside these jobs and pay arguments we were also negotiating with the unions on changes to the NHS pension scheme. Apart from GP pensions, we made good progress on pension changes for other NHS staff and curbing the NHS costs of an increasing pensions bill. The normal retirement age would increase to 65 from 60; contributions by employees would increase from 5% or 6% to 5% to 8% depending on pay level, with the employers' contributions frozen at 14; and there would continue to be a final salary scheme based on an average of the best 3 consecutive years in the final 10 years of work. I wanted to protect final salary schemes for NHS staff, especially the lower paid. We managed to do this by raising the retirement age substantially and getting the higher paid to pay larger contributions for their pensions. Work by able staff in DH and NHS Employers enabled us to reach agreement with the unions on a new NHS Pension Scheme to start in April 2008.

I was much less successful in cutting NHS spend on agency staff as a way of preserving NHS jobs and reducing the £1 billion a year then spent on agency staff. DH had set up an ALB – NHS Professionals – to try to reduce the cost of hiring agency staff but it was loss-making. I tried to float it as a commercial going concern without success; but did manage to reduce its subsidy and the spend on nursing agency staff. I made speeches and found NHS people who had reduced agency spend to share conference platforms with me. By the time I left the progress made on reducing nursing agency spend was not matched by that on medical and scientific/technical staff, which continued rising. A Parliamentary Answer by Care Minister, Helen Whately, revealed NHS expenditure on agency staff in 2019/20 at £2,4 billion, in real terms roughly double that in my time as a Minister.

The events of 2005/6 showed that Ministers trying to manage the NHS efficiently could expect little support from public sector unions. As an ex-public sector manager, I wasn't surprised by union behaviour, but my elected colleagues were less phlegmatic. It took the Chancellor, Gordon Brown, introducing public sector pay restraint, with no NHS exemption, for NHS unions to realise the good times were ceasing to roll. Throughout this period, I had remained sceptical about the return on the large investment Labour had made in extra NHS staff because I could see no evidence of improved NHS productivity.

The Office of National Statistics (ONS) measured productivity in public services and how healthcare compared with other public services. Essentially, they calculated the growth in the index of inputs and the same for outputs and took the former from the latter. In June 2009 ONS published a paper covering the period from 1997 to 2007. The ONS data showed healthcare inputs going up from 100 in 1997 to 157.3 in 2007; but productivity dropping from 100 to 95.7 in the same period. In each year outputs were less than inputs – about 65% of which were likely to be accounted for by the pay bill. The decline in productivity increased in every year to 2005. Only in 2006 and 2007, after the tougher approach to pay and the curb on jobs' growth described above did productivity start to improve, although inputs still exceeded outputs by some margin.

There has been a long running argument about how to measure healthcare productivity and take account of improved healthcare quality. ONS agreed quality was not captured by their input/output analysis. Nevertheless, the ONS data showed nearly a 60% increase in inputs over 10 years producing a 4% reduction in outputs. Such a large gap was unlikely to be covered by quality improvements. In 2009 I asked a Parliamentary Question on NHS expenditure, finished hospital consultant episodes and health care productivity. The DH answer on 16 July 2009 supported my scepticism. NHS expenditure increased between 1996/97 and 2007/8 by 63% in cash terms and 52% in real terms. In the same period finished consultant episodes increased by 28%. The UK Health Care Productivity Index figures in that Answer revealed improved productivity only in 2006 and 2007, apart from a blip in 2001.

There is an ongoing debate about NHS productivity. Changes in clinical practice like generic prescribing and earlier hospital discharge can improve productivity but these improvements are modest relative to the budget increases in the pay bill. The big surge in NHS staff pay and numbers between 2002 and 2005 seem likely to have reduced NHS productivity even if they helped secure improved service access through target regimes (see below). If there is to be another big surge in NHS funding and staffing post-Covid19, the Government would do well to try to measure outputs and outcomes relative to input increases.

Training More UK Doctors and a New System Fiasco

One staffing problem that increased NHS costs was caused by the EU, not the NHS. This was the 1993 European Working Time Directive

(EWTD) as interpreted by the European Court of Justice (ECJ). This Directive reduced the number of hours that doctors worked. A reduction to 52 hours a week by August 2007 was in progress with a further reduction to 48 hours to be made by August 2009. Problems had been created by two ECJ rulings – the SIMAP and Jaeger cases – which effectively deemed doctors to be working if they were resident on call and sleeping in the curtilage of a hospital. These rulings created serious rostering problems in many hospitals and specialties and required the UK to employ more consultants. Change was needed and inevitable but the ECJ rulings made managing that change much more difficult and expensive. My job was to try to buy more time for transition – up to 2012.

I tried getting the PM to argue at EU summits for special UK dispensations on SIMAP/Jaeger and slower progress on reducing doctors' hours. Other EU Leaders simply saw this as further UK obstinacy over the Social Chapter provisions for shorter working weeks. I worked with the Attorney General, Peter Goldsmith, to see if we could use patient safety and training arguments to secure exemptions for particular specialties like obstetrics and for more sparsely populated areas. The EU legal eagles said if we wanted a derogation from the 2009 deadline for a 48-hour working week for doctors, then we would have to agree this on a case-by-case basis. This meant a major data collection exercise. BMA junior doctors refused to rule out legal action against any hospital trust that didn't apply the SIMAP/Jaeger rulings, even though this would reduce their training. DH had little choice but to accept extra costs of about £0.5billion a year and try to make the best case for an EU derogation.

This was the position when I left at the end of 2006, but the saga continued. At the end of 2008 DH accepted that the NHS could not achieve the 48-hour maximum working week for doctors in training by August 2009. It secured a limited derogation for some of these doctors that was extended to 2012, with the Government pumping in more money to the NHS. The saga of reducing the working week for junior doctors had lasted two decades. But it had become a relatively minor problem compared to the new scheme for training more UK doctors to reduce NHS dependence on overseas doctors from less developed countries.

This new scheme – Modernising Medical Careers (MMC) – had been devised by the medical profession under the supervision of the four UK Chief Medical Officers (CMOs). Although MMC came within my workforce brief, I thought this was a professional matter best left to the four CMOs. How wrong I was. It gradually became apparent that the doctors leading MMC had little understanding of how their scheme related to overseas doctors already working in the NHS or to changes.to immigration rules.

Overseas doctors had propped up the NHS in unglamorous places like Grimsby, Rochdale, and Oldham, with a significant proportion coming from India. The respectable reason for their coming to the UK was to enable them to extend their training and experience before returning to their own country. The reality was that few of them did return home – until near retirement – but many were unable to secure the specialist training that would enable them to fill consultant posts. Some were stuck in local jobs without the pay and status of a consultant. Some turned to general practice. Some left for the USA where money and status were better. Many of these doctors had UK citizenship or the right to remain here. Others were here as junior hospital doctors completing training and seeking a post-graduate qualification. They had been allowed to come here for this training without work permits.

Growing public concern over immigration caused the Government to change the immigration rules, first in 2004 and again in 2005. These changes reduced the number of people coming to the UK without work permits, unless they came in under a new Highly Skilled Migrants Programme (HSMP). The immigration changes had a significant impact on all those overseas doctors – mainly Indian – who traditionally trained here without work permits. This in turn impacted on MMC which was soon to transition from the old system to the new. Under MMC, graduates completing medical school would then do two Foundation years involving post rotation (in place of the old junior and senior house officer jobs). After that they would have to apply for specialist training posts. When this training was completed satisfactorily and specialist qualifications obtained, doctors could apply for consultant posts.

I began to realise MMC had a serious flaw that its architects appeared not to have noticed. It could produce more new UK doctors ready for specialist training without enough posts to accommodate them if large numbers of overseas doctors already here competed for the limited specialist training posts available. The MMC masterminds had constructed a system under which they had no control over the number of specialist training posts made available. That was because it was down to the NHS to decide how many such posts they could afford to fund. To further complicate matters, training posts might well not be in parts of the country to which UK trained doctors had traditionally wanted to go – especially the offspring of UK doctors. But these less popular posts would not be an obstacle to overseas doctors seeking training posts. MMC professional leaders were heading DH towards a major political row.

The first MMC Foundation year one intake began in August 2005 so they would complete their Foundation years in August 2007. I needed to start turning off the tap of overseas doctors coming into the country for training as quickly as possible. The least bad way - to do this was to use the new immigration rules to require work permits for doctors coming here to train. However, we needed transitional arrangements for overseas doctors already in the UK to complete that training. This required DH, the Home Office (HO) and the Treasury to agree on what should be done, never an easy task. It took a while to agree new immigration rules across Whitehall with transitional arrangements. News of what we were up to started to leak and the balloon went up when the new immigration rules were published on 26 April 2006.

Overseas doctors could no longer automatically seek training placements. Hospitals had to prove that they could not recruit a junior doctor from Britain or the EU before they could shortlist candidates from other countries. Cries of betrayal rang out. The British Association of Physicians of Indian Origin (BAPIO) claimed 15,000 doctors might have to leave Britain heavily in debt without completing qualifications: the BMA said it was 9,000. Hundreds of overseas doctors protested outside DH and lobbied MPs, with BAPIO in the lead. MMC medical leadership disappeared when I was accused of betraying overseas doctors. They had been allowed to come here for decades to complete training in junior doctor posts without work permits, with some posts specially reserved for them. Many of these doctors stayed on after completing their training, working in general practice, as locums or in sub-Consultant hospital posts. In parts of the country these doctors had been critical to the local NHS, sometimes comprising two-thirds of all the NHS doctors in a particular area.

I went on the Today programme to explain that as we became more self-sufficient by training our own doctors, we had to reduce the inward flow of overseas doctors. We had increased the medical school intake by 70% in recent years, so we had to have sufficient post-graduate specialist training posts for that higher output. The public, for the most part, seemed to accept my explanations. MP lobbying was modest, concentrated on areas with high numbers of Indian doctors. I met the courteous Indian Ambassador who accepted change was inevitable but wanted improved transitional arrangements. I agreed to do my best and we protected some longstanding medical training schemes between particular UK and overseas institutions. In June the Ambassador sent me a copy of Amartya Sen's 'The Argumentative Indian,' with just a hint of irony. By the Recess it looked as though things had calmed down.

Then officials brought me bad news. An unusually high number of overseas doctors were applying successfully to the HSMP. Until February 2006 on average about 200 overseas doctors a month came into the UK under this programme. By Spring the numbers were around 600 a month and still rising. Overseas doctors - some living in the UK - who had gained Royal College medical qualifications were using the HSMP to secure NHS positions. I suspected this was with the collusion of NHS employers. By the autumn 2006, about 10,000 overseas doctors would be in a position to compete for NHS specialist training posts in August 2007, alongside the first group of UK graduates of MMC. This would mean huge numbers of qualified UK and overseas doctors failing to get specialist training posts.

Civil servants and I began a Whitehall campaign to close what was obviously an HSMP loophole. Eventually we got the HO on side with the then Immigration Minister, Liam Byrne, agreeing to introduce new immigration rules. Bizarrely, the Treasury refused to agree, despite a robust correspondence and several angry telephone calls I had with their Ministers (including the Chief Secretary). One Treasury Minister told me they thought more overseas doctors coming into the UK would increase competition for consultant posts and so cut pay rates for NHS doctors. Treasury Ministers thwarted closure of the HSMP loophole.

By the end of September 2006, it looked as though we could offer about 22,000 specialist NHS training posts in 2007. This would cover most UK candidates, but injecting another 10,000 overseas doctors into this competitive process would produce an even bigger row than earlier in the year. News there could be insufficient specialist training jobs leaked out. The BMA junior doctors started campaigning that over 11,000 doctors would be unemployed as a result of MMC. Some claimed that junior doctors would be left unregistered and would not be able to perform life-saving procedures. Senior doctors with offspring in medical training took to the media. Hysteria was whipped up. I tried to calm things down with media interviews, but the situation worsened when MMC's new IT and selection process failed.

The new Medical Training Application Service (MTAS) introduced by those masterminding MMC had two new features. There was a standard online application form and selection for interview was made on the basis of anonymity. This was intended to tackle alleged racism under the old paper-based system. Published research had shown British-trained doctors with Asian names were less likely to be short-listed than those with English names. Anonymity and standardisation of the MTAS system had been designed and trialled by the medical deaneries and agreed by professional leaders and the four CMOs. I explained this context publicly, but CMOs and other medical leaders again failed to provide any public support.

There were serious problems with the IT when it went live. Pressing the "send" key turned out to transmit multiple applications to large numbers of hospital trusts. This made short-listing a nightmare and wrecked any remaining reputation MTAS had. A predictable row blew up when the offspring of eminent doctors failed to get their expected choices. I went on the Today programme and other media yet again to reassure an angry cadre of junior doctors and the BMA. After my departure, the plane crashed as the Treasury continued refusing to close the HSMP loophole and the IT system failed totally after being swamped with applications. The online system was abandoned in the spring of 2007. Patricia Hewitt set up an independent inquiry into MMC under the Chairmanship of Sir John Tooke, Dean of the Peninsula Medical School. This produced interim proposals for consultation and a final report in January 2008 which did not fundamentally change the MMC structure.

Angry applicants and their parents attacked the Government as more than 13,000 doctors from UK medical schools failed to get specialist training posts - roughly the number created by the HSMP loophole. The media was full of stories of young British-trained doctors emigrating. The medical establishment rose up in arms against MMC even though it was their own system, blessed by the four UK Chief Medical Officers who were now invisible. DH issued guidance saying that overseas doctors (including those in HSMP) could only be considered for specialist training posts if there were not suitable UK and EU graduates.

BAPIO challenged the legality of this guidance and in November 2007 the Court of Appeal ruled in their favour, saying overseas doctors should be allowed to compete. Late in the day, the Treasury agreed to close the HSMP loophole and in April 2008 the Law Lords dismissed the DH appeal against the Court of Appeal judgement in favour of BAPIO. The MMC saga limped to a conclusion with medical deaneries and Royal Colleges handling the transfers to specialist training. The medical establishment and Treasury took no responsibility for the significant contribution they had made to this fiasco and remained unaccountable.

Targets and Improved Health Services Delivery

The era of NHS targets began with the NHS Plan launched by Tony Blair in July 2000. This plan followed a wide-ranging consultation process and provided the development and investment the NHS had waited 60 years for:

- 7000 extra hospital and intermediate care beds
- Over 3000 GP premises modernised and 250 new scanners
- Over 100 new hospitals by 2010 and 500 new one-stop primary care centres
- Cleaner wards overseen by modern matrons and better food
- A modern IT system in every hospital and GP surgery
- 7500 more consultants and 2000 more GPs
- 20000 extra nurses and 6500 extra therapists
- 1000 more medical school places

- By the end of 2005 the maximum waiting time for an outpatient appointment would be 3 months and for inpatients 6 months
- Shorter waits for heart operations
- Rapid-access chest pain clinics across the country by 2003
- A big expansion of cancer screening programmes
- An end to the postcode lottery on prescribing cancer drugs
- Breast screening for all women 65-70 years
- By 2004 new intermediate care packages costing nearly £1billion to allow older people to live more independent lives

After the 2001 Election, a Prime Minister in his pomp, outflanked his Chancellor by announcing on television that by 2008 the UK would be spending at the EU average on healthcare. This meant nearly a 50% increase in the proportion of GDP spent on healthcare in the decade to 2007/8. The NHS budget would rise from about £36billion in 1997 to over £100billion in 2007/8 – a threefold increase in cash terms.

In effect Blair had committed to funding the NHS Plan and had increased the NHS funding commitment beyond that in Gordon Brown's March 2000 budget. The NHS was heading toward annual budget increases of 7% in real terms. Whether DH and the NHS had the planning and management capability to execute this Plan and spend this huge investment wisely was another matter. A mechanism was required to ensure the extra money produced better services and patient access to them. The mechanism chosen was targets.

Labour has been criticised over targets by clinicians and other NHS staff. Academics and commentators have also weighed in. When things have gone wrong clinically as in the Mid-Staffordshire Trust, targets have been blamed in preference to facing up to straightforward clinical and managerial failure and incompetence. 20-20 hindsight is a wonderful thing. It is easy to forget that in 2000 there weren't many tools in the Ministerial delivery toolbox for galvanising a tax-funded, monopoly NHS used to 'make do and mend' for two decades.

The NHS had no experience of managing growth on this scale. Large parts of it – including many clinicians – accepted long waiting lists as a fact of life and a reasonable way of rationing a tax-funded healthcare system. The doctors did the rationing, with some doing very nicely from private practice that benefited from long waiting times. The NHS had a poor track record on innovation and was often reluctant to change clinical and administrative practices. Clear targets driven through a chain of command made sense in a national service where the government needed to show results for the huge increased investment. In this situation any government would probably have done something similar, to hold the NHS to account for this large dose of extra taxpayer money. The current government will be faced with a similar problem after Covid19 is brought under control and the NHS is expected to tackle the huge backlog of treatment that has built up.

The main focus of the New Labour targets was on a matter of genuine public concern - access to services without long waits which could be life-threatening. Leaving elderly patients on trolleys for 12 hours in A& E Departments was a national disgrace. People did not see why they should wait two weeks to see their GP. The long waits for elective surgery may have been good for consultants' private practice. but they were a continuing source of complaints by patients. On occasion, people were waiting up to 3 years for an NHS operation. The UK had some of the worst cancer survival rates in Europe because of the length of time it took to see a specialist, achieve a diagnosis and secure treatment. Pre-Covid19, the NHS was returning to the pre-target era of longer waits for services and the public had noticed.

Many NHS staff thought the targets were too demanding; but there was evidence the NHS was let off lightly. A 2006 Report by the left of centre IPPR, "Public Expectations in the NHS" suggested the public were tougher than government on waiting times. The target for seeing a GP was within 48 hours, but the public's average "reasonable" wait was less. For A & E waits, the public's average "reasonable" wait was 2½ hours, not the Government's maximum wait of 4 hours. Two- thirds of people thought they should be seen in A & E in two hours or less. The public's view of a reasonable wait for a non-serious outpatient appointment was up to five weeks on average, not the 13 weeks of the Government target. Nearly half the public thought two weeks was long enough. With Covid19 under more control, government and opposition would do well to establish public expectations on waiting times, rather than leaving the NHS to decide.

When I became responsible for NHS delivery, targets had produced good progress in key areas like heart disease. By the end of 2001 about 108 people out of 100,000 died of heart disease and strokes compared with 140 in 1997 and the figures continued dropping. There was a 30% increase in NHS heart operations between 1999/2000 and 2002/2003. The maximum waiting time for heart operations had fallen from 18 months to 6 months in four years and was well on the way to 3 months. Over 80% of patients who had just had a heart attack were receiving clot-busting drugs within a half hour of arrival at hospital compared with only 38% in 2000. Nearly 2 million people were receiving cholesterol-lowering drugs to reduce risk of a heart attack. Death rates from coronary heart disease dropped significantly.

Patient experience was improving significantly. At their peak NHS inpatient waiting lists had contained nearly 1.3million people and were private health care's best recruiting sergeant. In March 2004 waiting lists were down to 906,000 and dropped another 100,000 or so by the 2005 Election. The maximum waiting time had reduced from 18 months to 9 months for inpatient treatment and was down to 6 months in March 2005. The number of people waiting more than 3 months for an outpatient appointment had fallen by about 200,000 since 2000 and the maximum wait was now 17 weeks compared with 21 weeks in 2003. The NHS Plan had set a target that the maximum waiting time in A & E from arrival to admission or discharge should be 4 hours. By March 2004 services had improved to the point that nearly 94% of patients were treated within 4 hours. By March 2005 this was to reach 98%. On medical advice, John Reid had accepted this meant the target had been met because 100% could never be achieved for clinical reasons relating to emergencies.

Delayed patient access to GP practices had been a long running source of public complaint. Targets had been set for people to be able to see their GP within 2 days and a primary healthcare professional within 1 day. By March 2004 the percentage of patients able to see their GP within 2 days was just over 97% compared with about 75% two years previously. It was the same for accessing a primary health care professional within a day. Technology has now made it much easier to access GP services, but speedy access face to face remains an issue.

A follow-up to the 2000 plan, the NHS Improvement Plan, was published in June 2004 with a foreword by Tony Blair. It set out the progress made by using targets data, particularly in treating killer diseases. Death rates from cancer were falling steadily by about 3% a year. An additional 200,000 women had been invited to breast screening in the 3 years since 2001. Virtually every patient with suspected cancer was being seen by a specialist within 2 weeks of GP referral, compared with 63% in 1997. There were 1000 more cancer consultants than in 1997 and over 1000 more MRI ad CT scanners, linear accelerators and pieces of breast screening equipment. Many more new cancer drugs were available on the NHS.

In mid-2005, it was clear that targets were doing the job they had been asked to do – show that the NHS was using the extra money to improve access and healthcare performance for patients. My job was further improvements without alienating the NHS too much. A key priority was continued progress on cancer under the leadership of the excellent cancer czar, Mike Richards, who continued to see patients at St Thomas's. By 2007/8, 99.5% of people with suspected cancer were seen by a specialist within 2 weeks; and 99.6% diagnosed with cancer began treatment within 1 month. The UK still had a problem with early diagnosis compared to France, but our figures were a huge improvement on a decade earlier. The rate of premature death (before age 75) from all cancers was 116 per 100,000 people in 2006, a drop of over 18% compared with 1996.

The picture on survival was even more dramatic with heart disease. There were 91 deaths per 100,000 people in 1996 but this had dropped to 45 per 100,000 in 2006. Early deaths due to stroke had also fallen markedly to 15 per 100,000 people – a fall of 44% in 10 years. Not all these improvements could be attributed to targets, but better access to GPs and shorter waiting times for specialist appointments had played a major part. Targets were also producing major improvements in emergency care. In 2007/8, 98% of people were seen within the 4-hour target, compared with 91% in 2003/4. Ambulance services had played a part in improving emergency care through the target regime. Again in 2007/8, 77% of top priority 999 calls were responded to by ambulances within 8 minutes. Moreover, both ambulances and acute hospitals were ensuring 80% or more of people with heart attacks received thrombolysis within an hour of a call for help.

The A and E target had also caused acute hospitals to increase efficiency by examining how they used beds and avoided delayed discharges. A group of A & E clinicians came to ask me not to drop the

4-hour A & E target, despite the calls to do so from some medical leaders. They said that the target had forced the NHS to take A & E work more seriously, improve the status of emergency staff and improve services to patients, including saving lives. These improvements in the way hospitals were run and the closer working of ambulance and acute hospital trusts also helped the NHS manage a perennial problem - winter crises.

My main target pre-occupation was the waiting time commitment made in 2004 - a maximum waiting time of 18 weeks from GP referral to hospital treatment. This included the first outpatient appointment, all diagnostic services and admission to hospital. When I became Delivery Minister, most DH officials told me this couldn't be done. I didn't agree, but I accepted it might be impossible in a few specialties where there was no data base like psychological therapies and audiology. This would mean some criticism of "hidden waits." but it also meant the NHS would have to pay more attention to improving access to these neglected services. And it did.

I monitored progress on the 18-week target at regular monthly meetings. We set milestones for the various stages along the patient journey. We were always lagging behind but by sending teams to help trusts improve their performance and getting poor performers learning from high performers, we started getting closer to the milestones. There were problems with specialist hospitals like Great Ormond Street who often received their referrals for highly specialist treatments very close to the 18-week deadline. Despite these problems and the financial crisis described above, we made better progress than expected.

About two-thirds of acute trusts had achieved the 18-week target by March 2008, 9 months ahead of the deadline. When the Care Quality Commission (CQC) assessed performance on 18 weeks at the end of 2008/9, it found that 89% of acute and specialist trusts had consistently achieved this indicator in the 3 months January to March 2009, with 6% underachieving it and 5% failing it. However, in crude terms the December 2008 deadline for 18-week waits had been achieved for the 840,000 admitted patients and 2.3 million outpatients in that 3-month period. Perhaps, more to the point, the average time for patients on the journey from GP to hospital admission was down to around 7 weeks and "hidden waits" in services like audiology had virtually disappeared.

Targets and monitoring created a level of NHS service improvement for patients that was unimaginable in 1997.

I saw how targets improved NHS data collection and use. They became embedded in the NHS regulatory framework and performance measurement. The Healthcare Commission (and its successor CQC) used target data to assess the NHS performance locally and nationally. Monitor, the FT independent regulator, used target achievement as part of its licencing system. Targets were used with some success in areas I haven't mentioned, like stopping smoking during pregnancy, reducing healthcare-acquired infections (discussed more fully in the previous chapter) and with mental health trusts. I acknowledge they had not worked well with some areas like teenage pregnancy and Chlamydia screening, where individual behavioural change was required rather than NHS performance improvement.

Despite the criticism of targets patient satisfaction surveys in this period suggest they were more popular with patients than critics recognised. Targets may also not have been as unpopular with staff as some have suggested. NHS staff satisfaction ratings stayed consistently over 80% in all types of trusts for most of the noughties. A staff survey in acute and specialist trusts in 2008/9 for the CQC showed a satisfaction rating of 88%.

I still consider that New Labour Ministers made a reasonable judgment to drive NHS performance improvement through central targets, given the huge extra investment. The targets were relevant to patients and the NHS was given a reasonable amount of time to deliver them. Ministers repeatedly said in public that targets should not overrule clinical judgement. If anything, the access targets were on the generous side given the scale of the extra investment. The commitment to the targets approach came from the very top, the Prime Minister, who set up his own Delivery Unit under the leadership of Michael Barber who had improved performance in schools. This unit rigorously monitored performance across Departments and provided expertise and muscle if you needed it. It is interesting that Boris Johnson, who has been advised by, now Sir Michael Barber, is now setting up his own version of a Delivery Unit to drive his 'levelling up' agenda.

I recognise there was an unforeseen consequence of NHS targets when some top managers in DH and the NHS became too obsessed with target delivery. As NHS Chief Executive, Nigel Crisp had the authority for approving the accountable officers of each NHS trust. Local NHS chief executives knew who they were really accountable to and who called the shots on their careers – the NHS Chief Executive - not their local Boards. I thought this sometimes created an inward focussed senior management system that was over pre-occupied with protecting their own. Failing chief executives were usually found another managerial slot and some became like Flying Dutchmen wandering the high seas of the NHS. Some got really lucky and were paid off before returning as consultants on generous daily rates. This closed managerial system seemed to exclude doctors, with talented clinicians like National Clinical Directors (or 'Czars') using their own clinical networks to secure change. For me, this clinical talent pool looked excluded from the DH/NHS senior management 'brotherhood.'

Gradually, clinical buy-in to service delivery targets reduced because they became seen as a chief executive's agenda in which managers ruled the roost locally and ran things through a parallel management universe that often seemed to exclude clinicians and Board non-executives. As a result, many local trusts started to look upwards rather than outwards to their communities. Apart from those trusts with a thirst for autonomy who moved to become Foundation Trusts, the chairs and non-executives could too easily be side-lined and become disengaged from trust management by management teams taking orders from the centre. Quite a few trusts chairs and non-executives were to talk to me about this disempowerment both when I was a Minister and afterwards.

These unfortunate side effects of targets were not inevitable or planned. Nevertheless, they happened and led to a loss of goodwill across the NHS which was revealed when the financial meltdown and pay rows happened, as described above. With hindsight it would certainly have been better to have managed the targets regime with greater clinical and local board engagement but that does not mean the targets approach was inappropriate. The scale of development and the sums of taxpayer money involved required a system that measured progress regularly and improved NHS accountability. Whether one calls the system targets, standards, guarantees or whatever, seems to me a matter of semantics, not substance.

359

Anyone who has managed large organisations – which usually excludes most elected politicians – knows that whatever gets measured gets done. Some way of measuring NHS performance and demonstrating improvement was required in 2005 and is still required today. When the pandemic has eased and the performance of the NHS is assessed, we will find shortcomings and a huge backlog of people awaiting treatment, some of whom will die before they are treated. Reducing this backlog will need a system for measuring performance and the use of the additional funding required. If targets are dismissed as unsuitable for a tired NHS, Ministers need to identify an alternative.

Strengthening Regulation but Failing to Deal with Failure

Targets are good for securing and measuring volume increases in services, but they tell you little about day-to-day quality and safety in individual services and institutions. That requires a regulatory system. Until 2000, the NHS relied on professional bodies to regulate individuals; and medical royal colleges to inspect teaching hospitals to see that they were suitable for training doctors. Private health and care facilities had more inspection and regulation than their NHS equivalents. The NHS Plan set a new direction for regulating the NHS when Alan Milburn established the Commission for Health Improvement (CHI) following the 1999 Health Act. CHI was the first organisation to assess clinical performance in NHS hospitals in a systematic and regular way. Its aim was to improve the quality of NHS patient care by assessing organisations and publishing its findings; investigating serious failure; advising on best practice; and checking the NHS was following national guidelines.

In June 2003 I became responsible for CHI and its annual star rating system for hospitals, giving them one, two or three stars. CHI had delivered one set of star-ratings and I had to oversee publication of its second and final report in July. The decision had been taken to merge it with the private hospital functions of the National Care Standards Commission (NCSC) and some of the NHS performance review functions of the Audit Commission. A new enlarged Commission for Healthcare Audit and Inspection (CHAI), later to be called the Healthcare Commission, was to be established to take over these

360

functions, together with reviewing unresolved NHS complaints and handling complaints about private hospitals. CHI had been competent but there were tensions internally and with DH.

The new Commission came into operation in April 2004 through the 2003 Health and Social (Community Health and Standards) Act which I piloted through the House of Lords. This Act also brought into being Foundation Trusts, (FTs) – see Chapter12 - along with their own regulator, Monitor. Suddenly the NHS had two new, powerful regulators: one for quality, the Healthcare Commission, and the other more akin to an economic regulator, Monitor. The latter relied on the Healthcare Commission for quality information but assessed the financial strength and business acumen of hospital trusts along with the quality information, to see if they were capable of becoming independent FTs. After licensing FTs, Monitor supervised their financial and clinical performance and could suspend or withdraw licences. Monitor could also agree mergers of FTs and the takeover of other trusts by FTs.

The 2003 Act also created a new social care regulator, a Commission for Social Care Inspection (CSCI) which assumed the responsibilities of the DH Social Services Inspectorate for adult social care together with the inspection work of NCSC and the Audit Commission's social care value for money activities. During the passage of the legislation, I was fairly criticised for reorganising health and social care inspectorates so quickly. Defending these decisions was not my finest hour as a Minister. The new regulators had been set up too quickly without realising the importance of integrating health and social care and how the new FTs would be licensed. I later incurred further wroth by merging the Healthcare Commission and CSCI into the Care Quality Commission (CQC) – today's integrated regulator of health and social care. I reached the right end point but in a messy way that was hard on the staff involved.

During its time – 2004 to 2009 – the Healthcare Commission was a success. NHS performance improved and public satisfaction with the NHS increased. The proportion of the NHS that met national standards and targets increased, with evidence to show this. The Commission carried out over 30 national reviews of services; and when they followed these up, they found their recommendations had generally been acted upon. Its surveys showed the NHS found their reports were important drivers of improvement. The Commission expanded the volume and quality of information about NHS performance. This information was seen as independent and credible by MPs, journalists, DH, patients and clinicians. It also began the process of moving more information to an outcomes basis by monitoring death rates, length of stay and re-admission rates. It initially struggled with the high volume of complaints it received for review but redesigned its processes and reduced the time it took to close complaints by nearly two-thirds. It had become respected and trusted both by the NHS and those outside when it closed its doors in April 2009.

CSCI also improved the quality and cost-effectiveness of regulating adult social care. It had inherited a disparate system of local authority inspections with highly varied customs and practices; and a rigid system of annual inspections that failed to target places where change was most needed. CSCI had done much to create an effective and modern inspection and regulatory system covering a wide range of social care services. But it lacked the scale and heft of the Healthcare Commission.

In the 2005 Budget the Chancellor simply announced there would be a single health and social care regulator that would incorporate the work of the Mental Health Commission. The new body was to be established during 2008 subject to legislation and come into operation as the CQC in 2009. To achieve the merger of the two bodies I wanted to fold CSCI into the Healthcare Commission. This would have enabled us to retain the considerable talents of the Commission's Chairman and Chief Executive who had been responsible for its success. Unfortunately, the merger coincided with budget cuts and my powers of persuasion were inadequate. The political and public mood was turning against the cost of public sector regulators and the Government had established a Better Regulation Taskforce to reduce regulatory costs. There was concern about reducing the frequency of care home inspections by CSCI, but I received short shrift from Ministerial colleagues for reduced cuts when I took my regulatory proposals to a Cabinet Committee chaired by John Prescott.

Monitor had proved a robust and effective regulator of FTs. I had to make it clear to No.10 there would be no bar-lowering by Monitor to secure more FTs by the next Election and Tony Blair accepted that.

Some FTs failed to maintain standards – clinical and financial - but remedial action was usually taken promptly. Two exceptions were Mid-Staffordshire and Basildon and Thurrock FTs which inexcusably slipped under the Monitor net. There remained a question about whether FT regulation should remain separate from the new CQC or whether Monitor should become a fully-fledged economic regulation policing competition and handling service failure like an insolvent hospital.

By Spring 2006, despite all these regulatory changes, it was apparent that there were still some wider issues to consider, particularly the relationship between regulation and the performance management role of SHAs and economic regulation. Patricia Hewitt chaired a Ministerial seminar with officials and regulatory experts from outside the NHS to discuss the regulatory intellectual landscape. Looking at other industries like rail, telecoms, the Royal Mail and water, there was no obvious model that could be applied to the NHS.

With other state monopolies it was clear that the key purpose of regulation was to support competition. Quality and price regulation were handled differently in different industries. Government and regulators had restructured industries to separate monopoly segments (gas pipes, electricity transmission, telecoms local loops) from competitive segments (gas and electricity supply, retail telecoms) so that there could be full de-regulation of the competitive segments. I thought the NHS could consider this model of segments where there was scope for competition among providers (some diagnostics, elective surgery and pathology) and some where there wasn't (A&E and highly specialist services). However, among Ministers and DH officials I was in a minority of one. There was little appetite for significant regulatory change to promote competition or give Monitor more powers. Minimal change was the DH and NHS default setting, particularly with the prospect of a new Prime Minister reluctant to upset the unions by promoting NHS competition. Further research was duly commissioned.

On 27 November 2006 the work on regulation was rounded off by publishing a 70-page consultation document – "The Future Regulation of Health and Adult Social Care in England." This set out an analysis and rather unadventurous conclusions. The proposed future regulatory structure gave most of the regulatory power to the new integrated regulator, CQC. For the NHS, CQC would share with SHAs promoting choice and competition and assessing commissioner performance. Stewardship of public assets and financial distress and failure would also be shared with SHAs (for non-FTs) and Monitor (for FTs). This sharing of responsibility was a muddle, with a lack of clarity about what happened when things went seriously wrong. DH remained responsible for price-setting and resource allocation. The Office of Fair Trading would be responsible for competition in the private healthcare sector and adult social care. The document was published for a three-month consultation.

I thought the document was a missed opportunity to challenge NHS monopoly. I would have liked to see Monitor turned into an economic regulator with powers to encourage competition in segmented parts of the NHS like elective surgery, diagnostics, pathology and community services). I also thought Monitor's experience with FTs might make it a suitable body to handle failing NHS trusts, a continuing problem that has never been resolved satisfactorily. But I recognised I was in a minority of one and would be resigning shortly. As it turned out, final proposals were not decided until Gordon Brown became Prime Minister and his Health Secretary, Alan Johnson, had little appetite for NHS competition (see Chapter 12).

During the Brown premiership the NHS regulatory framework became much more complex. In May 2008 Alan Johnson published a 'Framework for Managing Choice, Cooperation and Competition,' supposedly to help SHAs get the balance right in terms of choice, cooperation and competition. Or, as sceptics suggested, to ensure that SHAs did not behave in too red-blooded a way over competition. A new entity was established – with the contradictory title of a Cooperation and Competition Panel. The Panel was advisory to SHAs, the DH and, in relation to FTs, Monitor; but it could not decide anything itself.

Then in September 2008 the DH launched a low-key consultation on dealing with unsustainable NHS providers. Failure would be kept within the NHS family with a convoluted legal process involving SHAs, the NHS Chief Executive, a new 'Trust Special Administrator' and ultimately the Health Secretary, described in legislation as the 'Receiver-General.' The rules for winding up a failing trust were eventually set out in the 2009 Health Act. Transferring services between hospital trusts remained subject to a lengthy public consultation process, with contested cases being considered by an Independent Review Panel. They advised the Health Secretary, to whom all roads finally led. Weaker NHS providers were swathed in sufficient bureaucratic process to protect them from dangerous external competition, whatever its benefits for patients.

How right I was to resign at the end of 2006. The scope for change was narrowing quickly. I knew I was unlikely to be part of a Brown Government, even if I wanted to be. I told Tony Blair privately that I wanted to leave at the end of 2006. He was understanding and we had a relaxed and enjoyable farewell chat in No.10 about the past decade working with him.

11. Computer Games are Not Just for Geeks: 2005-2006

National Programme for IT: Origins and Structure

The National Programme for IT (NPfIT) was the most frustrating job I have ever been involved with. It was a ten-year programme ending in 2013/14 and estimated to cost over £12billion plus local NHS costs of implementation. Its main aims were to provide a single transferable electronic patient record for all NHS patients; and connect up over 30,000 GPs with over 300 hospital trusts and thousands of pharmacies. In 2005 this programme was said to be the largest civil IT project globally. It was at the heart of the Labour Government's attempts to bring e-Government to public services reluctant to embrace IT. It aroused considerable passion within an NHS that had little experience of networked IT and was used to working in management silos with their own information systems. It provoked civil libertarians opposed to giant government databases holding personal data. It was a target for any who doubted government's ability to implement large-scale computer programmes.

No sensible Minister would want to be responsible for this project, particularly after its history of false starts. Prior to 1997 the NHS had been working to a 1992 NHS Information Strategy that tried to create a new infrastructure for IT based on national standards These theoretically enabled local systems to operate with each other. The reality was lots of local initiatives but little inter-operability. To move information from one place to another the NHS relied on paper or word of mouth. When patients changed GP their bulky paper records went by Royal Mail to the new GPs. Most arrived with the new GPs many weeks later, with some lost on the way. Unkind, but largely accurate, critics have described the pre-1997 NHS as one of the last bastions of garage-built computer systems and paper.

In 1998 Labour launched a new national strategy to support the development and implementation of electronic patient records but relying on each health authority creating their own local implementation strategies. An electronic record pilot programme known as ERDIP produced a few successful but small-scale local installations. This programme failed to be taken up nationally for three main reasons. There was a lack of local funding for IT because budgets were not ring-fenced and were used for other purposes. Second most hospitals continued to work with separate unintegrated departmental clinical systems because hospital consultants could not agree on an integrated system. Thirdly the cost inefficiencies of buying one-off local systems made this approach unaffordable nationally. ERDIP only lasted three years and led to a new DH strategy group chaired by Sir John Pattison, then Director of Research, Analysis and Information.

This group produced in 2002 a report which became the genesis of NPfIT. There were four key strands: a lifelong patient record with details held locally and a summary record available nationally; a system to deliver prescriptions electronically between GPs and pharmacies; another to enable electronic booking between GPs and hospitals; and a fourth was an NHS broadband infrastructure – later to be called N3. Despite later rewriting of history by critics that there had been little consultation with NHS users, the 2002 strategy was the result of learning from ERDIP pilots and extensive consultation with NHS frontline users by the then NHS Information Authority. This revealed major affordability problems with the local approach. Whatever the failings of the NPfIT one of its achievements was that it did learn from NHS experience of previous mistakes. In fact, the NHS consultation led to two significant later additions to the 2002 strategy document.

The first and most significant of these additions was Picture Archiving and Communications Systems (PACS) which arose from the NHS's wish to move to film-less hospital diagnostic imaging departments. For the previous hundred years film had been almost the exclusive medium for capturing, storing and displaying radiographic images of patients. Much like a digital camera PACS captured X-rays and scans and stored them electronically. Images became more quickly available because they did not need to be transported by hand – often from hospital basements; and they could be studied at different locations. Lost X-rays – up to 12% of the total – became a thing of the past; and the NHS no longer had to give over space storing X-rays. The second addition was an online GP payment system, following the 2003 GP contract negotiations, which was implemented by NPfIT in six months.

By the time I arrived as the responsible Minister in May 2005 the shape and scale of the NPfIT had been largely settled, with a complex set of inter-related programmes. Each element had its own purpose, but most contributed to a common goal of moving patient clinical information around a complex and dispersed healthcare system spread over thousands of outlets. Some projects like a new broadband system for the whole NHS provided the foundation for other parts of the system to operate. Many of these 'foundation' projects had to be delivered first which meant that the clinical advantages of NPfIT took longer to show. A wholly transferable electronic patient record was not possible without a functioning spine containing a Personal Demographic System (PDS). The sheer scale and complexity of what was being attempted was rarely acknowledged by many of the programme's critics.

At this time my focus was on the eight core projects to be completed:

- N3 – the new secure broadband national network for the NHS.
- The NHS Care Record Service (CRS) which was at the core of the new system with a PDS which stored basic demographic information about each patient and their NHS number as an identifier. When complete the CRS would enable patient information from different parts of the NHS to be linked electronically with detailed records kept locally and a Summary Care Record that would be available across all NHS organisations in England to meet the needs of out of hours and emergency care. (Scotland, Wales and Northern Ireland had declined to be part of this system.)
- Picture Archiving Communications Systems (PACS) which would replace film-based systems with digital X-rays and scans.
- Electronic Transfer of Prescriptions (ETP) which would enable prescriptions to be sent electronically from GP prescribers to the pharmacy to reduce errors and costs and increase patient convenience.
- Choose and Book (CAB) which was a new electronic booking system enabling GPs and patients to book first outpatient specialist hospital appointments so that patients could choose the most convenient available appointment from different hospitals.

368

- Support for general practice IT, including several programmes: choice of GP systems; GP2GP which transferred patient records electronically when people changed GP; and QMAS a new system for paying GPs under their new contract.
- NHS mail (or Contact as it was re-named) which provided a secure e-mail and directory service for the NHS.
- Secondary User Services (SUS) which provided the NHS with high quality data to enable investigation of trends and emerging health needs that could inform health policy. SUS was of particular benefit to researchers and had a capacity to anonymise individual patient data for the benefit of research.

These core projects were demanding enough, but the programme had accepted many other projects not originally intended. These included Single Assessment Process systems for care of the elderly; the Map of Medicine which provided electronic support to prescribers; radiology, A & E and theatre systems; and replacement of patient administration systems (PAS) because so many were on the verge of collapse. There were new ambulance communication systems; community, clinical and child health systems (for immunisation and vaccination programmes); and systems to support care in prisons. I also discovered new systems to support processes such as datamining and placing orders, as well as the new 'Smart Card' registration system to ensure access security. The reasons for this mission creep depended on who I talked to: empire building by the programme; political/top management pressure; or just trying to please end users. Each item was easy to justify on its own but together they increased substantially the scope for things to go wrong and programme costs.

As an incoming Minister there was little I could do about the programme's enlarged scope because the commitments had been made and untangling projects would have been time-consuming and disruptive. The hand had been dealt. I had to play it as best I could, whatever the increasing noise level from critics and poor DH advocacy for the project. The same was true with the contracts and contractors for the NPfIT – or Connecting for Health as it been optimistically renamed a month before I arrived.

Contracts, Contractors and Momentum

Public sector IT contracts – including earlier NHS experiences – had been bedevilled by substantial cost overruns and non-delivery to time by contractors. Government departments had been criticised for agreeing contracts that placed all the risk with them and none with contractors. Protecting taxpayer in NPfIT contracts had been taken seriously by Richard Grainger who had become DH's Director-General of NHS IT in October 2002. Richard had been involved with large scale IT programmes including the London congestion charging scheme. He was said to be the highest paid civil servant, earning more than the Prime Minister, which attracted regular media attention. Richard was the architect of the contract system for purchasing and running NPfIT.

The contract architecture Grainger had devised was divided between national and local programmes. For local programmes England was divided originally into five "clusters" – Southern, London, East and East Midlands, North West and West Midlands and North East. A Local Service Provider (LSP) was contracted to deliver NPfIT in each of those areas. This structure avoided dependence on a single supplier and introduced a measure of competition. The original five LSPs were CSC for North-West and West Midlands; BT for London; Accenture for both North East and East Anglia and East Midlands; and Fujitsu for the South. The benefits of this approach became apparent later when two LSPs – Accenture and Fujitsu – withdrew (see below).

Alongside LSPs were National Application Service Providers. They were contracted for services common to all users like Choose and Book and the Care Record Service (CRS). BT was responsible for CRS and the new national broadband network (N3). ATOS were chosen for Choose and Book and EDS for NHS E-mail. Underneath these main contractors were a series of subcontractors, the most significant of which were those chosen to produce the software for the CRS which became the programme's biggest problem.

When the NPfIT contracts were let in 2003 they were seen as a model for government IT procurement with their transfer of risk to the private sector. Giving evidence to the Public Accounts Committee in 2005, the then Chief Executive of the Office of Government Commerce, John Oughton said: "I think the procurement process for Connecting for Health was an exemplary example of procurement. It was run to a very tight and rapid timescale; it started when it was intended and completed when it was intended; and it produced a very good result. I do not think any of the suppliers were disadvantaged in that process." Richard Grainger was still the golden boy of government IT contracting when I became responsible for NPfIT in 2005, whatever came later. Whether he was popular is another matter.

When I went to Cabinet Committee meetings, other government departments struggling with their IT programmes were encouraged to look at the DH experience. Contractors were paid only when they delivered. They had gone into the contracts with their eyes open and were global companies with armies of lawyers and accountants who wouldn't be bamboozled by Richard Grainger and DH civil servants. At my meetings with senior managers from the main contractors, it was clear they knew what the score was on contracts. They knew that Warner and Grainger would stick to the contracts if things started to go wrong. I supported Richard in paying only for what had been delivered. The only thing that was certain was that in a project of this scale and complexity some contractors would fail. The issue was who picked up the tab for failure, as had happened before my arrival.

In March 2004 EDS had their ten-year contract to supply NHS Mail terminated and they were replaced in July by Cable and Wireless. In 2005 IDX Systems Corporation were starting to fail to meet deadlines in the Southern Cluster. In August 2005 Fujitsu cancelled the IDX contract and were replaced in September with Cerner Corporation. Shortly after I arrived there were problems with CSC's subcontractor supplying PACS in the North West and West Midlands. In early 2006 CoM Medicare were replaced by GE Healthcare. All these examples showed the strength of the NPfIT contracting architecture. If main contractors were being let down by subcontractors and didn't get paid, then they replaced the subcontractors with no financial consequences for taxpayers.

A former Chief Executive of BT, Ben Verwaayen, told the Sunday Times in an interview on 14 May 2006: "Richard Grainger is doing a good job. He's one of our most difficult, demanding and therefore capable customers." Verwaayen said Grainger's critics had got the scale of NPfIT's problems out of perspective and needed to understand the extent of the changes being implemented. Few of the project's critics took much notice of this experienced Chief Executive's view.

371

As I began to realise, protecting the taxpayer was all very well, but it tended to slow down progress. It took time to replace failing contractors and deadlines for implementation slipped. We were two years into the project and there were few frontline systems in operation which damaged NHS support for the project. In Spring 2005 there were well under 100 local systems installed and working, nearly all of which were relatively small – Choose and Book, GP systems and Single Assessment Process systems for the elderly. No new PASs had been implemented and the NHS frontline had little to show for the national programme. GPs were being restricted on the IT systems they could choose and might be required to relinquish systems they had developed personally. Local people were waiting for NPfIT to replace systems that were falling apart, sometimes believing misguidedly that NPfIT would pay for all the transition to new systems. The gloss was wearing off and main contractors were struggling to secure payment because of their slow delivery. We might be protecting taxpayers, but we were not transforming the NHS electronically as quickly as we needed to.

By the autumn 2005 the programme was heading for a big underspend. This helped the DH budget overspend (see Chapter 10) but not with progressing Connecting for Health. At my meetings with Grainger and his team I accelerated take-up of Choose and Book systems as part of the choice agenda and encouraged more action on the electronic transfer of prescriptions and PACS which was proving popular with the NHS. Some local patient administration systems were on the verge of collapse and I wanted more of these replaced quickly. I had some difficult discussions with Richard Grainger about the growing unrest among GPs over the slow replacement of their systems. He often showed little understanding of the need to keep the NHS onside with the project and an excessive rigidity about contract application. After a lot of pressure, I persuaded him to give GPs more choice and let them use existing suppliers, providing there was compatibility with NPfIT systems' architecture.

My efforts did increase the number of local systems installed in 2005/6, despite the NHS financial problems. Between April 2005 and March 2006 over 5000 local systems were installed, more than 4000 of them Choose and Book systems. About 60 PASs and over 300 GP systems were also installed. Unfortunately, few new patient administration systems were in big acute hospitals where they were most needed, as I found on my visits. Still frontline activity was a big improvement on the previous year. This was just as well given our problems with the software for electronic patient records.

IDX was in financial difficulties and concerns were being expressed publicly about the business practices of Isoft, the software company working in the North. Isoft issued a huge profits warning in mid-2006 and revised their previous year's accounts. The value of their shares dropped by 90%, leading to the sale of the company and a lengthy Financial Services Authority inquiry. The Isoft solution for the patient record, Lorenzo, was popular with doctors, but remained a major problem in terms of successful hospital implementation. The timetable for most of the core projects was slipping and people were beginning to notice. The National Audit Office started an enquiry.

In early 2006 main contractors increased their complaints over payments. My growing suspicion was that as global demand for IT skills expanded, many of the contractors were struggling to attract talent. I also thought we needed a wider range of sub-contractors, but Grainger's team didn't agree. We started to see more progress as we increased pressure on main contractors to demonstrate delivery if they wanted paying. This exposed the problems of Accenture, who in Spring 2006 made public that it was making provision in its accounts of $450million (£237million) for losses on NPfIT because of delays in delivering software by Isoft. I knew things were serious when at a regular meeting with Accenture UK, a colleague from US headquarters turned up. Marty looked as though he could audition for The Sopranos.

The Accenture situation continued to deteriorate. Driving back from Scotland from a break with my family I had to pull off the road to take a call from Richard Grainger. He said that unless we coughed up more money by their next Board meeting then Accenture might well walk away from the project. I regarded this as crude blackmail and thought if we gave in then we'd have trouble with other main contractors. I told Grainger to hold them to the contract and only pay for what had been delivered. It became increasingly clear to me that Accenture were out of their depth – accountants and consultants, not an IT company. The crunch came in August when Accenture said they wished to withdraw from their contract.

We could have said 'See you in Court' which would have led to a lengthy hiatus in delivering the NPfIT or tried to negotiate new terms. This would have involved giving them more money when their delivery record was poor and encouraged others to pull the same stunt. There was an option of transferring the hospital work to CSC, leaving Accenture to deliver the primary care element. This would have lost economies of scale and pushed up the total programme cost by well over £0.5billion eventually. I rejected these options and decided to transfer the whole contract to CSC for 9 years at the same price as we would have paid Accenture – nearly £2billion. This enabled CSC to continue supporting Isoft – a British company – and those NHS organisations using Isoft. I agreed Accenture should be paid for the work they had done (about £50million) and not the huge sum they were seeking. I let them keep implementation of PACs which they were doing effectively. These were my negotiating instructions to Richard Grainger; and this was the deal that was done.

Accenture had let us down badly and the temptation to go after them publicly was enormous, particularly when I discovered that Sainsbury's and Centrica had had bad experiences with them. However, a lengthy virility contest with them would have distracted us from our main objective, delivering the NPfIT. We were not totally blameless because our monitoring had also been slow to pick up the difficulties with Isoft and their Lorenzo software (which continued to cause problems). We now found ourselves with a PAC enquiry to handle, so I was glad to get some media support for our approach. Michael Cross in The Guardian on 19 October said: "Congratulations to the NHS for facing down Accenture" and added they "should have known that the NHS faced a technical challenge of unprecedented complexity." Slightly backhandedly, he even congratulated Ministers for holding their nerve.

Despite all the brouhaha we maintained momentum on frontline implementation. I even managed to pause Jeremy Paxman on Newsnight by saying I would resign if we hadn't implemented Choose and Book by March 2007. By the end of 2006/7 about 9,000 frontline systems had been installed. Nearly 8,000 of these were in the Electronic Prescriptions Service and Choose and Book systems. But there were also another 300 GP systems installed and the GP2GP patient record transfers were beginning to take place at scale. Another 50 PASs were installed; and virtually all local programme projects had some progress to show. Connecting for Health had momentum when I departed and was well on the way to 15,000 local project installations according to a DH report in 2008.

The contracting system had stood up to failure by a main contractor without the cost of failure being transferred to the public purse or the momentum of the project being significantly affected. In its report on NPfIT published on 16 June 2006, the National Audit Office said the programme was much needed; well managed; based on good contracts; had made substantial progress; and the central expenditure was being managed within budget. It said that the programme had the potential to deliver substantial financial, safety and service benefits for patients and the NHS. The NAO drew attention to the fact that the programme had strong Ministerial and senior management support and was an example of best practice arrangements and structures for delivering the programme. Savings had been achieved by using NHS centralised buying power (for example, some of the lowest Microsoft costs in the world) that provided estimated savings of £860million. The NAO said the tough contract negotiations at the outset had lowered prices from bidders by £6.8billion.

I thought this was a strong endorsement from an independent source not noted for showering praise on Government Departments. Despite the NAO report, criticism continued, both from within the NHS and outside. Why this hostility?

Geeks Need Operational Plans

I had realised for some time that there were fundamental flaws in the way this highly centralised project was being managed by DH and these flaws went much wider than the contracting process. All the focus had been on managing contracting and contractors, rather than thinking about the impact of this huge project on the NHS itself. It would mean massive changes to the working practices of doctors, nurses and many other NHS staff. Such IT systems as the NHS possessed had been largely designed and implemented by groups of local clinicians in GP practices and hospitals. Grainger and the Connecting for Health enthusiasts were trampling over these beloved creations with a networked system that demanded architectural compatibility. To see through successfully the level of change required by NPfIT required a major clinically focussed operational and communications plan.

To move from where they were to a fully networked IT system GPs and practice managers, hospital consultants and managers and commercial pharmacies all had to invest a lot of time, effort and money. They had to replace their paper-based, film-based and unnetworked (and often obsolete) IT with new kit. Moreover, the new kit was to a great extent going to be dictated by people at the centre, or contractors on their behalf. The fact that these arrangements might save money and improve efficiency and benefits for patients did not always convince staff of the merits of change. There was also the matter of who paid for the local transition work of changing processes, training staff and using this centrally driven kit.

By the end of 2005 I knew the DH attempts to sell and manage this transition to the NHS were inadequate and I should have been more challenging. The fundamental problem was that the DH Management Board never owned the project, despite a paper trail pretending it did. The Board saw NPfIT as Grainger's project and responsibility. The project was never integrated into the narrative on NHS reform. The NHS Chief Executive failed to operationalise the work into the priorities of SHAs and local trusts. When his successor attempted to do this there was a lot of ground to make up. Ministers must take some responsibility for this failure but primary blame rests with DH top management.

I found it difficult to persuade the CMO, Liam Donaldson, to become a strong personal advocate for the programme to the medical profession, despite its potential to improve patient safety. Early on he had appointed one of his deputies, Dr Aidan Halligan, to work alongside Richard Grainger but Halligan left DH and was never really replaced. Able clinical leads for parts of the programme were appointed who I met periodically; but their efforts would have been aided enormously by a CMO willing to go on the stump for Connecting for Health with the BMA and the medical Royal Colleges and to feature the programme prominently in his annual reports. It was not to be.

At the local level the absence of clear messages over the priority NPfIT should receive was a significant problem, made worse by the lack of clarity about what resources the local NHS had to find for implementation. This problem was exacerbated by the low base the NHS started from in terms of IT expenditure. In the US the equivalent of the average well-run acute trust would be spending 4% or more on IT and would secure a lot of clinical benefit and management efficiency in return. In the UK in 2005 it was probably less than 2%. To run an IT system that secured the benefits of Connecting for Health the NHS would have to spend much more annually on IT to achieve the efficiency gains and patient benefits. At the point of transition, with staff training and moving data into new systems, the annual cost would be more before the benefits were achieved. The management effort for the transition would be considerable. DH and NHS top management failed to explain any of this properly to the local NHS or built it into their annual operating plans and priorities.

In the Spring of 2006, the programme's critics started scare stories about costs being out of control and the ten-year programme costing £30billion. The true published figures – accepted by the NAO – were £6.8billion for core national contracts; £2.2billion for national implementation activity and new projects; and £3.4billion of local expenditure on NHS implementation of CRS and PACS. This was a total of £12.4billion at 2004/5 prices over a ten-year period. I thought this might be an under-estimate, but a figure of £30billion over ten years was fantasy. I considered that the NHS might well be expected to spend an average of £1billion a year or so on IT as more of the programme came on stream alongside the central contracts. I couldn't see how a total cost figure could exceed £20billion over 10 years, with considerable offsetting benefits/savings coming on stream before the programme's full implementation. To counter the exaggerated stories about NPfIT costing £30billion, I gave an interview to the Financial Times. This set out my views on costs and explained why the electronic patient's record would be delayed. This appeared on 30 May 2006.

This did little to quieten the critics who were quite unwilling to accept that central contracts had always been only part of the costs or that the NHS simply spent too little on IT for a modern healthcare system. The local NHS declined to accept that they would be wise to spend more on IT while extra money was available in order to secure the future benefits. DH was too slow in producing an effective narrative for the NHS on the benefits of Connecting for Health. This was one of the few criticisms made by the NAO. I had tried to prod DH management into action on explaining NPfIT's benefits to the NHS but without much success. It was not until August 2006 that action was taken to operationalise NHS responsibility for implementing NPfIT by the new NHS Chief Executive, David Nicholson. He made clear that responsibility for the implementation and benefits realisation rested with the SHA and PCT Chief Executives under a new NPfIT Local Ownership Programme (NLOP). Even then it took until July 2007 to transfer management responsibility and resources to the SHAs.

It was to be long after my departure that in late 2008 DH finally published the first coherent "Benefits Statement" for NPfIT, covering the period to March 2007. This revealed that over 14,000 frontline systems had been installed under the programme by then. For the first time the DH was able to show the actual and recurring savings on the money spent in that period. There were cash-releasing savings of over £200 million at the end of March 2007, which in the seven remaining years of the contracts (to the end of March 2014) would produce over £1.1billion of NHS savings, with the recurring savings stretching into the future. This was the return on the £2.4billion spent by NPfIT on the systems delivering those benefits. It took no account of the benefits that would accrue from an electronic patient record; or what the NHS would have had to spend to keep old, outdated systems going. This meant that by early 2007 Connecting for Health was representing good value for money, but the story had simply not been told by DH. Even if it had, it might well have been drowned out by malicious critics.

Dubious Critics

By the second half of 2006 the absence of a clear narrative on costs and benefits, contractor failure and delays and the lack of clinical and NHS buy-in was providing fertile grounds for a growing band of critics. The lack of progress on the electronic patient record and increasing noise about the confidentiality and privacy issues relating to that record only encouraged persistent sniping at Connecting for Health. Much of this came from a group of information technologists and Conservative Party supporters, with Computer Weekly as their vehicle of choice. Some of this was traditional Opposition politics which I didn't take too seriously. Some of it was IT people deeply suspicious of any big government IT programme with large databases and networked systems. There was a strong civil libertarian strand to this criticism which thought giving personal data to government IT systems was inherently bad because it was bound to be misused and would not be secure. Any facts or arguments on patient benefits, true costs, realistic timescales and security systems were simply disbelieved.

As a Government Minister it is difficult to complain about an orchestrated campaign against a government programme like NPfIT without appearing paranoid and over-sensitive. Richard Grainger and his team were more convinced that the criticism was orchestrated than I was, but they had some evidence to support their views and many of the critics were unpleasant, unfair and difficult to expose. Grainger was an effective contracts designer and manager; but he was not the person to sell Connecting for Health to the outside world. He should never have been put in that position by his line manager, the then Permanent Secretary. He became, unfairly, a personal focus for the critics; and his naturally combative style only attracted more gunfire. As the responsible Minister I needed to defend him and the programme but with little DH capability or bottle to mount an effective counterattack.

It was only after my resignation as a Minister that the true extent of an orchestrated campaign against the NPfIT was brought home to me by a large volume of emails sent anonymously to me at the House of Lords. These covered the period of 2006 and 2007. I was able to draw on these in a House of Lords debate on 21 June 2007 on Public Sector IT projects. It is worth quoting verbatim from Hansard for that date, some of what I said in the debate:

"Some of my puzzlement over hostility to the programme has been removed, since leaving office, by discovering people working together to campaign against this programme. The campaign seems to be made up of the Foundation for Information Policy Research, the Big Opt Out organisation, the Conservative Technology Forum, Computer Weekly, Medix surveys and the Worshipful Company of Information Technologies, which I only recently discovered. An energetic presence in this network is a Cambridge professor called Ross Anderson. Some interesting e-mails of his have found their way to me. One e-mail of 27 November 2006 says:

"The Big Opt Out Org will be a separate campaign (which many of those help). The principle (sic) organiser is Helen Wilkinson" – who I believe is a Conservative Councillor. Another e-mail of 13 February, talks about, "how we might put the IC on the spot".

"The IC is, of course the Information Commissioner. Another e-mail of 8 March, after Professor Anderson had been asked to be an adviser to the Health Select Committee, says: "Well I said yes on the grounds that I can probably do more on the inside than on the outside.""

"Another e-mail which I particularly like is of 24 May 2007 sent after a lunch with Conservative front bench spokesmen Damien Green MP who is quoted as saying: "The Tories had taken an uncharacteristically principled line on the ID card and now felt exposed.""

"Ross was asked to provide some other arguments – a little less principled, I assume. Finally, in a quote from an e-mail of 20 December 2006 we have something a little closer to home: "After speaking to Andrew Lansley, Tim Loughton, Malcolm Harbour and Lord Lucas I may be starting to get the message across.""

"I have insufficient time to entertain the House with more extracts. I am willing to let them be seen on a private basis by my honourable friend in the other place who chairs the Health Select Committee. In a spirit of bipartisanship, I would encourage Conservative parliamentarians to look closely and sceptically at some of the sources of advice they appear to be using. The Connecting for Health IT programme should not be a political football. Too much is at stake for patients and the NHS."

It appears that the maligned Richard Grainger was right to be a little paranoid - they were out to get us. I noticed that after this debate and a robust defence of the NPfIT in the House of Commons on 6 June 2007 some of the more rancorous criticism abated. The slow progress on the electronic patient record is a different story and rightly continued to be criticised.

The Electronic Patient Record: Delays and Disputes

The jewel in the crown of Connecting for Health was to be an electronic patient record (EPR). This record would be available to locally networked services, with the national system able to transfer around the country a summary record of an individual patient's key details if there was an emergency. Such a system required a large measure of national agreement on the information to go in the EPR. For all this to work local NHS hospitals needed a modernised PAS but many of these hospital systems were not fit for purpose and needed to be replaced. Some were on the verge of collapse. Outside hospitals, most community and mental health systems simply didn't have a PAS that could move patient details around electronically.

Before significant benefits from an EPR could be realised it was always going to be necessary to re-equip the NHS with better local patient administration systems. DH completely failed to explain effectively to the NHS and the public that there was a massive modernisation of NHS local IT to be accomplished before people could have an electronic NHS Care Records Service (CRS). The NPfIT was never going to be able to make this happen in 3 or 4 years without a massive clinical engagement and marketing effort, together with generous local financial incentives. Even then it would have needed most NHS clinicians to be convinced that there was a working EPR that was going to meet their clinical needs at the end of the process. The failure to incentivise and persuade the acute hospital sector to transform and maintain its IT has held back modernisation of the NHS – and I suspect stills does in some places.

At the time we were trying to introduce a networked version of an electronic patient record there was still much public distrust of government placing vast quantities of personal data on central databases. Arguments about improving efficiency and quality of public services didn't convince people who saw these large, networked databases as threats to civil liberties. Their suspicions were confirmed when civil servants carelessly lost discs with huge amounts of personal data. For these critics, records of individuals using public services should be kept locally, not networked. Many in the NHS shared these views. Some still do.

Persuading NHS professionals that a networked system of patient records would both work and benefit patients was difficult. Most doctors wanted systems designed around their own circumstances and working practices. This is what GPs had done in the past and why I had to convince the NPfIT to be more flexible about the systems on offer to

GPs. The more standardised hospital systems offered by NPfIT tended not to provide all the bells and whistles of current local systems that clinicians had crafted and wanted to retain. There were few examples of local networked healthcare systems being implemented, let alone national systems. To make matters worse the subcontractors who would instal new local systems weren't doing a great job of convincing the NHS frontline to use their products.

Cerner's anglicised version of an American system, Millennium, had significant problems with its deployment in London and the South. In the Midlands and North West, the problems were even worse. I was endlessly told how positive clinicians were about Isoft's Lorenzo software and how they preferred it to Millennium. Just be patient Minister it will come right in the end. Release after release was postponed but contractually it was difficult to dump the Lorenzo product, particularly when CSC, the LSP main contractor, took responsibility for it. You wouldn't want to dump a British company would you Minister? Well actually, I should have done so.

The NHS was quite unrealistic about the effort they had to make with staff to successfully deploy and implement these new systems. Contractors were concerned not to bankrupt themselves by picking up costs they regarded as not covered in their contracts. The scope for dispute between NHS, LSPs and software subcontractors was considerable. Amongst the subcontractors there was an absence of specialist system deployers who were permitted to choose alternative software systems if the main suppliers could not deliver. I began to doubt Connecting for Health's ability to deliver EPR.

To convince myself that it was possible to make a networked EPR work in a major healthcare system I went to Washington DC to look at the US Veterans Administration (VA). When I lived in the US in the 1970s (see Chapter 1) the VA was a byword for inefficiency but in the late 1990s it had transformed itself. At the heart of that transformation was implementation of an Electronic Health Record (EHR) networked across all the VA outlets in the US with over 200,000 employees. The EHR operated across all inpatient and outpatient environments and I saw how a patient's information followed them in all clinical situations wherever a US veteran happened to be.

It had taken the VA ten years to design and implement their system and to secure the clinician "buy-in" to use it. I spoke to doctors who had been opposed to the whole idea and were very similar to their English counterparts. They now supported the EHR including its summary version. This was because whenever and wherever they saw a patient they could retrieve up-to-date data. The EHR was also a mechanism for optimising and standardising clinical practice – a particularly threatening issue for doctors in the UK. It provides real-time error checking, clinical support and was the primary means for generating corporate and individual provider performance data.

The EHR had been the main basis for improving the safety, quality and efficiency of care within the VA. A good example of this was the simple measure of what they called "patient chart availability". In 1995 patient charts had been available in only about 60% of patient/clinician encounters. Ten years later it was virtually 100% according to a 2006 report by Dr Jonathan Perlin. The efficiency gains of the EHR were considerable. In the US one in five lab tests were repeated; and one in seven hospitalisations occurred because previous records were not available. Yet the VA's EHR costed about $80 a year per patient to operate, the equivalent of not repeating a moderately inexpensive lab test.

I returned to the UK convinced that the VA was the best example of a live large-scale networked EPR with clinical buy-in. It demonstrated to sceptics how such a system improved patient care and healthcare efficiency. On my return I discussed with officials, especially Harry Cayton, the DH's National Director for Patients and the Public, how we might expose the BMA and other sceptics to the VA experience. I agreed that Harry should lead a group of clinicians to see the VA system in action and learn from their experience. While this did not solve all our problems the visit did quieten down some of the noise and did change some attitudes. There was, however, still the issues of privacy and consent to be resolved if patient information was ever to be networked by loading it on to the national spine.

Controversy over Privacy and Consent

In June 2006 I decided to try again to secure the medical profession's agreement on the consent issues surrounding the EPR. There were disagreements between GPs and hospital doctors and within each group, all of which had compounded the problems of delay. Some GPs argued that patients should be consulted before any of their information was uploaded to the network and wanted to restrict severely the amount of information recorded nationally. I asked Harry Cayton to chair a new taskforce that would develop by the end of 2006 "a detailed action plan" for speeding up implementation. With this I pressed DH to produce the long-promised information campaign that would explain the benefits of the EPR to the public. I decided to speak at the annual conference of local medical committees to announce this to GPs together with a firm date for a new set of pilots to test the uploading of personal data to the national system. I asked them to exercise more clinical leadership to ensure that patients received the benefits an EPR could bring.

This new initiative built on work that started in 2005 when we set up a Care Record Development Board to ensure that ethical issues were properly considered. This Board represented users of the care record, including patients, and provided independent oversight of how the care record was used. An NHS Care Record Guarantee had set out the rules governing use of patient information and what control patients had over it. The Guarantee had provided some reassurance to patients but there were continuing calls in the media to give patients a clear right to opt out of the Care Record Service. Critics wanted doctors to secure formal consent from all patients to loading their medical records on to the national database. This would be time-consuming; and the government had resisted it.

I thought we would have to give ground, particularly when The Guardian ran a write-in campaign to enable people to opt out of uploading their data nationally. I asked the Care Records Board for advice and they recommended giving people the opt-out of national uploading providing it was explained to them that this could have adverse consequences for them in accessing appropriate healthcare. I was determined to make progress on uploading summary patient data on to the national spine, as this was the only way to progress the new Care Record Service. After publishing the Board's recommendations, I decided to make concessions and start a pilot scheme in several areas. In December 2006 I gave an interview to John Carvel of The Guardian saying that we had changed our policy: "Minister admits U-turn on NHS database amid privacy fears" as The Guardian headlined it on 19 December. 20

I said I thought the fears of unauthorised disclosure of medical histories were groundless, but if patients didn't want their data uploaded, they could stop it. I made it clear – and the Guardian printed it – that campaigners did not have the right to stop the scheme or prevent the majority of people having their information shared or uploaded because of the protests of a minority. I pointed out that in Scotland where they had created an Emergency Care Record with uploaded data, only 250 people out of 6 million patients had asked for their data to be withheld. People would not have to give reasons for stopping uploading but they could not delete all their GP's data from his or her computer unless they could demonstrate mental distress. I made clear that patient control over their medical records was not absolute.

Just before my departure at the end of December, I launched trials of uploading data in Bolton, Bury, Bradford, South Birmingham and Dorset. Connecting for Health wrote to nearly 650,000 patients in the five trial areas and ran public information campaigns there on people's right to protect their data. When the trials ended two years later about 2,500 people opted out and 500 said their records could be uploaded provided NHS staff asked their approval every time their file was accessed. My compromise approach and the pilots enabled progress to be made. At the end of the pilots 635,000 patient records in the pilot areas were uploaded to the national database. The Care Record Service could make progress. After legislation the Care Record Board became a statutory body, the National Information Governance Board in 2009.

The Slow Death of Connecting for Health – or Resurrection?

In my time I had managed, with Richard Grainger and his team, to take Connecting for Health a fair way towards completion of its mission, despite DH management. Although the original contracting model protected the interests of taxpayers in terms of costs, it proved to be too inflexible for such a large diverse and cantankerous organisation as the NHS. A wider range of software and service providers were required with more local choice. The real failure, however, was not technical or the contracts manager but a fundamental failure of leadership and commitment to the project by DH top management – medical and lay. They did not produce and manage an operational and communications plan that ensured implementation across the NHS and took people, especially doctors with them over a period of years. They just left it to Grainger until 2007.

Despite the DH top management failure and a barrage of ill-informed and organised hostile criticism a lot was achieved. Nearly 14,000 frontline systems had been installed when I left. The National Spine and a secure e-mail and directory for the NHS were operating. The new system was highly reliable with system availability scores consistently over 99.9%: this meant it operated 167.9 hours of each week's 168 hours without unplanned breakdowns.

Choose and Book was fully operational and supported by GPs but was too often thwarted for patients by poor hospital PASs and uncooperative hospital management. Nearly 100 PACS systems had been installed to give the NHS digital imaging instead of film and these were clinically popular. With about 4000 pharmacies and GP practices covered, the electronic prescription service was making steady if unspectacular progress. The row over patient confidentiality and opting out of the national database had been calmed down and the governance structure around a Care Record Service was being strengthened. The central contracting system had been endorsed by the NAO and had coped with the failure of one of the four original Local Service Providers.

At the end of 2006 the big unresolved technical and operational problem was what to do about the large number of acute hospitals without the modern patient administration systems (PAS) needed to support electronic patient records (EPR); and who were unable to agree on the new software to support new systems. Connecting for Health's inability to produce convincing PAS/EPR products had made it difficult to persuade many of these hospitals to make the effort to replace their antiquated systems. They needed help from top management to resolve the problem.

After my departure (and later Richard Grainger), DH struggled to respond effectively to Fujitsu's decision in May 2008 to walk away from their £1.1billion contract for the South of England. This created a legal dispute with associated costs and a serious loss of momentum on new systems installation that lasted over 2 years. When Fujitsu jumped ship the new central team at DH and the three SHAs involved were unable to agree with Ministers an alternative implementation strategy. The Northern SHAs and hospital trusts were unwilling to abandon Isoft's Lorenzo product, despite its significant problems. BT struggled in London with financial problems in its Global Services Division and were slow to fix problems with Cerner installations.

The technicians seemed to be left to resolve problems they couldn't do on their own. Viewed from outside, the DH top management including Ministers totally lost their grip on this project and the ability to give direction to the NHS. In May 2008 the NAO estimated that the care record system was four years behind schedule and identified particular problems over deployment of the Lorenzo system They said delays meant only £3.6billion has been spent on NHS new IT services.

Yet outside the acute hospitals it was a quite different story. The answer I was given to a Parliamentary Question on 6 January 2010 revealed that nearly 7000 GP practices would have an Electronic Prescription Service by March 2010 and over 9000 pharmacies would. Over 7500 Choose and Book systems had been installed and over 1100 modernised GP systems. Over 5000 GP practices then had GP2GP medical record transfer systems. There were over 400 new clinical specialist systems in A and E, mental health trusts, community services, operating theatres, radiology departments and child health services. PACs were in over 300 hospitals, virtually completing the programme. Even PASs had been installed in over 60 acute trusts.

Eventually Connecting for Health was abandoned in 2013 following the Health and Social Care Act of 2012. It had still not achieved an interoperable EPR. It was folded into the Health and Social Care Information Centre and given the fancy new trading title of NHS Digital. The new organisation's mission statement is collecting, transporting, storing and disseminating the nation's health and social care data. The EPRs are now called Personal Health Records but without being interoperable nationally. NHS patients and clinicians still don't have the benefits of an interoperable personal health record that was working across the USA in the Veteran's Administration over 20 years ago.

In mid-2021 NHS Digital seems to have plucked up courage to transfer 55 million individual patient records to a national data base unless patients opted out. Success was jeopardised by indicating that in anonymised form this information could be made available to commercial interests. This led to protests about the short time given for patients to opt out and concerns over security and the purposes to which data might be put. This has led to delay in in making any such change. It remains unclear whether Connecting for Health will be resurrected from the grave dug for it.

12. Challenging the NHS to Change: 2005-2007

The Rise and Fall of NHS Commissioning

For its first 40 years two ideas dominated thinking on how to reform the NHS: reorganisation (including integration of service areas) and better management. A well-run healthcare system does require the right organisational structure and good managers but there is little evidence that these alone have improved NHS performance or prevented regular financial crises. That is because such changes do not resolve the inherent problems with a tax-funded single-payer healthcare system like the NHS, where demand regularly exceeds supply. New clinical technology and rising public expectations push up costs which cannot be met by charging users more, as in other industries. Governments want the NHS to stay free at the point of clinical need but are usually reluctant to raise taxes to provide more money.

In this situation the NHS needs to do things it has found difficult, like keeping the nation healthier, improving productivity or using more cost-effective ways of delivering services. Its performance has also been highly variable geographically. At the heart of this unresolved conundrum is the way the NHS chooses to use its funding– capital and revenue. Over the nearly 75 years of its existence, the NHS has financially favoured acute hospitals at the expense of preventative and community-based services which tend to be cheaper than hospitals which have expensive overheads and high running costs. Instead, successive governments have allowed the biggest kid on the block, with the most expensive toys – the acute hospital - to largely control the healthcare agenda. Aided and abetted by TV soap operas, the British public has developed a 75-year love affair with hospitals.

Nothing reveals this more than events during the Covid19 pandemic, with policy being driven by the needs of acute hospitals and their inability to cope with increased demand. The mantra "save our NHS" has really been about saving acute hospitals: even if this meant in March 2020 discharging large numbers of patients to care homes without Covid19 tests. What this means is that the NHS has become an extreme case of what economists call "provider capture," in which one group of providers – acute hospitals – dominate consumption of finite healthcare resources.

To try to combat this problem the idea of commissioning was developed 30 years ago along with the linked ideas of markets, competition and increased patient choice. The aims were a better balance in the distribution of finite resources, improved capability in managing demand and greater financial stability. The commissioning approach had been used earlier in local government (see Chapter 4) but it was introduced into the NHS by Ken Clarke, 30 years ago. In 1987 the NHS had probably the worst financial crisis in its history, with its Finance Director, Ian Mills, telling Ministers that the NHS was "technically bankrupt." Thousands of beds were closed in an attempt to balance the books, doctors marched on Downing Street and Thatcher announced a review on the BBC's Panorama programme.

Two years previously a US professor, Alain Enthoven, had published a little noticed pamphlet on the management of the NHS. This suggested creating an internal market in which health authorities were able to buy and sell services from each other and the private sector. This idea was latched onto by Ken Clarke when he became Health Secretary in June 1988. On holiday in Galicia Clarke came up with the idea of GP fund-holders using budgets to purchase services for their patients. In January 1989 Clarke, transported by riverboat to Limehouse, launched his White Paper 'Working for Patients.' This totally transformed the NHS with a purchaser/provider split: health authorities and GP fund-holders were to do the commissioning of services and hospitals (public or private) were to provide services. Despite Thatcher getting cold feet, Clarke stood his ground and in April 1991 the most fundamental changes to the NHS since 1948 were introduced.

Labour opposed GP-fundholding and after the 1997 Election banded GPs together into Primary Commissioning Groups (PCGs) which in 2002 morphed into statutory bodies - 302 Primary Care Trusts (PCTs). These trusts were to be commissioners of all services including GPs and other primary care contractors; but they remained providers of community health services, so were totally conflicted. More significantly PCTs were never properly trained for commissioning and there were far too many of them. To add complexity a version of practice-based commissioning (PBC) by GPs had been initiated just before the 2005 Election but on a voluntary basis so that GPs could decide whether or not they wished to commission and PCTs could decline to cooperate. This was a case study in how not to do commissioning.

This was the mess Patricia Hewitt and I inherited in mid-2005 but with a Manifesto commitment to 'streamline' the NHS and advance PBC. We had to start somewhere and did so by halving the number of PCTs from 302 to 150 (as described in Chapter10). I thought we only needed 40-50 PCTs, given research evidence and the fact that there was to be some GP commissioning. Unfortunately, I couldn't persuade those above my pay grade politically to do what was needed, despite the evidence for fewer, bigger commissioners. In California, Kaiser Permanente commissioned services on a state-wide basis. In Australia hospital services were commissioned and paid for on a state-wide basis. In New Zealand the 21 District Health Boards came together in four shared service organisations covering over 1 million population, each to commission specialist services.

I tried to get across to officials the three essential elements of PCT commissioning. First a local needs analysis which involved understanding and measuring the population's health needs. Second identifying the services required to meet those needs in some priority order. Third, within the resources available, contracting for the services needed from the most appropriate providers (whether in the NHS or not), monitoring performance against those contracts and changing providers when they did not perform. High class commissioning required a set of analytical skills and the nerve to stand up to powerful big spending acute hospitals and switch providers when they didn't perform. In 2005 most PCTs fell a long way short of being able to commission in this way. They usually had some form of contract system in place but were still attached to cosy contracts with local acute hospitals and to letting hospitals shape their spending patterns. The result was neglect of community needs for mental health services, care of chronic conditions or health promotion.

Most PCTs lacked the bottle or skill to change providers, whether it was underperforming GPs or particular hospital services such as elective surgery. The result was that PCTs paid the local acute hospital what it claimed it needed, often using national targets to justify their financial demands. There was little appetite for shifting service delivery outside hospitals. Powerful figures in the NHS and at the top of DH had built their careers in managing acute hospitals so few had any real interest in commissioning - either in theory or practice. And they knew Ministers moved on. As a government we were pouring increasing amounts of money into a failing commissioning system with targets as the only weapon in our armoury. Unfortunately, most targets helped powerful acute hospitals to demand more money to implement them. As more hospitals became FTs the position was likely to worsen.

In this situation I thought the best we could do was press on with PBC, tackle specialist commissioning and try to enhance the commissioning skills of the 150 PCTs we were stuck with. This was best done by linking commissioning to the patient choice and market reforms being pursued; and incorporating all these changes into an operational programme the NHS was required to follow that would manage demand within budgets. A tall order. Through autumn 2005 Ministers worked with officials to produce a document showing how the strands of NHS reform fitted together – "Health Reform in England: update and next steps." This was a reform route map, something not provided before. An appendix explained to PCTs what the purpose of commissioning was and that PBC would be a key part of their future.

During this period, I also took action on commissioning specialist services, many of which required populations much larger than those of PCTs. or even consortia of them. The failure to reduce the number of PCTs sufficiently made commissioning specialist services much more difficult. I decided to establish a review of commissioning specialised services under the chairmanship of Sir David Carter – a former Chief Medical Officer in Scotland. Sir David did a good job in achieving consensus in a disputed area and worked with me to ensure continuing political support for the changes needed. I accepted the recommendations in his May 2006 report; and we began to implement it.

In the December 2006 NHS operating framework document, the 10 new SHAs were required to implement Carter's specialised commissioning changes. This involved the establishment of a new National Commissioning Group based in the London SHA and 10 regional Specialised Commissioning Groups (SCGs) composed of PCT representatives that would collectively commission a minimum of

10 specialised services by 2008/9 and continue commissioning most specialised services for their populations. But the pace of change slowed; and in the Operating Framework for 2008/9 the NHS was still having to be told "to create pooled budgets to commission the majority of specialised services."

Back in the first half of 2006 I met weekly with the head of a new Strategic Policy Directorate and his staff on a range of NHS reform issues but particularly on commissioning and PBC. These meetings teased out the detailed operational consequences of the Government's reforms alongside the emerging NHS financial problems. Managing demand through commissioning was an integral part of this work but was a totally new idea for most NHS managers and clinicians. Much of this work was tested informally with NHS contacts to assess understanding, acceptance and workability. I had access to a small cadre of reform-minded people who could help operationalise NHS reform. The result in July 2006 was an update on reform for the NHS and an 80-page annex on commissioning.

This work revealed the NHS's poor understanding of commissioning and how few champions it had. The collective memory of DH top management seemed to have forgotten what had been done under Ken Clarke – or else they weren't letting on. However, we ended up in July 2006 with a workmanlike document that explained how commissioning would help PCTs achieve the best value within the resources available. It tried to terminate the endless arguments about inadequate funding with a firm statement. "Some PCTs continue to argue for a greater share of resources. We will keep the funding formula under review, but allocations made for 2006/7 and 2007/8 would not be changed. It is the responsibility of PCT Boards to operate within the cash limit." This robust approach was required because Ministers kept being told by managers and Boards that they couldn't use commissioning to change providers because of underfunding. The attitude that we will only change if you give us more money is alive and well in today's NHS and will be paraded in Covid19 recovery.

To help build commissioning capacity, we developed a new Fitness for Purpose Improvement programme for PCT boards and senior managers. We used websites to provide a database of demand management and commissioning initiatives; and undertook a national procurement to enable PCTs to call off a range of commissioning skills and services from private sector companies. This produced a lurid Guardian front page story on 30 June 2006 about how we were just working to privatise the NHS. Patricia Hewitt and I had angry meetings with the trade unions; and I was cross-examined on this by the Health Select Committee. We stuck to our guns and the DH website provided a menu of services and providers that PCTs could draw upon under this procurement, although many declined to use it. We needed the new SHAs to push their PCTs to improve much more than many of them did.

To strengthen commissioning, we introduced a new model national contract for PCTs to use with acute hospital trusts, together with a more effective disputes resolution system. Many of the acute trusts were adept at incorporating new costs into their contracts and stringing out dispute resolution. The acute hospital bias in DH management made for difficulty in resolving these issues. Some PCTs were foolish enough to enter into very long-term contracts – a 30-year contract came to my attention which had to be reviewed. Patricia Hewitt and I wanted the default position on disputes to be in favour of commissioners. We wanted firm deadlines so disputes could be resolved within a financial year for existing contracts or at the beginning of the new year where a new contract was involved. We managed to get to this position, with considerable persistence, in new guidance settling a new draft national contract as part of the operational framework for 2007/8.

Alongside this team effort on commissioning, I pursued a personal crusade on practice-based commissioning (PBC) where there was no real plan to ensure PCTs cooperated with or helped GPs who wanted to do PBC. I decided to move from a voluntary approach – which was going nowhere – to incentivising GPs. My target was virtually all practices undertaking some PBC by the end of 2006. DH officials and PCTs were reluctant participants in this mission, so I looked for GP allies. Two supporters were Dr James Kingsland of the National Association of Primary Care (NAPC) and Dr Michael Dixon of the NHS Alliance. The Royal College of General Practitioners were also cooperative. Sir John Oldham, a reforming Peak District GP, agreed to set up and run a network system for training GPs in PBC through the National Primary Care Development Team that he managed: he did this despite resistance in DH. The BMA's General Practitioner Committee was cautious but interested to see how PBC might benefit GPs financially. I sweetened their mood by agreeing a scheme to reimburse practices for the cost of engaging with PBC.

There was predictable resistance to setting a deadline for participation in PBC and giving GPs a cash incentive, but No.10 were supportive. Ministerial will, plus internal and external GP support trumped bureaucratic inertia, at least temporarily. I launched in January 2006, with a personal foreword, a document setting out what needed to be done to achieve full GP coverage of PBC by December 2006. It instructed PCTs in some detail on what to do to provide GPs with the standards and information they would need to make PBC a reality and how to set indicative budgets for PBC. It laid out the issues of accountability, governance and arbitration between GPs and PCTs. I followed up the January document by asking GP leaders to produce guidance on where clinical gains for patients could be produced quickest through PBC.

As private contractors, I have found GPs responsive to financial incentives (often quite modest) that help meet the clinical needs of their patients. I preferred to risk overpaying GPs to do something we wanted done than giving it to PCTs to spend on something we didn't. I went further, against the wishes of civil servants, PCTs and probably the Treasury. I said that "practices should be entitled to access and redirect at least 70% of any freed-up resources; the remaining 30% to be used by the PCT to meet a wider need across the whole PCT area". I was backing the financially shrewd entrepreneurs in general practice against bureaucratic caution. I believed that if we wanted more NHS resources diverted to services outside hospitals, chronic conditions and preventative health services we had to put GPs more in the commissioning driving seat. Tackling health inequalities and personalising services required more localised commissioning with greater GP involvement.

Opposition to PBC continued. PCTs wouldn't provide data; GPs couldn't be trusted; PBC would wreck demand management; and so on. Most resistance was simply an unwillingness by PCTs and their DH supporters to share commissioning power with GPs. I tried to end the battle of principle when we published in July 2006 a fuller document on commissioning for PCTs and SHAs. An annex stated unequivocally:

395

"Through PBC, practices will have indicative budgets and the freedoms and incentives to exercise devolved responsibility for aspects of the commissioning and redesign of services." PCT resistance continued but I thought we had achieved a workable balance between public accountability for taxpayer's money with freedom for clinicians to innovate and deliver improvements for patients. In November 2007 the Audit Commission said in a report on PBC that: "The combination of an incentive payment to practices, together with the requirement on PCTs to provide a supporting infrastructure has helped to introduce and implement PBC."

PBC had been established nationally when I ceased to be a Minister but was a long way from playing a full part in NHS commissioning. PCTs continued to give inadequate support and information for PBC and to reject many GP plans for new services under PBC. Many PCTs failed to hand over budgets to GPs. The incentive payments to GPs produced insufficient innovation in the services commissioned according to a Kings Fund study in November 2008. Despite these shortcomings, this two-year study argued that the Darzi Review (see below) was right to commit the Government to persevering with PBC. In December 2008, a national framework was established to provide practical support to PBC groups. When I later checked on progress with a Lords Parliamentary Question, the reply I received on 8 July 2009, was that in March 92% of GP practices were part of a PBC group. I thought Ministers were not pushing PBC very hard because handing more power and budgets to GP commissioning undermined the already weak rationale for 150 PCTs. Merging small PCTs and losing NHS jobs had no appeal for Labour Ministers as an Election approached.

When I left DH at the end of 2006, the foundations for a commissioning-led NHS were established with an NHS Operating Framework for 2007/8 that I agreed before departure. There was a coherent NHS structure for commissioning that stretched from micro-level commissioning (PBC) through local commissioning by PCTs to 10 regional Specialised Commissioning Groups with PCTs in consortia and a National Specialised Commissioning Group for highly specialised and expensive treatments. Despite halving the number of PCTs there were still far too many of them, with too many weak ones – especially in London – unable to manage demand or change providers. We had

396

moved the dial on commissioning but not enough to loosen the grip on resources of acute hospitals.

It looked as though things might change at the top of DH when the new NHS Chief Executive, David Nicholson, said in December 2006 that "a truly patient-centred NHS has to be driven through commissioning and we need to see a qualitative shift in the quality and nature of commissioning in this country". The arrival of Mark Britnell in 2007 as a new and energetic Director of Commissioning enabled PCT commissioning to be driven harder through a "World Class Commissioning" initiative launched in December 2007. Britnell described PCT commissioning and purchasing skills as 'featherweight' compared to the strength of the acute hospital sector.

The new initiative placed a stronger emphasis on commissioning for health outcomes and reducing health inequalities. A set of commissioning competencies was published together with an assurance system for assessing health outcomes, providing governance competence and building capability, including using expertise from the private sector. The 2008/9 NHS Operating Framework issued in December 2007 consolidated the work in progress on commissioning that Patricia Hewitt and I had left behind. There was a final version of the national contract for PCTs to use with all acute trusts; PBC was integrated fully into PCT governance frameworks as the best way of generating local services; and the new system of specialised commissioning was embedded. "World Class Commissioning" was to be pushed by SHAs as an important part of NHS development.

In early 2008 it looked as though PCTs might be transformed from bodies that simply handed out cheques to providers of services, into bodies that implemented 5-year health and wellbeing targets to improve the health of their local populations. However, what Britnell's initiative exposed was a yawning gap between the most and least competent PCTs and a political unwillingness to tackle this by merging PCTs and bringing in more external expertise. Mark Britnell left the DH in 2009 and the drive to transform commissioning effectively collapsed because it lacked Ministerial support for challenging NHS lethargy.

Autonomous Provider Organisations had been created by SHAs within PCTs; but there was no political appetite for separating them from PCTs after a robust process of market-testing. In September 2009,

Andy Burnham, the then Health Secretary, effectively killed off commissioning by telling the world that for him the NHS was the preferred provider. There was no political willingness to tackle the large number of underperforming PCTs, despite the clear evidence for doing so from the Care Quality Commission. Their NHS performance ratings for 2008/9 revealed that only 3 out of 152 PCTs were rated "excellent" for service quality, with 71 rated "fair" or "weak:" All 4 PCTs in NE London were "weak." On financial management no PCT was rated "excellent" and 71 were shown as "fair" or "weak". After 7 years of generous funding and a lot of development effort, PCT commissioning had simply not delivered.

That was the view of the Health Select Committee whose March 2009 report summed up their frustration. "The Department argued that its World Class Commissioning programme will transform PCTs. While the programme has only been in place since July 2007, there are few signs yet that variations between PCTs in their commissioning capability have been addressed. The NHS purchasing/commissioning function was introduced nearly 20 years ago, and its management continues to be largely passive when active evidence-based contracting is required to improve the quality of patient care."

PCTs had their chance to show their worth and the great majority had failed dismally. Overall SHAs were unable to performance manage a sufficient number of them into an effective piece of NHS machinery or to separate provision of services from commissioning. Too many PCTs frustrated the commissioning by GPs who were capable commissioners. The original number of 302 PCTs was far too large. I had lacked the political support to reduce that number to the 40-50 needed and that could be staffed with competent people. This lack of competent people had been revealed during the financial crisis in 2005/6 when 175 PCTs had to be visited by turnaround teams because their finances were in such a mess. In one PCT, two thirds of the ineffective management was made redundant according to the Humana CEO speaking at a conference in October 2007.

The brutal truth is that when Tony Blair ceased to be Prime Minister, elected Labour Health Secretaries and Ministers were unwilling to significantly reduce the number of dysfunctional PCTs, replace large numbers of staff unable or unwilling to commission and subject PCT inhouse community services to a competitive tendering process. What needed to be done to make commissioning work and to create competition in a monopoly NHS provider market, was strongly opposed by NHS unions and many NHS staff. The successors to Blair and Reid lacked the political appetite to challenge entrenched staff attitudes in the cause of patient choice and a more cost-effective NHS.

The Battle to Increase Patient Choice

Over the years there has been much talk about the NHS being patient-focussed and patient-led and giving patients more say over services. Professional bodies have exhorted doctors and nurses to listen to patients who in turn have continued to complain about their voices not being heard. and having too little say over services. At the heart of this issue is whether NHS systems and behaviour facilitate patient choice or block it. Producing a patient-led NHS involves difficult practical issues around information, choice and commissioning that no political party has yet resolved. New Labour had a go during my time as a Minister.

The NHS Plan of 2000 had a strong patient focus and talked of giving people 'a real say in the NHS'. But that plan was more about seeking patient views, having advocates, patients getting copies of doctor's letters and patient surveys. The only real choice patients were offered related to cancelled operations. Things changed with the arrival of John Reid as Health Secretary who saw that patient choice could appeal as much to working-class Labour voters as to the middle classes that New Labour had been wooing. Shortly after John's arrival a major public consultation was launched in which over 100,000 people were involved, along with hundreds of bodies and organisations.

This consultation revealed that people wanted to share in decisions about their health and healthcare and to make choices about that care. 90% of people said they needed more information to make their choices. People wanted to be treated as individuals and not forced into NHS systems. They wanted extra NHS capacity to be provided, especially for long-term conditions, and they supported continuing reform. More power should be devolved locally but system changes had to deliver more choice. The NHS had to do a better job of listening to patients and the public. As I went round the NHS on Ministerial visits and held local staff engagement meetings it was clear that most NHS staff were not on the same page as the public in terms of patient choice and voice. Hoping that local staff would have a change of heart without more high-level intervention was wishful thinking.

John Reid's response to this consultation was the publication in December 2003 of a White Paper – "Building on the Best: Choice, Responsiveness and Equity in the NHS." This identified six main changes:

- Giving people a bigger say in how they were treated with the provision of their own Health Space linked to the electronic health record which would enable people to make their preferences known to clinical teams.
- Increased choice of access to a wider range of services in primary care.
- Increased choice of where, when and how to obtain medicines.
- Enabling people to book appointments at a time that suited them from a wider choice of hospitals, with a promise that by the end of 2005 patients requiring surgery would have a choice of four or five hospitals.
- Widening choice of treatment and care, starting with maternity services and end of life care (relating to where they wished to die and how they wanted to be treated)
- Ensuring people had the right information at the right time.

The Foreword made it clear that "without an increase in capacity in the NHS, we cannot deliver the degree of choice that we want for patients." This Ministerial message on the link between choice and capacity was very clear in 2003. But as I found over the next 3 years, many in both the Labour ranks and the NHS were not keen on hearing this message. John Reid kept his foot firmly on the choice accelerator and egged on by No.10, he followed up the December 2003 document with another blast in June 2004 when the "NHS Improvement Plan" was published.

The Prime Minister was now in full flow on public service reform, with patient choice a weapon in his armoury. A Foreword by Tony Blair made it clear that there would be no slowing down on NHS reform and no apology for driving reforms from the centre. The NHS Improvement

Plan contained some new and radical proposals that were not fully grasped by the NHS at the time.

- "Patients will be admitted for treatment within a maximum of 18 weeks from referral to their GP and those with urgent conditions will be treated much faster."
- "Patients will be able to choose between a range of providers, including NHS Foundation Trusts and treatment centres."
- "They will be able to be treated at any facility that meets NHS standards, within the national maximum price that the NHS pays for the treatment they need."
- "We anticipate that by 2008, the independent sector will carry out up to 15% of procedures per annum for NHS patients, paid for by the NHS."
- "By 2008 all NHS acute trusts in England will be in a position to apply to become NHS Foundation Trusts, working as independent public benefit corporations, modelled on cooperative and mutual traditions."
- "The Healthcare Commission will inspect all providers of care and provide assurance of quality of care wherever it is delivered."

Improving delivery through central targets was extended with a new demanding target of a maximum of 18 weeks from GP referral to specialist operation. But there was much more emphasis on personalisation and devolution to counter the criticism of an over-centralised 'command and control' NHS. More personalised care was promised, and more care was to be delivered closer to home, with a better deal for people with complex long-term conditions. Local communities would have greater influence and say over how their services were run. All hospitals were to be removed from Whitehall control by becoming FTs by the end of 2008 - a hopelessly optimistic target.

NHS patients would be "able to choose from a growing range of independent providers" who by 2008, would "provide up to 15% of procedures on behalf of the NHS." For the first time the expansion of private sector capacity was linked to patient choice. Two future choice benchmarks were laid down. "From the end of 2005 patients will have the right to choose from at least four to five healthcare providers."

"In 2008 patients will have the right to choose from any provider," subject to meeting NHS standards and keeping within NHS tariff price. The 15% figure was immediately attacked by the unions, outraged that someone with John Reid's Labour pedigree could agree this. John said it was an estimate not a target, but Tony Blair continued to regard 15% as a target.

The commitments in the December 2003 and the June 2004 documents were carried through into the 2005 Election Manifesto ('Britain Forward not Back'). This promised to expand capacity and choice in primary care, not just hospitals. By 2009 all women would "have choice over where and how they have their baby and what pain relief to use". More patients with cancer would have a choice to be treated at home. In social care there would be "personalised budgets" so, "people can decide for themselves what they need and how it should be provided. Yet when I arrived in my new job after the 2005 Election my induction pack made no mention of choice or competition, apart from a single slide on the independent sector. DH senior civil servants had no enthusiasm for the choice and competition agenda and there was no plan for delivering a choice of 4 or 5 hospitals by the end of 2005.

The literature on patient choice showed strong support and that it could not just be dismissed as a fad of Ministers. There was good survey data showing that over 60% of patients thought choice of hospitals was very or fairly important. This compared with over 75% in relation to schools where there had been more public debate on parental choice. Choice was more important to women than men, so there were some gender politics as well. The 2005 British Social Attitudes Survey revealed that support for choice of hospitals was spread throughout the socio-economic groups. If anything, support for choice was stronger in the poorer groups who often received a worse deal from the NHS than the sharp-elbowed middle classes. Armed with this information and the arrival of a few more enthusiastic civil servants, I was able to go on the stump around the NHS about choice being a key issue. We set up a raft of seminars with PCTs to push the agenda and found some PCT champions – largely women - who were enthusiastic about choice.

Back in the DH we grappled with how to give people the information needed to exercise choice. A duff pilot effort and booklet for each area had to be aborted, at some cost. There were lengthy debates about what performance data for each hospital should be included and tortuous discussions about the reliability of the local data. I wanted to use published data and was able to persuade the Healthcare Commission to help us with data provision. We settled on a traffic-light system for each of seven hospital measures (including waiting times and infection scores) so that it was easier for the public to understand. We had to pressurise some areas to include private sector providers so that people had a wider choice. There was a printing screw up which added to the costs and my woes. Eventually, we distributed booklets around the country at the end of 2005 so that, at least in theory, people could exercise the choice of hospital promised. I authorised a publicity campaign in early 2006 and we set up later an NHS Choices website using Dr.Foster (see Chapter 9).

Although we had enabled people to exercise choice of hospital, many clinicians (including GPs) and managers were less enthusiastic and found choice threatening. Some NHS staff tried to scare local people about going to hospitals outside their area because the loss of income would threaten the future of local hospitals. Some acute hospitals and their consultants refused to put available appointments on the Choose and Book computer system to prevent patients exercising choice. Some GPs said the data on quality was unreliable. The tensions and conflicts over choice within the NHS were reflected in the views expressed in professional journals and by the commentariat, with many journalists siding with professional self-interest. Although the civil servants working directly to me on choice were very supportive, the top echelons of DH, the NHS and SHAs were far less keen on patient choice.

Despite having public opinion on our side, the government received little credit for pushing on with choice. Most of the media presented choice as something Ministers were inflicting on a hard-pressed NHS and that the public didn't really want. There was virtually no coverage of the view that parts of the NHS were simply engaging in restrictive practices to suit provider convenience. We surveyed the public later in 2006 to see how many people had experienced increased choice. This revealed much local variation. In the new SHA areas 6 out of the 10 had between a third and a half of people reporting a choice of hospital, with the rest reporting under a third. About a quarter of the new PCTs reported over half their population saying they had a choice and about a dozen reported over two-thirds. We were able to compare this data with unoccupied and available beds. With the exception of rural areas like Devon, Cornwall and Cumbria, most parts of the country had reasonable bed availability within an hour's travel time of people's homes.

When I resigned at the end of 2006, we had delivered in 18 months choice of hospital to at least a third of the country and to half the population in some places. We had shown a significant proportion of the public had an appetite for choice of hospital and were prepared to travel if they could get treatment quicker. King's Fund research published in 2010 revealed that many patients were denied a choice by the behaviour of NHS personnel. Many GPs were resisting patient choice, and rarely pointed patients towards performance data to help them choose. Although information was available to help people choose, they did not always know about it. Patients were relying for help with exercising choice on NHS personnel who were too often reluctant to assist patient choice.

Some NHS staff resisted patient choice on the grounds that patients didn't want to go to a non-NHS hospital; but our own survey information at the time didn't support this view, as I repeatedly told NHS audiences. In April 2005, a Mori Survey indicated that 71% of the public were happy to use the independent sector to provide NHS treatment: 16% had no preference and only 11% were unhappy with the idea. Patient satisfaction levels on ISTCs were consistently higher than those with NHS hospitals overall. Every ISTC patient I spoke to was delighted with their care and treatment but often surprised that they could get this level of service on the NHS. They particularly liked the customer-focus of private providers, compared to their previous NHS experience.

Once Labour Ministers like Andy Burnham said that the NHS was their preferred provider, as he did in 2009, they undid the work of their Labour predecessors and effectively killed off patient choice. It is difficult to provide widespread patient choice without access to independent sector service providers. Those providers have been discouraged by Ministers. Once NHS staff knew that Ministers were opposed to competition they quickly reverted to their old monopolistic ways and let waiting lists build up. Covid19 has ensured a huge backlog of NHS patients awaiting urgent and elective treatment. Many of these

404

people would be willing to travel further for faster treatment if Ministers had pushed the NHS into facilitating this. Patients can only exercise choice if they are helped to do so by political leaders pushing the NHS in this direction. During Covid19 there were plenty of underemployed surgeons who could have undertaken NHS elective surgery in independent facilities at NHS rates, with much of this being day surgery. The NHS was allowed to prevent this happening.

The monopolistic NHS has effectively seen off commissioning and patient choice – with the help of elected Ministers. It was almost as though most of the NHS has no interest in patient convenience and wish for speedy relief of pain and discomfort. The NHS was to prove equally unwelcoming to the third strand of the Blair government's NHS reform agenda – competition. These three strands came as a package, aimed at making a lethargic NHS more receptive to rising public expectations and advancing technology. To change the NHS culture of largely monopoly providers dictating the terms of trade and the use of the budget, all three of these strands were required. Availability of alternative providers of NHS services remains critical to patient choice and improving NHS performance.

Creating an NHS Market - Foundation Trusts

I was speaking to a packed audience of doctors at the Royal College of Surgeons in the 2005 Election campaign and advancing the virtues of choice, competition and other works of the devil. This was all too much for an angry orthopaedic surgeon. He burst out "Lord Warner, my patients don't need choice, they know I am the best". This encapsulated the views of many NHS staff. Certainly, most of the Labour Party and trade unions were hostile to markets and the private sector providing health care. For 60 years the NHS had operated on a basis of local monopolies with a GPs acting as gateways to specialist care that heavily constrained patient choice as well as rationing demand. The default-setting of the NHS was local monopoly and central control. This was the favoured position of many civil servants, NHS managers and elected Ministers - with a few honourable exceptions. But in 2005 it wasn't the view of the Prime Minister.

Tony Blair had tried centrally driven targets, but they hadn't produced enough change at sufficient speed. Now he was on an impatient mission of public service reform focussed on health and education with choice and competition as the new main drivers, but without abandoning national targets. Blair drove change through a small cadre of Ministers and advisers in No.10 and the main Departments, with some key civil servants in both places. The 2005 Election manifesto was intended to bury Labour's opposition to competition in the NHS and a healthcare market. The groundwork for creating a diverse group of providers was the move to Foundation Trusts(FTs) provided for in the Health and Social Care (Community Health and Standards) Bill that I had piloted through the House of Lords in 2003.

The Bill that arrived in the Lords gave financial freedoms to FTs and placed them outside Ministerial direction. This enabled them to make their own decisions on adapting services to local needs. Diehard statists in the Labour Party disliked the idea of independent hospital trusts outside Ministerial control, even though FTs were not-for-profit-public benefit corporations, based on Cooperative movement principles of mutualism. These critics had persuaded the Government to insert a cap on the private patient income FTs could generate. This was an own goal because it reduced the private income FTs could generate to increase NHS services; and simply made it more difficult for some trusts to become FTs.

During the Bill's passage Labour critics, egged on by trade unions, worked themselves up into a lather over NHS privatisation. They disliked the idea that FTs could raise their own capital for development (within a prudential borrowing code) and that I made clear FTs would not be rescued if they went broke. The Conservatives supported the idea of FTs but wanted to exploit Labour divisions. They worked with the Liberal Democrats to embarrass the Government. Over a two-month period I moved 200 amendments to placate a joint Opposition that could always outvote the government. This was to avoid losing the Bill in a Parliamentary session that was to end by 30 November. Eventually matters came to a head over an Opposition amendment to delay the process for approving the first waves of FTs.

When the Commons rejected the Lords' amendments a furious game of 'ping pong' ensued between the two Houses through the night of 20 November. I shuffled between the Lords and the Commons trying to agree with John Reid cosmetic concessions that would not do too much damage to the Bill. Eventually we agreed that after Monitor – the new FT regulator – had approved the first two waves of applicants, there would be no more applications until there had been a review of the impact on the NHS of the first two waves by the new Healthcare Commission. I ended up at 5am on the 21 November arguing furiously with the Opposition but finally agreeing the Bill with a manageable amendment on a review. Shifting gear through the night between emollience and attack dog mode improved my street-cred with John and elected colleagues.

Once the Parliamentary tempest had blown itself out the move of trusts to FT status started smoothly. The first tranche of 10 were authorised in April 2004, mostly high performing hospitals. Like their successors they were keen to escape Whitehall control and performance management through Strategic Health Authorities. They favoured the ability to access capital on the basis of affordability instead of the old system of centrally controlled allocations and lengthy capital approval processes. If they made revenue surpluses, they could invest these in new services locally rather than having them removed to prop up failing hospitals elsewhere. Although my concessions made FT governance more cumbersome, they still ended up as membership organisations of local people. Their boards comprised patients, staff and local people elected as local stakeholders.

The peace process of the Healthcare Commission review took place in 2004. When the Commission's report was published it found the NHS had not been noticeably affected, although it was probably too soon to make a final judgement. The Commission's report cleared the way for further FT applicants. When I took over responsibility for FTs in May 2005, I found that 32 FTs had been approved but we had no pipeline of FT applicants. Officials and I developed a process for producing a steady flow of applicants to Monitor. The first five waves were given free assistance to get themselves in a fit state to become FTs. All applicants first needed to satisfy the responsible Minister – me after mid-2005 – that they could go forward to Monitor for a rigorous assessment of their business plan. It became apparent that only 60%-70% of applicants got through at their first application.

Those who failed usually did so because of financial over-optimism, poor risk assessment in their business plans and overall doubts about the robustness of their governance and financial management capability. The enthusiasts for FTs had overestimated the ability of many acute and mental health trusts to make successful applications. The new Regulator, Bill Moyes, did not want to seem a soft touch or to repeat the Conservatives mistake of the early 1990s of letting through inadequately managed hospital trusts to a higher status. Moyes declined to indulge the NHS tendency to regard all geese as swans. It was also clear to me that letting candidates go forward on the basis of historical performance wasn't sufficient.

The available data suggested that by the end of 2008 – the Prime Minister's deadline - we might with hard work achieve about 100 FT approvals. That would still leave the majority of hospital trusts outside the FT magic circle. I had to make it clear to Tony Blair and Patricia Hewitt that it was going to take a lot longer than they wished for all NHS trusts to become FTs. I did not think we should reduce standards to meet an Election timetable. I broke the bad news to Tony Blair who, a bit reluctantly, accepted that we should not lower the bar.

There were four main reasons why so many NHS hospitals could not become FTs. They had high reference costs because they were too expensive and inefficient; poor financial management; inadequate performance ratings from the Healthcare Commission; and a lack of business planning and other skills to get them through the Monitor authorisation process. This was a considerable indictment of the state of the NHS's governance and management into which large amounts of public money was being poured. These problems were at the heart of the 2006 NHS financial meltdown described in Chapter 10. Endless wittering about the virtues of the "NHS family" in the DH top echelons was no substitute for an effective financial and performance management regime.

I wanted DH management to agree with Monitor a process that was likely to produce a higher success rate. We commissioned a diagnostic tool that allowed SHAs to assess each acute trust's state of readiness to apply, together with an action plan process in two pilot SHA regions for getting people up to speed to apply. This approach was then rolled out across the country as a whole. We invested money in it and also gave financial help to those trusts who would go forward to Monitor in the first five waves. I asked for candidates for the next wave to come forward by December 2005 to go to Monitor for approval from April 2006 and for a further wave from July 2006. This injected some momentum.

By the time I left at the end of 2006 there were 54 fully operational FTs and 59 by the end of March 2007. These FTs were generating an annual surplus for reinvestment of about £130million and had consolidated cash balances of nearly £1billion. Only four of them had poor financial risk ratings on which action was being taken by Monitor. In 2006/7 only 48 hospital trusts were rated 'excellent' in their use of resources by the Healthcare Commission, and all were FTs. This pipeline continued to produce a steady flow of candidates. Monitor reported that in September 2008 there were 105 NHS FTs, 31 of them mental health trusts. They were generating revenues at an annual rate of about £20billion. It was clear, however, that geographical enthusiasm for becoming an FT was varied. London, West and East Midlands and the South East Coast SHAs had only a third or less of potential FTs approved when five other SHAs had over 50% with one of them reaching 80% of Trusts.

At the end of 2008/9 Monitor had approved 114 FTs who had recruited over 1.2 million members; employed approaching 400,000 staff; and had a combined turnover of over £22billion a year. As businesses FTs were in rude financial health compared with non-FT hospitals. The gap between FTs total income and their operating costs in 2007/8 was about 8%, way beyond what the rest of the NHS was achieving. They were improving their efficiency and profitability much faster than the rest of the NHS at a time of reduced public expenditure. But all was not well. The Care Quality Commission's annual report for 2008/9 showed that only about half the 230 hospital trusts had become FTs. The pipeline of applications to Monitor had virtually dried up, with the Brown Government having little appetite for markets and competition.

Without seeming to realise it, the Brown Government was now presiding over a two-tier NHS hospital service. The higher tier of about half the trusts were independent, well-run and financially sound with good governance and local accountability. The other half were not as well-run and couldn't make the effort to change and go through the approval process to become FTs – still allegedly the Government's

409

preferred NHS trust model. Major hospitals like the Oxford Radcliffe, Great Ormond Street and Barts and the Royal London were still not FTs. In half the ten SHAs, the majority of acute and mental health trusts had simply not applied for FT status. These included more than half the 25 hospital trusts with the largest annual turnovers in the NHS (over £400million a year). The NHS Chief Executive, David Nicholson, asked SHAs to identify those Trusts who wouldn't be FTs by 2011.

Many of these non-FT trusts were simply not robust enough financially, whatever their clinical performance, to be standalone FTs. What was lacking was the political will to tackle the issue of failing and financially unsustainable hospitals and to require the mergers and realignment of hospital services that were needed. FTs had been successful and proved their worth and were providing a superior service to many, if not most, of the non-FT hospitals. A large proportion of patients were relying on NHS providers operating within an inferior model for financial management and, who, as a consequence, often had lower clinical quality. The Healthcare Commission's annual health checks had shown that financially weak trusts were frequently unable to focus on clinical quality. In 2008 the Commission's final report showed that of the NHS trusts rated "excellent" for use of resources, 91% were rated "good or excellent" for quality of services – as were 86% of trusts who were rated "good" for use of resources. Compared with these figures, the Commission's data showed that of those rated "weak" for financial management, only 45% were said to have "good or excellent" services.

In 2008 Gordon Brown brought in as a Health Minister a pioneering surgeon, Sir Ara Darzi to conduct a review of the NHS that shifted the focus to quality and quality accounts. Darzi's Next Stage Review didn't argue against FTs and said: "It is our clear ambition that in future hospital care will be provided by NHS foundation trusts." Unfortunately, that didn't seem to be the view of Brown's two Health Secretaries, Alan Johnson and Andy Burnham, who had no enthusiasm for markets.

There was no longer any political pressure to move trusts to FT status. Some did make the journey and in 2019 there were about 150 FTs; but they found, along the way, that many of the FT advantages of the Blair years, had evaporated. The long period of austerity saw raids on their accumulated surpluses; the cap on private income thwarted the build-up of surpluses for new developments; and there was the disruption of the Lansley re-organisation. The political failure to follow through on FTs was reflected even more graphically in another strand of the Blair initiative on markets – competition.

Opposition to Competition: ISTCs

Alongside FTs the key battleground over establishing an NHS market of providers was the creation of new Independent Sector Treatment Centres (ISTCs) These would be built and managed by private sector companies for use by NHS patients at NHS prices. The ISTC programme was centrally driven and aimed at breaking the NHS monopoly over elective surgery which had caused long waits. ISTCs were intended to provide choice and were a clear statement of Tony Blair's intention of forcing public sector reform through greater competition. Periodically private sector providers came into No.10 and were given encouragement and support. Whether they wanted to be Tony's shock troops remained less certain. There was little Labour enthusiasm for markets or competition, but if there was to be an NHS market, succeeding with ISTCs was essential.

The ISTC story began with a change of clinical practice in the 1990s when some NHS doctors proposed separating elective surgery from emergency surgery. Mixed emergency and elective lists had led to many patients with less serious conditions being "bumped" for operations by emergencies. Repeat cancellations were a significant issue and the loss of productivity for hospitals was a problem. In 1999 the first treatment centre in England dedicated to elective surgery – the Ambulatory Care and Diagnostic Centre – was opened at the Central Middlesex Hospital. The NHS would probably have separated elective and emergency surgery in a leisurely and piecemeal way but in 2002 things speeded up.

In April 2002 DH announced it was creating a programme of NHS Treatment Centres but later that year it decided to commission a number of what were called Diagnostic Treatment Centres from the private sector because of the shortage of NHS capacity. In December 2002 the DH invited expressions of interest from private providers; but before new centres were commissioned, a joint venture between the

NHS and BUPA – the Redwood Diagnostic Treatment Centre – opened in Redhill in January 2003. The private sector now had a foot in the NHS door alongside the spot-purchase of care in its own facilities that it had long provided. In an early meeting of the new 2003 Ministerial team John Reid wanted to agree what to call these new beasts. We settled on Independent Sector Treatment Centres.

At this time the procurement exercise was still in progress under the direction of Ken Anderson's new DH Commercial Directorate. Ken, a Texan, had considerable US health care experience. He was technically a civil servant but with a salary, style and access to Ministers (including the Prime Minister) very different from Whitehall mandarins – which irritated many civil servants. In September 2003 DH announced the preferred bidders for the majority of ISTCs. Contracts were awarded on the basis that bidders met the core clinical standards required by the NHS, provided high standards of patient care, brought additional staffing capacity from outside the NHS and represented good value for money. The first contracts were signed in September 2003 - some involving new builds and some the adaptation of NHS premises. The first ISTC opened at Daventry in October 2003.

This first wave of ISTCs involved renewable five-year contracts and was worth about £1.7billion. I became responsible for this wave in mid-2005. By mid-2006 there were 19 fully operational ISTCs; 6 partially operational and 4 still under negotiation. The specialties covered included ophthalmology, orthopaedics, urology, general surgery, gynaecology, plastic surgery, gastroenterology, oral surgery, rheumatology, and many diagnostic procedures such as endoscopies.

Alongside the Wave 1 ISTC programme the Commercial Directorate negotiated another system of private sector NHS elective care. This was the General Supplementary Contracts (GSsupp). Under these contracts Nuffield and Capio provided extra activity on a call down basis in ENT, general surgery, urology and orthopaedics in areas with long waiting lists. A further GSsupp contract later in 2005 concentrated on orthopaedics. These contracts reduced the unit price to the NHS. By the end of 2005 about 250,000 NHS patients had been treated by the private sector as a result of these various contracts, over 50,000 of them in new ISTCs.

The reaction within the NHS and the BMA to the Wave 1 ISTC programme was hostile. The ISTCs were said to be cherry-picking easy patients, they didn't do any training, they diverted money from the NHS, they didn't contribute much to reducing waiting times and their standards of patient care were lower. This latter point was driven mainly by the British Orthopaedic Association (BOA) who seemed ill-disposed to the foreign-trained doctors brought into the ISTCs, even though their qualifications had been recognised by the General Medical Council. The Health Select Committee's report of on ISTCs of July 2006 chastised the BOA for "the strident and alarmist criticisms of clinical standards" when data for comparing NHS and independent sector performance was not available. It was accepted that the additionality' rule stopped the new ISTCs poaching NHS clinical staff.

The critics of Wave 1 chose to ignore the need to increase capacity to reduce waiting lists, the way the price of spot purchases was cut and the fact that the plans for extra capacity were drawn up locally. This last point was well made by Ken Anderson in his evidence to the Health Select Committee in 2006:

"The capacity planning was done at the local economy level. It was not for us [the Commercial Directorate] to try to determine at our level. We would not have had the capability because we don't have the granularity of data to go out and make those decisions for a local health economy".

If the numbers were wrong that was the fault of the local people not Ministers and DH. It was totally fanciful to believe that the Commercial Directorate could have achieved 147 expressions of interest from the private sector and over 25 contracted ISTCs after a lengthy, arduous and costly contracting process unless there was a genuine capacity gap to be filled.

Just before the 2005 Election a further substantial procurement of elective surgery and diagnostic capacity from the private sector had been launched. This would more than double the size of the Wave 1 procurement. When the new DH Ministerial team arrived in May 2005 the scene was set for the next stage of the battle over competition – the Wave 2 ISTC programme covering elective surgery and diagnostics. The latter had been added to the programme because diagnostics had

413

become a major blockage to reducing to 18 weeks the period from a GP referral to receiving hospital specialist treatment. Too many patients were experiencing long waits for hospital diagnostic procedures before a specialist could decide what action to take. Extra capacity was still the main driver of the Wave 2 programme.

The plan I inherited was ambitious. It involved delivering up to 250,000 new procedures a year and creating an Extended Choice Network (ECN) of independent sector providers who would deliver up to an additional 150,000 procedures a year on a call-down basis. The additional capacity would be provided through a variety of facilities: existing ISTCs, new build centres, refurbishments and existing NHS facilities. The Wave 2 programme would cost £4billion over five years with a quarter of it diagnostics, which were faster to deliver. The aim was to start signing contracts in the summer, with service delivery starting in 2006.

The diagnostics contracts were less contentious than ISTCs because the lack of NHS capacity was clearer and they were less threatening to hospital trust income. I used three key arguments to justify Wave 2 ISTCs - the extra capacity needed, greater choice for patients and the scope for the NHS to learn from ISTC innovation in terms of layout, patient experience and speed of response. I could also show better value for money. The NHS spot-purchased about 100,000 operations a year from private providers at premium rates 40% to 100% higher than under the new contracts. This was a useful argument with the many critics in Parliament, the unions and the media who continued to claim that doctors didn't have UK qualifications; patient safety was inferior; and ISTCs didn't do any training of clinical staff. The real reasons for opposition were xenophobia and resistance to competition.

Once ISTCs were established we required them to take on training responsibilities which for the most part their doctors were keen to do. ISTCs did make mistakes but there was no evidence that they made any more than their NHS counterparts, as the Health Select Committee said in its July 2006 report. The ISTCs provided more up-to-date information on clinical performance than NHS centres did. The "British-trained doctors are best" arguments rumbled on with little supporting evidence. Patients continued giving high satisfaction ratings for their ISTC experiences, higher than their general responses for NHS care. DH top

414

management commitment to this programme was lukewarm – outside the Commercial Directorate. Lurking in the background was a Treasury keen to use value-for-money arguments to scale back the programme, headed by a Prime Minister in waiting who had shown little support for extra private sector capacity to facilitate choice and competition.

With No.10 support, I pressed on with opening new centres. In July 2005 I opened the new 40-bedded Barlborough Centre in the Trent region providing about 5,000 orthopaedic operations a year. The patients loved the experience and its South African owners enjoyed working for the NHS, despite a suspicious local NHS. Another ISTC I opened later in Kent proved less popular because the owner/operator had failed to persuade the local GPs to refer patients because they preferred not to upset their local NHS hospital consultants. Restrictive clinical practices were alive and well in Kent and this ISTC struggled with an occupancy rarely above 50% after opening.

While working on the Wave 2 programme, I became aware of the variation in costs of NHS pathology and the large amount of spare laboratory capacity in some hospitals. There seemed to be little sharing of laboratory capacity between hospitals and little interest in variation in unit costs for the same tests. The excess capacity was apparent when I opened a large new laboratory at the Royal London Hospital that would be very underused. I also found there was no NHS interest in testing the market to see if private laboratories could provide a more cost-effective and speedier service for high-volume tests. I decided to commission an independent review chaired by Lord Carter of Coles that reported to me in August 2006.

The evidence in the Carter Report on NHS pathology services suggested there was scope for at least 20 -25% savings in a sector then costing the NHS at least £2.5billion a year. The unwillingness of boards, clinicians (especially pathologists) and managers to group facilities in networks, improve transport and IT and put work out to tender was deeply entrenched in the NHS. I accepted the findings of the report and announced this at the annual dinner of the Royal College of Pathologists. Lord Carter worked with DH to take forward his report but progress on implementation was very slow. He produced a second report in December 2008 which went over similar ground to the first report which had produced little change.

In a Parliamentary answer on 15 July 2009 Lord Darzi told me that DH was working with five SHAs on 'developing approaches that responded to Lord Carter's recommendations.' This was DH-speak for saying that they were making haste very slowly. In January 2010 I was sent a Pathology Programme Update showing everybody beavering away but with no indication of how much, if any, of the £500million of savings estimated by Lord Carter had actually been achieved or what consolidation of services or contracting out had taken place. The review of pathology was a classic case of DH/NHS procrastination over securing greater efficiency when changes to clinical practice were required.

Back in 2005 I continued working on the list of Wave 2 ISTC projects and reported progress to the Prime Minister. In total the schemes amounted to about £550million of ISTC business a year for five years when fully operational, with another £200million plus a year of diagnostics work for the same period. Market analysis had been done to try to identify the scale of government business required for the private sector to remain committed to competing in the NHS market over the longer term. The Commercial Directorate view, shared with the PM, was that Waves 1 and 2 needed to produce a steady market of about £1billion a year of NHS business for the private sector to remain interested.

I had some doubts about this figure, but it was clear that if Wave 2 was too small the private sector would lose interest. They needed a stable market with a guaranteed investment return to convince their investors to stump up money. The cumbersome and costly public sector procurement processes won few private sector friends. What I lacked were reliable figures on the scale of private sector provision we had to generate to guarantee continuing competition with NHS providers. It was that competition Tony Blair wanted. I found myself caught between the PM, Commercial Directorate and the private sector wanting a programme of at least £1billion a year; and a sceptical DH and NHS, with the Treasury behind them, insisting on no target figure and signing off each project one by one on the basis of value-for-money.

The Office of Government Commerce (OGC) was brought in to do a Gateway Review of the programme and I worked hard on them. Its October 2006 internal report showed the Wave 2 programme was well matched to the requirements of the NHS and represented good value-for-money. But I was still faced with a Wave 2 programme whose individual projects were variable in quality and local commitment. The processes of the Commercial Directorate depended on local assessments of service needs and the underpinning data which were decidedly shaky in some places. I decided to break Wave 2 into three groups of projects with the weaker ones to be dealt with last and some further work done to bolster them. Our public position remained that we were determined to deliver a Wave 2 worth £550million a year. This minimised agitation from the PM and an industry with access to him. Patricia Hewitt supported this approach; and the DH top management and Treasury were reluctant to challenge it, given the PM's involvement.

In the first half of 2006 we had over £200million worth of projects moving through the contracting process. I dropped a few smaller projects as sops to NHS critics but without too much agitation from No.10. I said I was preventing the private sector making poor investments – which had the advantage of being true. We survived a review by the Health Select Committee whose report in July 2006 was hardly flattering but accepted that the "threat of competition from the ISTCs may have had a significant effect on the NHS." We headed off trouble from medical critics about quality of comparable international clinical standards by announcing a review of ISTC care by the Chief Medical Officer. We added an initiative of private sector Walk-In centres near stations for London commuters.

MPs put pressure on Wave 2 projects in places where ISTCs would have significant impact on the income of their local hospitals and the viability of some departments. Some pressure came from Patricia Hewitt's Cabinet colleagues lobbied by local hospital consultants – in Blackburn for example. I had a few adjustments made to projects by using some of them more for clinical assessments of hospital referrals instead of elective surgery and cancelled a few weak projects. The NHS financial problems in 2005/6 carried over into 2006/7 and made some trimming inevitable; but the diagnostics part of Wave 2 held up well because the NHS so obviously needed extra capacity. Elective surgery projects remained under considerable pressure from a reluctant NHS and consultant cadre.

By the time I left at the end of 2006 the Wave 2 programme in its entirety was still heading towards a total value of over £400million a year – compared with the £550million we had originally envisaged. I had approved nine large new projects and ruled out five, mainly small ones, as unviable both in NHS terms and commercially. Most of the remainder were, in my judgement, likely to be viable with commitment from Ministers and the Commercial Directorate. But the private sector's champions departed. Ken Anderson had also gone at the end of 2006 and Tony Blair left in mid-2007. I had warned the private sector that Gordon Brown didn't share Blair's enthusiasm for competition. After Ken and I left the contracts in the system drifted and were eroded by ISTC opponents.

A new Prime Minister and Health Secretary in the summer of 2007 had little enthusiasm for the ISTC programme. Alan Johnson's speech to the Labour Party Conference in September 2007 made no mention of markets, competition or choice and Unison expressed public delight at their absence. The Financial Times headline was "Johnson signals end of NHS Reforms." The DH Commercial Advisory Board resigned with a blast at Ministers about scrapping the Wave 2 ISTC programme. After a lengthy period of silence Alan Johnson announced on 15 November 2007 that 6 further schemes were cancelled and 7 more were under review. Only 3 new projects, worth about £200million, were announced to deliver nearly 20,000 PET-CT diagnostic scans and 120,000 kidney dialysis sessions a year.

In February 2008 the FT claimed that DH had suppressed evidence from independent review teams looking at local plans for Wave 2 ISTCs. These plans were said to "be well-matched to the [NHS's] requirements" and were "very good value for money." The review made clear that the ISTC programme had forced the NHS to become more productive and had helped to contain cost increases in elective surgery. It argued that even if the whole Wave 2 programme had gone ahead there would have been only "localised pressure" on NHS providers; and that without a sufficiently large private sector "there will be no competitive tension" to drive down cost, raise quality and improve accessibility.

Negotiations on the outstanding ISTC schemes limped on inconclusively but expensively for the private sector. DH acknowledged that Wave 1 projects (worth £1.4 billion) had provided 800,000 elective procedures diagnostic assessments and episodes of primary care through 23 ISTCs, a mobile ophthalmology service, a mobile MRI scanning service, a chlamydia screening service and six Walk-in Centres. Johnson recognised the private sector had helped improve the NHS by speeding up treatments and galvanising it to raise its game. But enough was enough. By the end of 2007 Brown and Johnson had effectively ended private sector competition in the NHS and its threat to underperforming acute hospitals. The more emollient Lord Darzi would work with the NHS in his Next Stage Review and move the agenda from markets to quality. Though even he had his problems with his NHS colleagues by suggesting more treatment and care should be delivered in the community (see Chapter 13).

The pioneering days of trying to create an NHS market with robust competition ended with the Blair premiership. But as the competition tide went out, it left on the beach one of its requirements - an NHS tariff.

Constructing an NHS Tariff : Payment by Results

Unlike in local government, the private sector would not be competing on price in the NHS. For most services there were benchmark NHS prices and increasingly an acute hospital tariff. Initially NHS competition was more about patient choice, innovative new capacity and improving NHS performance; but over time competition might drive down price as well. Apart from ISTCs there was a growing internal NHS market with an increasing number of FTs competing with each other and non-FTs for those patients willing to exercise choice. The decision had been taken to create a new tariff system for the bulk of acute hospital work called Payment by Results (PbR). This would enable payment to follow the patient and move away from block grant funding of hospitals used since 1948. PbR was a misleading term because payment was for an activity not an outcome. In reality it was an item of service payment that incentivised activity but with higher volume unit price ought to drop.

In May 2005 this new tariff system had been under development for three years and was in its second year of limited trialling. It drew on international experience of activity-related funding of hospitals which started in the 1980s when the US Medicare system introduced Diagnosis-Related Groups (DRGs) to pay for inpatient services for elderly people. In the 1990s, Sweden, Italy, Germany, Norway and Victoria State in Australia had all introduced a version of DRG payments for hospital care, with Finland and The Netherlands following in 2000 and 2003 respectively. The international evidence supported the view that activity-related funding promoted greater cost-efficiency in acute hospital services.

Studies in Sweden and Australia suggested that costs per case dropped by about 10% when hospitals were funded on a mixed-case averaging DRG system. An OECD study suggested these systems raised activity levels which would help reduce waiting times. The system also improved management information systems, especially medical coding. This was important in the NHS where the Audit Commission had shown 14% of hospitals didn't bother to code some activity – which under PbR would have meant no payment for work done.

However, PbR was not risk-free. Hospitals might "cream-skim" by trying to avoid treating sicker, more expensive patients; they might try to reduce costs by discharging patients too early; they could openly 'game' by trying to code people within higher tariff DRG groups; and they could engage in higher levels of activity that would bust local NHS budgets. But there were ways of reducing these risks through protocols to regulate admissions and quality of care; independent audit of coding data; and risk-sharing agreements between purchasers and providers that limited levels of hospital activity attracting higher prices.

NHS anxiety about PbR was high because of the threat it posed to the viability of some hospitals. Specialist children's and orthopaedic hospitals had more expensive treatments, not adequately covered by the case-mix averaging of the DRG system. Some services were trying to exclude themselves from PbR for fear of income loss. Whenever PbR was introduced, we would have problems. I concluded that despite the downsides we should introduce PbR and then refine it over time. No country had started with a perfect system or perfect data and coding. In most countries governments had imposed the system to improve efficiency and then amended it over time. The NHS would be no different but first I wanted to see a big DRG system in operation, so I went to Germany. They had been working on their system since 1996 and it had gone live in all hospitals in 2004 and 2005.

I made the German visit with the official who had been working on PbR, Bill McCarthy; and in the British Ambassador's residence in Berlin, I recruited him to run the new DH Policy and Strategy Unit that Patricia Hewitt and I had decided to set up. The Germans had tackled PbR with a scary Teutonic efficiency, including establishing a central agency for setting the tariff. 10% of hospitals were sampled each year, on a paid basis, to update cost data. The German system had nearly 1,100 DRGs (and growing) but our system would have about 650 DRGs. This meant they had a more precise reimbursement scheme than we were envisaging. This involved them cancelling all leave in the tariff-setting agency for 3 months before the start of each financial year to assimilate new cost data and calculate the new tariff. Despite this elaborate system the Germans still found it difficult to absorb into the system highly specialist hospitals without making supplementary payments. Nevertheless, the German experience encouraged me to go for full implementation across the NHS.

On return from Germany, we had to decide what to do. We were part way through a 4-year transition phase for introducing PbR by 2007/8. The NHS was extremely twitchy and there were powerful DH and NHS voices in favour of abandoning the whole idea. After seeing the German experience, my view was that we should accelerate implementation; and in 2006/7 extend PbR to all NHS elective and non-elective inpatient care, outpatients, and A & E and critical care. I could see no point including mental health services – about 10% of NHS spend - because they had a poor track record of case-mix classification. Patricia Hewitt agreed to accelerating expansion of PbR in 2006/7 and settling the tariff no later than January 2006.

This provided just enough time to do some "road-testing" of the new extended tariff before settling firm figures for 2006/7. We hired a person who had worked on the Victoria State system and enlisted the help of the Audit Commission for a PbR assurance framework to support good behaviour by NHS trusts. We needed an authoritative body like the Commission to be involved because regular monitoring of payments and behaviour would be crucial to ensuring that PbR operated as intended. The Commission continued to play a key role in validating PbR in the NHS and their auditors helped check 'gaming'.

The most difficult part came when Patricia Hewitt and I sat down for two hours with massive spreadsheets and PbR experts to settle the acute hospital tariffs for 2006/7. We could see potential winners and losers and the impact of various options for securing efficiency gains and approving inflation factors. Although it was hard work fine-tuning the 2006/7 tariff, the PbR system clearly had huge potential for driving efficiency and quality in the NHS providing we didn't become too obsessed with its early-stage limitations. When the 2006/7 tariff was issued, we made it clear the system would in time cover more areas, embrace a service quality dimension and incentivise non-hospital care by unbundling the tariff. We encouraged local experimentation in these areas, although not a lot happened.

By the time I left the PbR tariff was part of the NHS furniture, with a new tariff for 2007/8 signed off as part of the NHS Operating Framework for that year. People had learned the tariff could be used to set efficiency gains and, to some extent, control healthcare's inflationary tendencies. It was flexible enough to make special payments to a limited number of highly specialist hospitals to avoid bankrupting them, providing the PbR purists were controlled. Work had begun on making the tariff more sophisticated and all talk of the NHS abandoning PbR had disappeared. The issue had become how rapidly it could be expanded to a wider range of activities, made more sophisticated and handed over to an independent body for tariff-setting which was not possible in 2005/6.

In February 2008 the Audit Commission published a report that found "PbR has undoubtedly improved the fairness and transparency of the payment system. It has, perhaps, had a positive effect on activity and efficiency in elective care. Day cases have increased and the length of stay for elective inpatients has fallen". The report recognised however that other factors, like targets, had played a part in these improvements. It considered that "PbR has now been largely mainstreamed by the NHS"; that "overall, interest in information and improving data quality within the NHS has increased as a result of PbR"; and that "in general there is no evidence to date that trusts are 'gaming' the system to gain unwarranted payments".

When Lord Darzi's NHS Next Stage Review, "High Quality Care for All" was published in 2008 it made several clear commitments to building on PbR and improving it. It wanted to reflect quality more in the PbR tariff and to cover other services. By the time Darzi's report was published the average hospital (in 2008/9) received over 60% of its income through PbR. By 2009/10 the tariff was being used to reward desired practice but also to restrain costs with only a 1.7% increase; and it was planning expansion into mental health. It was a more sophisticated way of curbing expenditure than the old block grant system. I felt vindicated in pressing on with PbR implementation when critics said Ministers should give the NHS more time. PbR did not get the media attention of other parts of the NHS reform agenda – mainly I suspect because it was too technical for journalists to write snappy stories. It would have been a key part of creating an NHS market if there had been the political will to do so.

Why Challenging the NHS is Necessary

Between 2003 and 2007 four key NHS reforms were pursued: more autonomous hospitals, FTs; the beginnings of an NHS market with competition between providers, some from outside the NHS; increased patient choice of provider, especially for elective surgery; and the start of a tariff system for paying hospitals on an activity basis rather than by block grant. Payment for NHS treatment outside an NHS hospital was made on the same tariff as an NHS hospital. By 2007 the NHS was part of a public sector which had a third of its services delivered by the private and voluntary sectors according to the DeAnne Julius Review in December 2007 which had been commissioned by John Hutton when Business Secretary.

With much effort a coherent system of commissioning from local to national was developed but never effectively established as a governing principle of the NHS, with an effective failure regime and a better balance between acute hospitals and community-based services. The basic problem with this system was that no Health Secretary would reduce the number of PCTs to 40 -50 and back them to replace under-performing providers. The situation was made worse by Andrew Lansley with his 2011/12 reforms when he replaced Labour's 150 PCTs with over 200 clinical commission groups (CCGs) who were no better at challenging under-performing acute hospitals than PCTs.

We had shown the public liked choice of hospital and would exercise choice if the NHS facilitated it. The NHS – particularly some clinicians and managers – had shown their capacity to thwart patient choice. Unless patient choice is driven politically, NHS staff as a whole are unlikely to facilitate it, despite a lot of rhetoric about patient-centred care.

There is published research showing that with expanded patient choice in a healthcare market with fixed price competition there are improvements in hospital care and lives are saved. The market was the NHS during the period described above. This research by Zack Cooper et al of the London School of Economics was published in the Economic Journal of August 2011. It cites similar research in the USA relating to the American healthcare system. This may not be what many NHS supporters want to hear but it shows that a monopoly service like the NHS needs challenge. I consider it was a major error of political judgement and against the interests of patients to abandon competition in the NHS service provider market. Coping with Covid19 would have been assisted by a more diverse NHS provider market.

The message for me from my time as a Health Minister remains clear. The NHS only undertakes sustained change when there is a strong and consistent political message, reinforced by action through a change management programme and an annual operational framework. Under Tony Blair the message was clear from 2002 onwards. The private sector was encouraged to compete for business within an NHS market that was part of a wider public sector reform process. How that market would work became increasingly clear.

Under Gordon Brown the messages were mixed and confused. Too often he seemed preoccupied with not upsetting Labour's paymasters in the public sector unions. Then he would make a speech saying how important the private sector was to public sector reform, particularly when John Hutton was Business Secretary. The private sector was confused about competing for NHS services, when bidding costs were high and outcomes uncertain. Brown's Health Secretaries discouraged competition, particularly when Andy Burnham made a speech in September 2009 about the NHS being his preferred provider of choice.

None of the reforms introduced under Blair were perfect instruments of competition. All needed further refinement, extension and support but they provided a challenge to an NHS legacy of complacency and monopoly. Public sector unions and many NHS staff continue to be staunch critics of competition and the private sector, even though the Blair ISTC initiative came nowhere near the 15% of market share thought necessary to provide the challenge the NHS needed. Critics of NHS competition completely overlook the mixed economies of service providers in many overseas healthcare systems and our own social care and education systems. It shows little confidence in the NHS to suggest it has to be protected from such modest amounts of competition.

Prime Ministers and Health Secretaries continue to have a choice. Do they want to serve the best interests of patients and give them more choice of provider? Or do they just trundle on with the same old unchallenged monopoly hospital providers, whatever their performance? The Covid19 pandemic has produced an NHS backlog of millions of people awaiting treatment, sometimes for conditions from which they will die and usually in pain and discomfort. No amount of saucepan banging will reduce these waiting lists. It is time to bring in a wider range of service providers to get the lists down and let them continue to provide NHS services at NHS tariff prices. That would demonstrate true commitment to the NHS.

13. Neglected Services and NHS Sustainability: 2005 to date

The Demographic and Disease Profile

Health Ministers spend too much of their time concerned with hospitals. Yet most people are using services outside hospitals. These are not the glamorous services that TV soap operas or documentaries focus on. Hospitals are where all the exciting kit is being used and the dramas are taking place. As Covid19 has shown it is when the hospitals might be swamped that the politicians get excited and the public bang saucepans. George Clooney made his reputation in a hospital emergency room, not a GP surgery or a care home. It is hospitals where about two-thirds of the NHS's budget is spent, with their expensive overheads and skilled staff.

The last four chapters have been largely about hospitals. This one is about the less glamourous bits that look after most people and try to keep them out of hospital. These are the areas of the NHS that government neglect, where services are often poorly aligned with the UK's demography and disease profile and less reliably funded. Yet it may be these less-fashionable services that ultimately determine the sustainability of the NHS, given that demographic and disease profile. Back in 2005 when the NHS was in financial turmoil, a team of Ministers, of which I was one, attempted to rebalance the NHS so more services were delivered in communities. This attempt and its aftermath is the topic of this chapter. This rebalancing is still much needed.

In 2005 UK longevity had improved significantly since the mid-1980s, with average life expectancy increasing for men by about 5 years and for women by more than 3 years. But not everybody was living longer. The gap in life expectancy between the most deprived areas and the population as a whole had continued to widen. There was a difference of 10 years in the life expectancy of men living in the least and most deprived areas in England. In London the 7 stops eastwards on the Jubilee Line between Westminster and Canning Town had a 7-year difference in life expectancy. The disease profile across the population was getting worse, as were the health inequalities in an NHS founded on equity of care. Many people were living longer but often with poor health. More recently even increased longevity has stopped.

Most NHS activity is related to the 15 million people in England with longer-term health needs. Every decade the number of people with these conditions increases by about a million from ageing alone. As the population ages, dementia has been growing faster than the care system can respond to adequately. About 850,000 people and their families are struggling to cope, with the prospect of this number growing. At end of life most people want to die in their own homes, not hospital; but we have managed to achieve the exact opposite for many people – along with a poorly funded end of life care system.

At the other end of the age spectrum the picture remains alarming. Obesity in childhood has continued increasing. Physical exercise has declined as car and bus replaced walking to school and as school PE and sport declined. All types of diabetes have been increasing among children and young people and are often not well-managed in terms of blood sugar control. As an increasingly obese younger population grow into adulthood, the result will be an increased prevalence of circulatory diseases, cancer and diabetes. We face the prospect that unless our children's lifestyles change, many will not live as long as their parents.

The working age population, who fund the NHS, have their own problems. In 2005 22% of men and 24% of women were regarded as obese and obesity rates were rising. They had nearly doubled for men and increased by about 50% for women since the early 1990s. In the 2004 Health Survey for England only 37% of men and 25% of women were achieving the recommended physical activity levels of 30 minutes or more of moderate-intensity activity for five days a week. Alcohol-related deaths in the UK almost doubled between 1991 and 2005. Excessive drinking was rising fastest amongst women. Despite efforts to deter people from smoking, it remained the single biggest cause of illness and premature death in England – killing over 85,000 people a year and accounting for a third of all cancers. Sexually transmitted infections continued to rise. Mental illness and stress-related conditions remain the most common cause of sickness absence from work.

The NHS needed a change of direction in 2005 – and still does – to meet the UK's health challenges and to reduce health inequalities. The contradictions in health policy were and are striking. There are fewer

GPs per head of population in areas of greatest need. Dissatisfied with the availability of GP services many Londoners flock to A & E for their urgent care. The more we improve A & E Departments and neglect primary care, the more people chose, quite rationally, to go to A & E. We focus on driving down hospital waiting times but fail to put the same resources and effort into services to prevent hospital admission in the first place. Throughout my working life the NHS has had the wrong balance of effort between hospital and community-based services. About 90% of people's contacts with the NHS take place outside hospitals but the funding doesn't follow them.

For 70 years we have failed to re-engineer services so that more people can receive more treatment, care and support without going to a hospital. Patients go back and forth to hospitals for tests and consultations under arrangements that serve professional convenience rather than patient need. The NHS has done an excellent job of protecting the budgets of its acute hospital citadels and of convincing public and politicians to protect these institutions. Management and clinical elites, professional bodies, unions and career structures reinforce hospital-based services at the expense of those in the community. In the competition for resources acute hospitals always out-muscle community services and prevention. As Sir Roy Griffiths pointed out 30 years ago, social care remains a poor relation of the NHS.

Rebalancing the focus of NHS services away from hospitals is difficult and politically risky. This was demonstrated by the Covid19 mantra about 'saving our NHS' which was really about saving our hospitals. In 2005 four health Ministers – Patricia Hewitt, Caroline Flint, Liam Byrne and me – tried to change this focus. As I was responsible for GPs and community health services, I took the lead in producing a new White Paper on developing services outside hospitals. Tony Blair, impatient for reform as his time as Prime Minister shrunk, wanted a new strategy by the autumn of 2005. We persuaded him that he would get a better product if he gave us until the turn of the year.

We did not start work with a blank sheet of paper. A consultation paper on social care had promised more control and choice for service users, wider use of direct payments and piloting individual budgets. The need to improve the skill and status of the social care workforce was recognised but there was no commitment to extra funding. There had also been several attempts to produce a stronger focus on public health and better health outcomes. Virginia Bottomley's 1990s document was well-intentioned but without funding nothing much changed. In 1999 Labour published 'Saving Lives: Our Healthier Nation.' Its emphasis was on using targets to reduce deaths from the main killers: cancer, coronary heart disease, stroke, accidents, mental illness. It reduced many unnecessary deaths but found it more difficult to reduce mortality rates in deprived groups and achieve behavioural change by individuals. Most of the extra money had been spent in hospitals, not on changing population behaviour.

In 2004 'Choosing Health: making healthy choices easier' promised Government-wide initiatives to improve public health: campaigns for healthy living, more school nurses, health trainers and better obesity and sexual health services. There would be action to improve the nation's diet and to increase physical activity, especially amongst young people. But this statement of intent lacked any operational plan to change the way NHS services were delivered. Acute hospitals would continue consuming the lion's share of growth money.

The 'Our Health, Our Care, Our Say' Consultation

We had 6 months to come up with a different game plan for the NHS which placed more emphasis on improving health rather than providing healthcare. We also had to ensure that adult social care was given proper attention. Most senior DH staff lacked understanding of how social care could help the NHS in caring for people with long term conditions and were distrustful of local government. DH policy capability on social care was weak and Liam Byrne who was responsible for social care wisely reached outside DH for advice. We needed a process for discussion with the main NHS professional interests, so I chaired a group of senior people to secure their involvement in preparing a White Paper. Most important of all we needed to find out the public's real preferences and priorities.

Patricia Hewitt wanted the White Paper to be informed by a large-scale engagement with the public: something that went beyond the usual surveys and consultations. She took personal responsibility for this by hiring Opinion Leader Research (OLR). Throughout the processes devised by OLR's Deborah Mattinson and her team we wanted to demonstrate that Ministers were genuinely listening to what the public were telling us. Too often public consultation is tokenistic, but on this occasion, we did our best to engage directly with people, to find out what they thought about services, how they wanted them changed and to feed back our thinking to a group of fellow citizens.

This exercise was called 'Your Health, Your Care, Your Say'. Its scale was large for the time available. Some civil servants thought we were mad because we might be given messages that would be difficult to respond to. It was also clear that Patricia was putting Deborah Mattinson, not the civil service, in charge of the processes. The scope of the programme was considerable and the views of over 40,000 people were heard. There were four regional deliberative events accompanied by a range of local events and activities which involved about 10,000 people. Special efforts were made to include seldom-heard groups. A questionnaire was available to people who wanted to have their say but were not involved in a deliberative event: this attracted a response from 30,000 people. This material was supplemented by magazine surveys which attracted several thousand responses.

This whole process culminated in a national event in Birmingham on a Saturday with about a 1000 people attending from across the country. The Ministerial team attended to hear views and observe the voting process for determining people's priorities. We established a 'citizen panel' to ensure the consultation was genuinely citizen-led, with ten members matching the demographic profile of delegates at the deliberative events. Ages ranged from 23 to 82. One member was unemployed, and others included a retired machine operator, a fashion designer, a gardener and an underwriter. The panel vetted material to make sure language and format were easy to understand and free of NHS jargon. The panel also met the Ministerial team before the White Paper was written to act as a sounding board for likely policy themes. I am unaware of any similar public engagement process leading to a government White Paper.

We linked findings from this consultation to those from the social care consultation. Both revealed a strong desire for more help to support people maintaining their independence, with more emphasis on tackling loneliness and isolation among older people and carers. People knew prevention was better than cure and wanted the NHS to focus more on prevention than treating illness. 86% of the nearly 1,000 people who attended the Birmingham Summit thought that GP practices should provide people with more support to manage their own health and well-being. They wanted to see a wider range of professionals – particularly community nurses and pharmacists – involved in health improvement, disease prevention and the promotion of independence. The public believed regular health check-ups could be cost effective if done in the right way.

This consultation made clear the public wanted services to fit the way they lived their lives and not fitted around the way public services found convenient. Their priority was a wider range of times when services were available, especially GP services. They did not expect 24/7 services from GPs but did expect more flexibility around evenings and early morning opening times and on Saturday mornings. Participants at Birmingham confirmed my view that the 2003 GP contract had gone too far in enabling restricted access times for patients. The public were – and still are – in a different place to many NHS professionals on service access and the way they are treated. Many want to be treated more as customers – an idea most health professionals reject. People have had to show more flexibility in their own working lives and don't see why public sector professionals shouldn't do the same.

A common complaint throughout this engagement process and the separate social care consultation was the way different agencies assess people and make them repeat the same information to every professional they meet. The public simply do not understand or accept that the public services couldn't integrate their assessment processes better. They were much more relaxed about agencies sharing personal information if it improved services than many campaigners against data-sharing would have us believe. They expected more personalisation of services and this was reflected in strong support for individual budgets and direct payments. People knew their own priorities and told Ministers repeatedly that they wanted advice and support from professionals not excessive direction and control.

The culmination of this public engagement was voting on people's top priorities at the Birmingham summit. Much of the day was spent in groups discussing the findings from the regional deliberative events and the 36,000 questionnaires; and then testing arguments with each other. This led to a list of 13 specific changes that attendees wanted Ministers to deliver in the White Paper. Ministers wandered round the groups listening to the arguments, responding to questions but declining to influence people's thinking. About 1000 people were then asked to vote 'yes' or 'no' for 13 items they had identified as the most important.

A regular health check for everyone, with 75% support, was the clear top priority. The big surprise was the second priority with 62% support which was for more focus on mental well-being. The public were telling Ministers something they hadn't realised. They were seriously concerned about an increasing mental health problem across society. More and more people were feeling unhappy about their lives, anxious, depressed and generally miserable. The term 'well-being' was put on the political agenda by this engagement process and featured much more in DH discussions. Politicians had been slow to appreciate that increasing national prosperity had not prevented many people feeling miserable about their lives. Today political leaders want to measure wellbeing alongside GDP, but in 2005 that was still a novel idea.

The third and fourth priorities, with just over 40% each were more help for carers and a trained nurse as a first point of contact for patients. In fifth place there was a lot of support – about 30% - for incentives for healthy behaviour if we could find the right incentives. Others however wanted to take a punitive approach: the ninth priority was penalties for inappropriate use of services and the tenth, penalties for unhealthy choices. We still struggle with finding effective incentives and sanctions. One surprising feature was the level of concern about transport, with a quarter of attendees considering transport a problem for accessing health and social care services. This supported the idea of bringing more services closer to home.

The messages from these consultations were clear and consistent. People were positive about services and the expertise of professionals. They praised many recent innovations such as social care direct payments, NHS Direct, walk-in centres, on-line booking of appointments and text message appointments. But they thought service quality was uneven and that they had been lucky to get good service. They wanted more personalisation, more preventative work and more say in how services were designed and delivered whilst recognising limits on money and staff time. They wanted more emphasis on supporting people and carers in their own homes and monitoring long-term conditions such as diabetes. Over half the people at the summit supported in principle moving some hospital services to community settings, whilst recognising this had implications for general hospitals.

On social care people supported the March 2005 consultation document but this was hardly surprising given that most of its ideas were what people had wanted the government to do for some time. The difficult bit was delivering this vision when there was little, if any, growth money for adult social care; and there was a political reluctance to ask families to pay more out of their own pockets as the population aged and personal wealth increased. Having asked the public for their views we now had to produce a White Paper that reflected them.

New Direction for Community Services: the 2006 White Paper

In November 2005 we had a Ministerial away day with officials to settle the structure and content of the White Paper. Ministers had made it clear they intended to set a new strategic direction for the NHS and DH that would help people to live more independently in their own homes and focus much more on their own wellbeing. This strategic shift was to support choice and give people more say over decisions affecting their daily lives. We wanted the White Paper to realign the way the health and social care systems worked, with more services delivered closer to home to suit the needs of individuals rather than the convenience of service providers.

DH top management had shown little interest in the public consultation exercise, but Nigel Crisp decided to attend the awayday now Ministers were talking about transferring money from hospitals into ring-fenced budgets for health promotion and preventative services. The architects of NHS financial meltdown (see Chapter 10)

433

were now advising Ministers how difficult this would be and the importance of detailed costings.

Under pressure from No.10, we produced a White Paper called "Our Health, Our Care, Our Say – a new direction for community services" by the end of January 2006. This set out key recommendations to help people to improve their own health and well-being. A new NHS 'Life Check' service would be developed and evaluated to help people to assess their own risk of ill health, based on a range of risk factors and awareness of family history. Expansion of psychological (or "talking") therapies was proposed, starting with two demonstration sites focussed on people of working age with mild to moderate mental health problems and taking forward computerised cognitive behaviour therapy (CBT). The Quality and Outcomes Framework (QOF) in the new GP contract would be focussed on wider health and well-being outcomes. A range of activity was promised to improve service integration.

There were four recommendations which promised tough negotiations with the BMA. Patients would be guaranteed acceptance onto a list shown as 'open'. Successful practices would be encouraged to expand through contractual incentives. There would be a national procurement of additional practices in under-doctored deprived areas. And we would push hard to secure GP opening hours that reflected patients' preferences. All these changes required a major change of attitude by many PCTs, GPs and the BMA, with few financial sweeteners available.

A review of the complicated urgent and emergency care system was proposed to try to simplify it: apart from A & E Departments and GP services, there was NHS Direct, some new walk-in centres, minor injuries units, pharmacists, local out-of-hours services and for mental health, crisis resolution teams. A new screening programme for bowel cancer would be provided; piloting self-referral to physiotherapy would be undertaken; there would be more choice for women over the place of their babies' birth would be provided; and easier access to immunisation services.

Coordination of end-of-life care would be improved through establishing networks of services. In social care use of direct payments would be expanded, with the prospect of individual budgets spanning health, social care and possibly other services. The Expert Patients

Programme would expand to train more people in self-care. Integrated care plans covering health and social care for those with long-term conditions would be developed, together with increased support for carers.

While the White Paper was in preparation, I chaired a group of professional leaders to consider which specialties had the best prospects for transferring work out of hospitals. They identified six: ENT, trauma and orthopaedics, dermatology, urology, gynaecology and general surgery. I set up six groups under expert leadership to identify sites where promising work was in progress or in prospect with the scope for assessing the potential for wider application. These groups reported back positively in time for including in the White Paper a proposal that over the next year the DH would work with specialty associations and Royal Colleges in 20-30 demonstration sites to define safe patient pathways and models of care for doing work outside hospitals. There were nearly 45 million outpatient appointments in England every year. For some specialties there were reliable estimates that up to half these could be provided in community settings. I agreed that Manchester University should be appointed to carry out an independent evaluation of all these projects.

There was evidence that community hospitals provided better (and cheaper) recuperative care than DGHs but in some parts of the NHS they were busily closing community hospitals. The White Paper committed the Government to a new generation of community hospitals providing diagnostics, day surgery, rehabilitation and outpatient facilities where specialists could work with community-based staff. Community hospitals would be one of the places where we expected to see more co-location of services – health, social care and other public services. We wanted to expand the 350 or so existing community hospitals and also stop the inappropriate closures. The White Paper said that any PCTs threatening to close community hospitals would be required to demonstrate that not only had they consulted locally but they had tested their proposals against the principles in the White Paper.

The White Paper made clear that "we intend to shift resources and activity from acute hospitals to local settings, in direct response to patient feedback". PCTs, SHAs and acute hospitals were required to review their capital plans accordingly. We too readily accepted civil service advice to back away from a firm commitment to start shifting resources from secondary care to primary and community care, as I had argued for. Instead, the White Paper said that from 2008 we would look at PCT annual plans to see if this was happening and would "examine the case for setting a target for the percentage shift from current secondary care to primary care and community services." This was the most I could achieve but it was a major mistake not to insist on a specific shift of revenue resources.

The White Paper showed that the UK lagged behind the US, Germany, Netherlands and France in the proportion of its health expenditure that went on prevention and public health. It promised to establish an expert group to develop robust definitions and measures of preventative spending and to look at establishing a 10-year ambition for preventative spending based on comparisons with other OECD countries. In six months, four Ministers with a few supportive officials and external professional leaders had produced a potentially game-changing NHS White Paper, despite DH top management indifference. The question was would DH and the NHS implement it?

The White Paper's clear message to the NHS was that people only went to acute hospitals when it was really necessary, not as a matter of routine. The NHS should make a fundamental shift to care being provided closer to home, with expenditure moving away from acute hospitals to preventative and community work. Unfortunately, we published the White Paper when NHS finances were in meltdown (see Chapter 10) which provided an excuse for avoiding change. This meant delaying publication of a road map for local change in line with the White Paper's vision. In October 2006 we finally managed to publish "Our Health, Our Care, Our Say: Making it Happen." This explained what needed to be done over the next three years, including what DH would deliver, together with a timetable for specific actions. The delay was caused by battles with DH and the Treasury over money to start implementation in 2006/7 and continuing it in 2007/8.

The NHS and DH had so mismanaged their budgets that there was little money to kick-start a new agenda that would use NHS resources more effectively. It was a classic public sector Catch 22; the financial situation was so bad you couldn't finance the changes that would improve it. We used the delay to start a wide-ranging programme of pilots and demonstration sites so that practical applications of White Paper ideas were distributed across the NHS and social care. This programme included:

- Pilot schemes to test self-referral to physiotherapy.
- 3 pilot sites covering a population of a million people to test whether a comprehensive integrated approach to care supported by assistive technologies like telecare could show a significant shift from hospital care – the so-called ICAT demonstrations.
- Testing and evaluating of individual budgets on 13 sites over 2 years.
- 30 demonstration sites covering 6 specialties to define and test new care pathways for national use to shift care closer to home for dermatology, ENT, general surgery, gynaecology, orthopaedics and urology.
- Scoping and designing the online health and well-being assessment tool for NHS 'Life Checks' and an associated website, along with 4 pilots for teenage health demonstration sites that would start by the end of 2006.
- 18-month pilots to run at two sites to establish the evidence base for psychological therapies to support people in and to return to work, including the use of computerised cognitive behavioural therapy.
- Partnerships for Older People Projects – about 30 in over two phases – to show how innovative partnerships could lead to improved outcomes for older people, thereby reducing hospital admissions and residential care stays.
- Testing the idea of information prescriptions that would signpost people with long-term health and social care needs and their carers to the information and advice that would enable them to self-care better. Most were to start in 2006/7, would last up to 2 years and would be independently evaluated.

Alongside this work I tried to re-energise the community hospital building programme that had been promised in Labour's 2005 Election

Manifesto and again in the 2006 White Paper. This turned out to be an uphill struggle with little enthusiasm for it among officials. I found that DH never spent their full capital allocations so there was capital money in the current year which could be earmarked for expenditure in future years. Defining what we meant by "a community hospital" proved more difficult. I ended up with a broad definition that covered a wide range of services and encouraged co-location but excluded complex medical procedures. It was left to local people to come together to agree and configure the services they wanted in particular buildings.

In July 2006 I launched, with a personal foreword, an invitation to the NHS to come forward with bids for new or refurbished community hospitals and services. PCTs and local communities could bid for money from a £750million fund created for a 5-year building programme. We envisaged 3 different funding models: straightforward public capital through the NHS; Local Improvement Finance Trusts (LIFTs) which was an existing model for bringing together public capital and private sector expertise; and community ventures, which was a new approach for capital investment using a joint venture between PCTs and a partner such as a private or voluntary organisation. We wanted PCTs with advanced plans to submit them by the end of September 2006 and for schemes ready in 2007/8 to come forward by the end of December.

I stopped further closures of community hospitals without full scale reviews. I had to personally intervene to halt the proposed closure of nine community facilities in Gloucestershire that would have taken services back into larger hospitals – the complete opposite from what was in the January White Paper. This was a classic example of local NHS managers totally ignoring an elected government's community-based policy favoured by local people in order to protect incompetent acute hospitals in financial difficulty.

In 2007 when I had left DH, the Hewitt Ministerial team had set up a range of pilot schemes and provided a road map to take forward the ideas in the 2006 White Paper for bring services closer to home. There was a capital building programme in place for providing more community hospitals. A wider role for the voluntary sector and social entrepreneurs was promised which did lead to the setting up of a Social Enterprise Unit in the DH before I left as a Minister. What we had failed to do, however, was put in place a financial system that guaranteed moving resources – money and staff – away from acute hospitals to community-based services that concentrated more on health promotion, undertook more work outside hospitals and were integrated with social care. We had left the acute hospital barons and their DH friends enough room to regroup after the innovators moved on.

Alongside this Ministerial work the London SHA had asked Professor Sir Ara Darzi, a prominent surgeon, to carry out a review of London's healthcare system. His report published in early 2007 provided further support for the ideas in the 2006 White Paper. Darzi described a radical change in the models of healthcare he thought London needed. The most significant of these was "a new kind of community-based care at a level that falls between the current GP practice and the traditional district general hospital". He called these polyclinics. (I tried to persuade Ara to call them "community hospitals" which I thought would be more publicly and politically acceptable, as 'hospital' sounded more significant than 'clinic.')

Darzi called for more healthcare to be provided at home and in polyclinics, with local hospitals providing the majority of inpatient care and elective surgery centres providing most high-throughput surgery. Major acute hospitals should be handling only the most complex treatments, with Academic Health Science Centres being developed as centres of clinical and research excellence. Darzi's proposals were what London needed but they would have involved major upheavals for London's hospitals and GPs. True to form the BMA quickly protested about polyclinics which were redefined so that groups of GP practices could be regarded as a polyclinic if a diagnostic hub was provided. Most of the hospital changes never happened because, as I discovered later, there was little appetite – political, clinical or managerial – for the reconfigurations required. Then in June 2007 Gordon Brown became Prime Minister, keen to put his own imprimatur on the NHS.

Slowdown – the Darzi Next Stage Review

Brown's political strategy was to look different to Blair and to reassure the NHS workforce and the public sector unions after the turbulence of the Blair health reforms. Competition and care closer to home posed threats to hospitals and their staff and were less popular with the new Prime Minister. The 2006 White Paper disappeared into a new review. Ara Darzi became a Health Minister in the Lords, charged with providing a new vision for the NHS in time for its 60th birthday in July 2008. It looked like a political masterstroke to put a doctor in charge of an NHS Review. But it also meant Brown would be stuck with what Darzi proposed. For a while it looked as though the person setting the NHS agenda was the surgeon from Imperial College and St Mary's Hospital – who still carried on operating on Fridays and Saturdays. He was said to have the Prime Minister's mobile number and the new Health Secretary, Alan Johnson, seemed almost invisible.

Darzi quickly produced an interim report in October 2007, saying he had detected little enthusiasm in the NHS for doing something completely different from the NHS reforms and that they should be seen through to their conclusion. He went on to say that "No-one should see this Review as a way of slowing down or diluting what we need to do. If anything, we should... be more ambitious." The immediate steps proposed for primary care were very much in line with the 2006 White Paper. New GP practices – 'whether they are organised on the traditional independent contractor model or by new private providers' – should be brought into those areas where they were most needed starting with the 25% of PCTs with the poorest provision. Darzi wanted new health centres in easily accessible locations; and more choice over when patients could see their GP by expanding opening hours in evenings or at weekends. His emphasis was on a safer, more innovative NHS, with a new combined health and social care regulator – as I had proposed – with tough powers backed by fines for hospitals with poor hygiene and infection control.

But this interim report lacked the dynamism of Darzi's London report with its emphasis on alternatives to hospital and grouping more hospital services in fewer major specialist centres. The next step was for staff groups in each region to discuss how to achieve a fairer, more personal NHS, delivering more effective and safer care in a locally accountable manner. Each SHA was to conduct their own change agenda through clinical leads. The review became staff-led rather than

440

the user-led approach of the 2006 White Paper. Darzi boxed himself in over changes to hospital services by indicating that changes could only be initiated when there was a clear and strong local clinical basis for doing so and resources could be made available to open new facilities alongside old ones closing. This apparently sensible approach made it easy for local opponents of change to frustrate it. The review looked as though it wanted to avoid upsetting the acute sector or take professionals out of their comfort zone.

The Next Steps Review Final Report, 'High Quality Care for All' was published in June 2008 along with 10 regional reports covering maternity and new-born care; children's health; planned care, mental health; staying healthy; long-term conditions; acute care; and end of life care. These were heavily influenced by staff views, although ideas from the 2006 White Paper survived in both the regional and national reviews. What was new was the emphasis on quality issues: stronger enforcement powers for the CQC; independent quality standards and clinical priority-setting through NICE and a new National Quality Board; new quality accounts; best practice tariffs for paying hospitals. There was also more emphasis on supporting innovation; improving NHS staff education and training; enhancing clinical and Board leadership. A major proposal was for an NHS Constitution that it was claimed would secure the NHS for the future in terms of its 'enduring principles and values'.

Although the 2006 White paper was little acknowledged, some of its thinking was identified in Darzi's final report:

- Every PCT was to commission comprehensive well-being and prevention services in partnership with local authorities to tackle obesity, reduce alcohol harm, treat drug addiction, reduce smoking rates and improve sexual and mental health.
- There was to be a Coalition for Better Health between the Government, private sector and voluntary organisations to improve health outcomes, focusing initially on obesity.
- A new programme of vascular risk assessment was to be provided for people ages between 40 and 74.
- GPs were to help individuals stay healthy by improving the QOF to provide better incentives and indicators.

441

- Choice of GP practice for patients was to be extended by providing more information on the NHS Choices website about primary and community care services.
- A personalised care plan was to be provided for everyone with a long-term condition and individual health budgets were to be piloted.
- Practice-based commissioning was to be reinvigorated and more freedoms were to be given to high-performing GPs.
- New integrated care organisations covering health and social care were to be piloted; and the NHS would be encouraged to set up social enterprise organisations and other enhancements of community services.

The ideas in Darzi's final report on quality, innovation, health outcomes, inequalities and personalisation were all perfectly sensible. What was missing was any operational plan to move services closer to home at scale or any assessment of the implications of doing so for acute hospitals. By promising no further structural change and leaving everything to local determination by professionals, what the Next Stage Review ended up doing was to duck the hard choices that have to be made if NHS priorities are to change and more services are to be provided outside acute hospitals. The NHS cannot improve health outcomes, bring care closer to home and concentrate specialist services to improve quality but simultaneously continue to pump more money into a mixed bag of acute hospitals with the same service configurations.

Leaving an unnecessarily large number of weak PCTs in place – most of them uncomfortable with replacing failing NHS service providers – was never likely to deliver Ara Darzi's vision. The world of adult social care – the NHS's poor relation – which had been brought into the fold in the 2006 White Paper had been largely cast adrift again and received virtually no attention in the Next Stage Review. There was no more talk about 'reform.' Instead, the NHS was on 'a journey,' without much clarity about the destination. Darzi had been joined on this journey by 2,000 clinicians and other professionals but not apparently by any managers because the word 'manager' is completely absent from his Final report. I thought the political handcuffs had been placed on Ara Darzi as political parties vied with each other to promise the public that their hospitals would be saved if people voted for them in the 2010 Election. Only after that Election would there be another attempt to tackle the neglect of social care.

The Failure to Fix Adult Social Care

The NHS and local government adult social care have a symbiotic relationship although the mutualism is too little recognised publicly. The NHS is basically free but social care is means-tested and the mean-test is an ungenerous one. As an ageing population increases it makes more demands on a social care system that depends for funding on local government and self-payers. The latter are means-tested and have to reduce their capital assets to a low level to have their social care bills paid by the State. This may mean them selling their house and not leaving it to their children. The issue of being forced to sell your house to pay for care has been a contentious political issue for three decades, with any new funding arrangements sometimes called 'death taxes.'

Funding adult social care is a longstanding problem, with an increasing number of older people and those with disabilities needing services funded by local authorities. A decade of austerity since 2010 has made the situation worse by reducing local authority funding for social care – both for adults and children, where demand has also increased. The funding shortfall has adversely affected the volume and quality of care available for an increasingly frail and dependent population. The problem has become worse in poorer areas where there are fewer people able to pay for their own care and the tax-base of local authorities is less resilient. As the funding of adult social care worsens the NHS effectively becomes the carer of last resort, with many patients kept in acute hospitals by the shortage of social care. Lack of local authority funding has caused providers to leave the sector or accept only self-payers.

The risk of the publicly funded adult social care sector collapsing was growing pre-pandemic. Brexit added a further twist because this sector was heavily dependent on care staff from the EU willing to work in the care sector for relatively low wages: pre-Brexit 40% of London's care staff was from the EU. Many of those staff have left. During the pandemic many care home residents have died and staff working there

443

have been less well treated than NHS staff. The state of adult social care is precarious in many parts of the country as the UK recovers from the pandemic and the NHS tackles the huge backlog of patients needing treatment. In 2019 the current Prime Minister promised to fix social care quickly, notwithstanding the failure of his four predecessors to do so. The fix is still awaited.

In 1999 a Government-appointed Royal Commission published reform proposals including a more generous means-test and free personal and nursing care. Scotland introduced free care but has found the cost difficult to fund in practice, despite the generous funding of the Barnett formula. Little changed in England as a result of the Commission's report. In 2009, the Labour Government's Green Paper proposed a National Care Service. This was followed by a White Paper proposing a two-year cap on social care charges, with free social care after 2015. Just before the 2010 Election Gordon Brown tried to rush through a Bill on free social care. This was delayed in the Lords because it provided free care to those who could afford to pay and was highly unlikely to be affordable in the state of the public finances. For these reasons I helped to oppose this Bill which I regarded as an unaffordable Election gimmick. It fell because no cross-party compromise could be agreed before the Election.

In July 2010 the Coalition Government set up a three-person Commission on the funding of care and support. I was a member of the Commission chaired by Andrew Dilnot, an economist. The moving force in establishing this Commission was the Liberal Democrat part of the Coalition. We were asked to achieve deliverable recommendations on how to meet the costs of care and support as a partnership between individuals and the state; how people could choose to protect their assets (especially their homes) against the cost of care; how public funding could best be used to meet care and support needs now and in the future; and how our preferred option could be delivered. It was clear that a deliverable solution was required that could be implemented within the 5-years of the Coalition.

At the time public funding on adult social care was about £14.5billion a year in England, with just over half of this spent on services for older people. We found a significant proportion of people were exposed to very high care costs which they could not anticipate or insure against in advance. There were unacceptable variations in eligibility for services across the country: eligibility criteria needed standardisation nationally and assessments made portable across the country. Funding was inadequate, with provision failing to keep pace with demand. For 15 years, adult social care had been funded substantially less generously than the NHS. The system for funding care and support was complex and difficult to understand. Many people (over half in an Ipsos MORI survey we commissioned) did not understand that social care wasn't free like the NHS, until it was too late. After collecting a lot of evidence and discussions with a wide range of interests we published our report 'Fairer Care Funding,' in July 2011. We believed our main proposals had a wide measure of support.

We made five main recommendations. To protect people from extreme care costs an individual's lifetime contribution to costs should be limited to between £25,000 and £50,000, with £35,000 our preferred figure. The threshold for means-tested help should be raised from £23,250 to £100,000. People with care and support needs in childhood should automatically receive free state support for their care when they became adults. We thought that eligibility for service entitlement should be fixed nationally. For those in residential care there should be a higher standard cost for normal living costs like food and accommodation. There were other recommendations for better information and awareness campaigns, improved carers assessments and improved alignment of disability benefits with a new care funding system.

Our report made clear that more needed to be spent on social care immediately and in the future. We considered the Government should both implement our recommendations and ensure there was "sufficient and sustainable" funding for local authorities. We estimated that "our recommended changes to the funding system would cost from around £1.3billion for a cap of £50,000 to £2.2billion for a cap of £25,000." Most of the cost was on the cap. From informal soundings of the Treasury and the Shadow Chancellor, Ed Balls, an implementation cost of about £2billion looked likely to be politically acceptable across the political spectrum.

After publication there were niggles about some of the details but general support for the ideas of a cap and a more generous means-test threshold. Some argued that we had been too generous to the well-off. There was much discussion about the details of a system for capturing lifetime costs spent by individuals to count against the cap. There was a long silence in government about the level of the cap and funding of the reforms. Local government wanted plenty of time to put a new system in place and for the Government to fund the administrative costs of doing so. In 2012 a vehicle emerged for implementing our proposals, but the Government had still not decided whether to accept them.

The vehicle was a new Care Bill published in draft in 2012. This set out the obligations on local authorities to assess people's needs for social care and the needs of carers. The draft Bill was effectively a major overhaul of the social care system, but it made no provision for reform of the charging system. (There were also some changes to NHS quangos). The draft Bill was considered by Joint Select Committee of which I was a member. It made recommendations for changes that the Government largely accepted. Eventually the Bill in modified form was introduced in the House of Lords in May 2013. This version included a section on charging that would enable the Government to make regulations introducing the Dilnot 'cap and floor' proposals if they wished to do so. The Bill was passed in May 2014 with still no Government decision on our recommendations.

After the Conservatives won the 2015 Election, George Osborne postponed implementation of the Dilnot proposals until 2020. He was helped to do this by local government complaining about the timescale for implementation. Since that decision local authorities have had to rely mainly on increases in council tax to meet the rising demand for adult social care – latterly presented as a social care precept. There was a one-off social care grant in 2017/18 and funding transfers have been made from the NHS through a Better Care Fund. These short-term funding measures have been totally inadequate for meeting realistic care costs.

In 2011 the Dilnot Commission identified an annual funding shortfall of about £1billion relative to eligible demand. In a May 2018 report by the Health Foundation and the Kings Fund ('A Fork in the Road') the authors suggested that "Restoring the system to 2009/10 levels and restoring the level of eligibility that existed at that time… would require an additional £8bn in 2020/21." That forecast is likely to be an underestimate in the light of Covid19 and is continuing to grow as the over-80 population increases. This funding shortfall of over a third of the current budget, has seriously damaged three groups: the people needing services and their families; the service providers, especially those relying on public funding; and the NHS, the carer of last resort if social care is unavailable.

Back in 2018 Age UK estimated that 1.4 million older people, 14% of those aged over 65, had unmet care needs. There has been a big decline in the older and disabled people able to access publicly funded adult social care, despite a rising population who would be eligible. The Health Foundation put this number at 400,000 in 2013/14 and it is now much higher. Surveys show that what this means is many older people are unable to maintain the basics of washing, dressing and visiting the toilet, with a fifth saying they go without meals. The pressure on families is enormous. There are now over 6 million unpaid carers with about a quarter providing over 50 hours a week of care and the majority suffering mental and physical ill-health.

As local authority budgets have shrunk, so have the fees they have been willing and able to pay care providers. The Institute for Fiscal Studies has shown that in the most deprived local authority areas, adult social care funding per head decreased by 17% between 2009/10 and 2017/18. Effectively care providers have been paid reducing fees at a time when those they care for have higher dependency levels. The result has been that care providers are handing back contracts for publicly funded care to local authorities. A 2018 ADASS survey stated that care providers had handed back contracts to over 60 local authorities, over 40% of those with social care responsibilities.

The Competition and Markets Authority estimated that in 2016 self-funders paid 41% higher fees than the local authority rate which meant self-funders were paying a huge subsidy to those funded publicly. This is not a sustainable position in areas where providers can rely on self-funders for whom they could provide a better and cheaper service without the cross subsidy. The result is the potential collapse of publicly funded adult social care in many parts of England. Persistently low local authority fees make it impossible for care providers to borrow money to invest in new developments involving publicly funded care. The sector's regulator, the Care Quality Commission, has drawn attention to the fragility of the adult social care market and the implications of collapse for those needing care and for the NHS.

If vulnerable people cannot obtain adequate social care, a good proportion of them will end up in an acute hospital bed because the NHS is the carer of last resort. Once in hospital they will be difficult to discharge, as the NHS has found. A decade or so ago there was research showing that about 25% of patients in medical acute wards stayed longer in hospital than they needed to, largely because of problems with arranging social care. The increasing loss of publicly-funded social care significantly reduces the capacity of the NHS to treat working age patients including those with cancer, cardiac conditions and diabetes. This loss of capacity will have a major impact on the NHS's ability to reduce the backlog of patients whose treatment has already been seriously delayed by Covid19.

Fixing Social Care Funding

The failure over two decades and five governments to agree a robust funding system for adult social care is a national disgrace. The disgrace looks set to continue even though the Johnson Government seems likely to implement a version of the Dilnot proposals, with a lifetime cap on care costs of about £86,000 and a more generous means-test threshold. Although our proposals are fairer for individuals facing unpredictable and uninsurable care costs, they do not solve the massive and worsening underfunding of adult social care. Even back in 2011 we estimated that the social care system had a shortfall of £1billion and attracted less generous annual funding increases than the NHS.

To fund adult social care to the eligibility standards of a decade ago, most informed opinion calculates that the publicly funded care system now needs an annual funding injection of about £8billion. This would stabilise the system, stop the exit of service providers and provide decent pay and training for care staff so they stayed in the sector and had pay parity nearer to that of NHS staff. Instead of building up funding increases to this level the Johnson Government has committed to no more than an increase of £5.4billion after 3 years – or under £2billion a year. A good deal of this extra money will go on implementing our capping recommendations and benefit users not service providers.

The Government's approach largely leaves the social care funding problems with local authorities. They now face having to make huge increases in council tax just to maintain services but without the capacity to remedy systemic underfunding. This is because the current system of council tax, with its out-of-date house valuations, lacks the capacity to cope with the endemic underfunding and rising demand for adult social care. Only central government can produce a buoyant social care funding system.

By providing adult social care with so little of the money it is raising by a 1.25% national insurance levy, the Government has missed an opportunity to stabilise the sector's funding longer-term. This is likely to mean that care providers, their investors and their staff will continue moving away from providing publicly funded care, particularly in the areas where the Government wishes to 'level up.' NHS beds will continue to be occupied by people who needn't be there. The Government has suffered the political pain of the national insurance levy without being able to guarantee delivering their promise to fix social care funding.

What to do? Some will argue that we should abandon means-testing social care and make it free to everyone, like the NHS. The main argument against this, which I support, is that many people can afford to meet their care costs without State aid. There seems no very good reason to give the better off free care. This would increase demand, involve a high 'dead weight' cost to the Exchequer on introduction and be difficult to sustain over time, as Scotland has found. There is, however, some scope for shifting the boundary between means-tested social care and the free NHS, although this is rarely discussed.

One option, which has some supporters, would be to treat serious dementia as a disease – which it is – that is eligible for free NHS care. To limit eligibility and to reduce cost, entitlement could be limited to people whose dementia required admission to a nursing home. We know that about 850,000 people have dementia but many fewer are in care homes. Laing and Buisson, experts on the sector, estimated in 2016 that about 40% of those in care homes had dementia. This would mean giving less than an extra 200,000 people free NHS care.

Another way of altering the boundary would be to make nursing homes (but not residential care homes) the responsibility of the NHS. This would make it easier for the NHS to use these homes as cheaper step-down care to free up beds in expensive acute hospitals. A cheaper variant of this option would be to limit free care in nursing homes to those who would otherwise be in hospital. This would require assessment and increase complexity, but it might improve throughput in NHS acute hospitals. Both these variants would increase NHS expenditure but reduce the money to be found for publicly funded social care and provide more guaranteed funding for some care providers. It would also shift costs from council taxpayers to general taxation.

Given the problems with funding the NHS, neither of these boundary-shifting options seem likely to have much political appeal at present but the problem of funding adult social care adequately remains because so much of the national insurance levy is going to the NHS. There are essentially two options: central government grant to replace or top up council tax, thereby increasing general taxation; or some form of social insurance. Both approaches raise the issue of who should pay for social care – those who benefit (mainly the elderly) or the wider working age population. A social insurance approach would likely require the working population at some time in their working life – say age 40 – starting to contribute to a social insurance fund to pay for care later. This is essentially the system in Japan and Germany, but both systems require some topping up from central government.

A social insurance fund would take time to build up; while the current state of funding for social care makes it almost inevitable that central government will have to step in again sooner or later and do something more decisive than their national insurance levy. It is difficult to see that levy being increased further and adding to the burden placed on the working age population, either through national insurance or income tax. Reluctant though the Government may be, it is time to look at taxing accumulated wealth by the older population, mainly through property, as a revenue source for social care. One way of doing this would be a substantial increase in inheritance tax. Another would be to uprate property values for increased council tax and inflation-proofing those values each year.

The Johnson Government has bought some time with the national insurance levy and moving to implement the Dilnot recommendations; but they have not fixed the funding of adult social care. There remains a real risk that publicly funded adult social care will collapse in some parts of the country where local authorities cannot fund care providers adequately. There are big question marks over whether providers and their investors will continue to put money into care homes with a substantial number of publicly funded residents. There remain doubts about whether some care homes will have the resources to recruit and train sufficient staff to satisfy the regulator. In many places the NHS will remain the carer of last resort keeping elderly patients in acute hospitals who shouldn't be there and impeding their efforts to reduce the backlog of patients whose treatment has been delayed by Covid19.

The absence of a durable solution to funding adult social care adds to the continuing doubts about the sustainability of the NHS in its present form. These doubts have been strengthened by the mixed performance of the NHS and the Department of Health and Social Care during the Covid 19 pandemic and the resulting huge and growing backlog of untreated patients. There is nothing new about questioning NHS sustainability. It has been aired frequently over the past decade.

NHS Sustainability – Questions Still Unanswered

Since 2010 the NHS has experienced a series of potentially existential challenges, one of its own making. It declined to change a failing business model when funding was plentiful. It was a strategic mistake not to move care closer to home, focus more on prevention and public health and concentrate specialist services on fewer hospital sites. Some of us, including Ara Darzi, had urged the NHS to do this but to no avail.

But it wasn't the NHS's fault that Governments failed to fix adult social care and made its job harder. It was the Cameron Government that imposed the ill-judged NHS reorganisation under the 2012 Health and Social Care Act that disrupted NHS work for three years and wasted £3billion. This reorganisation left the NHS frontline with a collection of competing quangos making demands on them and over 200 clinical commissioning groups. Alongside this debacle the Cameron/Osborne financial austerity programme required the NHS to operate for much of the decade with annual budget increases of about 1% a year in real terms, a totally unrealistic expectation. It was hardly surprising that by the 2015 Election many were questioning the sustainability of the NHS.

The May Government was so preoccupied with Brexit that it paid little attention to the NHS for most of its term, apart from issuing a discredited white paper on public health that looked to have been edited by the food and drinks industry. No heed was paid to warnings about the adverse impact of Brexit on NHS and social care staffing, with its curtailment of easy access to EU staff. Only towards the end of her time did May commit to a substantial increase in NHS funding to implement a 10-year plan prepared by NHS England and launched by Simon Stevens in January 2019. However, there was little time to implement this plan or take advantage of the extra funding before the Covid19 pandemic hit and dominated NHS work.

During this decade I have joined with many others arguing unsuccessfully for fixing adult social care and making the NHS more sustainable. After my time as a Minister, I chaired a new body for the London SHA, the Provider Agency, to help take forward ideas in Ara Darzi's London Review before he became a Minister. The Agency's purpose was to concentrate more acute hospital services on fewer sites and free up resources for community services. The SHA were working on the concentration of stroke services which eventually reduced the number of London stroke centres from 32 to 8. (This was later shown to have improved patient recovery and saved lives and money.) It proved difficult to apply this approach to other specialties. There wasn't the political and managerial appetite for facing down local clinical and public opposition and tackling failing hospitals. I left after a year.

Over ten years there have been many reports arguing for a change of approach to financing, staffing and delivering health and care; and the need to take a longer-term view. I have contributed a couple of pamphlets, including one on more devolution of control as is happening in Greater Manchester, together with endless speeches. In 2017 a House of Lords Select Committee, of which I was a member, produced a report on the Long-Term Sustainability of the NHS and Adult Social Care. This criticised the culture of short-termism of successive governments: and the lack of long-term workforce planning. It criticised the 'feast and famine' approach to funding and the absence of realistic and consistent funding for health and social care. It was particularly critical of short-sighted and counter-productive cuts to public health budgets. It said the "Government should restore the funds which have been cut in recent years and maintain ring-fenced national and local public health budgets for at least the next 10 years."

The Government did accept the Committee's recommendation to change the DH name to the 'Department of Health and Social Care' and there were improvements to workforce planning. The criticism on short-termism seems to have hit home because two years later NHS England produced a 10-year plan. Nothing happened on safeguarding public health budgets. We still have no system for dealing with failing hospitals, concentrating specialist services on fewer hospital sites and changing at pace the business model to more community-based services. Social care and public heath remain unaligned with our demographic and disease profiles.

Covid19 has revealed how unprepared the NHS was for a pandemic in terms of equipment, laboratory capacity, ventilators and the reorganisation of hospitals to cope with a pandemic. There was no effective contingency plan; and the UK had an early death rate much higher than most of Europe. Matters were made worse by a decade or more of neglect of adult social care so that patients were discharged from hospitals to underfunded, understaffed and underequipped care homes. This unsatisfactory situation has been rescued by the UK life sciences industry and courageous decisions to back new vaccines and ensure their speedy administration by the NHS. We await an independent inquiry into the chaotic handling of the pandemic.

What we do know is that the NHS has a backlog of over 6 million people requiring treatment that has been deferred as a result of the pandemic. Many of these patients, some with cancer, have been waiting over a year already. We also know from a recent NHS Digital report that in 2019-20 there were over a million hospital admissions in England for which obesity was a primary or secondary cause. This was a 17% increase on the previous year and a 600% increase on 2009-10 when there was fewer than 150,000 admissions linked to obesity. The fastest rate of increase was among children under 16. Obesity is the strongest risk factor for diabetes and a strong risk factor for heart

453

disease, heart failure and lung and kidney disease. This surge will continue without radical changes by government and the NHS to community-based preventive services rather than dealing with the problems when hospital admission is inevitable.

In February 2021 the Government published a White Paper on the future organisation of health and care in England after consultation with the NHS and local government. Legislation to make the proposed changes was introduced in the House of Commons in July 2021, with implementation starting in April 2022. The main change is replacing clinical commissioning groups (CCGs) with 42 NHS Integrated Care Systems (ICSs). Each ICS will have an ICS Health and Care Partnership involving local government and other partners. The declared aim is to improve integration of health and care services and secure more focus on whole population health. These are laudable objectives. Replacing the large number of CCGs with fewer larger ICSs is an improvement on the Lansley 2012 legislation and similar to the smaller number of PCTs I wanted to secure in 2005/6, without success. However, the Competition and Markets Authority is removed from NHS involvement; and it seems to be for the NHS to decide how much competition there should be, even when services are failing.

Although the emphasis on integration and whole population health is welcome, it is difficult to see this latest NHS reorganisation altering the dominance of acute hospitals in the allocation of the NHS budget. There is nothing to stop acute hospital trusts carrying on much as before, arguing that they have to concentrate on reducing the backlog of cases caused by Covid19. Many ICS staff will be preoccupied with job changes rather than reshaping budgets. For me the jury is definitely out on whether public health, social care, community health services and mental health will secure a larger, more appropriate share of the health and care cake under these new arrangements. The changes do correct some of the mistakes of the 2012 Act, but I remain doubtful that they will change the NHS business model fundamentally.

There remains a big question mark over the sustainability of a universal NHS because governments continue to struggle to rebalance the NHS away from an ill-heath service dominated by acute hospitals. A rebalancing of this kind requires a consistent shift in resources – money, staff and management effort – over a longer period of time than a single Parliament. The time has come to provide governments with some independent external help of the kind that the Office of Budget Responsibility offers. OBR has provided Chancellors and the Treasury with a level of independent advice and oversight that has increased public trust and improved the quality of economic decision-making. The iconic nature of the NHS and the size of the health and care budget would support doing something similar for health and care. That is why I proposed such an idea to the House of Lords Select Committee who took evidence on it from the former head of OBR, Sir Robert Chote.

The Select Committee recommended as an antidote to short-term fixes, establishing an Office for Health and Care Sustainability reporting to Parliament. Such a body might look 10 to 15 years ahead and publish data on changing demographic and disease profiles, their expected impact on workforce numbers and skill mix and advice on how to align future expenditure on the NHS and social care without lurching from feast to famine. After the Committee's report was published in April 2017, this recommendation was ignored by the then Health Secretary Jeremy Hunt; but in an interview in the Times of 26 June 2021 Hunt recommended such a body to keep his successors 'honest.' I agree. If we want to make the NHS sustainable and fix social care for the longer term, we need to think more radically than we have done so far.

14. Epilogue: Red Bench Reflections

Life in the Lords

You know when you are in the House of Lords and not the House of Commons. The carpets and benches are red, not green. I first sat on the red benches in July 1999 as a Labour Peer. At that time a Bill was before Parliament to remove hereditary peers in accordance with the 1997 Labour Election Manifesto. The Bill was a messy compromise with the Conservative Opposition that left 92 hereditary peers in place who could retain their number by elections to replace any who died. (The replacements became the only elected members of the House of Lords.) One of my early acts was to speak and vote on the House of Lords Bill which secured Royal Assent in November 1999. This reduced Lords membership from 1330 in October 1999 to 669 in October 2000. There are now about 800 members, compared with 650 MPs. I resigned from the Labour Party in 2015 and moved to the Crossbenches.

During 22 years in the Lords, I have made several hundred speeches from both the backbenches and despatch box, asked and answered countless Parliamentary questions and piloted 5 Government Health Bills through the House and many regulations. I have served on 5 Select Committee inquiries: Genomic Medicine, Behaviour Change, Nuclear Research and Development, Public Procurement and NHS Sustainability. And also on 3 Committees undertaking pre-legislative scrutiny of major Bills: Modern Slavery, Care and Adoption. I have been a member and chair of various All-Party Parliamentary Groups (APPGs) ranging from Assisted Dying, Humanism, Palestine, Qatar, Personalised Medicine, Autism and many others. I have been part of Parliamentary delegations travelling abroad and even led two. In short, I have experienced how the UK Parliament works from the inside and met a wide range of leaders from home and abroad. It has been both an interesting and frustrating experience.

As a Minister, the House of Lords is a nuisance. It takes a lot of time out of your day which you could be spending more usefully. You have to be polite to people you would usually avoid at any other gathering. As a backbencher you start by being amused by the Lords' idiosyncrasies and then become increasingly irritated by them. But if you like clubs – which I don't – it's the place for you. Fine speeches are made, clever plots are hatched, and the government can be defeated occasionally. In the time-honoured phrase, the Lords can ask the government to think again. But as Brexit demonstrated, on major issues, it rarely does – especially when it has a large Commons' majority. The House of Lords is good at evidence gathering and analysis but hasn't much of a track record at securing significant changes.

However, it is a useful place from which to campaign for unfashionable or unpopular causes. I have a small collection of these on which I have been able to make a nuisance of myself over the years: assisted dying, humanism and Palestine deserve special mention, alongside the NHS, social care, children's issues and legislation on modern slavery that Theresa May bravely promoted as Home Secretary.

I have been involved with trying to make assisted dying legal in the UK for two decades. As a Minister I had to pretend neutrality but doubt I convinced many people. The Lords has been braver on this issue than the Commons, even though it has some hardcore opponents. It has attempted to pass two Bills, so far without success, despite increasing UK public support and the spread of legislation permitting this around the world. Physician-assisted dying (as it is called in many countries) is now legal in Belgium, Canada, Luxembourg, the Netherlands, Spain, Switzerland and ten American states plus Washington DC and four Australian states. Columbia, Germany, Italy, Portugal and New Zealand are at various stages of legalising assisted dying. The UK is now way out of step with maintaining a legal ban using 60-year-old suicide legislation that punishes terminally ill people who wish to end their lives peacefully. Moves are afoot in Scotland to change that. I hope to be able to use such legislation in England, should I need it, without having to go to Switzerland on my own.

The British Humanist Association (BHA) has been a strong supporter of assisted dying legislation, along with Dignity in Dying. I had the privilege of chairing the APPG on Humanism for five years. A lot of that time was spent encouraging the Government and Ofsted to take action against unregistered fundamentalist schools (Muslim, Jewish and Christian) that failed to follow the national curriculum and restricted children's education to dubious religious tenets, including

457

creationism. There were similar concerns over the growing appetite for home schooling. More attention is now being paid to closing down some of these schools and regulating home schooling, so children are safe and receive an education more likely to fit them for the modern world.

During the Coalition Government Nick Clegg produced a Bill on reforming and shrinking the House of Lords. The APPG on Humanism and the BHA saw this as a chance to reduce the number of bishops, or even remove them all together. I led a small group to see the Minister handling this Bill who seemed amenable to reducing the number pro rata, but without committing the Government to a specific number. On a personal level I like many of the bishops, but they are an anachronism, particularly over conducting prayers at the start of each day's Lords' proceedings. This requires Peers to enter the chamber, face the walls, put one knee on a bench and communally recite the Lord's Prayer out loud. A duty bishop then says various prayers for members of the royal family, wise counsel and other things. Then the unbelievers come in and scramble for what seats are left.

The 2019 edition of the British Social Attitudes Survey stated that "our report charts a continuation of a long-term decline in religious identity, religious observance and religious belief in Britain." Only 12% of the population identified themselves as 'Church of England' and a third of these people were over 75 and threequarters over 55. The daily prayers performance demonstrates how out of touch this unelected House is with the views and identity of the population it is supposed to serve. The Scottish Parliament simply has a short period of reflection on the first weekday it is in session, led by outside speakers from a range of faiths. Canada, Australia and New Zealand are all questioning praying at the start of political proceedings and moving away from this practice at different levels of government. No other Parliamentary chamber has its own in-house clergy of 27 leading it in prayer. In March 2020 I asked the Chairman of the Procedure Committee to review this practice. So far, no response. Praying for wise counsel hasn't had much payback.

Supporting Palestinians

If removing bishops from the House of Lords is difficult, removing illegal Israeli settlers from land belonging to Palestinians makes it look like a stroll in the park. I remain ashamed of the duplicity of the 1917 Balfour Declaration and the way the UK failed Palestinians when it administered the UN mandate for Palestine, a land where 90% of the population were Arabs at the time of the Declaration. I have seen many injustices in my working life, but none compare with those inflicted on the Palestinian people - made worse by their own quarrelsome and geriatric leadership. Since 2007 I have spent much time in Parliament and in Gaza, the West Bank, Israel, Egypt and Qatar with like-minded colleagues drawing attention to the suffering of ordinary Palestinians, especially children.

I have seen the terrible damage done in Gaza by two Israeli invasions. I have been in the Hamas tunnels and in an armed compound with Hamas leaders and four Parliamentary colleagues. We tried to persuade them to recognise Israel's right to exist and make their peace with Fatah. I had a similar situation with a Sinn Fein politician as we tried to persuade Hamas to try peace. I have met the widows of Palestinian 'martyrs' and heard their misery. I have met Palestinian doctors and nurses in Gaza trying to provide healthcare with unpredictable power cuts, few drugs and a mass of young children with chronic diarrhoea because the water supply is so polluted. I have sat in a West Bank court and watched shackled juveniles (hands and feet) being prosecuted in Hebrew for throwing stones at armed Israeli soldiers with no independent evidence. Then spoken to these children's mothers who have seen their children taken in the middle of the night and been unable to visit them. I have met UNWRA officials repeatedly to discuss their lack of aid money to feed Palestinians and provide schools.

I have received Bedouin hospitality in a West Bank village as they wait to be evicted so their land could be transferred to illegal Israeli settlers. I have visited a West Bank farm owned for generations by Palestinians where settlers have cut off their water supply. I have seen a Palestinian home firebombed by illegal settlers, killing a mother and two children, with no prosecution. I have walked round Hebron, a Palestinian town, with a former member of the Israeli Defence Force ashamed at what he and his colleagues were expected to do to clear the place for settlers. These courageous ex- soldiers have formed an organisation, 'Breaking the Silence,' to bring home to Israelis what their government is doing in their name. I've hosted a lunch in the

Lords for a Palestinian farmer/author and non-violent activist whose son was killed by the IDF. I have had to call the police in the Lords to evict Israeli activists disrupting a private meeting of Palestinian supporters that I was chairing.

These are just a few of the direct experiences I have had with colleagues across all political groups in the UK and Irish Parliaments. After each visit, a report is sent to the FCO and a debate is usually secured. The Israeli Government always briefs a group of Peers to put their point of view. The pro-Palestinian speakers are reducing as people die or retire. There is also growing anxiety among Palestinian supporters that criticising the Israeli Government will be regarded by Israeli supporters as antisemitic, which it most definitely is not. In debates the FCO Ministers show sympathy, criticise Israeli settlements, decline any sanctions and recite a mantra about seeking a two-state solution and only recognising a Palestinian state when it best serves the interests of peace. We have reached an impasse in the UK Parliament which no amount of evidence can shift. For Palestinians the misery and death of innocent people continues, especially in Gaza's blockaded open-air prison – David Cameron's phrase.

I have made many visits with others to Arab countries to show there are UK Parliamentarians sympathetic to the Palestinian cause and to see if they can help. Two visits to Egypt at the time of the Arab Spring revealed the difficulty of securing Arab attention to Palestinian issues. The first after the fall of Mubarak, with elections in prospect, found the young leaders of Tahrir Square totally unable to organise themselves to fight an election, despite all the outside advice given to them. This was in contrast with the well organised Muslim Brotherhood led by Mohamed Morsi who we met and who looked the part of a President, which he duly became. On the second visit (which I led) in 2013 Morsi was in jail following a coup in July by General Abdel Fattah Al-Sisi who Morsi had appointed as Chief of the Defence Staff. I was interviewed live by Al Jazeera about whether I agreed with Senator John McCain that there had been a coup. I confirmed I did and added that I hoped the result of the election would be respected. The young interviewer was promptly jailed.

After the coup it became impossible to enter Gaza through the Egyptian crossing at Rafah. In 2014 one of the organisations that I had gone to Gaza with was declared an "illicit" organisation under Israeli defence regulations. I raised this with FCO Ministers who challenged the Israeli Ambassador but were no more successful at getting an explanation or the ban rescinded. Since then, it has been virtually impossible for Parliamentarians to enter Gaza. We have been confined to visiting the West Bank where we have witnessed a surge in illegal settlements under Netanyahu's premiership that have made a two-State solution virtually impossible. The elderly Fatah leadership continue to avoid elections, 17 years after their last one or to make peace with Hamas. Unsurprisingly, Gulf Arab countries have lost interest in the Palestinian cause and made their own accommodations with Israel.

The exception is Qatar which ceased trade with Israel after its first invasion of Gaza. It was blockaded by Saudi Arabia, UAE, Bahrain and Egypt between 2017 and early 2021 because of its independent foreign policy (good relations with Iran and Turkey) and criticism of Gulf states by Al Jazeera. I visited Qatar both before and after the blockade, including leading a cross-Party group in 2018. Meetings with the Emir and his Ministers have always been cordial. Qataris have been willing to improve their treatment of foreign labour when pressed. I assisted them by raising with the FCO human rights issues caused by the blockade for some Gulf families with different citizenships. I have always found it possible to discuss the Palestinian situation informally and constructively with the Qataris but their ability to help is inevitably limited by their circumstances, even though the blockade has now been lifted.

The final indignity for the Palestinians was the so-called Trump Peace Plan published in June 2019. The Lords finally debated Trump's plan on 27 February 2020, just before Covid lockdown and after a muddled response by the UK Government. As most speakers said, this plan abandoned the norms of international law about non-acquisition of territory through military force. Instead of the 95% of the West Bank being returned to Palestinians as Bill Clinton proposed in 2000, Trump gave the Jordan Valley and 30-40% of the West Bank to Israel. His plan left 600,000 Israeli settlers in the new Palestinian State, protected by the Israeli military. The new State would have no capital in Jerusalem; no airport; Gaza would have no port; and Israel controlled water and the electro magnetosphere. The Palestinians had not been consulted and rejected the plan totally. In our debate even pro-Israel speakers were

461

embarrassed, but the Minister couldn't bring himself to criticise it. Until the UK Government changes its approach, there is little more UK Parliamentarians can do to help Palestinians.

Brexit and Lords Reform

My time supporting the Palestinian cause revealed for me the limitations of the House of Lords. The British media has been reluctant to use Lords' evidence to expose the illegal activities of Israel or the excessive use of force used by its government in responding to attacks by Hamas. Compared to the plight of Syrian children and others, the suffering of Gaza's children has generally failed to reach the British media's shock threshold. For me the Lords' limitations were exposed even more clearly by Brexit.

Lords Ministers simply declined to engage with arguments about the way the 2016 referendum result was interpreted or the way the Government was going about exiting the EU. The warnings about the problems Brexit would cause for Northern Ireland were just brushed aside and predictably have come back to haunt everybody. Brexit has exposed that when there is a major constitutional issue fundamentally affecting the UK's future, the second Chamber cannot stop a bullying Government controlled by one political party from forcing through highly flawed legislation that will do long-term damage to the UK's economy and international standing.

As some of us tried to point out, the mandate from the 2016 referendum result was nothing like as clear cut as Ministers claimed. For a start it was an advisory referendum and only provided a binary choice to a complex issue. The electorate excluded groups significantly affected by the referendum's outcome, namely 16-18-year-olds and British citizens living in the EU. Its result was hardly a ringing endorsement for leaving the EU. 38% of the electorate voted to leave, 34% voted to remain and 28% didn't express a view. Such a low percentage in favour doesn't reach the threshold for calling a public service strike. These arguments were made in the Lords and brushed aside as irrelevant by Ministers. If the second Chamber had some clearer, more democratic role on major constitutional changes, I suspect the outcome on Brexit would have been more measured. Even if it had led to a decision to leave, this might have been executed more smoothly.

There was no need to rush out the EU door shouting 'take back control' and doing things that were positively self-harming. It was clear that most people wanted to retain many of the existing environmental and employment protections and to continue participating in research programmes with EU partners. Showing some understanding of how much our economy, especially the NHS, depended on EU labour could have led to a less precipitate loss of personnel. Negotiating better arrangements for sharing criminal justice information would have made our country safer. Focussing negotiations more on service industries might well have safeguarded more jobs. We were forced to leave Euratom because it was subject to the jurisdiction of the ECJ who had never intervened in a nuclear safeguard issue since Euratom was set up in 1958. We are now stuck with a raft of damaging decisions caused by a gung-ho approach to Brexit that a stronger second Chamber might well have prevented.

Even without these Brexit arguments, House of Lords reform is long overdue. The House is far too large at 800 members and likely to grow. Its procedures are antiquated and a source of amusement externally. Hereditary Peers and Bishops are anachronisms in a 21st century second Parliamentary Chamber. As currently constituted, the Lords has not a shred of democratic legitimacy that justifies it challenging an elected House of Commons. Its geographical legitimacy is suspect; its functions are poorly defined; and as a self-regulating body it decides how it wants to conduct its affairs. It needs fundamental reform with a clearer statutory basis.

A good starting point would be to shrink the Lords with a statutory cap like the House of Commons. I see little justification for a second Chamber of more than 400 members; and no case for life-time appointments. I would introduce term appointments of five years, with provision for reappointment of a second term. 25% of members could be appointed by an independent commission required to secure certain areas of expertise, particularly related to constitutional and judicial expertise. There would be geographical constituencies for the remaining 75% of members settled by the Boundary Commission and of roughly equal size. The allocation of these seats between political parties might reflect the popular vote in the latest practical general election. It could be for the parties to choose candidates on a list system as was the case with EU Parliament elections. It would probably be necessary to allow Prime Ministers to choose people outside the cap, say 15 or so, to fill Ministerial posts. I think there is also a case for an age limit.

A reform along these lines would not overrule the democratic sovereignty of the House of Commons but it would increase the legitimacy of the second Chamber to challenge the Commons, especially on constitutional matters. It would require a new name for the second Chamber and its occupants, possibly Senate and Senator. It would not stop the Monarch appointing Peers, they just wouldn't have a role in governing the country. Such a change would probably be opposed by many current Peers, but they are of course a vested interest. Ways could be found of sweetening the pill by transitional arrangements. The UK badly needs its political parties to start thinking in these terms and to see the advantages such changes could bring to 'levelling up' and enabling devolved administrations to participate more fully in the government of the UK.

Building Back Better – Thoughts on a Reform Programme

Writing this memoir has clarified for me the main weaknesses of our system of government for delivering public services. The ability to sack a government every 4 or 5 years is a rather blunt instrument for dealing with under-performance and doesn't always improve matters anyway. Recovery from Brexit and Covid19 makes systemic change to UK government more important than ever, and probably inevitable. Let me start with Parliament.

Having a revising second Chamber is not much use if it cannot effectively challenge an elected House of Commons where one political party has a large majority. This becomes a particular problem on major constitutional issues like Brexit. The current House of Lords is not fit for purpose and requires major reform along the lines I have outlined. That reform is unlikely to be delivered by any government with a large majority in the House of Commons. The most that is likely to be achievable is a cross-party Constitutional Commission charged with remedying two key weaknesses of our current governmental arrangements: the first is the functions, powers and size of the second chamber; and second, the relationship and powers of the UK Parliament relative to devolved administrations and local government in England, especially tax-raising powers. For such a commission to be agreed, I suspect the majority of its members would have to be Parliamentarians, but with an independent element and chair.

Making a constitutional change of this kind would be difficult and time-consuming. But there are other behavioural and machinery of government changes that might be easier to make if there was the political will. These have to do with the nature and conduct of elected politicians and the permanent civil service. The former, tend to have little experience of managing organisations, come to Ministerial jobs with little preparation and stay a short time. They find themselves reacting to events rather than pursuing considered strategies for change. Senior civil servants are analytical, usually good at policy and getting Ministers out of short-term jams but far less good at operational delivery over time and the longer-term planning of services. Few in either camp are natural change agents, although politicians are more likely to try something new than their civil service advisers.

However, most Ministers are creatures of their political party and to some extent captives of party ideology. The trouble with ideology is that it's not a particularly useful basis for operating public services, as rail privatisation has shown. Too often the political right has had a misguided confidence in the virtues of markets. The political left has too often been obsessed with public provision of public services and unwilling to accept private or even voluntary service providers. Too often the result has been unchallenged monopolies running public services. We see that most strikingly in the NHS as I have shown, and, at present, we seem destined to continue with this approach.

The trouble with monopolies – whether public or private – is they are not usually in the best interests of service users in terms of access and value. Some monopolies are unavoidable but there are few public services where some degree of challenge is not beneficial to the end user and taxpayer. Perhaps more to the point, the public generally doesn't care much who provides services as long as they are accessible and meet user needs. This was demonstrated in my time as a Minister with private provision of NHS elective surgery and diagnostics. The NHS will need extra capacity from the private sector if it is to tackle speedily the post-Covid backlog of patients needing operations. Even when Ministers want to change the way services are provided, too often they find their civil servants acting as trade bodies for the status quo. Many Ministers assume, mistakenly, that once they have settled the policy, they can rely on the civil service machine to implement it. If only!

Looming over our machinery of government are some deeply entrenched attitudes towards the value of competent management at the centre of government, both its place at the decision-making table and its role in implementing change over time. In the period covered by this memoir, Margaret Thatcher was the only Prime Minister who came to office determined to improve management at the centre of government and used two external advisers – Derek Rayner and Roy Griffiths - to help her effect change. She made clear to her Ministers and to Permanent Secretaries that they were supposed to manage their departments. This didn't go down well with either. Of the Ministers, only Michael Heseltine made a serious attempt to manage his department. The Financial Management Initiative introduced by Thatcher had a lasting impact but seems to have been set aside during the pandemic.

In the 1960s Harold Wilson used the Fulton Report to open up civil service entry and set up a Civil Service College to improve training – later abolished by Thatcher. It took Tony Blair until his second term to realise that giving the public sector more money without improving its management was a mistake. Targets, a No10 Delivery Unit and competition were his instruments of choice for improving management accountability. They did so while he was in office but like so many initiatives introduced by one government, they fell by the wayside under successors - although a delivery unit seems to have reappeared under Boris Johnson.

This top-level – political and official – inattention to competent management is a significant problem, especially when public services seriously fail and damage users. In my experience these failures are usually down to poor management or professional incompetence or a combination of the two. This was the case in the Mid-Staffordshire Hospital Trust. It didn't need a lengthy investigation by a lawyer and a fat report with 297 recommendations to explain what went wrong. What was required was speedy replacement of local personnel and systems rather than turning this example of local failure into a show trial for the wider NHS. A more knowledgeable top management at the centre would have spotted this and saved a lot of time and trouble and avoided unnecessary wider NHS reputational damage.

These individual service failures are invariably nothing to do with whether the public services are run by public or private providers. Whether it is cleaning hospitals, running prisons or performing elective surgery, it is the quality of management that matters, not whether the provider is in public or private ownership – as I have tried to demonstrate in this memoir. However, where there are continuing service and financial failures, the public services are too often reluctant to change management or market-test across the public and private ownership boundary. Yet we have seen academy schools replace failing state schools. The private sector runs most nursing and care homes. Local government has been commissioning its services at scale from the private sector for 40 years. Most of our European neighbours use private and voluntary providers to run State-funded acute hospitals.

A feature of virtually all public services – health, care, schools, universities, welfare, social services, police, criminal justice – is that they are staff intensive. About two-thirds of NHS costs go on the workforce. Ministers brag about the extra doctors, nurses, teachers or police officers they've funded, but they pay little attention to how these expensive resources are used. It seems to be an article of faith that increasing staff numbers will improve the quantity and quality of services. I have seen little evidence of Ministers or senior civil servants paying much attention to measuring output, outcomes or productivity on a regular basis. To do so would require paying attention to issues like staff recruitment and retention, pay and conditions of service, sickness absence, skill mix and staff training. These issues are rarely on Ministerial agendas unless there is a major industrial dispute disrupting services. Yet the performance of public services and value for taxpayers' money turn to a great extent on the way these staff resources are secured, trained, used and paid.

What all this points to is some fundamental weaknesses in the organisation, staffing and management at the top of the big spending Departments, both politically and officially. If one leaves aside the Treasury, FCO/ Overseas Aid, Cabinet Office and the Ministry of Defence, the remaining departments are responsible for about 90% of public expenditure. They are big businesses but without the top management business talent to run them. They don't have experienced Chief Executives or Chief Operating Officers. Instead, they have Permanent Secretaries and Director-Generals, largely responsible for policy areas. Service delivery is mainly hived off to agencies or local government, without much capacity to hold them to account or improve productivity. Little attention is paid to longer-term planning or workforce recruitment until there is a crisis. UK public services have relied heavily on overseas recruits, now in much shorter supply as a result of Brexit and Covid19. Factoring research, innovation and technological change into longer-term plans and budgets is little practiced.

The biggest service spender of the lot is health and care. Only recently has the NHS been given any idea of its budget for five years ahead, now torpedoed by the pandemic. For most of its history its budget has been either feast or famine. The agency responsible for running it, NHS England, is not responsible for planning its future workforce and there has been little attempt to plan for the longer-term staffing needs or changing the skill mix. Its partner service, social care, has had funding famine and no planning, with no credible solution to its funding and staffing problems in sight. One immediate step that could be taken to free these vital services from political short-termism, would be to establish an Office of Health and Care Sustainability to plan a decade ahead. It should publish regular data on demographic and disease profiles; their impact on workforce numbers and skill mix and advice to the Government and Parliament on aligning future expenditure on the NHS and social care. This could either be a new body or be part of the Office of Budget Responsibility.

The last serious review of the civil service was the Fulton Royal Commission set up by Harold Wilson in the 1960s. The time has come, not for another Royal Commission, but for a managerially driven independent review of the top management of the main spending departments, reporting to the Prime Minister and the Public Accounts Committee. Its purpose should be to establish a better regime for managing these big businesses, politically and officially. There are six particular changes I would like to see considered:

1. First, the ability of the Prime Minister to appoint Ministers who are not members of either House of Parliament on a time-limited basis but able to account to Parliament for their actions.

2. Second, to make available to MPs accredited management training and experience relevant to managing government departments.
3. Third, enabling Secretaries of State to appoint their own management adviser.
4. Fourth, replacing Permanent Secretaries and some Director -Generals with a Chief Executive and Chief Operating Officer, by open competition and with term limits and salaries to attract people from industry and the external public sector.
5. Fifth, reviewing the current arrangements for Departmental Management Boards with a view to strengthening their service delivery capability and annual accountability for delivering public services.
6. Sixth, reviewing the number, cost, scope and accountability of operational arms-length agencies and advising on the changes required to improve their effectiveness and efficiency in the delivery of public services.

There are three public services I consider require specific changes sooner rather than later - the NHS, police forces and the Prison Service. Even allowing for clearing the Covid backlog of treatment, a start should be made on rebalancing NHS funding, workforce and management effort between acute hospitals and community-based services. A bigger share of the NHS funding cake should go to community services (especially mental health), primary care and public health to bring care and treatment closer to home. Acute hospitals need a more effective failure regime that enable more specialist services to be concentrated on fewer sites and more elective surgery concentrated on larger surgical hubs. These hubs, imaging services, routine pathology, community health services and primary care should be open to competition from private providers.

To improve efficiency a review of police forces in England and Wales should be undertaken with a view to reducing their number, as has been done in Scotland (which has one police force) and for ambulance services in England (which were reduced from 40 to 10 in 2006). The Home Office should be required to produce annually a dashboard for each force showing their performance on key indicators of greatest concern to the public. I would like to see an experiment with a police force having a chief executive who is not a police officer.

The monolithic Prison Service should be broken up as part of a strategy to reduce the use of custody and shrink the prison population. Chapter 9 shows how the use of custody for juveniles was reduced by about two-thirds over a decade, using a bespoke system of prevention, punishment and rehabilitation for that age group. That system should be extended to 18 to 21-year-olds, as was originally envisaged. A similar system should be established for women, as proposed by Baroness Corston some years ago. A new system should be established for non-violent, short-term male offenders, making maximum use rehabilitation programmes and technology alternatives to custody. This approach would be assisted by decriminalising possession of illegal drugs (but not dealing) drawing on experience in Portugal. The Prison Service should retain responsibility for high security, violent and longer sentence offenders. Back-office services like finance, personnel, IT and building maintenance could be provided on a common service basis.

A reform programme of this kind is needed if governments are to avoid an almost inevitable decline in our public services in a post-Brexit, post-Covid19 era that could easily stretch to a decade and beyond. Building back better will require radical change, not more of the same. As Guiseppe di Lampedusa said in his 1957 classic, The Leopard: "If we want things to stay as they are, things will have to change."

Author's Notes

The main sources for this book are my personal papers, accumulated over the past 50 years. Chapter 2 draws on Barbara Castle's Diaries for checking dates and who was present at which meetings. My time with Barbara taught me most of what I needed to know about government.

I have frequently dipped into the three editions of The Five Giants, Nicholas Timmins' masterly biography of the Welfare State. Whenever I was a bit unsure about the order of events, I knew I could go to the much-thumbed editions on my bookshelves to resolve doubts. Over the years these books have helped me research many speeches and papers, as well as providing a great deal of pleasure. Nick has encouraged me for some time to get this book out of my system.

The efficiency studies in Chapter 3 are taken from two papers I wrote in the early Thatcher years for a periodical now extinct, 'Public Administration.'

In writing Chapters 6 to 8 I consulted the Home Office chapters in Jack Straw's memoirs, 'Last Man Standing.' However, these chapters are sourced mainly from my personal papers. Chapter 6 is a shorter version of a diary I kept in 1997. In shortening it for space reasons, I have tried to avoid sanitising it. This chapter is intended to show what it was like managing a major Government department when a political party has been out of office for 18 years. Given the accident-prone reputation of the Home Office, I still think an inexperienced Ministerial team did a respectable job in the first Blair Government.

I wrote an earlier book about my time as a Health Minister - 'A Suitable Case for Treatment.' I have gone back to many of the sources for that book. I was too kind in that book about NHS resistance to reform, competition and patient choice. I continue to believe that NHS staff deserve better policies and management than they often receive from their political and official leaders.

I recognise that some people who feature in this book may take a different view from me of events I describe. I have tried to be fair to them on the evidence available to me.

In producing this book, I have been helped enormously by my good friend and technical guru, Peter Chatterton. Without Peter's help my messy Word documents would have remained just that – a mess. He has also contributed a great deal to the design of the book's cover.

Finally, my wife, Suzanne, has been amazingly patient about my lockdown preoccupation with this memoir.

Index

475

Note by author

Chapter 6 is a shortened version of a diary of events kept at the time. That diary had far too many individual references to the author and Jack Straw to include them all in the Index. The entries for both have been simplified to be more useful.